# The Kinship Parenting Toolbox

*A unique guidebook for the kinship care parenting journey*

**Edited by Kim Phagan-Hansel**

EMK

EMK Press • Warren, New Jersey

EMK Press, a subsidiary of EMK Group, LLC
16 Mt. Bethel Road, #219
Warren, NJ 07059
www.emkpress.com

Publisher's Cataloging-in-Publication data

The Kinship parenting toolbox : a unique guidebook for the kinship care parenting journey /
edited by Kim Phagan-Hansel.
p.cm.
ISBN 9780972624473
Includes bibliographical references.

1. Kinship care. 2. Adoption. 3. Foster care. I. Phagen-Hansel, Kim.

HV875 .K56 2015
362.73/3 --dc23                                    2014957437

Manufactured in the United States of America

To Leonard & Jeanne
and the thousands of other grandparents
and family members who have stepped in
for the kids they love.

And to my many friends who have walked various
aspects of the kinship journey and for their
willingness to share their perspectives in this book.

*Kim Phagan-Hansel*

*Throughout the book you will find wisdom from people who are caring for children in kinship relationships. Many of the quotes are from anonymous sources but the emotions, observations, and feelings you might recognize as some that you are experiencing. Please know that you aren't alone.*

KINSHIP

More than 5.8 million American children live with their grandparents and another 2 million live with "other relatives," according to the 2010 census. That's more than 7.8 million children in America being raised in kinship care. Those numbers are startling, so I guess when I started thinking about people in my own life touched by some form of kinship care, I shouldn't have been surprised at the large number I came up with. My own mother-in-law has been raising two grandsons for 18 years, and is still their main family support as they become adults. Other friends, colleagues, and acquaintances had grown up in kinship care raised by aunts, uncles, and grandparents, while others had stepped in when the youngest members of their extended families needed them most. Many of their stories are shared throughout this book.

While kinship care has been happening informally for thousands of years, the latest generation of kinship care comes with a handful of unique challenges. Generations ago, multi-generational families lived together or in close proximity to each other, making it easy to raise children in an extended family setting. While those villages of generations gone-by provided strong foundations for children, today's kinship caregivers face difficult and daunting challenges when they step in to care for family. Often times the children's parents have alcohol or drug dependencies. The children have witnessed violence and drug use firsthand, while others have been neglected or abused – physically, mentally, and sexually.

These early childhood traumas create unique challenges for kinship caregivers. Unlike foster parents who are required to go through hours of training in preparation for many of the challenges they face, kinship caregivers are delivered children with little to no warning. While foster parents are provided funding through monthly reimbursement checks and support through caseworkers, CASAs, and others, often times kinship caregivers are left to face financial challenges alone, with little comfort or support. These families become parents, many for the second time around, with little financial or emotional support, no training, and little guidance. For many of these families, they are struggling on fixed incomes and without a life support of resources and professionals to guide them through the new-age world of parenting children from tough beginnings. Unfortunately, these struggles are something I have witnessed firsthand.

So before *The Foster Parenting Toolbox* was barely started, a number of people suggested we also tackle the topic of kinship care. So, here we are delivering *The Kinship Parenting Toolbox* to you. I will admit, this book provided its own set of unique challenges and for good reason. It was more difficult to find writers and resources for this book. For families, it is difficult to "air the dirty laundry" of their loved-ones. It's one thing to write about other people's problems, it's entirely different when those "other people" are family members that you love and have been hurt by. It was difficult to find resources because there are few out there, however as more and more child welfare agencies emphasize family placements, more resources are slowly becoming available.

I hope *The Kinship Parenting Toolbox* will highlight many of the same things you have experienced on your kinship parenting journey. I also hope it will provide you with resources and information to turn to when you're struggling with the children in your care. By providing you with this information, we hope to help make your parenting journey just a little bit easier and give you some tools to help you raise the children you have stepped up to parent. May your parenting journey – whether it's the first, second, or third time around – be blessed with the resources and guidance you need when you need it most.

*Kim Phagan-Hansel*

Kim Phagan-Hansel
Editor

# The Unexpected Role

# Getting Organized

# Your Legal Toolbox

# Your Financial Toolbox

# Our Changing Family

# Guilt, Shame, & Love

# Perspective of the Child

# Finding Support

# Parenting Children from Tough Starts

# Understanding Attachment

# Behavior and Discipline

# Working with Schools

# The Unexpected Role

> *"Something I didn't consider when I first got the call to foster my granddaughter was how it might change the way she thought about me if I said I couldn't take her in."*

*At 58 years of age, she had planned to work a few more years and then retire.*

# More Than Stand-ins:
# Real Parents and Real Struggles

*By Karen J. Foli, MSN, PhD, RN*

She spoke to me about how hard it had been, assuming the care of 5- and 7-year-old boys, her grandsons. The constant hum of the washing machine and the frequent trips to the grocery store were things that she had to reorient herself to after living alone for so many years. At 58 years of age, she had planned to work a few more years and then retire. But her son's death and her daughter-in-law's troubles with drug addiction and then, the law, had changed that plan when the boys came to live with her. She was lucky, she told me, because she was self-employed and could meet the additional expenses the boys created. Still, it was hard. She missed her son and she could barely keep up with the boys' therapy appointments, the parent-teacher conferences, and the disruptions the boys' mother caused after visiting. There was no permanent legal arrangement, but as a foster parent, she had visits from the social workers often enough. She was sad and depressed she said, so her doctor had pre-scribed an anti-depressant for her. The good news was that the boys were stabilizing. They needed her to be the parent, the mother.

Kinship parents — grandmothers, grandfathers, cousins, aunts, uncles, siblings, and close friends — who assume the primary care for children become more than stand-ins for those who gave birth to these children: you become parents. And as with many parents, kinship parents may struggle with depression. You may become immersed in a mist of loss that can threaten to engulf you at times.

Here are some common losses experienced by kinship parents:

- Loss of a (functioning/independent) birth parent: Either through death, incarceration, or disappearance, the relative or friend who gave birth to the child is no longer in the envi-ronment. Or if the parent is in the environment, he or she is incapable of parenting the child.

- Loss of a "healthy" grandchild/child: The child you are car-ing for may have multiple, complex needs, including medical, developmental, emotional, and educational. At times, these needs may overwhelm you and thrust you into a world of special needs children that seems foreign and complicated.

- Loss of developmental role: An additional loss may be the mismatch between your chronological age and developmental role. Perhaps you may have assumed that you would enjoy freedom from the confines and responsibilities of being a parent, and be able to concentrate on moving forward to a new stage in your life that had included personal freedom.

- Loss of control over your life: Tied to this mismatch may be a sense of loss of control over your life: suddenly, you are tethered to a child who depends on you for emotional and physical well-being. Finances may be a constant source of stress.

- Loss related to the trauma or neglect the child may have experienced and a sense of guilt over those experiences. Had there been a way to prevent all this from happening? You may ask yourself whether you could have been a better parent the first time around.

- Loss of a partnered relationship: Perhaps your spouse is the primary kinship parent. The relationship has changed and you may feel that what was once a second chance at a partnered relationship has been diminished because of the energy your partner expends toward the children.

- Loss related to aging, which may be amplified due to your new role of caregiver: You were already aware of the effects of aging on your body. You may even have been diagnosed with an illness. The additional physical and emotional energy to parent has taxed you to the point where you feel chronically exhausted or ill.

- Loss of being current: It is a new generation, filled with an affinity toward technology, trends and the use of gadgets that you simply cannot keep up with. You try to understand and control the environment, but it often becomes too much for you.

- Loss of a predictable future and feeling secure: You are not sure, now, what the future will bring to your family. Should you pursue legal adoption of the child(ren)? What about retirement? Should you move to a larger home to accommodate everyone? In exchange for predictability, you now have abundant change.

*Suddenly, you are tethered to a child who depends on you for emotional and physical well-being.*

## Signs and Symptoms of Depression

Depression can sometimes grow insidiously. You may have found yourself sleeping more/less, eating more/less, feeling anxious, and helpless during the past several weeks or months. While there are several screening tools used for depression, one is especially short and useful, and requires the answer to the following questions.[1]

During the past two weeks, how often have you been bothered by any of the following problems?

|  | Not at all | Several days | More than half the days | Nearly every day |
|---|---|---|---|---|
| Little interest or pleasure in doing things. | 0 | 1 | 2 | 3 |
| Feeling down, depressed or hopeless. | 0 | 1 | 2 | 3 |

If your answers to these two questions total **3 or higher**, you should seek a healthcare professional to verify the screening result. Remember this is a *screen* for depressive symptoms, not a diagnosis; however, it indicates the need for further evaluation.

## Strategies:

While there is often no one treatment plan for individuals who experience depression, there are common strategies that might help:

1. Get a physical evaluation. Know if there are physical problems that can be effectively treated and also rule out illnesses that can mimic depressive symptoms or make those symptoms worse. Your primary care provider can also refer you to a mental health professional if symptoms of depression are reported.

2. Try to build a support network. From your own personal environment to the larger environment, many Internet resources have been created that are credible and helpful. You are far from being alone: approximately 2.7 million people care for children of close friends and relatives.[2]

3. Know and use your tangible resources. Government agencies, AARP and other organizations now offer information on available resources, common challenges, and state listings of available assistance. Cities are now recognizing housing as a common problem for grandparents raising grandchildren and are beginning to respond to this need.

4. Educate yourself on your child's needs. A child's behaviors can frustrate and exhaust you; however, understanding the causes, symptoms, and best ways to respond to them will help both of you. The world of special needs children can be better understood by reading about their unique needs. Most libraries have solid collections of books that can promote empathy and appreciation of the child's world.

5. Let yourself grieve. Most mental health professionals see grieving as a normal part

of life. The losses listed previously can evoke grief, anger, sadness, and regret. Acknowledging loss and allowing oneself to grieve — and forgive — can be healing.

## The Effects of Parental Depression

While it may be difficult to seek help, research findings describe potential negative outcomes to children who are in homes with parents who experience depression. Children's intelligence scores have even been affected by mothers who experience depressive symptoms.[3] The children under your care have already been through many transitions and even traumas. They are sensitive to the environment, which includes their parents, and need caregivers who are able to engage and interact. It is not easy to admit that you may be depressed. Despite how society has accepted struggles with mental illnesses, the stigma of reaching out for help can be a real and difficult barrier. So, know this: when you hesitate to obtain the help you need, be selfless once again and do it for the sake of your family and those who you care about. By helping yourself, you will help them.

*Karen J. Foli, MSN, PhD, RN, is an associate professor at the Purdue University School of Nursing in West Lafayette, Indiana. She is the co-author of **The Post-Adoption Blues: Overcoming the Unforeseen Challenges of Adoption** (Rodale, 2004) and conducts research that examines nursing care of the adoption triad and depression in adoptive and kinship parents. Foli has been interviewed by journalists from The Washington Post, The New York Times, The Philadelphia Inquirer, and O! The Oprah Magazine for articles discussing post adoption depression.*

[1] Kroenke, K., Spitzer, R.L., Williams, J.B. (2003). The Patient Health Questionaire-2: Validity of a two-item depression screener. *Medical Care*, 41, 1284-1294.

[2] The Annie E. Casey Foundation (2012). Stepping up for kids: What government and communities should do to support kinship families. Retrieved from: *http://www.aecf.org/KnowledgeCenter/Publications.aspx?pubguid= {642BF3F2-9A85-4C6B-83C8-A30F5D928E4D}*

[3] Hay, D.F., Pawlby, Sharp, Asten, Mills, & Kumar (2001). Intellectual problems shown by 11-year-old children whose mothers had postnatal depression. *Journal of Child Psychology and Psychiatry*, 42(7), 871-889.

*"I had no idea that I could be this tired. My 62-year-old legs are no match for his 3-year-old ones! But he does keep me going and his smiles are worth everything to me."*

## Raising A Grandson

*By Stephen Fisher*

My wife and I are in our mid-fifties, and are raising our 5-year-old grandson. We have been his sole support financially, spiritually, mentally, lovingly, and have raised him as our own pretty much since he was born. Within a few months after he was born, his father took off and has never seemed to have any interest in seeing him. From day one, his mother, our daughter, never seemed to have the motherly instincts. He has always only been important to her when she could use him to her advantage. If our daughter didn't get what she wanted from us, she would pull him out of our home and go from place to place. We would never know where he would be each evening and wonder every morning if he was the only one awake laying there hungry and scared. Due to our daughter's lack of interest and effort in becoming a responsible mother, her putting him in unstable and dangerous situations, her using him to attempt to get what she wanted from us and constantly threatening to leave with him and never allow us to see him again, and her choice of using drugs and hanging out with bad people, we decided to seek legal custody of him.

Nearly two years ago, after more than two years of calling Social Services when she would put him in dangerous situations, documenting concerns of her legal and drug problems, and working with a court appointed attorney for our grandson and court appointed social workers and completing professional home visits and inspections, we received legal custody. For the most part he has adjusted well and is happy. During the home visits, inspections, and social workers visiting and interviewing the staff at his daycare; all reports came back that he was a happy and well-adjusted boy. I say for the most part, only because from time to time he will cry and ask for his mother. We have put a lot of time and effort into giving love, a stable family life and good Christian morals. Every time I think, "what are we doing," he will say or do something that makes it all worthwhile.

The other morning when I was getting him dressed for school, I asked him, "Do you know how special you are?"

He responded, "yes, Gampa, do you know why you are special?" I asked why and he replied, "Because you have a special boy — me!"

He loves all sports and is good for his age at any sport he decides to play. There isn't a day that goes by that either I, his grandmother, or his 20-year-old uncle doesn't play some sport with him. We are fortunate to have our oldest daughter and our other two grandchildren living nearby to spend a lot of time with him. He is also fortunate to have his uncle, who is a great role model for him and spends a lot of quality time with him.

His mom says she wants him back, but her life is a constant disaster, and I will not let her drag him back into it. She refuses to work and wants someone, and it doesn't matter who, to take care of her. For some reason she thinks, at age 24, she doesn't have to work, not even lifting a finger around the house when we allow her to stay because she doesn't have anywhere else to go. She has taken advantage of everyone else she knows. She is constantly asking for money and has no guilt in doing so.

We are involved in church, sports activities, a lot of school things and we pray together as we did when raising our own children. I constantly wonder how I could have raised such an irresponsible daughter and I don't know what went wrong. She started hanging out with the wrong crowd and using drugs at an early age and it has gotten worse from there. We had her in counseling and therapy a number of times throughout the years. Since age 18, she has been prescribed medications to stabilize her mood swings but refuses to take them. Throughout the years she has been in the legal system for driving without a license and domestic violence. She was put in jail for nearly 90 days for parole violations. Her mother and I had hoped being in jail would give her time to think about things and improve her situation, but she met people in jail who she now associates with and has gotten worse.

I am a firm believer that the confusion and chaos we are having now is a lot better than all the sleepless nights and worrying we would do if we hadn't received legal custody. It can be difficult when our own feelings clash with each other. While we love him and honestly believe this is the best thing for him, we wish and pray that something would click with our daughter and she would become the mother he deserves. We are doing our best to parent him and would never want for him what the alternative might be. I also go through periods of feeling that if I had done a better job as a father raising our own children, we wouldn't be doing this all over again.

Along with my younger sister, I was also adopted and raised by my grandparents — my mother's parents. On one hand I believe this gives me an advantage of understanding how he might accept and adapt to this, because as I went through childhood in this situation I remember always believing I was lucky and always felt loved and cared for. On the other hand, I see him after his mother has said she's going to be there to do something with him and then not shown up for days at a time. I remember how I felt when the same thing happened when I was his age. One thing is clear; our lives have changed with the addition of our precious grandson. The change has brought both happiness and sadness, and with that change has come stress. I understand that finding proper ways to deal with it is vital for our own emotional and physical health, as well as for our grandson's health, but I don't believe I am doing a good job at this.

After I grew up and left home, I remember my grandmother (legal mom) telling people and also telling me when she was on her dying bed, that when my sister and I were young and around other children with their parents, she always worried we may have felt bad that our parents were so old and wished for younger parents. When she told me that, I told her that I never felt that way and I remember always thinking how lucky I was as a child, she then cried and hugged me so tight. A few years ago, I told a neighbor who also raised her granddaughter this story. This brought tears to her eyes and she said she also always worried about that.

*Stephen Fisher is a Colorado grandfather raising his grandson after having been raised by his own grandparents.*

# Seven Tips for New Kinship Caregivers
*By Alison O'Donnell Caliendo*

I have had the privilege of working with individuals who are raising their relative's children for more than three years. New kinship caregivers often tell me they didn't think twice about assuming responsibility for their relative's children. When time came to take a relative's child or children into their care they opened their hearts and homes. However, amidst all the changes they soon discover it is extremely difficult to navigate the systems around them in order to support the children in their care.

In my office or over the phone, relatives relate their bureaucratic, financial, and emotional struggles to me, hoping for answers. A great-grandmother was in tears as she talked about being turned away for the third time from the Social Security office while trying to get a Social Security card for her great-granddaughter. A grandfather broke down in my office, disheartened after his application for welfare assistance for his four grandchildren was rejected. A grandmother told me about spending all her savings on a lawyer who hadn't even filed guardianship paperwork, something she only recently realized she could do on her own. A young aunt talked about how alone she feels raising her nephews while protecting them from their mother — her sister — who is an addict and a prostitute. My heart goes out to these individuals who are trying so hard to raise their relative's children only to be broken down by the systems around them. What they didn't realize is that much of these frustrations and heartache could have been avoided with a little knowledge and research.

As you begin to seek resources to parent your relative's child most effectively, I offer seven tips to explain some of the issues you may encounter and suggest strategies to overcome them effectively:

- Participate in a Support Group
- Understand How Programs Define You
- Beat Frustration with Preparation
- Decipher Local Labels and Acronyms
- Become an Internet Sleuth
- Learn About Child-Only TANF
- Know the Law

With a little guidance, caregivers can master some tricks in order to reduce some of the external frustration that can get in the way of the most important job you do: providing a safe and loving home for a vulnerable and deserving child.

## 1. Participate in a Support Group

The most valuable and yet often overlooked action a kinship caregiver can take is to join a support group. While it can be hard to explain your situation to friends or co-workers, fellow caregivers will understand and provide emotional support and encouragement. Finding others who are on the same path can provide great comfort. It is unlikely that you will say anything that will shock or surprise a fellow kinship caregiver. In addition, a support group of people who have encountered the systems you have yet to navigate will provide advice and information as you begin your journey.

Many states and counties now have support groups specifically for kinship caregivers. If this is not true in your area, you may find support in a local group focused on issues relevant to your situation, such as bereavement, mental illness, families of incarcerated individuals, or foster parenting. If you can't find something nearby, there are numerous alternative options: books and articles about raising a relative, online kinship support groups, blogs by relatives, Facebook groups, Twitter accounts, chat rooms, message boards and other ways to connect with people who will understand what you are going through.

Finding support is a crucial first step and provides a foundation for everything else that may come your way. After you have spent some time navigating the systems, you will also be able to provide valuable knowledge to those who begin their journey after you.

## 2. Understand How Programs Define You

While all kinship caregivers perform a similar role in the life of a child, not all caregivers are eligible for the same types of support in their state and community. Knowing how support programs will categorize you will be helpful in seeking out available resources.

Caregiver age and the custody status of the child are two variables that determine types of available support. A good starting place is to understand if you are considered a **formal** or **informal** kinship caregiver, two general categories that encompass the range of child custody statuses.

The majority of caregivers are **informal kinship caregivers**. Most often these individuals step in to take over parenting from the natural parents after death, incarceration, abandonment, or when they see abuse and neglect. Usually these caregivers have intervened before Child Protective Services removes the child from parental custody. Informal kinship caregivers can have physical custody only, temporary or legal guardianship, legal custody, or eventually become adoptive parents of their relative. Each type of custody has different legal ramifications for both the caregiver and the child.

**Formal kinship** caregivers work with the child welfare department in their state or county and are resources for child placement when a child is removed from the home by protective services. Depending on state law, formal kinship caregivers are either licensed (paid) or unlicensed (unpaid) relatives that provide full-time care of the child but usually have only physical custody.

Your **age**, in combination with the child's custody status, may also determine what programs are open to you. Some programs are only available to older individuals. For example, counseling and respite care may be available to grandparents or other relatives, 55 years of age or older, caring for a child through the National Family Caregiver Support Program administered by each state's Department of Aging.

Your state may also have a subsidized guardianship program. For example, in Nevada there is also a financial program through the Department of Welfare and Supportive Services called the Kinship Care Program available to relatives who have legal guardianship and are aged 62 and older.

Once you understand age requirements and what support is available based on the type of custody you have, you can more effectively pursue relevant avenues of support.

## 3. Beat Frustration with Preparation

Know this at the outset: the systems you encounter were not made to accommodate you. Because you aren't the biological or adoptive parent, each bureaucratic system you encounter will challenge you in some way. The key to survival is careful documentation and easy document retrieval. Designate a binder or folder that you can use to keep track of copies of important documents, appointments, notes, and numbers. Safeguard original documents and make copies of everything. Having everything together in one place will make all your appointments go more smoothly.

Don't be like the great-grandmother who was turned away from the Social Security office three times for three different reasons. Always call agencies and offices in advance to find out exactly what documents you need to bring and if you need to bring the child with you. Ask about hours and days of operation, and payment methods and prepare accordingly. Keep track of when you called and to whom you spoke within your binder.

When you do have an appointment, bring something to do while you wait, and reward yourself in some small way when it is over. Expect long lines and hassles at government offices. If you do get rejected, find out exactly what you need to correct the situation. Ask the employee to make you a list of documents or steps and get the name of the supervisor if you still have questions. I recommend having a few deep breathing exercises and calming mantras in your mental toolkit; you'll need them.

Take control of what you can before setting out by both physically and mentally preparing and you will actually minimize the amount of difficulty you experience.

## 4. Decipher Local Labels and Acronyms

First, there are many different names for what you are doing: kinship caregiver, kin carer, relatives as parent, grandparent as parents, relative caregiver, grandfamily, licensed relative caregiver, unlicensed relative caregiver — the possibilities seem endless. There is no consistency for kinship caregivers in the language of both academic literature and in welfare departments all across the county. Find out what labels are used in your area to define your role and you may find more support than you could without them.

Second, acronyms abound when you are searching for assistance. Much assistance is available through various government departments in your state. It is prudent to first understand your state department's associated acronyms so you can effectively research available support, especially while searching online. For example, each state designates their Child Welfare Department, Department of Aging and Social Services Welfare Department slightly differently, resulting in a variety of acronyms. For example, in Nevada we have the Department of Family Services (DFS) and the Department of Welfare and Supportive Services (DWSS). In California you will work with the Children and Family Services Division (CFSD), in the California Department of Social Services (CDSS). Take some time to figure out what these departments are called in your state.

Different assistance programs usually have corresponding acronyms. It is hard to seek help from TANF, SNAP, WIC, or FRC if you don't know what those programs are or if you qualify! In your binder of important information you may want a sheet to take note of acronyms you run across and the meanings.

Also keep in mind when seeking help that professionals often speak in acronyms. If you don't know, don't hesitate to ask questions. When professionals are speaking in the language of their work, ask them to repeat themselves using more general terms and to explain any linguistic shortcuts they use.

## 5. Become an Internet Sleuth

As you search online you will find that some information listed is no longer useful, or a program that was once active has recently been closed. Programs providing support today often do not exist tomorrow. The Internet is more a catalogue of all the efforts that have existed, and not always an accurate database of current help. Check the dates on data used and news articles posted. Call the programs listed or go directly to their website.

Remember, there are people and programs that do exist to support you. With some clever digging you can identify them. Keep careful notes of people, places, numbers, and websites that offer you relevant information so you don't have to do the sleuthing twice.

## 6. Learn about Child-Only TANF

Raising children is expensive. They eat a lot, quickly grow out of clothing, and even the most basic care can be surprisingly expensive. Make sure to learn about Child-Only Temporary Assistance for Needy Families (acronym: TANF, pronounced TAN-F) because it may be the ONLY financial assistance available to kinship caregivers in your state.

Many relatives have never applied for welfare before, and many think they wouldn't qualify based on their income. But there is a category of assistance available to Non-Needy Relative Caretakers (acronym: NNRC). This means that even if your household income prohibits you from receiving assistance for yourself, qualifying relatives can *apply on behalf of the child only* and will usually receive a small monthly cash assistance for care of the child.

Some relatives do not pursue the NNRC TANF assistance because by doing so the state may require participation in a child support enforcement program. Relatives who are balancing the needs of their child with the needs of their grandchild may not want to add additional stress on the entire family unit in this manner. It is helpful to talk to others who have been in your position as you consider the best decision for the child in your care.

If you do decide to apply, I always recommend that relatives write NNRC or CHILD ONLY in big letters across the top of their applications, as there may not be a box to check to designate the type of welfare assistance for which you are applying. When applying for child-only assistance, complete the application as if you were the child. For example, household income would be based on the child's income, which is usually zero.

This is another area where you may need to push professionals to assist you correctly. I have talked to countless relatives who were denied NNRC TANF assistance they were actually entitled to. They reapplied correctly and now receive a little extra assistance each month. Remember Tip #3: Beat frustration with preparation — and don't give up.

## 7. Know the Law

Lawyers can help you navigate the legal system and family law attorneys can be useful when you have questions about kinship care. Lawyers are also expensive and don't always get it right. If you are considering a lawyer, as a starting point check to see if your area has a legal aid clinic. For example, Southern Nevada has exceptional free legal support including guardianship classes, help filing uncontested guardianships and a family law "Ask A Lawyer" program.

You can also do some basic research online or in a library to understand more about the laws that govern parental rights, guardianship, visitation, custody, and adoption. A good starting place is **The Grandfamilies State Law and Policy Resource Center** (http://www.grandfamilies.org/), a "national legal resource in support of grandfamilies within and outside the child welfare system."

If you need an attorney, interview several before you decide. Many lawyers offer free consultations that can be valuable in expanding your understanding. Each one may tell you something slightly different, and out of all these conversations you will better understand where the common legal ground is and find someone who is a good fit for your circumstances.

As with everything else, the more knowledgeable you are, the more you can ensure that the professionals you hire actually do the work for you. Don't spend money unnecessarily like the grandmother whose lawyer had already taken $5,000 from her, but hadn't even filed her uncontested legal guardianship paperwork. She was beside herself when she found out that with some assistance from the free guardianship class she could have filed the paperwork herself. Had she known the laws governing guardianship and the free legal resources already available to her she could have saved time and money.

## Conclusion

These seven tips are just a few of the simple things you can do to more effectively find the resources and support you need in a timely fashion. Doing this research at the beginning of your caregiving duties should help you find time to do what is most important, be with the child in your care. So grab your binder or folder, and:

- Participate in a Support Group
- Understand How Programs Define You
- Beat Frustration with Preparation
- Decipher Local Labels and Acronyms
- Become an Internet Sleuth
- Learn About Child-Only TANF
- Know the Law

Stay with the process and don't let frustration get in the way of finding resources. Support comes in many different forms and with perseverance you will find what you need.

*Alison O'Donnell Caliendo is the founder and director of Foster Kinship, a non-profit providing support and resources for individuals raising their relative's children in Clark County, Nevada. She earned a master's degree in organizational systems renewal specializing in systemic healing (Seattle University 2009). Kinship caregivers can be traced in her family line for generations, and for that she is extremely grateful. More information and resources for kinship caregivers can be found at www.fosterkinship.org or by calling (702)KIN-9988.*

## From a Satin Duvet to a Washable Bed Spread
*Becoming a Foster Mom of a 5-Month-Old At 63*
*By Phyllis Stevens*

My husband and I have been married for 35 years and have five wonderful adult children. Four of the five children were adopted out of foster care. At this point in our lives we started to think about retiring and taking long naps. One telephone call changed my life forever.

I was working in my office when the telephone rang. I answered it as usual, "Together as Adoptive Parents, this is Phyllis," thinking it was a resource family needing help. It was a member of my church, "Joyce." She told me that her four-month-old grandson had been taken into foster care and what could she do? I told her of course I would help. We talked a long time about her and her husband becoming a relative placement for him. She loved that idea. Before our call ended she asked, "if we can't get our grandson, would you take him?" I said, "Yes, of course," not really thinking about my answer. I thought for sure her grandson would be placed with her.

I told her that I would recruit some members of our church to help me get her home ready before the caseworker came. A few days later I received another call from "Joyce." She said that she and her husband could not become relative caregivers because of their health. Remembering that I had told her that I would take her grandson if she could not, I was speechless. My mind was racing all over the place. Finally, I said, "Joyce" would you mind if I talk to our pastor to see if we could find a younger couple to become the resource family for your grandson?" She agreed.

There were several couples who were willing to adopt her grandson but none willing to become foster parents. When a child is taken into foster care the goal for that child is to be reunited with his or her birth mother or father. Only when that is not possible will the goal become adoption for the child. At this point, the goal for this little boy was reunification. It was time to call a family meeting.

"Are you crazy?" was the first thing my husband and I heard. "Mom are you and Dad ready for 3 a.m. feedings?" "Have you thought about bottles, diapers, car seats (my husband drives a 350Z convertible), doctor appointments and Children and Youth always in your home?" Needless to say, this was a long family discussion. In the end, all my children said that they would support us in our decision and that they would be available to help when needed.

My 25-year-old daughter Alex and her two-year-old son, who live at home with my husband and I, were excited. She loved the idea of having another baby in the house. She started talking about double strollers, and going through her son's clothes taking out anything that was too small for him and saving them for this little baby.

I started to prepare myself mentally. I emailed members of my bible study and asked them to pray that God's perfect will be done for this little boy.

I contacted Children and Youth to let them know that I knew the family and I would like to be considered for a kinship placement. To my surprise, I received a call back that day. The caseworker was nice and said that Children and Youth would need to see my home before we could discuss a kinship placement. In the meantime, would I fax over my driver's license?

Two weeks later two caseworkers for Children and Youth were sitting at my kitchen table discussing this little boy I will call "Jon."

During the conversation, one of the caseworkers made a comment about my age and the picture on my driver's license. He said that he had to make sure that he was calculating my age correctly after seeing the picture. I smiled and said, "Yes, I will be 63 in May." We took a tour of my five-bedroom home and talked a little more before they left.

I received a call a few days later from one of the caseworkers letting me know that they had approved my home as a kinship foster home. I was excited, happy and nervous all at the same time.

My youngest child was 25 years old. I had not parented a baby since 1966 when my son was born. The children my husband and I adopted were all toddlers. I started to think, OK what does a baby do all day? What will I do with a baby all day? How many times will he wake up at night? How many times will I wake up at night?

While I was walking around with a thousand questions going through my mind, my daughter Alex started to organize. Her first question:

"Mom what size diaper does he wear?"

"I would think a small," I replied.

"No, Mom what number does he wear?" she asked.

"Do diapers come in numbers?" I asked.

"Yes, Julius wears 2s," she replied.

"Whatever happened to cloth diapers?" I asked.

"Cloth diapers, I don't think I have ever seen cloth diapers before," she said. I simply responded, "Oh."

The permanency hearing for "Jon" was scheduled for the following month. I decided not to go, but wait at home to see what happened. Shortly after the hearing was over I received a call from the caseworker. He said that "Jon's" advocate told the judge that I was too old to parent a five-month-old baby. That he would be better in a home with a younger couple.

To my surprise, I was devastated. I wanted to cry. I tried to think of anyone I knew that may be able to help me. I called a lawyer friend of mine who has been working in the child welfare system for years. I explained to her the situation. She suggested that I call the advocate and ask to meet with her. One of the problems was that the advocate had never met me and knew nothing about me or my family. I thought it was worth a try.

I called the grandparents of "Jon" and told them the news. They were devastated as well. They did not want to "lose" their grandchild to the system. I asked them if the birth mother would be at the next permanency hearing. They said, "yes." I told them to tell their daughter that if she wanted her son placed with me she must tell the judge.

I emailed members of my bible study and asked them to pray. I asked them to pray that God's perfect will be done, that God would do what is best for "Jon."

At the next permanency hearing the birth mother told the judge that she knew my family and went to school with some of my children and that she wanted her son placed in my home.

I received another call from the caseworker and he asked if I was still interested in becoming a kinship foster parent for "Jon." I said, "yes." He told me when the next permanency hearing would be. I told him that I would be there.

I still had not met the advocate. I did not know what to expect when I arrived at court with the grandparents. They introduced me to the birth mother's lawyer who introduced me to the child advocate.

"Jon" was placed in our home as a foster child on January 30, 2012. My husband, daughter and I are having so much fun. "Jon" has taught me what is important in life and what is not. Missing a conference call that had been planned for weeks is not important. Having tickle time with "Jon" is.

I have put away my cashmere sweaters and silk skirts, at least when I am holding "Jon." I replaced my beautiful satin duvet for a washable bedspread. I have more time to play with my grandson and "Jon" than I ever had when my children were growing up. "Jon's" grandparents get to see him every Sunday at church, as well as every other Thursday.

Consider becoming a foster or adoptive parent, 63 is the new 40.

By the way; "Jon" is in a number 3 diaper.

*Phyllis Stevens and her husband Derek have been married for 35 years. They have five children, one birth child and four adopted. She is founder and executive director of Together as Adoptive Parents, Inc. (TAP). TAP is a non-profit organization that provides support, resources and help to the adoption, foster and kinship community in Pennsylvania. Reprinted with permission from* **Fostering Families Today** *magazine.*

*So, you're a grandparent raising a grandchild. . .*

*. . .Have you begun to wonder yet whether you will all be in diapers at the same time?*

## Kinship Toolbox
*By Jan Wagner*

So, you're a grandparent raising a grandchild. And you have probably figured out by now that it is even a bigger change of life for you than menopause. It takes more than a village to raise a young child at our age. If you haven't sat your other family members down by the time you are reading this book and told them you will need a lot of their support and help to do this, trust me, it's too late. You should have gotten it in writing from the get-go. They have their own lives to live. Life hasn't happened for them just as they were making other plans. By the time you get to be our age, you know you better go with the flow or you'll make yourself crazy.

How about those sleepless nights with a baby, or a toddler with an ear infection? Have you caught up yet? You never will. We don't have that much time left. Potty training? Have you begun to wonder yet whether you will all be in diapers at the same time? Those latches on their car seats were not made for arthritic hands, but how many of you know there are safety locks on the back car doors so they can't open the door while you are driving down the road? My kids used to sit in the back seat and wait for me to hit a bump big enough for them to hit their head on the ceiling. Now they are strapped in so tight they can't move. Don't you just love those little chairs in the preschool room? It's either that or the floor doing criss cross applesauce. Either way, they all grab an arm to pull you up.

When the kid on the playground tells you that you can't be his mom, you're too old, try to refrain from telling him to appreciate the fact that his teeth still have the opportunity to grow back. Just let your dentures slip and give them back the same gummy smile they gave you. Soon they will learn that when you come to the classroom they will just say Hey H, your whatever, whoever she is, is here. He will be the first in his class to have a car and special license to take us back and forth to doctor appointments. Just remember, you are raising your own caregiver. Graduation will be a breeze. They can just wheel you up to the front row. They will think Grandpa is so humbled he still has his head down after the benediction. Nope, he's sound asleep.

What is it really like to raise a grandchild from infancy to adulthood? It is probably the most spectacular thing you have ever done. Give yourself some credit for doing this. All the love and all the pride you had for your own children is multiplied into infinity with a grandchild. I never thought that possible, but I am living the dream. How many times have you looked upward and asked, "what have I gotten myself into and how am I going to survive." First of all, hang on to whatever bits and pieces of humor you have left and go for it. Remember, you're old, you can say anything. Cut yourself some slack. You don't have to be perfect. You weren't the first time around, and they are OK. Well, most of them anyway. Just be there. Love them and protect them. They need it and deserve it. Even if your spouse is hard of hearing and you're used to shouting at him to be heard, try to tone it down for the little one. He's probably heard enough and it will just make him cry and run from you.

**Be consistent.** I know it's a grandparent's role to love them, sugar them up, and return them to their parents. But, don't ever lose sight of the fact that you are the parent or you are going to be sitting up with the energizer bunny long past bedtime.

**Be a good role model.** You're only as old as you feel (not look), so eat right and eat together. Get out and exercise with them by playing. Kids love to take walks. Walks are nice, and slow when you're exploring nature. Remember when you were so busy working you just didn't have time for those things. Well, now you do.

**Listen intently to them.** They won't know it's because you are having trouble understanding what they are saying. They just like the intensity on your face. Let them know they are the most important person in the world. I know money is tight, but libraries, museums, and communities always have free functions. We didn't take advantage of those things years ago, but we do now. And make sure they have young families around. Many adults do not want another child to raise, but they make sure he gets picked up and thrown in the air just like their kids do.

How many times have we been told to take care of ourselves first or we won't be able to take care of anyone else. We have to take time to nurture us. I could never do it when I raised my first family, and I can't seem to wrap myself around it now. I get my strength and my joy from the simplest things. Just being with a child renews me. And the biggest bonus of all for me is to see the father my husband has become because he is not out working three jobs anymore. Our priorities have changed. What once was so important now has little significance in our lives. And seriously, we are not nearly as old as we would be without this child in our lives.

*After raising three children, 37 years of marriage, and at the age of 57, Jan Wagner started raising her then two-year-old grandson. Jan Wagner is now an advocate for kinship families and is involved on a state and national level. You can follow her blog Raising H at jdwags.blogspot.com. She is also available to speak or give workshops on Kinship/ Grandparenting issues.*

# To Grandmother's House We Go:
## *At the Intersection of Kinship Care and Foster Care*
*By Ron Huxley, LMFT and Catie Hargrove, MS*

For some children, a trip to grandmother's house is more than a casual one. It can be a safe haven from a living situation that is chaotic, unsafe, or confusing, and may be a more long-term living arrangement for the child. This placement arrangement, children living with relatives or near-kin, is known as "kinship care" and has similarities and differences to the more formal institution of foster care.

## Historical Basis for Kinship Care

Although it was not until the 1990s that the term kinship care became mainstream, there is overwhelming evidence that kin and near-kin caregivers are not a new phenomenon in child welfare. In many cultures, relatives are the parents of choice in various circumstances, and are almost always the alternative in situations where one or both parents are unavailable. Kinship arrangements may occur when birth parents are deceased, unable to parent, or to afford opportunities for education or to learn a trade. No matter how kinship arrangements evolve, family members stepping up to care for their own is as old as time and a natural part of our history across cultures.

## Kinship Care vs. Foster Care

Although a kin caregiver can also be a foster parent, this latter designation is usually understood to be a more formal, court-mandated living arrangement for children. Children who have been removed from their homes due to abuse or neglect live with guardians who have been approved and licensed by social service agencies. Along with this formal arrangement comes extra support. Foster parents are guaranteed a monthly stipend to help defray the costs of care and to cover any medical care or treatments for the child. While in foster care, the legal responsibility for the child resides with the court and/or public agency responsible for oversight of the child's well-being. Therefore, foster parents are required to obtain permission from the agency or the court to do things with and for the child (for example, taking the child on vacation, administering medication as prescribed by a physician, or even getting a haircut). The physical care of the child is the responsibility of the foster parent, and they must abide by all rules, guidelines, and stipulations set forth from the agency that has the legal responsibility and places the child in their care.

Kinship care is often similar to foster care, although there can be some significant differences depending on the type of legal arrangement that exists. Children can reside with relatives under any of the following arrangements:

1. **Informal Kinship Arrangement** — occurs when the parent or parents of the child arrange for the child to be cared for by a kin or near-kin, without the involvement of the legal system. This is the most common form of kinship care.

2. **Kinship Caregiver** — occurs when a child has been removed by authorities from the care of parents and is placed with a family member or near-kin caregiver. The

caregiver has physical, but not legal custody of the child. The caregiver may access some services directed toward kinship caregivers, although most of them are designed to assist low-income caregivers. Not all caregivers will be eligible to access these services, depending on specific eligibility criteria.

3. **Kin Guardianship** — a similar arrangement to the kinship caregiver, although the caregiver has physical and legal guardianship of the child, giving them the right to make decisions on behalf of the child. In some states additional services are available to kin guardians, including financial assistance and Medicaid coverage for the child.

4. **Kinship Foster Care** — occurs when the kinship caregiver is also a licensed foster parent. This typically allows the kinship caregiver to access more services and programs. Legal responsibility remains with the agency that placed the child in foster care, and kinship foster parents must meet and abide by all agency and court policies, procedures, and guidelines.

## Benefits and Concerns of Kinship Care Homes

A recent study (Sakai, et al 2011) detailed the benefits of kinship care. It found that children placed with a relative had fewer behavioral and social skill problems than children in foster care but they had a higher risk of substance abuse and pregnancy as teenagers. This study also brought to light the reality that kinship care providers are more likely to be older, unemployed, single and poorer than foster parents. Consequently, the researchers advocated for more support services to kinship caregivers to improve children's outcomes. Because kinship care is often done outside the child welfare system, it often does not include the financial or legal support inherent in the foster care system. Additionally, there are unanticipated emotional challenges that raising a kin member can also bring. Some of these challenges include:

- Dual roles/relationships — for example, a grandparent is both parent of their own child and "parent" of their grandchild.

- Confusion about who has final say on the welfare of the child.

- Feeling forced into a role of secrecy to avoid legal conflict and having children placed in the "system."

- Conflicted loyalty over making the child's placement permanent versus being able to prevent further harm to the child.

- Dealing with personal guilt over choices their child has made and how this has affected their grandchild.

- Holding on to child rearing practices that may conflict with current social standards and from the child welfare system.

## Who Belongs To The Child?

Historically, placement of a child has been in the service of adults. Children were seen as property and expected to be appreciative of anyone who would take them in. Decisions about permanency depended on who has the "rights" to a child. This line of reasoning makes sense from a legal perspective, but what happens when we see the situation through the eyes of the child? Instead of asking the question, "Who does the child belong to?" what different decisions would be made by asking, "Who belongs to the child?" Who is important to the child and where would the child feel safest? The answers that come from this new perspective will dramatically alter social work practice and placement decisions. History and research suggest that the fewer disruptions for a child, the better the outcome. This makes kinship care a natural solution for child placement decisions when and where possible.

When a child's preferences and needs cannot be met by a kin placement, then foster placement with a non-relative is a viable next choice. Even in this scenario, openness of relationship with kin is vital to the well-being of the child and will lead to better permanency outcomes. This open attitude, with visitation and honoring of relationships with the family of origin will prevent detrimental placement disruptions.

Relatives, especially grandparents, who become caregivers for their kin should be applauded for their dedication to keeping their family together. Alternatively, those who cannot become caregivers, but who are persistent in maintaining relationships with their kin, contribute to the health and welfare of their family's children by being supportive to the foster parents who partner with them to provide safety and well-being for children.

*Ron Huxley is a licensed child and family therapist and the director of Kinship Center services in San Luis Obispo, California. He is the author of the book* **Love and Limits: Achieving a Balance in Parenting** *and founder of the ParentingToolbox.com blog.*

*Catie Hargrove was director of Kinship Center's Education Institute in Salinas, California. She produces educational videos and develops curriculum for foster and adoptive parents, kinship caregivers, and the professionals who support them.*

## References:

Berrick, J. D. (1998). *When children cannot remain home: foster family care and kinship care.* **The Future of Children**, 8(1), 72-87.

Hegan, R. L., Scannapieco, M. (1999). **Kinship Foster Care: Policy, Practice and Research**. New York: Oxford University Press.

Sakai, C., Lin, H., Flores, G. (2011). *Health outcomes and family services in kinship care: analysis of a national sample of children in the child welfare system.* **Archives of Pediatrics and Adolescent Medicine**, 165 (2): 159.

# A Hard Road*

*By Anonymous, as told to Kim Phagan-Hansel*

By the time I was 60, my husband, Harry, and I had raised 11 children on our family farm. After selling the farm, we moved to town and our youngest son lived next door. At only 19, he and his girlfriend welcomed our grandson, Jeff, into the world.

As Jeff's mother struggled to overcome an infection after her caesarian, I took care of little Jeff starting at just two days old. I guess that's where my journey as a grandparent raising her grandchildren began. All of my other children had families and lives of their own, but my youngest son and his girlfriend struggled with the transition to parenthood. Because they lived next door, it was easy for them to come and go and depend on us to help with first, Jeff, and then 13 months later, Mikey.

At first, we would just have the boys on certain occasions, but as time passed those occasions happened more frequently. Then when the boys were about three and two their mother left and we didn't see her for several months. We became the easy answer for our son when he was working and wanted to do something in the evenings. At that time, the boys lived with us practically full time.

While we were frustrated with their mother and father, Harry and I loved those boys. Jeff had been Grandpa's buckaroo from the moment he arrived. But when Harry's health began to fail, it became more challenging to keep up with two little ones and care for Harry.

In time, Jeff and Mikey's mother began to take more interest in them, but with two additional children, she wasn't interested in caring for the boys full time. And our son remarried and his new wife didn't want to be responsible for the boys. Anytime the boys would stay with their parents they'd cry and say they missed Harry and I, so I'd run, pick them up and bring them back to my house. It was frustrating because we loved the boys and wanted to do what was best for them, but also wanted their parents to take responsibility for their children.

As the boys entered adolescence, Harry's health deteriorated. It was too difficult for me to keep up with it all, so the boys went to live with their dad full time. As Harry slipped into the final stage of his life, he would often voice his concern for the boys' future. Harry and I had showed them more love than anyone else.

After Harry died, it wasn't long before the boys were back staying with me. At 13 and 12, they were nice company for me during a really difficult time. But as they got older, they became more chal-

*"It was frustrating because we loved the boys and wanted to do what was best for them, but also wanted their parents to take responsibility for their children."*

lenging and had little respect for me. Today at 17 and 16, they are disrespectful. Unfortunately, their bad attitudes and circumstances have led them to make some poor choices.

While I love the boys, I think if I could go back in time, I would have chosen not to care for them again. I dearly love the two boys, but I would make it so they couldn't stay with me, but just come to visit. They had a Grandma and Grandpa, they never had a Mother and Dad. If we would have actually gone to court and established guardianship I think I would have felt more like I could discipline them and have more of a parental role. But at the same time, if we hadn't stepped up to take care of them, I truly believe they would have ended up in foster care or been in trouble at a much younger age.

Living on Social Security, it has been difficult to raise the boys. I have so little and children take so much to feed and clothe. It has been a struggle and something that has frustrated many of my other children. Unfortunately, it has driven a wedge between many of my family members as they believe Jeff and Mikey's dad should have stepped up and been responsible for his children. I agree, but I also know those two boys needed someone and I guess that turned out to be me, and while he was living, my husband.

Today, Jeff and Mikey still live with me. It isn't perfect and I would change things, but I love them both and I feel sorry for the way things have been for them.

*\* Names have been changed for privacy reasons.*

> *"Someone told me to keep the relationship with the parents as positive as possible and some days that is really hard. I have had my two grandchildren for almost a month now. Today I am feeling so overwhelmed as I have caught their cold and have been up all night with them. Of course, their mother is out partying. I am trying to accommodate everyone for the holidays so that they all get time, but between all these social workers, parental visits, and counseling visits for the kids, I barely know if I am coming or going most days."*

# Kinship Care — The History of a Name

*By Eileen Mayers Pasztor, DSW*

During the past two decades, the child welfare field has given much attention to research, policies, programs, and practices concerning the care of children by relatives, typically known as "kinship care." Just as children often are eager to know how they were named and, as adults, we seek family history concerning our names, here is how "kinship care" was named.

In 1990, the Child Welfare League of America convened the National Commission on Family Foster Care in collaboration with the National Foster Parent Association. Its mission was to focus national attention on strengthening family foster care as an essential service option for at-risk children, youths, and their families. The 49-member commission included two congressmen, the president of the National Foster Parent Association, public agency administrators and managers, private agency executives, foundation representatives, university-based educators and researchers, national advocacy groups, and two young people from the foster care system. CWLA staff and an intern with a masters degree in social work provided support. One of the first decisions of the commission was to commit to the term "family foster care" instead of the historical "foster family care," to emphasize the importance of putting family first.

It was in the first half of the first meeting that several commission members asked: "We're focusing on family foster care, but what about the relatives? How will the strengths and needs of relatives involved in the foster care system be addressed?

As the commission struggled with a definition of family foster care, as well as issues and recommendations, it also was challenged to have some kind of shared terminology for the "relative" part, but what? As the commission members came from across the United States, they shared their local perspectives. How about "relative foster care?" OK, but relative to what? How about "home of relative?" OK, but the acronym could be a problem. How about "de facto foster care?" No, not clear. As CWLA's national program director for family foster care and adoption, and the commission's staff director, I was charged with the task of recommending a name that would be child- and family-friendly.

When in doubt, go to history. I remembered that in my social work doctoral program one of the required readings was Carol Stack's "All Our Kin: Strategies for Survival in a Black Community," published by Harper and Row in 1974. A young white anthropologist with a preschool son and national funding from the then Department of Health Education and Welfare, now Health and Human Services, Stack lived for some time in a poor black community in a large urban mid-west city. Her book highlighted the strength of kinship networks. Many of the commission members remembered this book from their own educational programs. I proposed the name: kinship care. In 1991, CWLA published the commission's report in "A Blueprint for Fostering Infants, Children, and Youths in the 1990's" with a special chapter titled, "The Significance of Kinship Care." CWLA added kinship care as one of its major program areas, and I had the privilege of becoming CWLA's first national program director for kinship care.

In 1997, CWLA convened the first national conference on kinship care in San Francisco. Stack, then a professor at the University of California at Berkeley, was a guest speaker. She autographed my copy of "All Our Kin."

*Experienced as a foster and adoptive parent, Eileen Mayers Pasztor, DSW, is a social work professor at California State University, Long Beach, teaching courses in child welfare, social welfare policy advocacy and administration. Previously, she worked for the Child Welfare League of America, as its national program director for family foster care, adoption, and kinship, and director of its western and international offices. She is currently working on a new national competency-based curriculum for collaboration between kinship caregivers and caseworkers. Reprinted with permission from* **Fostering Families Today** *magazine.*

# Getting Organized

"*Providing kinship for my niece is like learning a new language. These people speak in code! If you don't understand something, speak up and ask. Also, I write down the name and phone number for anyone I meet. You never know when you might need it.*"

# Ten Things Kinship Caregivers Need
*By Allison Davis Maxon, MS, LMFT*

## Kin: *relatives, relations, family, connections, kindred of the same blood.*

For centuries, children have been raised informally by kin when their parents were unable to care for them. Currently, federal policy upholds the bonds children have and develop with their relatives by giving priority to "kinship caregivers." It is no surprise then that a quarter of the children in our child welfare system are placed with grandparents, aunts, or uncles. But how much do we really know about what kinship caregivers need? As an agency, we've been listening to the needs of the kinship caregivers we have been serving for more than 30 years. They have taught us well and have asked us to share their teachings so others may recognize and incorporate them into program planning, training, resources and supportive services unique to families built through kinship care.

## Ten Things Kinship Caregivers Need

**Answers:** Who has legal custody of the child? What's the difference between guardianship and adoption? What are the plans for permanency? What are the responsibilities of the placing agency, the birth parents, and other extended family? What financial supports are available for the child? Having access to legal counsel is imperative for the successful navigation of our complex legal system. In order to create an appropriate plan that best serves the child's needs for safety and permanency, kinship caregivers will need access to legal counsel and assistance in navigating the child welfare/court system. Many local law schools and bar associations offer clinical programs that provide free legal services by law students under the supervision of licensed attorneys.

**Resources:** Many of the grandparents we serve are raising two, three, or even four grandchildren on a modest and/or fixed income. Accessibility to resources in their community that can assist with basic needs; food, clothing, child care, and other needs are absolutely critical for family stability. More than one in five children living in kinship care live in poverty (nearly 1.3 million children) and without the links to the safety net resources in their community, these children and families are at risk.

**Peer Support:** Being around other kinship families decreases the sense of isolation that many kinship caregivers feel. The experience of being a kinship caregiver is unique and is recognized as a different form of parenting. Peer support allows members to share their collective experience and give/receive support to others with similar life challenges and experiences. Participating in monthly kinship caregiver support groups gives members the opportunity to be amongst kin — a normalizing and validating experience.

**Parenting Support:** Because young children experience the world through their relationships with parents and caregivers, those relationships are fundamental to the healthy development of the child's physical, emotional, social, behavioral, and intellectual capabilities, according to a 2009 report from the National Center for Prevention of Child Abuse. Kinship caregivers are typically parenting highly impacted children who have been exposed to multiple and/or chronic traumatic experiences. Parenting support that equips kinship caregivers with specialized interventions and tools to effectively manage the increased emotional and behavioral challenges that many children with complex trauma manifest will empower kinship caregivers in their parenting style. Specialized training that is adapted to the unique needs of kinship caregivers who are often balancing the dual roles of grandparenting and parenting is essential.

**Help:** Family members have raised others' children since the beginning of time, but the challenges facing these families have changed dramatically as of late. Feelings of guilt, anger, and embarrassment often permeate the caregiver's experience. Learning to ask for help and being able to access specialized supportive services is critical. Parenting multiple children can be challenging and exhausting at any age. Many grandparents who are raising children share that their greatest need is for respite. Some time to relax, take a walk, read a book, or sleep — is greatly valued. Often the first resource that is requested by the kinship caregivers we serve is for a few hours of respite support.

**Respect:** Being a non-nuclear family can be a challenge at back-to-school night, soccer games or parent-teacher conferences where community members are trying to figure out your family's dynamics. Kinship caregivers desire respect and acceptance like all other diverse family groups. Our most basic need as human beings is the need to belong; to feel we are amongst kin. Empowering kinship caregivers to actively advocate for their children's and family's needs certainly deserves our respect.

**Understanding:** Grief and loss permeate the experience of the kinship caregiver, the birth parents and the child. The core issue of loss is often times easily triggered and reacted to in these sensitized relationships. Assistance with grief and loss is key to healing and successful relationship building in kinship care. Children often feel angry, hurt, afraid, abandoned, and confused. Support groups for caregivers and children with professionals who understand the core issues of grief and loss that are experienced through each stage of development will assist in the facilitation/creation of healthy relationships and coping strategies.

**Sense of Humor:** In order to find joy in the present moment and overcome the many troubling memories/challenges that surface, one must use levity and humor. Emotions are contagious; it's easy to "catch" an emotion. One of the most effective tools caregivers can use daily to de-stress their home is to laugh often and frequently. Incorporating playful rituals into the home environment such as joke night at the dinner table, all-day pajama day, feelings charades, and Tuesday game night will all help to model and teach healthy coping strategies. Families that learn to de-stress together

*One of the greatest gifts any of us can give to our kinship caregivers is to extend to them our listening ear and an abundance of empathy.*

build in strengthened resources that help to sustain them through times of crisis/need.

**Empathy:** Kinship caregiver families are often loaded with painful experiences; parental drug addiction, incarceration, abandonment, abuse, and neglect. These families need to experience compassion and empathy from their supportive systems. Keep in mind that caregiver stress and unresolved trauma may lead to intergenerational trauma impacting both the caregiver and the child's mental health. Building bridges of support directly to the kinship family minimizes isolation and distress. One of the greatest gifts any of us can give to our kinship caregivers is to extend to them our listening ear and an abundance of empathy.

**Community:** The larger community; schools, neighborhoods, and faith communities offer opportunities for social connections that help to sustain and support the kinship family. Community networks that welcome and celebrate the unique contributions that our kinship caregivers are making throughout this nation become a powerful partner in helping to sustain our kinship families. It is our hope that you ask a kinship caregiver today... how can I help?

*Allison Davis Maxon, MS, LMFT, is the division director for the Kinship Center, a member of Seneca Family of Agencies. Maxon is a clinician, educator and advocate specializing in adoption/permanency, attachment and trauma. She is passionate about creating systems of care that are permanency competent and strength-based. She recently presented at the prestigious Georgetown University National Symposium on Children's Mental Health Systems of Care Conference on Kinship Center's clinical competencies of "permanency" focused, attachment-based mental health services for children who have experienced trauma, neglect and/or loss. She is the co-author and master trainer of* **ACT: An Adoption and Permanency Curriculum for Child Welfare and Mental Health Professionals** *and* **Pathways to Permanence: Parenting the Child of Loss and Trauma***. Maxon is also the creator of* "**The Ten Things Your Child Needs Everyday**," *a DVD with tools that help parents/caregivers strengthen their attachment relationship with their child.*

# Relatives and Kin Raising Children:

*What Are Some of the Needs of These Caregivers?*
*By Beth Powell, LCSW*

- *At least 7.8 million children live in households headed by grandparents or other relatives. These households include those where the children's parents may or may not also live.[1]*

- *2.7 million children (4%) of all U.S. children are being raised in grandfamilies or in kinship care situations.[2]*

- *Children placed with relatives make up more than a quarter (26%) of all children in the foster care system.[3]*

As a social worker, I work with a number of relatives and kin who are raising children. Below is a list of the most common needs that my associates and I have tried to help caregivers secure assistance with.

1. **Affordable Housing in "Safe" Neighborhoods**
   Too many of these children are being raised by single female caregivers who were already struggling financially. Just because children come to live with non-birth parents doesn't mean that these parents are financially reimbursed by state and federal agencies for the extra children they are caring for.

2. **Affordable Legal Assistance**
   Many caregivers can barely afford to meet the basic needs of the kids in care that they have, much less pay expensive legal fees to help these kids attain permanency with them.

3. **Beds and School Supplies**
   Yes, beds. In some homes, kids are sleeping several to a bed, on couches, mats on the floor, etc.

4. **Traditional Respite**
   In too many situations, too many young children are being cared for by only one, tired, older caregiver. Grandma needs a break sometimes.

5. **Therapeutic Respite**
   Sometimes traumatized kids are too much for already overly burdened relative/kinship caregivers to handle. These caregivers may be older and have health problems. Therapeutic respite using an In-Family Services model may be a cost/time effective way to help habilitate a child from hard places without relatives losing close contact with the child, without relatives having to turn a child over to an "impermanent state system" of revolving foster care and residential settings, and without relatives ceasing to become an integral part of the child's treatment plan.

6. **Knowledge of Resources Families Can Apply For and Most Importantly, How Relatives Are Supposed To Apply for the Potential Resources**
Many relatives caring for children aren't aware they may be able to get Medicaid for their little charges, Medicaid Transportation Reimbursement, Food Stamps, or other services. One of our local grandma's raising her grandchildren didn't want relative/kinship caregivers to have to go through what she went through trying to locate resources for the kids she was raising, so she created an organized template for where to go and how to fill out the forms for basic resources. With the help of social work interns we are expanding that template into *"Tina's Resource Manual: A Comprehensive Resource Guide for Relatives and Kin Raising Children."*

7. **In-Home Parent Assistants**
More adult hands in the home during high traffic and high activity periods can surely help the caregiver provide better supervision. They can help with transporting children to extracurricular activities, help cook, clean, assist with homework, help discipline unruly children and many other tasks.

8. **Emotional Support and Camaraderie of Other Relatives Raising Children**
It can get lonely and stressful having to do so much for so many in so little time. Caregivers need to "feed" each other emotionally so they have more water to give as they are the wells from which so many drink.

9. **Complimentary or Low-Cost Family Recreational Opportunities**
It's rare that many of our relative/kinship families get to have a family fun day such as a trip to the amusement park, a movie, an ice cream parlor, or even McDonalds. When someone can donate a pass to Splash Town or organize an Easter egg hunt for the families caring for others' children, it can be the highlight of a child's young life, not to mention a time when relatives and kin can recreate together and help support each other.

*Conroe, Texas-based psychotherapist and neuro-behavioral educator, Beth Powell, LCSW, specializes in helping traumatized children and the families who raise them heal. She understands the importance that relatives and kin have on a traumatized child's life from her own personal growing-up experience and acknowledges she wouldn't have the insight and ability that she has today to help others if she hadn't "walked a mile in the shoes" of the people who seek her assistance. For more information, visit www.infamilyservices.net.*

## References:

1. U.S. Census Bureau. *"Households and Families 2010: U.S. (April 2012)."*
2. Annie E. Casey Foundation Kids Count Data Center. *"Stepping Up for Kids: What Government and Communities Should Do to Support Kinship Families* (2012)."
3. Generations United calculated this figure based on the federal share of the 2000 average monthly foster care maintenance payment for 1 million children. The Green Book of the Committee on Ways and Means, U.S. House of Representatives estimates the cost at $545 per child. This is approximately half of the children being raised in grandfamilies outside of the formal foster care system. Half of the children are used for our calculation, due to a conservative estimate that the other half already receives some type of governmental financial assistance, such as a Temporary Assistance for Needy Families (TANF) child-only grant. Consequently, the cost of one million children entering the system would represent all new financial outlays for taxpayers.

# Kinship Care for a Son's Brother

*By Tonya Barker*

Birth mom contacted me again, she is expecting for the eighth time. My two adopted boys are the only two siblings together. The other brothers and sisters are in grandparents' homes, been adopted through foster care, or are being adopted through private adoption. They don't have contact with each other; they will never know each other until they get old enough to look for each other. Well, she has contacted me for the past two pregnancies interested in putting the baby with me and it didn't happen, so I'm not expecting it will happen. This time, regardless of the fact that I'm a licensed foster parent and have been for eight years, it doesn't mean that much to my local social service agency, nor does placing siblings together given the fact I tried to convince them to place the last two children with me so siblings could grow up together. Of course, it's cheaper for the state to put children in kinship care instead of foster care. I saw a significant shift and change from foster care to kinship care several years ago when the economy started going down.

Social Services started making budget cuts, and abused and neglected children were affected dramatically. Children had to try to live with every relative and nonrelative they could dig out from under a rock before being put into foster care. Many children have been moved so many times for the sake of saving the budget there is no way they can have a normal childhood. Stability and safety in placement offers time to cope with past abuse and neglect. Once children are able to quit wondering if they will go back to their birth home or stay in their current home, real healing can begin.

June 2012, I received a call in the middle of the night. "I'm having the baby, please come right now," the caller said. So I took off getting there just in time to witness the birth and get the dad's baby bracelet because the father was not in the picture. Yes, he was another drug baby, but what a beautiful little boy! He looked just like his brother, who I adopted. It was immediate baby love! When he tested positive I was absolutely sure they would take custody and place him with me as a foster child, but that's just not how it worked out. Social Services came to the hospital and somehow through all that baby love and fear of brothers not growing up together I was convinced to take kinship placement even though he was no kin to me or my husband at all. He was my boys' brother, they are part of me, and they want him, we want him. Someone else could want him, too. I was running on adrenalin from being up around the clock, making sure the birth mom finally gets her

> *This child needs permanency, his brothers need to know he has permanency, and we as a family need permanency.*

tubes tied, and having to endure viewing this different type of lifestyle for birth mom. Of course, this baby couldn't go home with her! I'd had two preemies already and he was the third. I knew what to do. I was not afraid. I'd had tons of foster parent training on a monthly basis. I knew most of the doctors, routines, and contacts. With eight years of experience as a foster parent, I was now a kinship caregiver. This side of care is different, and there are no boundaries. It was confusing to have to set the boundaries myself, set up visitation, and consider letting birth mom come to my home. It was an overflow of emotions and confusion.

Kinship care is shared parenting at the MAX! The social workers are amazed at the amount of shared parenting and tolerance level I have with this birth mom. I don't see any reason to be confrontational, cuss or run her down. She already knows her faults; I don't have to rub her nose in it. But, there is no way she's coming to my home to breastfeed every three hours — no, I'm not moving her in! The plan is to review his case and if she's not made progress for them to take it to court, take custody, and change my kinship care to foster care. I only wondered how quickly it would happen.

At six months now, the social worker has visited twice a month, which is one more visit monthly than foster care. Birth mom has backed off, she calls me sporadically, and went to church with me a few times in the beginning. I get to listen to her like a counselor over the phone when she's having problems. She wants to borrow money occasionally, and calls me to pick her up on the side of the road when she is left high and dry. She wishes I would have adopted her. She gets the baby's food stamps, while I care for him, and buy him baby food, and of course I'm not getting the foster care boarding payment. However, he is getting Medicaid for his health insurance. I did get to pay out-of-pocket for a minor surgery not covered by Medicaid. I get to buy his diapers and supply all his needs and yes, birth mom still has custody. She could call the shots at any time and change a plan of action. Social Services just sits back and makes sure they get their visits in. Our social worker is sick most of the time and cannot be contacted when I have questions. Well, by now you can feel the frustration in this, and all the while my boys keep asking, "Does he get to stay and when will he get our last name?"

The court paperwork is sitting on the social worker's desk now for a good five weeks waiting to be signed off on by a supervisor to get a court date. "There is no reason it's not completed," she says. She just has not had time. Once we get a date, how many times will it be laid over? What will the judge say? Will they take custody right away or will they ask me to continue kinship care? It will soon be seven months. Oops, she tells me on the phone, if he has been in my home for a year they can just give me custody and forget about going to court or foster care.

My brain is racing, but this child is a preemie with maternal drug use. There's limited to almost no long-term research on drug babies growing up. I've been down this road twice before and still living the health and behavioral issues these children have. This baby needs Medicaid until he's 18. He needs adoption benefits. He is a special needs child and we will need post-adoption support. Our family needs support! After all, they have him listed as medically fragile. My brain keeps racing to what I'm experiencing with my other adopted boys, both looking at double eye surgery in the summer, the other wearing a portable EEG home next week to check for seizures, the problems we have had with hydrocephalus and the shunt he has, the brain damage, the learning and developmental delays, the memory loss, the ADHD, the biweekly occupational therapy. I'm starting to see some physical therapy needs in the new baby; also one of his eyes is not looking just right. I know where this is leading. I've been told every child in this family has ADHD and what about all the substance abuse and mental illness in the family, and what about genetics? Stress, stress, and more stress! After all, we did get into this to foster, to adopt — what happened to that? What's a parent to do?

Well, the ball's in my court as I see it. If mom goes in and relinquishes to Social Services they will have to take custody, thus placing the baby in foster care with us, and giving us the support he needs. Oh yeah, we're no longer foster parents, the state would not renew us after we did all that renewal work to keep up our license. We are full they say, there are five kids in the home, so we will renew your foster care license once Social Services takes custody. I've had it! OK, so I call birth mom and say let's go. She meets me down there ready to sign her rights over. Social Services says, "We don't have time today." We will call you next week; we have to get it approved by our director. And so the story goes waiting, waiting, and more waiting. This child needs permanency, his brothers need to know he has permanency, and we as a family need permanency. We're giving, giving, and giving. I hope we don't give out!

Understanding this process is impossible. I have been given no instructions, no book, and no adviser. The only support I have is our local foster parent association, and the resources I have from our community, the resources that have taken me years to learn. What do other kinship caregivers do? How do they cope with this? Respite is a must, especially since the baby makes five boys in our home. You see I also have two birth children, they love their adopted brothers, and the new baby just the same as part of the family. They don't see them any differently. They too want the new baby to become a forever child. Respite is not provided like in foster care. Thank goodness for grandma, and a few special ladies that I go to church with.

We can do this, we are committed, and we are strong even through the stress. I don't know the future, but we are committed to this baby brother. One day it will all be over, the records closed and adoption papers in hand. Until then we will hang in there, be respectful, and professional, to our agency and birth parents. Our minds wander and race to how this will all play out, we lose sleep, pray, worry, cry, and think about future health and behavioral issues. It will all be worth it to give this child a forever home with siblings. Our earnest desire is they will grow up to be close brothers and thankful they had the opportunity to grow up together.

*Tonya Barker has been a foster and adoptive parent for eight years. She is the president of her local foster parent association. She represents foster parents on the local Child and Community Protection Team. Tonya is a homeschool mother to four of the five boys in her home.*

## Asking Others For Help
*By Beth Powell, LCSW*

Sometimes a request letter sent out on email lists is a cost-time efficient manner of soliciting help or even funds to help families. I sent a letter out to my email list to solicit help for my single moms raising children because the number of children with special emotional, neurological, and physical needs is rapidly increasing... and so are the number of single female parents. Below is a replica, with revised statistics, of that letter. Consider it as a template that can be modified to meet the service needs of one's clientele:

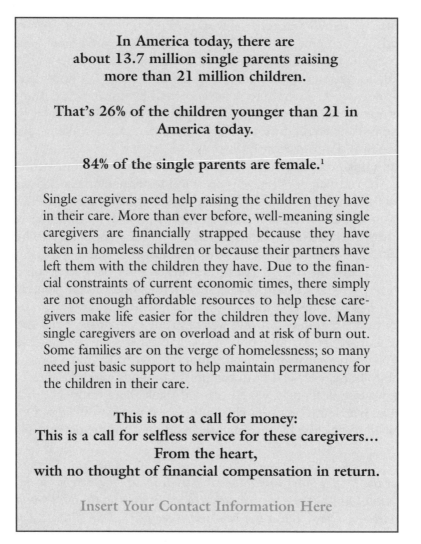

**In America today, there are about 13.7 million single parents raising more than 21 million children.**

**That's 26% of the children younger than 21 in America today.**

**84% of the single parents are female.**[1]

Single caregivers need help raising the children they have in their care. More than ever before, well-meaning single caregivers are financially strapped because they have taken in homeless children or because their partners have left them with the children they have. Due to the financial constraints of current economic times, there simply are not enough affordable resources to help these caregivers make life easier for the children they love. Many single caregivers are on overload and at risk of burn out. Some families are on the verge of homelessness; so many need just basic support to help maintain permanency for the children in their care.

**This is not a call for money:
This is a call for selfless service for these caregivers...
From the heart,
with no thought of financial compensation in return.**

Insert Your Contact Information Here

Below are ways in which you could help overly stressed and financially strapped parents create healing, helpful, healthy, and permanent homes for the children in their care, many of whom have special needs and have come from the "hard places" of abuse and neglect to live with non-birth but "forever" mothers.

### 1. In-Home Clean Up and Chore Assistants

Therapeutic parenting of numerous children or just one special needs child can be exhausting. The housework is a parent's last priority, and yet it is so vital to have a clean home for a calm mind. This particular service could so help free a caregiver up to have more time to spend with the children in their care.

In-Home Clean Up and Chore Assistants must be prepared for what they might find when they come into a home with special needs children from "hard places." For example, the carpets may have been urinated on; the toys may have been destroyed. Some children may have become visually overwhelmed with too much stuff and color in their bedrooms, so a child's bedroom may look spartan. People who come into the home to help must come with an attitude of service and non-judgment and a mind ready to learn about the neurological, physical, and emotional needs of the children in the home. Helpers could prepare a healthy meal, wash clothes, vacuum, clean carpets, sweep the porch, clean bathrooms, water plants, or even plant a garden…the list is endless.

### 2. In-Home Parenting Assistants

This could be someone who could conduct neuro-behavioral exercises with the children. It might be someone who could help with homework or other group activities with the children. It might be someone who could help parents take their kids on nature walks or enjoy other recreational activities. It may be someone who could help a harried, tired mom tag-team a house full of disturbed, traumatized kids to help them reach a place of safe-security and trust that the grownups around them can protect them and keep them safe.

### 3. Errands and Transportation Helpers

This could be someone who could go to the grocery store or take the car in for an oil change. Maybe a helper could even pick a child up from school or a sporting event or even help teach a child how to drive or to ride a bike.

### 4. Regular Respite Providers

Trained providers who could babysit while the caregiver takes a much needed break. Or someone who could be with the children when perhaps the caregiver needs to have surgery, go to the doctor, go to a meeting with a teacher, or attend a workshop or just get a haircut.

### Crisis, Therapeutic Respite Providers

This is the relief person who could hopefully be available, fairly quickly, when a parent needs to walk away from an angry, oppositional, and unpleasant-to-be-around child because the parent has been triggered and needs to find his or her center again. The crisis respite person would need to be someone who lives close by and could potentially get over to help fairly quickly. A crisis respite person could also help watch and occupy other children in a household while a parent therapeutically restrains a violent, out-of-control child until the child can calm down.

### 5. Complimentary Healing Workers

Many of our children with special needs are on Medicaid. This form of health insurance in Texas does not cover massage therapy, cranial-sacral therapy, nor other non-traditional healing modalities that caregivers and children could surely benefit from. The caregivers of these children are tired, stressed, and putting their own needs for healing on the back burner while they concentrate on the children in their care. A little bit of healing touch could go a long way.

*Conroe, Texas-based psychotherapist and neuro-behavioral educator, Beth Powell, LCSW, specializes in helping traumatized children and the families who raise them heal. She understands the importance that relatives and kin have on a traumatized child's life from her own personal growing-up experience and acknowledges she wouldn't have the insight and ability that she has today to help others if she hadn't "walked a mile in the shoes" of the people who seek her assistance.*

*Powell is also a CEU training provider, a social work supervisor of interns and externs as well as an adjunct instructor at Lone Star College's Montgomery Campus. She has created a unique systems'-based child-in-family approach that includes the child's caregivers as part of the treatment team. For more information, visit www.infamily-services.net.*

## References:

1. U.S. Census Bureau 2009 as found on *single-parents.about.com*.

# Kinship Care of Ryan

*By Dorrie Riley*

In September 2011, my daughter Jen came to me one night and told me that she needed to get some help. She said she was addicted to Valium. She wanted to know if I could take care of my grandson Ryan for about seven to ten days. But her Valium addiction actually ended up being a heroin addiction! While Jen was in detox getting help, she had a family friend tell me the truth. I just couldn't believe it, a few people had to confirm it for me.

At one point during this time she told an emergency room doctor that she had a son and that he was staying with me. They are mandated to report and that is how the Department of Children and Families became a part of my life. When my daughter called and told me that DCF would call me I was HORRIFIED. I was 47 years old and a mother of three grown daughters and I had never had DCF in my life. As a matter of fact, I had always heard terrible, scary stories about the people who worked for them. Jen's exact words, and I can still hear them to this day, were, "No, it's OK, Mom. It's a good thing. They are going to help me, us. Really." All I could manage was a, "yeah, OK." I was so overwhelmed.

Prior to September I basically didn't do much of anything. My partner, Chris and I just hung around the apartment, went shopping and did normal everyday things. She worked, but I have been on Social Security Disability for many years due to my depression, panic, and anxiety disorder. Now, here I was with a three-year-old who was scared and had no clue what was going on. And now I also had DCF involved in my life as well.

First was a phone call from an investigator. She came out and talked to me and then Ryan. During the talk with Ryan we found out there was physical abuse from both Jen and her boyfriend Timmy (also a heroin addict). Ryan described some of the things and I had to walk out of the room because I was crying. It was right then and there that I knew I had to do whatever I could to protect my grandson — anything and everything.

To help you understand why this became so important, I have learned through therapy, part of the reason is because I have guilt. When I was married to Jen's stepfather, he abused me and he also physically abused Jen and her half-sisters. Because of the abuse on me I felt there was nothing I could do. Now, with Ryan, I knew there were things in my power that I could do.

The DCF investigator explained that they would decide if there was enough to open a case for Ryan. If so, they would assign a caseworker and it would go on from there. Of course they did. This time, I had Ryan for seven months, a little longer than the seven to ten days Jen originally thought. When Ryan went home there was a safety plan in place, for her and for Ryan. There was a list of things Jen had to do and a list of people she could call if she felt she was in trouble. One of the things was that she could see Timmy, but he was not allowed around Ryan at all. I was taking Ryan to my house every other weekend. Ryan also started preschool through DCF so that there were eyes on Ryan and Jen. There were people watching and people she had to keep in contact with.

After Ryan went home I was lost, so I decided I needed a life. I was feeling better, became involved with MassRehab, and started doing some work to get back into the workforce. I signed up to do the MS Challenge Walk and I also started to volunteer for the MS Society. I lost some weight from all the walking and I was feeling good. My volunteering interrupted my time with Ryan, but instead of just switching weekends, Jen got angry and said that she would let me see him when she could. So my weekends got farther apart. In April 2013 I got a phone call from our DCF worker. She said Jen stopped therapy and she wasn't returning phone calls. She wanted to know if I knew anything. I told her about the visits and said I would try to get in touch with Jen. It all worked out that time — Jen lied her way through that one.

On May 14, I got a panicked call from the DCF worker. I needed to get Ryan. Jen was using again, Timmy was in the house. The house was a mess. It was bad. I got Ryan and he wasn't doing good. This time he was older, he wasn't that little baby who we could just cuddle and lie to. It didn't work that way this time. DCF went to court for temporary custody of Ryan. The next thing I know, I got a phone call from Ryan's new lawyer. My thoughts were "WHAT THE HELL…" no one explained any of this to me. I was getting calls from court investigators and the probation department from the court and another DCF investigator. I wish someone had told me about some of this BEFORE they all called me!

*YOU are the ONLY one who is looking out for that child's (or children's) best interest. No matter what DCF, lawyers, judges, court appointed anyone tells you, YOU are all that child has.*

So after I asked, I found out that DCF had to do another investigation even though they were already involved. The court investigator and probation department are ordered by the judge as "checks" on DCF to make sure there really is a child in need and that he is safe with his grandmother. Ryan's lawyer was court appointed because he needed someone looking out for his best interest even though DCF says that is what they were doing too.

Since May, I have learned so much. Some of it is hard to put into words, some of it everyone really needs to learn on their own because it is different for everyone, every case, and every child.

YOU are the ONLY one who is looking out for that child's (or children's) best interest. No matter what DCF, lawyers, judges, court appointed anyone tells you, YOU are all that child has. With any luck you will get a DCF worker who will at least listen to you. We are on our third DCF worker now. Shannon, the first one, I believe she started out thinking of Ryan, but then I think something happened. I think she spent too much time talking to my daughter and suddenly Jen became her focus. She lost her main goal in the case of keeping Ryan safe. We have since found out that she left certain key things out of the case and "lost" parts that are important. Then we got Tammy. At first, we thought she was going to be better, and she was, for a while. She seemed to put my daughter in her place, to hold her accountable, make her answer some tough questions. Shortly after it seemed all she wanted was reunification at any and all costs. When it became evident, by some statements she made that she didn't even read the whole case or the whole summary even, we knew we were in trouble with this one. She recently left her position. Now we have a new one. So far I am not impressed, but he has already taught me something else...

You have to stand up for yourself and for the child you have. I want to have my grandson tested for some behavior issues. I took Ryan to his doctor on the suggestion of Ryan's therapist. His doctor said she would refer us to Boston's Children's Hospital. I reported this to DCF at the Foster Care Review. All of a sudden they are telling me how Children's Hospital can take a long time, but that they can request the school do some testing in the meantime. Well, what do you know! The school never did the testing that Tammy requested. Now the new DCF worker, Kevin, comes along and does some follow up and he pushes for the school testing. I find out that the doctor never put the referral in to Children's Hospital. Now I am lost. Who do I turn to now? A friend tells me there is a place in Braintree I can go to. I run it by the supervisor at DCF and she doesn't answer. Ryan's doctor calls me back with the name of a colleague who can do a psychological evaluation on Ryan in February that is quicker than anywhere else. So I make the appointments. Now Kevin is fighting with me, saying that I am just trying to have him tested for no reason. He actually told Ryan's therapist that he feels I am just an overwhelmed grandmother. What was I supposed to do?

I fought back. It is hard for me. My panic and anxiety have returned. This whole thing is so uncomfortable for me. But I did it... I had to. Ryan NEEDS me to. His mother will NEVER do any of this for him. So, I wrote to his supervisor. I told her why I wanted the testing, where I wanted it. I told her what Kevin has said about me and I also asked her to sit with him and review the case with him because he was unaware that Ryan had been physically abused. You have to DO what you have to do.

No one is going to come to you and say, "what can I do to help you?" Oh wait, yes they will. I have my own caseworker — Jeremy. He does ask. But then sometimes he gives me the wrong information, telling me that I can get respite care, a foster care babysitter for Ryan that they will pay for. I am thinking GREAT, wonderful, since Ryan can't go with his own family. I can send him with total strangers. Then when the time comes and we meet a family willing to help out, Jeremy tells me they won't actually pay for it. I am on a fixed income, so this service isn't something I can use right now.

There is one thing that really bothers me the most, it is all the secrecy, or at least it feels that way. DCF and the lawyers all tell you nothing is going on, Jen is where she is and Ryan is safe and so there is nothing new to tell you. But then I find out they had a meeting to discuss when this or that was to happen, or they talked about what was going on with Jen, what her next move is. We had a court date and Jen missed it, one excuse or another. At that court meeting, DCF and everyone told me they didn't know what they were going for. They wanted Jen to move to a facility that would allow Ryan to live with her. Everything she needed was right there and Ryan would attend school in the community. They didn't know the exact locations of any of these so she could end up anywhere. The school system could be a good one or a bad one, who knew. (see what I mean, not looking for Ryan's best interest, let's just get them back together and end it). I argued against this, Jen even said she wasn't ready for this. DCF told me this was the plan they were moving forward with. At the next court date, I found out that DCF was going for permanent custody of Ryan. Of course, they had meetings talking about this, they all knew this was happening. No one took the time to explain it to me. He is in my care, I should have been included in this.

DCF thought I was just going to be a good little Nana. Just sit back and take care of Ryan and they will let me know when he goes home to Jen. They found out that I was NOT going to be that way. You have to speak up, you have to ask, you have to write down everything, and then bring it to their attention.

Everyone will tell you to document everything, to print out all of the emails, to write down all of the phone calls and other tasks. Do it. It is important. The only thing I don't do as much as maybe I should is to document every incident. If Ryan falls, I don't write down that he fell and bumped his knee. That's too much for me. I do document when he hurts the animals, when he has a major melt down, or when he is doing really well. These things are important to keep track of so you can look at how far you have come. You can see how much work you have put in and how much you have changed this child's life. Ryan came here in May and he had major temper tantrums, to the point that I would hold the bedroom door shut, he would yell, scream, and stomp his feet. He doesn't do that anymore. He didn't know how to sit at the kitchen table and eat a meal, now he at least sits there, but we still can't get him to eat right though.

Time and patience I guess.

*Dorrie Riley is a tired but happy grandmother to Ryan, taking each day as it comes.*

# Keeping Track:

*Help! Information Needed!*
*by Andrea B. Smith, PhD, and Linda L. Dannison, PhD*

One of the most important things you will need to do is to become an expert on your kin who will be in your care. Keeping track of information will make part of this process less frustrating. A three-ring binder with pocket to hold loose papers will be a life saver and allows you one place to keep all of the important information. Also, keep a journal, noting everything that you might want to recall in the future. (*Always think of the four Ws: WWWW — Who did you talk to, Where are they from, What did they talk about, and When did you speak with them.*) Get phone numbers and perhaps an address, and write down the gist of the conversation. Fill in this information as you locate it. Print clearly, in pencil in case some of it changes. This is the beginning of your record keeping and will help you get started. Below are items you will want to document in your binder.

## Information about the child(ren)'s parent:
Write down the parent's name, date of birth, social security number, address, phone number, and employment information. The child's other parent(s) names, dates of birth, other information including employment information is also helpful.

## Information about the child(ren):
This should incude: full names, social security numbers, any case numbers, court case or file numbers, dates of birth, present age, sex (m or f). *Spell everything correctly and double check all numbers.* **You want to be the best source for information about the kids, and you want to be an "expert" on them.**

List and keep track of any allergies, dates of all immunizations, special needs, doctors' names and addresses, who their school teachers are, anything that is special knowledge that you have. Know who the health insurance carrier is, if any, the policy holder and policy number, and how to locate the insurance claims office.

Get information on who might be involved and who might want to have a claim on the child's interests. Who are the other grandparents? Who are the other siblings? Who else might want the kids, and who else is working on the case?

# Where Do I Stand:

After you clarify your plans for your future and that of the children who are being placed with you, you can begin to assess, with some degree of certainty, whether those plans are realistic. These questions will help you begin to organize your thoughts and plans. Title a page in your notebook **Where Do I Stand** and include the following areas:

1. How did I get to be in charge of the child(ren)? (Who made this decision?) If I'm not in charge yet, do I want to be? What's the plan? Describe briefly, the events and circumstances that resulted in the child(ren) residing with you.

2. What agencies or departments are involved, and who are the players (people)? Make a short list of the people who have already been in contact with you about caring for the child(ren).

3. Is anyone else making a plan for the future? The child's future? Their parent's future? If so, who is in charge of those plans and what can I do about them? How can I become part of the planning? List anyone who is giving you instructions, advice, or directives.

4. Is there any paperwork out there that I have? Is there any paperwork I may need? If so, organize it in a file or notebook and keep good notes. Keep a list of the names and phone numbers of everyone you talk to, and don't be afraid to ask them to spell their name. Be kind and gentle, but be firm. This is a serious matter. Keep court records separated by court, and keep things pretty much in chronological order (organize them by date, with the oldest document on the bottom or at the back.) Use sticky notes or other ways to keep information attached to the documents. Try to keep clean copies, though, in case you or your lawyer needs to copy them for future court use.

## The Players — Who Do I Have to Deal With

Here are some of the people who may be a part of your case. Each state will have different people or names for the job they do.

**FIA Support Specialist**
**Protective Services Worker**
**Social Work Agency Caseworker**
**Social Work Agency Supervisor**
**Therapist/Counselor (adult child)**
**Therapist/Counselor (children)**
**CASA Volunteer**
**FOC Caseworker**
**Adult Child's Attorney**
**Juvenile Court–Judge/Court**
**WorkerChild(ren)'s Attorney**
**Circuit Court Judge**
**Other Parent's Attorney**

Tips on abbreviations: FIA: Family Independence Agency, CASA: Court Appointed Special Advocate, FOC: Friend of the Court

5. Keep a list of terms you run across that confuse you and find out what they mean. Always ask caseworkers or others if there is something you don't understand.

6. Know where you are and where you want to go with your responsibilities. Are we talking temporary or are we talking permanent? State, simply, your immediate objectives. And then state your long-term objectives.

7. Most important, recognize your relationship with the child(ren)'s parents, and the relationship of the parents with the child(ren). These relationships will ultimately be the ones analyzed for final (permanent) decisions.

The law doesn't try to define the "quality" of parenting — we've all seen both great parents and lousy parents. It may sound cold-hearted, but the law doesn't really care. What the law does care about is protecting rights — the rights of the parents and the rights of the kids. (Notice, we didn't mention any grandparents' rights or third party rights.) Here's where you have to make a decision — write all three choices down and choose one. Make your choice in pencil so you can change your mind!

1. I am going to manage things for the short term, and I want (expect) the child(ren) to go back to their parent(s).

2. I am in this for the long haul, whatever it takes.

3. I am going to wait and see what's going to happen.

## Tips When Seeking Information or Help

- Before you make contact decide if you have a specific need or are just looking for general information that might be helpful.

- Have pencil and paper handy to jot down what you learn from your phone call.

- When you make contact, be brief and polite. Often the person answering the phone is there to decide who can best answer your questions. If you are requesting help for a specific need, state your need and ask to speak to someone who can answer your questions.

- If you are seeking general information, explain that you are raising a grandchild and are looking for resources that might be helpful to you.

### Questions to ask:

- What are some benefits I might be able to get?

- What are the eligibility requirements?

- When and where can I apply? Can I have an appointment?

- What information and documents should I bring with me?

### When setting an appointment be sure to find out:

- Appointment date and time.

- Location (get directions including where to park, what door to enter, etc.)

- Name of person meeting with.

- Information and documents to bring.

- Time the appointment will take.

*If you have a disability or are otherwise unable to appear in person, ask if you can apply for assistance on the Internet or through the mail.*

### During your appointment:

- Arrive on time.

- Be prepared to wait.

- Have all of your information in order.

- Ask questions.

- If you are told you are not eligible for the assistance you are seeking, ask if there are other programs for which you might qualify.

- Ask for information on other services and referrals to other agencies.

- Be sure you understand everything before you leave.

- Get the name and phone number of the person you spoke with in case you think of other questions or run into problems.

- Do not be discouraged if things don't happen the way you would like them to. Be patient and polite and you will receive better service.

*Andrea B. Smith, PhD is a professor at the College of Education, Western Michigan University. Smith has more than 20 years experience working with kinship care families. She is co-director of the National Research Center on Grandparents Raising Grandchildren and co-executive editor of* **Grandfamilies: The Contemporary Journal of Research, Policy and Practice** *which can be found at scholarworks.wmich.edu/grandfamilies.*

*Linda L. Dannison, Ph.D., CFLE, recently retired as a Professor and Chairperson, Family and Consumer Sciences, Western Michigan University. She earned a master's degree and a Ph.D. from Kansas State University. Dannnison is a Certified Family Life Educator specializing in parenting education.*

*Smith and Dannison have worked together since 1996 to develop educational programs, resources, and trainings to support multigenerational families. They co-authored* **The Second Time Around: Grandparents Raising Grandchildren** *and* **Grand Ideas for Grand Kids**. *It can be found at: www.wmich.edu/grandparenting/resources/second-time.html.*

> "Everything will be
> okay in the end.
>
> If it's not okay,
> it's not the end."
>
> unknown

# Glossary of Acronyms Used by Social Service Departments
*Compiled by Angie Hurley*

AAL = Attorney Ad Litem

ADD/ADHD = Attention Deficit Disorder/Attention Deficit Hyperactivity Disorder

ASD = Autism Spectrum Disorder

AW = Adoption Worker

BMom or BF = Bio mom or bio father (sometimes BD is used for bio dad, not to be confused with bio daughter)

BP = Bio Parent

BS or BD = Bio son/bio daughter

CASA = Court Appointed Special Advocate

CPS = Child Protective Services

CW/CM = Case worker or Case Manager

DHS/CPS = Dept of Human Services and Child Protective Services. Different states call them different things

FAS = Fetal Alcohol Syndrome

GAL = Guardian Ad Litem

ICPC = Interstate Compact on the Placement of Children (adopting/fostering kids across state lines)

IEP = Individual Education Plan

ILP = Independent Living Program

MH = Mental Health

NAS = Neonatal abstinence syndrome (born dependent on a legally prescribed or illegally obtained drugs used during pregnancy)

OCD = Obsessive Compulsive Disorder

ODD = Oppositional Defiant Disorder

PTSD = Post Traumatic Stress Disorder

RAD = Reactive Attachment Disorder

SA = Sexual abuse or substance abuse

SPD = Sensory Processing Disorder

SW = Social Worker

Time In = an alternative to Time Out that provides children with comfort and safety while still addressing the behavior

TANF = Temporary Assistance For Needy Families

TPR = Termination of Parental Rights

WIC = Women, Infants, and Children (supplemental nutrition program for children up to age 5)

*Angie Hurley is a foster parent and a co-moderator of The Foster Parenting Toolbox Support group on Facebook.*

# Your Legal Toolbox

*"The most important thing you can do is to know what options you have for taking your kin. Take the time to look at your options and pick the one that is best for you, not your caseworker. If you don't understand, ask questions. I wish I had done more of that."*

# Formal Vs. Informal Kinship Care

*By Jan Wagner*

One of the most frequent questions I am asked by kinship caregivers is "how do I find financial resources to raise the child now that he or she is in my care?" The answer depends almost entirely on how the child is legally residing in your home. At a time when you are on overload by suddenly finding yourself caring full time for a child who is not your own, you need to make decisions based on practicality rather than emotion.

## Formal Kinship Care

Formal kinship care, by definition, is the placing of children in the home of a relative or close friend with a familial relationship through the child welfare system and by the court. The caregiver has the option, because of the open child protective services case, to become a licensed foster care home and foster parents to the child. In most states this will entitle you, the caregiver, to receive all the benefits of the foster care system, including financial reimbursements for the children. You will receive training and education in parenting children with special needs, have a case manager, support of a social worker and most likely a parental visitation and reunification plan. You must be transparent in your home and the care of the child in order to receive these benefits. The child welfare department will make the legal decisions involving the child, including terminating parental rights when reunification is not possible, allowing the child to be placed for adoption. The state will incur all financial costs for this process. If you feel you will need any of this in the future, you need to consider this option.

## Informal Kinship Care

Informal kinship arrangements occur because many relatives, particularly grandparents, hopefully assume that this will be a short-term agreement, often times involving biological parents and the caregivers as a way to keep the child out of the foster system, therefore waiving any child welfare or family court involvement with their families. There is also the fear that if the child goes into foster care the relative may never see that child again. The state readily accepts this type of arrangement due to cost savings. The downside of this becomes evident when the child remains in your home longer than a short period of time. If child welfare is not involved in an open case on the child, then they are not required to provide supportive services or reimbursements for their care. You become responsible for all decisions of the child, including any legal standing of the placement, but you will also be responsible for all of the financial costs, and you are on your own because you are not part of the system.

## Guardianship

The most common form of informal kinship is guardianship, which you apply for through family court. This can be temporary, partial, or full. There may be a parental visitation schedule drawn up during a formal hearing, and there will most likely be a reunification plan, which the parents are to follow before they can get the children returned. Your input into this hearing is important. Be meticulous in your documentations. By accepting guardianship of a child, you are accepting responsibility to act in their best interest and fulfill parental duties. The amount of court involvement varies, but you will, at the least, be required to file an annual report on the condition of the minor. But, your guardianship can always be challenged by the biological parent and overturned, so it is not a permanent arrangement.

## An Informal Guardianship Experience

My husband and I had an informal guardianship for our grandson. His mother left him with us temporarily when he was two. A hand-drafted power of attorney for medical treatment was left on the kitchen table per advice of a child services worker she consulted. I went to protective services to find out what our options were as my husband had recently lost his job and I could no longer work full time with a small, needy child. I was told that a parent has the right to leave their child with whomever they choose, as long as the child was safe and that if I pursued opening an investigation, they would simply require her to come and get her child. It was their determination that he was indeed safe with us, so there wasn't the criteria to open a case. I knew she was not capable at the time of parenting him and we felt it was far more important to keep the child from having to face any further hardship or risk. After six months of little contact and the period for the POA (Power of Attorney) had expired, we petitioned family court for emergency guardianship. She was served and temporary guardianship was granted by default. Two months later we had another hearing and received full guardianship. We were responsible for all costs, including filing fees. It was a good arrangement for us. We made all the decisions for education, medical, and travel. We did not have to ask the court or the state's permission for anything. But, there was always that looming fear that she would challenge us and he would be returned. Four years later, when we decided to adopt we found how important those first early decisions can be.

If you adopt a child from the child welfare system, even your own relative, the child qualifies for post-adoption services and subsidies, based on the child's need. You will qualify for adoption cost assistance, legal assistance, and a federal or state adoption refund, rebate or tax credit. If you adopt a child outside of the child welfare or foster system, neither the child nor you will qualify for any assistance. You must hire your own attorney and build your own case. All costs, including homestudies are your responsibility. It is expensive.

Because our grandson has some special needs emotionally due to early, pre-verbal trauma, we began to investigate the possibility of dissolving our guardianship during the adoption process, getting a foster license, have him placed under state ward and care in our home, and adopt him out of the system so that he would qualify for a medical subsidy. We were told that we would then be guilty of abandonment for failing to provide for our grandson under the responsibilities of being his guardian. Once you accept guardianship, you can't just give it back. Such an action could have jeopardized his remaining in our home, our ability to obtain a license, participate in school and sports activities, and the completion of the adoption itself. At the age of 61 and 62, we would be placed "on the list." We took this issue all the way to the state level of my Human Services Child Welfare Department and they would not support us. It was not a risk we were willing to take. On

September 27, 2012 our adoption was finalized.

## Consider the Options

You not only have to be the child's advocate, you have to be your own as well. Ask questions. Do your research. Don't make a decision based on what is best for the state, make your decision based on what is in the best interest of the child and for your family. Do not feel pressured into signing anything until you have had the time to consult someone. An attorney specializing in family law, members of a kinship support group, your family court judge or caseworker. Then, consider the options, based on the possibility that this may just be permanent. After all, if you think you loved that child before this happened, wait until he or she have lived in your home for a period of time. It multiplies, believe me.

*After raising three children, 37 years of marriage, and at the age of 57, Jan Wagner started raising her then two-year-old grandson. Not finding support services for her family, she soon became an advocate. She has served in a variety of positions including kinship chair of the Michigan Foster Adoptive and Kinship Families (MAFAK), kinship chair of a sub committee under Diversity for the National Foster Parent Association (NFPA), a member of the Child Welfare League of America's (CWLA) National Kinship Advisory Committee, and as a member of the Michigan State Kinship Coalition through the MSU Kinship Resource Center. Jan does kinship/grandparent trainings, workshops for conferences and speaking engagements. "If it has Kinship or Grandparents Raising Grandchildren as a title, I have explored it. ...I always wondered what my purpose in life was, or what I wanted to be when I grew up. Now I know." Jan can be reached at her blog site Raising H at jdwags.blogspot.com.*

# Legal Relationship Options
*by Generations United*

Below, find a summary of legal relationship options that can apply to grandfamilies.It is important to note that because this area of the law is created at the state-level, how these options are defined and which ones are available can vary significantly by state. For information about which laws are available in your state visit the Grandfamilies State Law and Policy Resource Center at www.grandfamilies.org.

**Adoption** – One of the most critical differences between adoption and other options is that it severs all of the biological parents' rights and responsibilities. The relative caregiver becomes the parent in the eyes of the law. This fact makes access to services on behalf of the child much easier. It also means that the biological parents cannot simply reappear one day and go to court to reclaim parental rights and responsibilities.

**Open or Cooperative Adoption** – About one-third of the states have this option available. As part of an adoption, the relative caregiver, birth parents, and child develop an agreement for post-adoption contact with the birth parents. In some states, siblings may also receive contact privileges through the agreement. If a party breaches the agreement's terms, courts can order remedies to enforce it. Invalidation of the adoption, however, is never a possible remedy.

**Guardianship** – The most significant distinction between adoption and guardianship is that guardianship does not sever the biological parents' rights and responsibilities. Parents typically retain the rights to visit the child and must consent to adoption and/or name change. They also keep the obligation to financially support the child. For caregivers, the guardianship designation allows them access to services on behalf of the child that otherwise might prove impossible. Unlike adoption, the parents can go back to court and ask for the guardianship to be terminated. Many states offer monthly guardianship assistance for children exiting foster care with their relative foster parents.

**Standby Guardianship** – This option exists in more than a third of the states. It allows a terminally ill parent to name a "standby guardian" to take over the day-to-day care of a child in the event of a triggering event, such as a parent becoming incapacitated, without the parent's rights being terminated. These laws were originally designed in response to the AIDS crisis.

**Legal Custody** – Legal custody is similar to guardianship, but is usually granted by a different court with varying procedures. The status of "guardian" may give access to more services and rights than "legal custodian." Consider, for example, how many times you read or hear the phrase "parent or guardian" without any mention of "legal custodian."

**De Facto Custody** – Because of difficulties with bringing legal custody cases and proving that parents are unfit, some states have enacted innovative laws that may help relative caregivers. These laws essentially provide that if a relative has been raising a child for a significant period of time, the first step in proving the case is met. Then, the relative can go on to prove that he or she should be awarded legal custody, because it is in the child's best interests. Kentucky was a pioneer in this area when it passed the nation's first de facto custody law in 1998.

## Consent and Power of Attorney Laws

In some states, relative caregivers who do not want or have a legal relationship to the children in their care have laws that make it possible for them to complete an affidavit and access health care and educational services on behalf of the children. About a third of the states have educational consent laws which effectively allow children being raised by relatives to attend public school free of charge. More states, about half, have some form of health care consent law.

Another option for those caregivers without a legal relationship may be a power of attorney. Parents execute a form or handwritten document that states what type of authority they are conferring to the caregiver. Some states allow parents to use power of attorney to confer school-related and health care decision-making authority. Like the consent laws, these laws do not require going to court.

Both consent affidavits and power of attorney documents can be easily revoked by the parents.

## Legal Assistance

Once a decision is made that a legal relationship is needed or wanted, finding an affordable lawyer can be difficult, if not impossible. There are some no- and low-cost alternatives available. Area Agencies on Aging, legal aid clinics, local law schools, and bar associations may provide legal assistance. Grandfamilies may be able to access referral services through local programs, including support groups.

For state specific resources, download your state fact sheet at www.grandfactsheets.org.

© 2014 Generations United. This article is used with permission from Generations United, www.gu.org

*For nearly three decades, Generations United has been the catalyst for policies and practices stimulating cooperation and collaboration among generations, evoking the vibrancy, energy, and sheer productivity that result when people of all ages come together. We believe that we can only be successful in the face of our complex future if generational diversity is regarded as a national asset and fully leveraged. The National Center on Grandfamilies is a critical part of Generations United's mission and strives to enact policies and promote programs that support relative caregivers and the children they raise. For more information visit www.gu.org.*

# The Interstate Compact on the Placement of Children (ICPC)
*by Janna Annest, JD*

## What is the Interstate Compact on the Placement of Children (ICPC)?

The ICPC is a contract between all the U.S. states and territories that establishes a uniform process for handling interstate adoptions. Many people are surprised to learn that every state has its own adoption laws, and no two are exactly the same. As a result, when a child from one state was adopted by a family in another state, he or she potentially could be subject to two different sets of laws.

Before the ICPC, once a child left a state, he or she left that state's adoption laws behind. Thus, if a California family adopted a child born in Texas, the child forfeited any protections available under Texas law, and if anything went wrong with the placement, Texas had no ability to fix it. Likewise, if the child was entitled to any benefits or support from state social services, Texas could shift all the responsibility to California.

By the 1960s, all states had signed the Compact, which established a mechanism for determining future financial responsibility for the child, ensured that appropriate safeguards were in place before a child left the state, and allowed the sending state to retain jurisdiction over the child. Each state now employs one or more ICPC administrators who must review and approve a placement before a child can cross state lines.

## Does the ICPC apply to kinship placements?

The ICPC applies to the placement of **any** child in state custody, regardless of the relationship between the child and the adoptive parents. If a child is not in state custody, placements among close family members are not subject to the ICPC process. Specifically, the ICPC does not apply to a child whose parent, step-parent, grandparent, adult sibling, adult uncle, adult aunt, or legal guardian places him with a parent, step-parent, grandparent, adult sibling, adult uncle, adult aunt, or legal guardian located in another state. Placements between more distant relatives, however — for example, adoption of a first cousin's child — are still subject to ICPC.

## If ICPC does apply, what will they need from us?

Each state's ICPC office maintains a checklist of information it requires. Although the adoptive parents' homestudy may not contain all of the information necessary for ICPC, it will include most of the key elements. Along with the interviews, home visits, and financial and medical information, the adoptive parents must have their FBI fingerprint clearances and state patrol and child welfare checks complete. Typically, those reports need to be less than 12 months old, but some states will accept them up to 18

*The ICPC is a contract between all the U.S. states and territories that establishes a uniform process for handling interstate adoptions.*

months. No ICPC request can be approved without a completed homestudy. ICPC may require additional information as well — for example, more detailed information about the child's medical needs and an explanation of how the adoptive parents plan on addressing them.

The attorney, agency, or caseworker handling the adoption will prepare a packet containing all of the information required by **both** states' ICPC offices, and send the packet to the ICPC administrators in the sending state. That administrator will review the packet, and if everything is in order, sign a form called the 100-A and mail the packet directly to the ICPC office in the receiving state. Although some offices now accept electronic submissions, it is still wise to include a pre-paid overnight mail envelope for the sending state's ICPC office to use to send the packet to the receiving state. When the receiving state has reviewed and approved the submission, its ICPC administrator will sign the 100-A and fax or scan it to the agency, attorney or caseworker. Only when the 100-A has been signed by both state administrators may the child cross state lines.

### How long does the ICPC process take?

The answer depends substantially on whether the child is in state custody or the kinship placement was privately arranged. If the child is not in state care, adoptive parents may receive approval within a week or two of submitting all the documents required by the sending and receiving states' ICPC administrators.

For the adoption of a child in state custody, the adoptive parents' homestudy will likely be completed by a social worker employed by their home state's Department of Social and Health Services (or its equivalent). It can take substantially longer for a state worker to complete a homestudy than a private social worker or agency. Despite their best efforts, state social workers often have more cases on their desks than they can keep up with, and emergent situations take first priority. You can help move the process along by educating yourself about the sending and receiving states' ICPC requirements. Many states have a checklist online, or if not, you can call the ICPC administrator directly. Information about each state's laws and procedures is available at *http://www.icpc.aphsa.org/content/AAICPC/en/home.html*. It is wise to research and review both states' checklists as early in the process as possible. This is especially true if the adoptive parents are relying on a privately-prepared homestudy to adopt a child in the custody of another state, because homestudies prepared in anticipation of private placements may not include all of the elements required for the adoption of a child in state care.

While some items on the checklist may be entirely in the hands of the social worker (e.g. interviewing you and drafting the narrative portion of the report), you can take charge of other aspects yourself, such as gathering references, and getting medical and financial reports. Keep copies of all the components of your homestudy, and have them readily available in electronic or hard copy form so that if anything gets misplaced, you can replace it immediately.

Remember that interstate adoption of a child in

**To determine the requirements for your state visit:**

http://icpcstatepages.org/

state custody involves considerations not present in private adoptions. For instance, if the child is entitled to benefits or services due to special needs, the states need to decide which state will bear those costs going forward. Naturally, this will slow the ICPC process. The most commonly reported reasons for delaying the ICPC process are incomplete homestudies or obtaining background checks, resolution of states' financial responsibility or medical services, obtaining background checks, and staffing and workload issues. Be realistic, and treat the social worker and the child's caseworker politely and respectfully, of course, but experience does show that the process moves faster for adoptive parents who are proactive, communicative, and persistent.

### Will anyone really know the difference if the child comes home before the ICPC process is complete?

It does matter. Don't do it. Particularly in private kinship placements, families may be tempted to transfer the child to his or her adoptive parents before the ICPC administrators in both states have signed the 100-A. However, courts have dismissed adoption petitions, revoked birth parents' consents, or vacated orders terminating parental rights as a penalty for ICPC violations. You do not want to have to hire a lawyer to explain to a judge why you should not be penalized for deliberately violating the law. ICPC is one of the final steps in a lengthy and often exasperating adoption process, but do not put the adoption at risk by cutting corners.

*Janna Annest is a shareholder at Mills Meyers Swartling in Seattle, Wash, practicing adoption law, estate planning, and business law. She graduated cum laude and with high honors from Dartmouth College in 2000, and earned her J.D. at the University of Washington in 2003. She has been named to the Washington Rising Stars list of outstanding lawyers each year since 2009, and is a member of the Board of Directors of World Association for Children and Parents (WACAP) and Adoptive Friends and Families of Greater Seattle (AFFGS).*

"I am not there yet but I am closer than I was yesterday."
- Maria Carry

# Basic Etiquette for Courtroom Attendance

*by Andrea B. Smith, PhD and Linda L. Dannison, PhD*

Everyone you deal with probably receives their salary from a government- or community-funded source. They aren't wealthy and there aren't many benefits. Taking on the wrath of a third party isn't considered one of the perks of the job!

In almost all instances, the workers are jammed up with more than they can handle. The more you help to lighten their burden, the more they might like you.

Problem solvers generally get appreciated (although not enough!) People who want to fight the system(s) — verbally or physically — are a dime a dozen, and you can't tell anyone something they haven't already been bored with.

Rest assured, you won't "make anyone's day" with abusive or threatening language. So no matter how bad your day is going; no matter how upset you might be at telling your story for the seventh time, and no matter how hurt you really are deep down inside, sit on it!

Courtroom manners are important. Assuming you don't come into court with a history (you verbally beat up on the judge's clerk, or you got a social worker so upset she went home from work — these are all rumors that do make it to the back rooms, and from there into the courtroom!), there is generally a level playing field. The court has its job to do. Follow this advice:

A. Since you are a third party, you probably won't be asked to speak. You may be allowed to speak after everyone else is through. Take notes while you are there!

B. Vocalizing and speaking out loud, making comments under your breath, calling people names, and other similar outbursts often result in an invitation to remove your conversation to the waiting room. Once you get kicked out, you probably won't be allowed to return.

C. If invited to speak, always address the judge directly and begin with "Thank you, your Honor," then continue. If you have organized some notes, refer to them but don't read them. You're already an expert on what you want to say.

D. Some emotion to show you are earnest and you really care is good. Too much of a good thing, however, can kill the effect. Avoid speaking "down" to anyone, calling anybody names, or referring to people as titles (Mrs. Smith, when it's really your daughter Judy).

E. You have a right to accuracy in court, and it is certainly permitted to offer correct information and point out incorrect information. Usually someone gets appointed to find the true answer.

# A Simplified [Generic] Lower State Court Structure
Here is an overview of what each court is called and what they can do.

## Court of General Jurisdiction

- may be called Circuit Court, Superior Court, or Court of Common Pleas

- has general jurisdiction; can hear any matter that comes before them unless state law reserves jurisdiction on the matter to a different court

- hears, for example:     felonies

    high-valve civil cases

    equity (justice)

## Courts of Limited Jurisdiction

- may be called Police and Traffic Court, District Court, County Court, Magistrate's Court, or Probate or Surrogate Court

- are only allowed to hear matters that have been assigned specifically to them by state law; all other matters go before the court with general jurisdiction

    **Traffic Court/County Court** hears, for example:
    traffic tickets

    misdemeanor offenses

    debtor/creditor cases

    small-value contract and damage lawsuits

    **Probate Court/Surrogate Court** hears, for example:
    estate matters

    guardians/conservators

    juvenile offenses, abuse and neglect cases

    medical/psychiatric commitments

    **Small Claims Court/Justice of the Peace** hears, for example:
    small claims

    small civil infractions

    landlord/tenant disputes

    ordinance violations

## See You in Court: *Tips for Preparing Kids For their Adoption Finalization*
*by Beth O'Malley, MEd*

When the big day is set and an adoption is going to be made legal how can social workers help families to prepare and children and teenagers to understand and celebrate this momentous occasion? After all, do you know anyone who likes going to court?

### Before the Court Date:

Devote at least one home visit to meet with the entire family and explain what will actually happen in court. If the children are old enough, I ask, "Have you seen Judge Judy on TV?" They usually laugh and say "Yes." Typically they relate a judge to some sort of punishment. Perhaps they have an image of a Judge harshly saying, "Go to jail" while banging down a gavel. Kids often think sending people to jail is the only thing judges do. I say, "A judge is a wise person who gives answers when people can't agree on something." Sometimes the disagreement involves money, land, or a family situation such as a divorce. In a child's case, decisions center around who will parent them. Remind children that judges can be young, old, man, woman, and any race. If you know which judge will hear the finalization it helps to have their name to personalize the process.

### Creative Reframe

Rosemary Broadbent, adoptive mom and adoption social worker for 26 years, tells all families, "Adoption is a process, not just an event." She explains that all of the time they have spent getting to know, love, and trust each other, they have actually been in the process of "adopting each other." In this way, she honors the entire time a family has spent together and acknowledges the adoption legalization as a milestone in a usually lengthy process. This concept is especially effective for older children who want to feel that their adoption is something they are involved in and not something being "done" to them.

### Let's Play Court

Nothing helps ease nervous jitters like role playing. During a home visit "play court." As the social worker, take the lead by playing the judge and have child (and other siblings and/or parent(s)) play themselves. Have them sit and waiting for the judge to enter. Instruct them about basic courtroom etiquette which dictates that they are supposed to stand when the judge enters, that all cell phones, beepers and toys be shut off and that proper dress be worn.

The judge will then tell the family, "You may be seated," and ask siblings a few simple questions, such as, "How old are you? What grade are you in? What sorts of things do you like to do?" and wait for them to answer. Role play the actual "adoption part" as well. I'll tell families that once the judge signs the adoption papers -the child is officially adopted. I'll say, "Well I've read the reports and I think this adoption is really wonderful. You are all very lucky." The family should then practice clapping and yelling, "Hurray! If they are shy, cue them by saying,"1, 2, 3." Be sure to complain that they weren't loud enough when they celebrated. Do this part repeatedly when each family member takes a turn being the judge. Don't be surprised at how much they love bossing each other around.

## How Long Does it Take?

This is the loaded question you should expect. After many rollercoaster years and sleepless nights, the actual adoption takes all of 10 minutes (OK, sometimes 5). It helps families to know ahead of time how quickly it goes. Some judges have their own rituals, which makes it a longer as well as an unforgettable day. Some read a formal statement or let the adopted child/teen sit in their chair and bang the gavel (you may have to ask — but I've never heard a judge say no). Most judges enjoy adoptions and are often heard saying, "This is the best part of my job." However, some judges are more subdued so families might have to make the day special all on their own. Encourage the family to eat out after the court ceremony and/or to have a party and celebrate the adoption anniversary like a birthday - that day and for years later.

Children should be allowed to help plan the celebration and to invite special guests. Don't let families start party planning too early (before the appeal period is over). Nothing like waiting 18 more months to put a damper on things! Tell them to invite extended family and friends. Let them know that while they will have to walk through a security check (similar to an airport) that balloons, flowers, and cameras are all allowed in the courtroom. I often volunteer to take pictures so they can focus on the actual event.

## Older Kids: Rituals

A picture is worth a thousand words. One Boston social worker filled up her bulletin board with photos of families on their

## Common Court Language

**Lower Court:** references to a "lower court" are to the court that has original jurisdiction to hear and decide a matter presented to it.

**Higher Court:** references to a "higher court" are to the Court of Appeals or the Appellate Court system and are beyond the scope of these materials.

**Standing:** authority to come before the judge with a legal matter or issue.

**Fiduciary:** legal responsibility to act for another's best interests; more than ordinary care of another's property.

**Power of Attorney:** appointment of another person to serve as "attorney in fact" to represent the grantor of the power for the purposes specified; a written instrument properly executed and certified.

**Complaint:** a complaint filed with a court upon some stated or statutory grounds; initiates court action requiring the defendant to answer the allegations.

**Petition:** similar to a complaint; a request formally presented to a court and requesting specific action or relief.

**Family of Origin:** the family into which one was born.

**Third Party:** a party other than a parent, legal guardian, or the child. Grandparents, most often, are "third parties."

**Status:** legal term that can be applied to the relationship between the grandparent and the child(ren) in their care.

Adoption Day. When kids would come to the office they were mesmerized by the pictures anticipating adding theirs to the mix. Here's another idea. Create an album (simple three-ring notebook) with a page for each of the families you have worked with through finalization and bring it with you on a home visit. This will provide a visual for "getting adopted" and prove that this "adoption thing" really happens.

## Bittersweet Feelings:

No matter how loving an attachment between adoptive parent and child, the legal finalization officially signals that the child has "lost" his or her first family and possibly previous foster families too. There are no more chances the birth parent(s) will return to the parenting role or that previous biological or foster siblings will share the same parents or roof. If a child is getting a new last name this may be troubling. While they may be happy about their inclusion in their permanent family they may be sad to give up a rare possession that they have carried with them - their last name. Or, they may feel disloyal to biological family members for changing the name. Other children have practiced the spelling of their adoptive name from Day 1, craving the security and permanence offered through adoption.

While the adults usually celebrate the end of an arduous, labile process — it's important to remember that this occasion may bring up sadness for the older child. On the day of the finalization, and during anniversary celebrations, the child needs his or her complex feelings honored. On anniversaries, a child once happy about her finalization might become sad or a previously grieving child might feel joyous. Feelings can change hour to hour or year to year.

## Saying Good-bye Families

As the social worker, acknowledge your shifting role. An adoption finalization likely means you will no longer have regular home visits, not to mention legal custody. Sometimes it feels like you are losing good friends — while other times families are glad to no longer have the "state" sitting at their kitchen table. Acknowledge the feelings of family members as well as your own.

For me, I've found in my role as a social worker, there is nothing as important to me as making families. I am honored and awestruck every time I witness a family being formed through adoption.

*Beth O'Malley, MEd, is a speaker and the author of* **Lifebooks: Creating a Treasure for the Adopted Child, My Foster Care Journey,** *and* **For When I'm Famous: A Teen Foster/Adoption Lifebook.** *To learn more about the books, call 800-469-9666. To receive free lifebook tips, visit www.adoptionlifebooks.com.*
*Copyright ©2012 Beth O'Malley.*

## Kinship Care: *A Child's Home Away From Home*
*By Melissa D. Carter, JD, Christopher E. Church, Esq., and Thomas B. Hammond, JD*

Relatives play a critical role in the response to child abuse and neglect. As an extension of the child and the child's family, relatives offer continuity, stability, and connection when a child cannot live with his or her parents. During the most recent reporting period, more than 3.7 million children were subjects of at least one child abuse or neglect report to a state child protective services agency. In that same time period, 252,320 children entered foster care. The majority of these children will return home after their parents have improved their parenting skills and are able to provide for and ensure the safety of the child through supportive services provided by the child welfare system. In the meantime, however, each of these children will need a temporary home that offers love, nurturance, and adequate daily care. Additionally, some children will not be able to safely return home from foster care. These children need and deserve a permanent alternative family to support their continued successful development. The honorable tradition of kinship care, through which relatives or other adults who have a family-like relationship with the child step in to provide temporary or permanent care for a child, offers a desirable solution for a child in a time of crisis.

> *Kinship care minimizes the traumatic effects of family separation and eases the stress of adjusting to a new environment.*

### Becoming Increasingly Common

Kinship care in all of its forms is becoming increasingly common. Recent child welfare data show that one in four children in foster care are living with a relative. Even more, we know many additional children are living with relatives or other close family friends informally, or without the ongoing supervision of the state, as an alternative to placing the child in formal foster care. Research demonstrates that kinship care offers unique benefits to children. Kinship care minimizes the traumatic effects of family separation and eases the stress of adjusting to a new environment. The existing bonds between the child and the kinship caregiver create a stabilizing effect that promotes the child's positive identity; preserves the child's connection to family, school and community; and maintains continuity of routines and traditions. Accordingly, children in kinship care are less likely to experience behavioral problems than children in the general foster care population.

In recognition of the importance of kin to achieving positive outcomes for children, federal law establishes a preference for relative caregivers over unrelated caregivers when determining with whom the child should be placed. To reinforce this preference, the law requires state child welfare agencies, within 30 days of a child's removal from parental custody, to identify a child's adult relatives and explain their options to participate in the care and placement of the child. The required notice must explain any services or supports that are available. If a relative does not step up early, he or she may lose the opportunity to do so later as the case progresses. Once involved, however, the relative caregiver must receive notice of, and be given a right to be heard in, any court hearings about the child. In this way, the kinship caregiver can share information about the child's well-being and needs with the judge, to inform the legal decisions made in the child's case.

## Kinship Care Presents Challenges to Family

Despite the popularity of kinship care, these arrangements present certain challenges. Kinship care can be disruptive to family relationships. For example, a grandparent caregiver may feel tension between supporting her son or daughter, who is the child's parent, and the child. Additionally, though emotionally rewarding, raising a child is expensive. The need for kinship care often arises from a crisis, and the caregiver may not be financially prepared to deal with the sudden challenge of parenting additional children, or parenting again. Moreover, children who have experienced trauma and disruption as a result of a history of abuse or neglect, parental substance abuse, abandonment, parental incarceration, or domestic violence are more likely to have physical and mental health disabilities, requiring expensive service interventions. Kinship caregivers are often unaware of the services and assistance available to them or are unable to access supports because of their legal status with respect to the child.

## Formal And Informal Caregiving Arrangements

Kinship care includes formal and informal caregiving arrangements. Informal, or voluntary, kinship care is based on a private agreement between the parents and the kinship caregiver. Though the child welfare agency may facilitate the arrangement, legal custody typically remains with the parents and no ongoing services or supervision are offered to the biological parents, kinship caregiver, or child. Kinship caregivers providing care on a voluntary basis are likely eligible for benefits through Temporary Assistance for Needy Families (TANF), which is available to support low-income families to become self-sufficient. Caregivers do not have to have legal custody to apply, but they do need to meet their state's TANF definition of a kin caregiver. Even if the family does not qualify, the caregiver can still apply and receive benefits for the children, which are available until the child's 18th birthday. Kinship caregivers may also be eligible for the Supplemental Nutrition Assistance Program (SNAP), or food stamps. The entire household income is considered as the basis for determining eligibility, and the children for whom the kinship caregiver is providing care can be included in the family size when determining the benefit amount. And finally, a kinship caregiver may be able to access health insurance through Medicaid or the state's Children's Health Insurance Program (CHIP), which provide coverage of health care expenses for low-income children and adults. Each state has different rules for eligibility and coverage, but the caregiver does not have to have legal custody to apply.

## Formalizing May Give Access to Support

Formalizing a kinship care arrangement may allow a caregiver to access additional sources of financial assistance, programs, and services that are not available in voluntary, or informal, kinship care. Formal kinship care arrangements involve the temporary transfer of legal custody from the parent to the child welfare agency, which then places the child in the care of the relative. When a child is in the legal custody of the state, the child welfare agency is responsible for ensuring the child is receiving all educational, therapeutic, health, and other services to ensure his or her safety and well-being. Formal kinship care involves ongoing court oversight until legal custody is transferred back to the parent or permanently granted to a substitute caregiver.

As a temporary caregiver, a relative has the option of becoming a fully licensed or approved foster parent by complying with certain training and evaluation requirements that are meant to ensure the child's safety. Doing so will allow the kinship caregiver to receive the same supports as other foster parents, including more structured involvement with the child welfare system to deal with the child's parents, school and healthcare providers. Relative foster parents also receive a foster care subsidy to offset the costs of the food, clothing, shelter, and other care they provide for the child, and child care assistance or respite care may also be available depending on state programs and resources.

If a child cannot be safely reunified with his or her parents, kinship caregivers are encouraged to consider becoming a permanent family for the child through adoption or legal guardianship. The federal law preference for relatives applies to permanent placements as well. Kinship caregivers may decide to adopt the child in their care. Adoption is the most legally secure permanency option as it requires the parents to fully surrender their rights or a court to terminate parental rights, legally severing the parent-child relationship. After the adoption is finalized, the guardian becomes the child's full legal parent and the child welfare agency is no longer involved. In 2011, 31 percent of children in foster care were adopted by relatives. If the child meets the state's definition of a "special needs" child, the family is eligible to receive ongoing adoption assistance, in the form of a monthly subsidy and access to one-time funds to cover the costs of legal fees or other special assistance.

## Permanent Guardianship

Permanent guardianships are a common alternative to adoptions. They are particularly appealing to older youth who want to maintain ties with their parents or to caregivers who prefer not to terminate parental rights. Once a guardianship is created, legal custody is transferred from the state to the guardian, and in most circumstances, the agency ends its involvement with the family. The guardian has legal and physical custody to act as the child's parent and make decisions, but the parents often retain visitation or other rights. These arrangements are often accompanied by a kinship guardian assistance payment, or subsidy similar to the payment received as a foster parent. The requirements vary by state, but additional incentives are available at the federal level to ensure the success of this permanency option.

## In Conclusion

When removal from the home becomes necessary for the protection of the child, kinship care offers one of the most stable and least traumatic placements. While certain challenges still exist in accomplishing these placements, the benefits for both the child and the

> *The kinship caregiver stands as a familiar guardian and protector in a time of crisis in the affected child's life.*

family are compelling. The kinship caregiver stands as a familiar guardian and protector in a time of crisis in the affected child's life. At times this relationship is only temporary, but in others, the kinship caregiver may ultimately fulfill the role of parent in the child's life, in effect becoming the child's new home away from home.

*Melissa Carter, JD, is a member of the Emory Law faculty and Executive Director of the Barton Child Law and Policy Center (www.bartoncenter.net). The Barton Center is an interdisciplinary child law program founded to promote and protect the legal rights and interests of abused, neglected, and court-involved children through legislative advocacy, policy development, and holistic representation and to develop dedicated and knowledgeable juvenile law professionals.*

*Christopher Church, Esq., is the Children's Data Manager at the Children's Law Center at the University of South Carolina School of Law. Prior to joining the Children's Law Center, Christopher was the Managing Attorney of the Supreme Court of Georgia's Committee on Justice for Children, at the Administrative Office of the Courts of Georgia. Christopher holds a law degree from Gonzaga University School of Law and a Masters in Mathematics from the University of North Texas. He completed his undergraduate studies at Concordia College in Bronxville, NY.*

*Juvenile Court Judge Thomas "Britt" Hammond of the Toombs Judicial Circuit in the state of Georgia was appointed to the bench on October 1, 2004. Prior to that, Judge Hammond worked as an agency (Georgia Department of Family and Children Services) attorney for eight years before becoming a judge. He is a recipient of the 2012 Georgia County Welfare Association's "Friend of Children Award" and the 2012 American Public Health Services Association's "Mitchell Wendell Jurist Award" for significant contribution to the field of children's law.*

# Grandparenting a Teenager

*By Sherry Howard*

It is not the normal order of things for a parent to need to go to court to protect a grandchild from their own child. When that happens, no one wins; yet, sometimes it is the only way to fully protect a child. Such was my situation nearly two years ago when I went to court to gain custody of my grandson. This brief synopsis of our situation in no way describes that for every word written, 10,000 tears were shed and countless nights were sleepless.

My journey to court started much longer ago than two years, however. As with most grandparents and other kinship caregivers, resorting to the court system was an act of sheer desperation. Nearly 15 years ago my precious first grandchild was born to my daughter and her husband. They lived happily with my husband and me for several years. We have precious memories of those early years, with Hunter the center of all of our lives. Then, when Hunter was only three, my husband died and soon my daughter and her husband divorced in bitter proceedings. Our happy little world was shattered.

*This brief synopsis of our situation in no way describes that for every word written, 10,000 tears were shed and countless nights were sleepless.*

Initially, my daughter had full custody of Hunter and he remained in my care. Sometimes his mother lived with us but usually she didn't. During Hunter's early years, his involvement with both parents was sporadic, with weeks or months sometimes passing without visits from them. Many nights Hunter cried himself to sleep, not understanding why his mother and father were not in his life. At other times, they visited regularly. Those early years of uncertainty were by far the worst; he was just too young for explanations.

Eventually, Hunter's dad got shared custody, after proving himself more dependable regarding his involvement with Hunter. From the ages of four to twelve, I was the constant in Hunter's life and his primary "parent," with no legal standing whatsoever.

Every situation in which a grandparent or other kin has to parent a child, there is a back story which is heartbreaking. Seldom does anyone outside of the home know the details, it is a silent shame too painful to discuss. Every story is different but the joys, sorrows, and frustrations bind people like us: raising someone we love and being completely unable to shield them from hurt! Our stories usually involve parental neglect or abuse, addiction, exposure to high risk situations, emotional turmoil, and mental instability or immaturity, oftentimes, all of these factors combined.

So, my journey that ended with court actually began many long years ago. Our problems were those I've just mentioned, and we were in constant turmoil trying to balance Hunter's involvement with his parents. Throughout the years, I consulted countless psychologists, attorneys, court workers, child welfare workers, police officers, church counselors, and anyone else who might be able to help us. I think I called every hotline and visited many chat rooms to find other people who understood the experience we were having, hoping for some answers. Over and over, I was told the same story. If the child is safe with you right now, the court is the only entity which can intervene. I was advised repeatedly not to "make waves" because it was likely that his father would get custody. I was told that courts always chose a parent and that "life style" choices were broadly interpreted to allow a host of unhealthy behaviors on the part of parents before child custody was jeopardized. I was told by a psychologist that a boy child is better off living with a father in a shack under poor circumstances than living without the father. This kind and supportive psychologist helped me through the worst of times by getting me to lower my expectations for "happily ever after" and helping me search for something, however small, to praise whenever possible.

Throughout the years, Hunter's father became more stable and Hunter loved to see him for brief visits. I had always worked hard to remain in a positive relationship with Hunter's dad, even at the worst of times. He had lived with us for years, and I loved him although I hated many of the things he did during the worst years. Conversely, my daughter's mental stability and involvement with Hunter deteriorated horribly. It was my daughter's emotional instability and a health crisis with Hunter that made me believe finally that I would have to risk the court system because Hunter's safety was being jeopardized by my daughter's bad choices and she no longer cooperated. Rather, she used my protectiveness toward Hunter and my love for her to "blackmail" me repeatedly just to keep him and her safe. If she didn't get what she wanted, she'd somehow find a way to put Hunter in the middle or appear so desperate that I took care of whatever monetary need she had. Hunter carried too heavy a burden, feeling responsible for and to his mother. He grew resentful and protective at the same time and increasingly frustrated by his interactions with his mother. He didn't want to visit her or go with her, yet we had no right to deny her the opportunity when she insisted.

Four years ago, I consulted a high-powered family court attorney. This attorney charged hundreds for a consult and asked for a $4,000 retainer, which he said would probably not go far toward the ultimate expense of such a case. He said that in our state, it was almost impossible for a grandparent to get custody. He did give me some good advice. He told me to continue to document everything regarding my daughter's behavior on a daily basis, including each day with no contact at all, since that was significant. He explained that I met the requirements for de facto custody status in our state but that a court would have to officially designate that standing. The attorney was not at all encouraging or compassionate and I was discouraged. Because of the expenses of caring for my daughter and her son, I didn't have the money for a long court battle. I still hoped that things would get better; I didn't want to make the sad choice to go against my mentally ill daughter in court.

Eventually, Hunter was in dangerous situations in his mother's care repeatedly. I desperately appealed to Hunter's dad to help me do something. He agreed and our journey through court began. We actually went to our courthouse and visited several offices explaining the dangers Hunter faced. Initially, we were just run in circles. Finally, someone came and talked to us and told us the correct paper to file to get a hearing on the situation. I had no legal standing; Hunter's dad had to initiate the request for a change in status. I was completely intimidated by the entire court process and frightened to trust an outside intervention; nothing such as this had ever occurred in our family.

Eventually, we had a court date, and I still had no standing legally regarding Hunter. I was allowed to sit in the back of court and the judge asked who I was. After hearing that I was a full-time caregiver and grandparent, the judge immediately gave me de facto custodian status and explained that I now had a legal voice in the proceedings. Hunter's father's unusual support of my efforts in court influenced the judge to give me temporary custody, although at this point, children are sometimes removed from the home. That had always been my biggest fear that Hunter would go into someone else's care temporarily. The judge also appointed a guardian ad litem, a court appointed advocate attorney for Hunter, to investigate our situation. More meetings, more unpaid days off work for my former son-in-law and a lot more stress ensued during this time. My daughter, her ex-husband, and I each needed to pay the guardian ad litem $200 to continue this process. I knew that it would drag out forever waiting for my daughter to pay, so I immediately paid the $600, which I was allowed to do.

Hunter's court appointed attorney then had me bring Hunter for a meeting with him and said he would do home visits to all three homes to assess the situation. I met with his attorney and provided the documentation I had. Eventually, the attorney never made home visits, deeming them unnecessary after the meetings with each of the four of us.

After multiple visits to the court and our involvement with the guardian ad litem, we had a last court appearance at which the judge spoke to us. My daughter sat on one side and I sat with Hunter's father on the other side. My daughter felt that was an ultimate betrayal, never realizing her deeds in bringing us to that point. She told the judge under oath that I was verbally abusive, this daughter who was the center of my world, but whose mental illness was so unpredictable.

We were allowed to go to a side room to reach an agreement, with Hunter's guardian ad litem documenting the details of the agreement. The guardian made it clear to my daughter that she stood to lose parental rights entirely based on what he'd seen. We all agreed at that time to more or less continue with things as they stood, only with legal status now. I was granted sole custody. I wanted no child support at that time, which was shocking to the court. Money had been too much at the root of problems with my poor grandson, having grown up with child support issues all of his life. And his dad was in school and his mom destitute. I felt blessed on this day beyond belief to have an end to the uncertainty. Yet, as I said, no one "won" anything that day.

## Advice if You Plan to Seek Custody

My advice to any "kin" seeking custody of a child is this:
- At any cost maintain positive interaction as much as possible with birth parents.
- Be as honest as is age appropriate with the child, but with the least amount of information needed for safety. They don't need much information.
- Document everything; you may need it. Facts count.
- Avoid court if at all possible; you are surrendering yourself to a process over which you have no control. The law is clearly biased toward birth parents.
- Never, ever speak badly about the child's parents to him or in front of him. Be sure he loves and is compassionate toward them.
- Forget about being right, just be an advocate for your child, even at the expense of

alienating your adult child. Hold yourself to high standards.

- Be firm and factual in court. The court is no place for emotional outbursts.
- Keep your daily life as normal as possible because the stress for your child is incredible.

I'd love to say that we all lived happily ever after. We are probably as happy as anyone can be in our situation. I no longer worry about Hunter's safety and his routine is certainly steady. He got something he wanted, which was to have some control over his time. He now gets one weekend a month to be at home. Although Hunter happily visits his dad most weekends for one night; he sees his mother at random when she visits us or occasionally stays with us. We talk to her most days and we both worry a lot about her mental status and well-being. Hunter has now, and will always have, a deep sadness that his life is not like most children who live with at least one parent. He loves me and "chose" me, but, as I said, it is not the natural order of things. A little sadness is always with us about this. With focus and perseverance we have brought some measure of peace to our lives. Hunter is an awesome young man and I hated seeing what he went through; I hope it will be a positive influence in some way in the man he becomes.

*Sherry Howard is a freelance writer and editor. Sherry's advanced degree and experience as an award winning school principal in one of the largest urban school districts in the United States provided her with a broad background on the growth and development of children. During her career in education, Sherry authored and edited many professional publications and earned her black belt in understanding kids! Sherry's other credentials include consulting with a major publisher, advocating for special needs children, and volunteer work in the schools she loves. Sherry's kinship experiences with her grandson influenced her to share the challenges and joy of a kinship caregiver through writing. Her own kinship experiences taught her that parenting chosen children is an especially rewarding journey. Sherry's current project is a mystery for adolescent readers inspired by her grandson and his friends.*

# Your Financial Toolbox

"*Biggest piece of advice:  we never expected it to go on as long as it did and we neglected to advocate for full reimbursement. Instead we used our own funds. DON'T! It goes longer and then you meet resistance getting help. It is money for the kids ADVOCATE for it from day one!*"

# Financial Resources for Relative Caregivers
*by Generations United*

Many grandparents and other relative caregivers face significant economic difficulties. About 22% of grandparents responsible for grandchildren live in poverty. Many younger caregivers must quit their jobs, cut back on work hours, or make other job-related sacrifices that can negatively affect their future economic well-being.

Caregivers who are either retired or are not working also suffer financially for taking in their relatives' children, often depleting life savings, selling belongings, and spending their retirement income to care for the child. Many older caregivers already live on limited incomes so caring for a child can severely strain their finances.

There are a few potential sources of financial assistance for relatives raising children.
- Temporary Assistance for Needy Families (TANF)
- Foster Care Payments
- Adoption Assistance
- Guardianship Assistance Program (GAP)
- Social Security
- Supplemental Security Income (SSI)

Where available, Kinship Navigator Programs may also provide caregivers with one-time financial help or connect them with other assistance and supports.

## Temporary Assistance for Needy Families (TANF)

TANF provides time limited assistance to families with very low incomes. It is the only option available to grandfamilies who are raising children outside of the formal foster care system. Each state determines the income eligibility for its TANF program and the amount of assistance to be provided to families. There are two basic types of grants a relative caregiver can receive under TANF.

### Child Only Grants
- Are typically quite small and may not sufficiently meet the needs of the child – in 2011, the average grant gave $8 per day for one child, with only slight increases for additional children.
- Usually consider only the needs and income of the child when determining eligibility.
- Because few children have income of their own, almost all grandfamilies can receive a child-only grant on behalf of the children in their care.

### Family Grant
- Are usually larger than child-only grants.
- Impose 60-month time limit and work requirements (states can exempt caregivers from these requirements and some do).
- Consider the caregiver and child's incomes when determining eligibility.
- Provides funding for the needs of the child and the caregiver.
- May not be appropriate for retired relative caregivers or for caregivers who will need assistance for more than 60 months.

## Foster Care Payments

Foster Care Payments provide monthly payments to relative caregivers on behalf of children in their care if the children are involved in the child welfare system. The vast majority of children in grandfamilies are ineligible because grandparents or other relatives stepped in to care for the children before the child welfare system became involved.

- Relatives must become licensed foster parents.
- Payments are typically higher than the TANF child-only payments grandparents or other relatives could receive on behalf of the children in their care (and usually higher than a "family grant") – in 2011, the average monthly payment was $511.
- Payments multiply (e.g. double, triple) as the number of children cared for increases.

## Adoption Assistance

Adoption Assistance provides payments to relative caregivers who choose to adopt qualifying children in their care. Children must have special needs to qualify. "Special needs" are defined by the state, but generally include characteristics or conditions that make it difficult to place the child with adoptive parents without a subsidy.

- Available in all states to children with "special needs" who are adopted from the child welfare system.
- Amount of payment varies by state – specific eligibility, benefit, funding, and other characteristics for each state's adoption subsidy program are available through the North American Council on Adoptable Children's website at www.nacac.org.

## Guardianship Assistance Program (GAP)

The federal Fostering Connections to Success and Increasing Adoptions Act of 2008 allows states and tribes to take an option to offer financial assistance to grandfamilies under the Guardianship Assistance Program (GAP). GAP provides monthly assistance to what are known as "Title IV-E" eligible children who exit the foster care system into a guardianship with a relative. The majority of states, the District of Columbia, and several tribes now offer GAP.

- Relatives must be licensed foster parents.
- The children must have been in foster care with the relatives for at least 6 months.
- Adoption and reunification with the parents are not appropriate options for the children.

The majority of jurisdictions with GAP also offer guardianship assistance to those children who are not Title IV-E eligible leaving the foster care system with relatives. Unfortunately, few places offer similar help to those children who have not first been part of the foster care system.

## Social Security

Children being raised by grandparents may be eligible for Social Security if the child's parent is collecting retirement or disability insurance benefits. If one of the child's parents has died and was fully insured when he or she died, the grandchild may also be eligible. Grandchildren may also qualify for Social Security based on the work record of the grandparents. More information is available at www.socialsecurity.gov/kids/parent5.htm.

## Supplemental Security Income (SSI)

SSI may be available to relative caregivers and the children they are raising if either the caregiver or child has disabilities that seriously limit their activities. In 2013, the average monthly SSI payment for children younger than age 18 was $633. The disability planner on the Social Security Administration website can help determine eligibility, www.ssa.gov/d&s1.htm.

## Food Programs

In addition to monthly financial assistance, there are programs that may help relative caregivers pay for food:
- Supplemental Nutrition Assistance Program (SNAP)
- Women, Infants, and Children (WIC) Program
- National School Breakfast and Lunch Programs
- Summer Food Service Program (SFSP)

## Supplemental Nutrition Assistance Program (SNAP)

SNAP, formerly known as "Food Stamps," may be available to relative caregivers to help get food for their grandfamily. Local offices, the state hotline, and each State's application are available at www.fns.usda.gov/snap/applicant_recipients/apply.htm.

## Women, Infants and Children (WIC) Program

The WIC program can help eligible relative caregivers meet nutrition needs of children they raise younger than age 5. Children must have certain types of health conditions to qualify. To apply, relative caregivers should start by calling their state office toll free. For those numbers, see www.fns.usda.gov/wic/Contacts/tollfreenumbers.htm.

## National School Breakfast and Lunch Programs

This program provides free or low-cost meals to eligible students, and is available through the children's schools.

## Summer Food Service Program (SFSP)

SFSP provides low-income children raised by relatives and others with nutritious meals when school is not in session. Free meals are provided to all children 18 years old and younger at approved SFSP sites. Visit www.whyhunger.org/findfood to locate sites using an online map.

## Federal Tax Credits

There are a number of federal tax credits available to relative caregivers.
- Earned Income Tax Credit (EITC)

- Child tax credit
- Additional child tax credit
- Child and dependent tax care credit
- Adoption tax credit

## Earned Income Tax Credit (EITC)

The EITC is refundable. That means relative caregivers who do not earn enough to pay taxes, can get a refund check from the IRS.

- Children must live with the relative caregivers for more than half the year.
- This tax credit applies until the children turn age 19 (or 24 if full time students).
- If the children are totally and permanently disabled, there are no age requirements.

## Child tax credit

This tax credit of up to $1,000 per child is available for dependent children younger than age 17. This credit is not refundable. So, if relative caregivers do not owe enough taxes, they cannot claim the credit.

## Additional child tax credit

This tax credit may help relative caregivers who do not owe enough taxes to benefit from the child tax credit. Unlike the child tax credit, this tax credit is refundable.

## Child and dependent tax care credit

This credit of up to $3,000 per child helps relative caregivers who have hired someone to help care for the children so the caregivers can work or look for work.

## Adoption tax credit

The adoption tax credit gives a credit for the money caregivers have spent to adopt children. The Affordable Care Act made the credit refundable for 2010 and 2011. Caregivers may file an amended tax return if they adopted during those years, and perhaps get a refund check. As of 2012, the credit is no longer refundable.

More information about all these tax credits is available at www.irs.gov. Please note that tax credits themselves are also not counted as income and will not be considered when applying for financial assistance or food support.

*© 2014 Generations United. This article is used with permission from Generations United. More information can be found here www.gu.org.*

# Financial Planning
*By Claudia Mott, CFP*

It may seem like the day-to-day bills are using up every spare bit of money, making saving for a rainy day impossible. What happens when something totally unexpected happens in your life, like your grandchild comes to live with you? Setting aside the money for a special purchase, an unexpected life event or paying off a debt isn't always easy, but without a spending plan or budget it can be next to impossible. Creating a budget isn't hard to do, especially with some of the computer-based tools that are available today. Getting started does require taking the time to organize bills and bank statements and thinking about the goals that you want to set for your spending plan. This will give you the steps that will help you create a budget and give you the tools to get on a path to planning for your families' needs and saving.

## Getting Started

To get started, there are some terms that are important to understand before we get into the budgeting process.

- **Income:** The money that comes into a household, which is used to pay bills and expenses is considered income. It may be a paycheck from an employer, a social security or disability payment, or other form of assistance.

- **Expenses:** The most common expenses are for housing, transportation, food, and clothing. These are considered staples (sometimes referred to as fixed or non-discretionary) and are those things you can't live without. Expenses for entertainment, vacations, and dining out are considered non-essential or variable and are often the areas where a bit of cutting back can create savings for other purposes.

- **Cash flow:** The difference between income and expenses is called "cash flow." When you have more income than expenses, your cash flow is positive. Negative cash flow happens when expenses are higher than the amount of income you have coming in.

- **Debit:** Money that is taken out of an account is called a debit. An online bill payment, a handwritten check, a withdrawal at an ATM or a bank fee are all considered debits.

- **Credit:** A deposit into an account is labeled a credit. This includes the direct deposit of a paycheck, a deposit made to a bank teller or through an ATM or interest paid on an account.

## Create a Plan

There are a few steps involved in creating a budget or spending plan. While it may take a little extra time and effort to get started, once you are up and running your monthly update should be easy.

**Step 1: Set both short- and long-term goals.** The reason most people want to track their spending is because they are trying to save for something in the future. Short-term goals are those that are going to be met within the year and long-term goals might not happen for five or ten years. No matter the timeframe, having a reason to want to put money aside can help keep you on track, because it will feel great when you are able to reach the goal.

**Step 2: Create an account for your savings.** With a savings goal in mind, having a place for the money that you are going to put aside to reach that goal is just as important. Opening a savings account at your local bank is the easiest and safest option. When our savings get mixed in with our regular accounts it is much too easy to say, "I'll just use this today and replace it next week," but then next week never happens and reaching your goal doesn't either.

**Step 3: Track your spending.** Before you can figure out how much to budget for both fixed and non-essential expenses, you need to know what you are spending. Some expenses are easy, like a mortgage, car payment, or student loan payment, but others can change from week to week. To get started budgeting, you'll want to know what you are spending over at least three months. Keeping track of where your money goes doesn't have to be a difficult task any longer. There are many tools that can be used to easily track both the money that you spend each month, but also the amounts that are credited (deposited) into your accounts.

- Mint.com (*www.mint.com*) is a free service that lets you link your online bank, credit card and loan accounts in one place. Each time you log into Mint, all of the transactions you have made since your last visit are added to your account and put into a category. Your bank may offer a similar service.

- Computer-based software such as Quicken lets you download your transactions and create your own categories and some people are just as happy downloading into an Excel spreadsheet.

- If a pencil and notebook work best for you, make a list of the fixed and variable expenses down the rows and create a page for each month, entering in your bills and transactions from your bank statements.

You'll also want to know where your cash goes. This may mean hanging onto receipts for the purchases you make with cash or jotting down cash spent in a notebook. If this seems like too much of a hassle, use a debit card because all of your transactions will be recorded on your bank statement.

**Step 4: Compare your spending to your income.** With a service like Mint or software like Quicken, a report showing your monthly cash flow is prepared for you automatically. If you have decided to create your budget in a spreadsheet or on paper, you'll want to total up all of your deposits and compare it to the sum of your expenses. When your cash flow is positive every month, you have found the money that you can now set aside in your new savings goal account. A negative cash flow number means going back to the variable (non-essential expenses) and finding categories where you can spend less.

**Step 5: Make adjustments and keep on track.** With a better understanding of where your money is going, you can make adjustments to speed up how quickly you meet your savings goals. You might decide to do some extra belt-tightening to reach your savings goals more quickly or if you are having trouble staying ahead with your bills. Once this system is in place, keeping up with it should be easy to do each month. A good rule of thumb is to update your budget when you sit down to pay your monthly bills.

## Savings Ideas

With your spending plan in place, here are a few savings ideas that may help stretch your dollars even further.

**Give yourself an allowance.** Using debit cards has become a way of life for most consumers these days. But, they make it easy to overspend. As long as the money is in the account, it can easily be drawn out with the swipe of a card. Ditch the debit card for all but the essential purchases such as groceries and gas and give yourself a weekly cash allowance for things like dining out and entertainment. Start with a number that you think is reasonable based on your budget and realize that once the cash is gone, you are done spending on non-essentials for the week. If you find you've got extra cash left at the end of the week, take out less the next time you visit the ATM.

**Leave the credit cards at home.** One of the easiest ways to reduce spending is to limit the amount that is purchased on a credit card. A good rule of thumb is that if you can't pay off all of the credit card purchases you make each month; you need to cut back using them. One of the easiest ways to do this is to leave them home when you go shopping and only have the cash you need for the purchases you are going to make.

**Pay off a debt, save the payment.** When you are done making regular payments on a credit card or consumer loan, take that money and put it in a savings account the next month...and the month after that. If you've been able to manage your budget without that payment amount each month, it can become a new source of savings for another goal you have.

**Review your insurance policies.** Each year it is important to review coverage and deductibles with your insurance agent to make sure they make the most sense for your home and autos. Increasing the deductible or eliminating some coverage options for an older vehicle can save on insurance premiums.

Creating a budget or spending plan shouldn't be a scary experience. The tools that are available can make it easy to collect your information and show you just where your money is going. Once you are able to reach your first short-term saving goal and enjoy whatever that might be, hopefully you'll realize that the process is worth a little bit of effort.

*Claudia Mott is a Certified Financial Planner® practitioner, licensed as a Certified Divorce Financial Analyst and has been specially trained to assist individuals thinking about divorce or working within the divorce process. She understands that financial needs and goals vary from person to person and works with each client to determine the individual needs of his or her own situation. She graduated from the University of Massachusetts Amherst and has her MBA from Boston University. Her firm is Epona Financial Services and can be found here www.eponafs.com.*

## Danger Signals in Money Management

Unfortunately, all too often there is not enough money. Many people find it difficult to talk about their finances. But if you have ever:

- wondered where your money went

- ran out of money before the end of the month

- borrowed money from "Peter to pay Paul"

*Then it is time to review your finances.*

At one time or another, everyone has money problems and can feel backed into a corner. Watch for these danger signals:

- unsure of how much money you owe

- not enough money to cover unexpected expenses

- unable to save money

- frequent arguments about money

- receiving past due notices

- borrowing money to pay for items usually paid for with cash/dipping into savings to pay bills/paying only the minimum amount on your charge accounts/ relying on extra income to pay bills

## Additional Danger Signs in Money Management

- Unable to save for upcoming expenses-back to school clothes, birthdays, holidays.

- Embarrassed about charging purchases at one place because they are behind on their payments, so they open new accounts at another store.

- Taking out a new loan to pay off an old loan or extending the loans for lower monthly payments.

- Seeing their monthly installment debts, revolving credit accounts, and loans (not mortgage) take more than 20% of their income.

- Constantly short of cash, so they use their charge card.

- Shuffling funds that were set aside for a specific purpose — such as insurance, a tax bill or a new refrigerator – and using the money to pay bills.

- No longer able to pay all the bills that come due, so only paying a few and ignoring the others.

# Kinship Care Finances

*By Shay Olivarria*

According to the *Expenditures on Children by Families 2011 Report*, it costs $990 per month to raise a child. That's a lot of money for any family. When you factor that many families involved in kinship care make the choice to take in a child with little preparation — physical space, furniture, clothing, daycare options — due to time constraints, that number looms even larger.

The average family involved in kinship care has access to little money, has a single caregiver, has little formal education and is caring for more than one child. Through all of these complications, kinship caregivers make the decision to help children in need, though sometimes that choice makes their lives more difficult.

## Background

Families that choose to take in a child are as varied as the children that they choose to take in. There isn't one specific profile however, there are themes that arise from looking at statistics. Let's take a look at some common themes for kinship caregivers.

- 41 percent of families involved in kinship care live below the federal poverty line. Almost half of all families involved in kinship care are living below the federal poverty line, which was defined in 2010 as $8,860 for a family of one, $11,940 for a family of two, $15,020 for a family of three and so on, according to Ehrle and Green in *"Children cared for by relatives: What services do they need?"*

- Between 48 percent and 62 percent of caregivers are single. In *"Kinship Care: Making the Most of a Valuable Resource,"* Rob Geen quotes multiple sources that put the number of single caregivers between 48 percent and 62 percent of all caregivers. That means that there is only one person to bring in money and there is only one person to provide child care.

- 32 percent of kinship caregivers don't have a high school diploma. Geen also notes that almost a third of caregivers have not earned a high school diploma. Not having a high school diploma makes it more difficult for caregivers to earn high incomes, which provides few options to have a job with benefits and rarely offers opportunities for caregivers to take time off.

- Number of children in care is also a factor. According to Shlonsky, Webster, and Needell in *"The ties that bind: A cross-sectional analysis of siblings in foster care"* about 70 percent of kids in foster care also have a sibling in foster care. Keeping siblings together seems to be a large motivation for those willing to provide kinship care.

- If it costs $990 per month to raise a child and now you've taken in two children, that's a cost of $1,980 per month. If the kinship caregiver is a licensed foster parent then they will receive the national average of $1,022 per month for both children which leaves them short by more than $900. If they aren't licensed foster parents, and have signed up to receive Temporary Assistance for Needy Families (TANF) benefits, then they will receive a measly $344 per month. I wish I was making these numbers up, but it's all documented in the *Expenditures on Children by Families 2011 Report.*

## Challenges

All that is to say, the families that choose to take in relatives are doing what they believe is right. They are opening their homes to children so those children can have a safe place to live, food in their bellies, a roof over their heads and clothes on their backs. They want to do those things, but sometimes those things aren't possible because the families are sometimes struggling themselves.

Remember that it takes $990 to raise a child every month. Half of kinship caregivers are living below the federal poverty line. If there are multiple children, then $990 needs to be multiplied by the number of children. Deciding to take in children you love shouldn't mean that everyone involved should have to live in poverty. Of course there are foster care payments and government assistance available, but many don't take advantage of those options due to ignorance or pride. Some are unable to take advantage of those options because they are not licensed foster parents.

To receive money to help take care of the children in their care, the caregiver(s) have to become a licensed foster care facility. That means that they have to take hours of classes, bring the home up to foster care codes, and open themselves up to scrutiny. For many families this seems like a lot of work when the money being offered won't cover the cost of care anyway. *The Expenditures on Children by Families 2011 Report* lists a national average of $511 as the monthly payment for one child in care. Some are willing to do the work, but doing everything needed takes months and children are usually moved within hours of the original notification.

The second option available to kinship caregivers is to use services provided by the government. Caregivers can look into help with bills (Temporary Assistance for Needy Families), help with food (Supplemental Nutrition Assistance Program), money specifically earmarked for special needs children (Supplemental Security Income), and money specifically for the nutrition needs of toddlers (Women, Infants and Children). Even with all of this help available, families will probably still not have enough extra income to cover the added expense. The national average of TANF payments for one child is $249 per month. Though almost 100 percent of kinship families are eligible for TANF funds, fewer than 12% receive TANF support, according to the *Expenditures on Children by Families 2011 Report.*

## Help for Kinship Caregivers

Obviously, the best thing for all stakeholders — kinship caregivers, children, communities, and others — is to keep families together as much as possible. Supporting kinship caregivers by making sure that they can provide the stable, loving homes that they want to provide is the best solution. To help kinship caregivers gain access to the financial resources available to them:

- Kinship caregivers have to be made aware of differences between licensed foster care providers and non-licensed providers.

- Kinship caregivers have to be made aware of financial resources available to them.

- Kinship caregivers should be provided contact information for each financial resource.

- Services should be offered to kinship caregivers, if requested, to help them transition to being full-time caregivers for the children in care.

*Shay Olivarria is a financial education speaker and author who grew up in kinship care with her maternal grandmother. Her book "Money Matters: The Get It Done in 1 Minute Workbook" is an Amazon.com best seller and is available at her website www.BiggerThanYourBlock.com.*

> **"How can I be fair to my other daughters who are and have always been good children? When I am gone, I have nothing now to leave them. We have broken the bank raising the grandchildren. I told my daughters I could make them a cross stitch pillow that says MY NIECES AND NEPHEWS GOT MY INHERITANCE."**

# Joiyah
*By Suzette Brown*

January 28

October 1 was the beginning of life for our ninth grandchild. You see my husband and I adopted eight children, seven females and one male. After the death of a good friend of mine who had adopted six females, we chose to keep two of the teens, so they wouldn't enter the system. My husband and I have been foster/adoptive parents for more than 25 years and were looking forward to not raising an infant again.

Around October 2, I received a call from one of my adopted daughters who already had three children, one on adoption status and two others with the paternal grandmother. My daughter called crying, that DeKalb County Department of Family and Children's Services was going to keep her baby girl. I did not quite understand because she was not on drugs to my knowledge, the father seemed OK, but again, now I know that God knows best. My oldest and biological daughter was having her second son and decided she did not want the baby bed she had purchased; I had taken it so I would have a bed for him when he came over. Charles and I also had been recertified as foster parents because of the two teens we had voluntarily taken into our home because of my friend's death.

After my daughter told me Department of Family and Children's Services stated she could not bring Joiyah home, I spoke with the Child Protect Services worker. To my surprise, Department of Family and Children's Services decided that because my daughter had an outstanding case with her son who was in an adoptive home and two children with paternal grandmother, they would not let Joiyah leave. I spoke with my husband and he was hesitant, but as usual, I convinced him, as my daughter and the father had committed to getting Joiyah back. I thought about the situation and everything seemed to be in place. I was working and had found online an in-home licensed daycare that was on my way to work. I kept thinking and convincing Charles that it was only temporary.

For two years of Joiyah's life, the parents seemed to be in their own world and my husband and I struggled to take care of her. We were receiving $421 and childcare when we were fostering her, but after being convinced by our agency to become a relative provider, we received $355 for relative subsidy and no compensation for childcare. At this time, we had four teens, a track athlete, a swimmer, and two girls in the band, as well as Joiyah. Joiyah's daycare was $550 a month and relative subsidy was $355 and no assistance from the biological parents or paternal family. Extremely financially straining! In 2010, I lost my job working for an adoption agency due to budget cuts and was working only part-time. We almost lost our home to foreclosure, my car was repossessed, my husband and I were battling with each other to the point we were on the verge of divorce, my friend's daughters were out-of-control and it was STRESSFUL! There have been days that I think back and wish I had said no to the "temporary" placement of Joiyah, because it truly was not. Joiyah's parents are not consistent with financial support or emotional support to Joiyah. Sad…

When the parents failed to complete their plan with Department of Family and Children's Services, the judge granted us full custody and I must say the financial strain is still here. We still struggle to pay childcare, which is still $500 a month and supply her other needs. I do work now, but we are so far behind in bills it will take a while to recover.

I personally have cried and prayed so hard for relief to get out of this slump and hope that one day we will. I have heard from some workers in my county that relative subsidy may be cut and that we need to look at adoption. I hope we do not have to adopt our granddaughter to get some financial assistance. We can't afford to pay the expenses of raising a now four-year-old who is active and steadily growing. In our sixties and starting all over again, it has been difficult and still is, but we know that Joiyah did not ask to be born and we are trying to give her the same opportunity for life that we gave her mother. We love Joiyah with all our heart and know, although we continue to struggle financially and emotionally, that God knows best. Please pray for us....

*Suzette Brown*

*Charles and Suzette Brown have been foster parents for more than thirty years. They chose to foster with Suzette having one teen biological daughter. Over the years they ended up with nine children in foster care, eight girls and one boy; eight of the nine were adopted. Suzette has worked for a private adoption agency and more recently has been working at the Atlanta Job Corps and as an adoption resource advisor for the Georgia Center for Resources and Support. Charles works for the Atlanta Public Schools as a bus driver. Suzette earned an associate's degree in business management at Shorter College in 2002 and a bachelor's degree in psychology from Argosy University in 2006 while parenting eight kids. While fostering they were involved in the local and state associations and have been highlighted in the media many times.*

*Suzette says, "I love working with foster, adoptive, and kinship parents because I have been there, done that. Nurturing parents is my passion. God is so good! I give him all the praise for all the challenges, successes, and whatever is yet to come. My husband is my greatest supporter as well as my 40-year-old daughter, Daphne."*

# Our Changing Family

"*I am in the beginning stages and feel hopeless at times. I am starting to give up on my daughter, not proud, but I cannot let my grandson go through any more. It is sad that the only stability he has is with me and his daycare. I only hope that things settle down for him. He has started to have nightmares, waking up and yelling Mommie! I pray that God gives me the strength and knowledge to accomplish what I must.*"

# Kinship Care and Strings Attached
*By Kim Combes, LBSW, MEd*

My wife once expressed to me her desire to swoop over the Middle East rescuing orphaned young people, bringing to America as many as she could gather. Her heart has always been tender toward young children, especially babies and toddlers in horrendous situations such as is the plight of all warring countries' children today.

Indeed, as foster/adoptive parents, our hearts hurt for the young people of any war-torn, impoverished, and disease-ridden nation. We would love to comfort fears and dry tears as great terror, loss, and grief is expressed. And we do. Some of us have gone through adoption agencies such as Holt International. Others may have initiated private adoptions domestically, while for yet others, such as Diane and I, the genesis of adoption was through fostering for a public agency. Some of us are strictly foster parents with no desire to adopt at all. In any event, our hearts are bent toward the unfortunate children who are experiencing their own terror and grief, even if they didn't come from the opposite end of the globe, but just from the other side of town.

As an ex-Iowa Department of Human Services worker and a former foster care specialist for private agencies, I have interacted with myriad foster children of all ages and foster/adoptive parents who do their best to love them. Some of those with whom I've worked have taken in as foster children their own nieces and nephews, brothers and sisters, grandchildren and even great-grandchildren. Federal laws dictate that the placing worker MUST first attempt to place a child in a relative home and document in the case permanency plan why that was not an option.

Kinship care, at least theoretically, is the best option when a child must leave the parental home. As a worker, I was not always privy to the "next of kin" when a court order was issued. And many times, for whatever reasons, the parents did not want their child going into a relative's care.

> *It is still my belief that when possible, family members should be considered as the first alternative to the biological home.*

Moreover, I have heard workers and foster parents verbalize that "the nut doesn't fall very far from the tree," meaning if a parent is "messed up," then the whole family of origin must have major problems. In some cases, this may be true, but an overgeneralization of such is always inappropriate. I have witnessed many devoted and committed aunts and uncles, grandparents and other family members give 150 percent to helping wayward youth get back on track. Whether or not the new addition chooses to do so is neither here nor there. These caregivers believed it was their ministry to do this. After all, family is family. They will, at the end of the day, rest assured they did the best they could to positively influence a young life.

Several years ago I had a nephew in foster care less than an hour away. My brother, long separated from the mother of his child who was NOT given custody, did not want his son getting a "reward" for misbehavior by living with me, his favorite uncle. Shawn was in care more than four years. His father died shortly before Shawn turned 18. Yes, it saddened all of us that events took this turn. However, I also believed that Shawn was being well-cared for and did much better with a greater chance of life success with the structure and guidance in his new environment, and his father reluctantly and sadly agreed. Would Shawn have chosen to do as well in my home had Dad agreed to let him come here? Honestly, I don't know. Given the more street-wise, delinquent boys I had in my home, Shawn might have been eaten alive. Ideally his new family would have allowed all of us to keep contact with Shawn. However, this did not happen and was explained away by the phrase *"best interest of the child."*

While my brother indeed had his issues, he loved his son. My family also loved him and had never been anything but nurturing and loving toward him. We are not monsters that would have harmed him, but generous and affectionate kin desiring only to help him be the best he could be. We missed him.

Workers and others in the system need to be reminded that we all have free will and that even those raised in the best of families can choose a wrong road and vice versa. Too, judgment should be withheld while simultaneously keeping an open mind toward those of the same blood. While not perfect, these people can be the child's greatest asset... and the worker's.

Anything anyone does can be closely scrutinized and critiqued. Kinship care is no exception. Say what you will regarding the view that the nut doesn't fall far from the tree. It is still my belief that when possible, family members should be considered as the first alternative to the biological home.

Scripture tells us we are to care for widows and orphans. May God raise up more of us to do just that, whether the "orphans" are related or not. Heaven knows the whole world needs it.

*Kim Combes, LBSW, MEd, is a private practice counselor and national presenter, as well as a former foster dad to 40-plus teenage boys since 1994. Currently he and wife, Diane, live in Colo, Iowa, with their five adopted children who range in age from 11 to 18. To contact Combes, write to kcombes@netins.net.*

# The Complex Relationships of KinCare
*By Mary-Jo Land, CPT, CDDP*

Last year, you picked up the kids for the weekend, spent 48 hours in pure joy and then dropped them back to their parents, tired and dirty. Then you went home and took a week to recover! Now your role as the fun grandparent, auntie, or great uncle is gone, replaced with parenting by necessity, not necessarily by choice. Your relationship with the children and their parents is changed forever. Navigating the complex changes in all the relationships is more than challenging.

As you assume the care of the children, they will struggle and you will struggle with them. Everything has changed. The children may expect that things will be as they were when they visited for the weekend: endless fun, late bedtimes, and more treats than at home. Having to now pack lunches, go to school meetings, doctor's appointments, supervise chores and brush teeth every day is new to the children and to you. They are not accustomed to the changes in routines that are now not only different from their parents' rules, but also different from your rules when they were visiting. The children will experience the loss of their former relationship with you while they are also experiencing the loss of their parents. You, too, will grieve the loss of your role as grandmother or special aunt, if you ever have time. It is important to talk about these changes and these losses with the children. You might notice with them what is the same and what is different; make a list of those changes and perhaps place a smiley face beside the changes that feel better and a sad face beside those that are sad. It can be an active and changing list. Your happy and sad faces can be on there, too.

One changing role that is particularly difficult is with the children's parents. Perhaps you are caring for your children's children, your sibling's children, or your niece or nephew's children. Your relationship is now much more complex. Perhaps there is conflict among the adults about the best plan for the children. Perhaps Child Protective Services has been involved and the children were removed for cause. Perhaps you agree with their decision to remove the children, thereby causing the parents to be angry with you. Perhaps you believe the parent is being treated unfairly, leaving you in conflict with Child Protective Services. One thing is certain, you are now in unfamiliar territory and you didn't ask to be here. You just want the best for the children and feel that foster care is less than optimal. You may now be responsible for some aspects of supervision of the access visits. This creates a difficult role for you: caught in the middle between the Child Protective Services, the court, the parents, the rest of the family, and the children. You may need to follow rules you don't agree with. Or, you may want to follow the rules but the parents pressure you to bend them.

One way to reduce some of these types of pressures is to

> *Last year, you picked up the kids for the weekend, spent 48 hours in pure joy and then dropped them back to their parents, tired and dirty. Then you went home and took a week to recover!*

clearly and in writing define everyone's roles, responsibilities and duties. This strategy creates clear boundaries for everyone involved. One way to achieve this is through a process called Family Group Conferencing. Ask if someone experienced in Family Group Conferencing can consult with your family. This process, in which everyone participates collaboratively, creates boundaries and limits for everyone. Having agreed to these conditions of kin-care, you will have a structure for daily living that is stable and predictable for everyone to follow. This will help the children (and the adults) adjust to the changes they are experiencing.

And finally, promise yourself and the children that one day per month, you get to have a day like it was. Be the fun grandfather, the favorite aunt, the soft grandmother that you were before being the new kincare parent. Plan it and do it. Enjoy them as you did before!

*Mary-Jo Land is a certified child psychotherapist and play therapist, a certified dyadic developmental psychotherapist, a certified sensorimotor psychotherapist level 1 and a certified attachment focused therapist, consultant, and trainer. She is a registered attachment clinician with ATTACh and currently president of ATTACh (www.attach.org). As a private practice therapist, she assists foster and adopt parents and children in their attachment and bonding while resolving early trauma and neglect. Land and her husband were therapeutic foster parents for twenty years. They have five children, one of whom is adopted and two grandchildren. Land can be reached at www.maryjoland.ca or homeland@sympatico.ca.*

# I Just Want My Mommy
*By Jan Wagner*

One question that comes up repeatedly in support groups from new caregivers is what do I tell them when all they want is their mommy? I think we go to the extremes to keep the child in our care from "thinking and feeling" about that one person who isn't there for them anymore. My son-in-law likes to refer to the "Look! Shiny thing!" method of distraction. In spite of all those efforts to entertain and distract, there will be times they are going to cry for "her." As a grandparent, witnessing those tears is doubly hard because as in my situation, it's my own daughter who is at the root of the heartache. I didn't understand why she left either, let alone know how to explain it to my two-year-old granddaughter. Words to a child that age meant nothing and it had to be as simple as possible.

### "Mommy's not here right now. I don't know why she didn't come back. I don't know when she will come back."

The important thing was to just keep reassuring her that it wasn't her fault, that she was perfect and loved. I told her that her mommy had to fix her own feelings because they were broken, but it wasn't because she didn't love her. She just couldn't be a mommy the way mommies are supposed to be, so she had me to take care of her. As she got older, she had a clearer understanding of her mom and that she wasn't capable of keeping her safe and providing a stable home, but it wasn't until her mom left her baby brother that she really understood that it wasn't her fault. She is almost a teenager now, lives with her dad and adoptive mom, but she still has questions for me. And I answer her as honestly as I can, without all the nasty details, because she has now reached a stage where she is concerned for her mother's well-being.

My grandson reacted completely opposite of his sister, even though he was also two at the time his mother left him. He never cried and never asked for her at all. So, I didn't talk about it either. I assumed it was because she was more detached from him almost from birth, when I should have realized that his behavior was a signal for much deeper loss — one he buried within himself. It wasn't until he was about four that he started talking about it. One night I said I was both his mom and his grandma, and he told me I couldn't be his mom, because his mom left him and I didn't. With him, the questions were about her.

> **Didn't she know it was wrong to break promises,
> to lie, to make a little boy feel bad? Didn't she know
> she was supposed to come home and live with him?**

He did not want to live with her, but she needed to come here to be with him. We ask God to bless her every night, and he wonders if she thinks about him. We do talk about her, but sometimes he will just stop and say he doesn't want to talk any more because he is starting to feel bad, and that's not a good feeling.

Although it was more painful for me to listen to my granddaughter cry for hours, she probably had the healthier reaction. At least she was able to grieve for her loss and eventually recognize it. My grandson's came out in behavioral issues, a lack of trust and sensory problems. He is struggling with school because of the emotional delays.

If you have any questions about how to talk with your child about why he or she is not with a parent, regardless of the reason, I would certainly talk with a professional. They can help to ease your mind and the child's. I don't think it matters how young a child was when the separation took place either, because children seem to have this memory bank that doesn't come with words, just feelings. What children really need is for us to recognize their feelings and help them recognize them also.

> **Don't take it personally.
> It's nothing you're lacking.
> It's who they are missing.**

*After raising three children, 37 years of marriage, and at the age of 57, Jan Wagner started raising her then two-year-old grandson. Jan Wagner is now an advocate for kinship families and is involved on a state and national level. You can follow her blog Raising H at jdwags.blogspot.com. She is also available to speak or give workshops on Kinship/ Grandparenting issues.*

# Tips for Dealing with Your Adult Child
*by Andrea B. Smith, PhD and Linda L. Dannison, PhD*

- Monitor positive and effective interactions with your adult child.

- Find ways for biological parents to remain parents even though you may be the primary care-provider for your grandchild(ren).

- If the adult child is unable to do so, be prepared to decide for yourself what is best for your grandchild(ren).

- Beware of manipulative behaviors of the adult child.

- Identify specific, situation-related ways for you to cope with the adult child and his/her problems.

- In your interactions with your adult child, it is important to be assertive and/or firm, but not controlling or bossy. You may be most successful if you set boundaries and give clear expectations. A written set of rules and goals may be used to clarify stated limits.

- Give yourself and others permission to make mistakes. The capacity to forgive is important.

## For Yourself:
Set Limits • Say no • Learn to let go • Have written guidelines/contract

## For the Grandchild:
- May need to protect them from their parents.
- Grandparents and their grandchildren must be truthful with one another. However, it is important that this honesty be tempered with kindness. Additionally, any honest information provided to the grandchild must be age-appropriate. So, if they ask, tell your grandchildren about their biological parents.

### Just remember:
- Be honest.
- Provide large pieces of information rather than details.
- Give age-appropriate information.

In addition, always encourage your grandchild to discuss his or her feelings.

## Visitation Tips

*by Andrea B. Smith, PhD and Linda L. Dannison, PhD*

Many grandparents have difficulty coming to terms with the relationship between their adult child and their grandchildren. Children often feel torn, and it is easy for them to feel guilty if they have a good time visiting with their parent while living with their grandparents.

### Suggestions for Visitation

- Reduce "pick up" and "drop off" conflicts. Make these times as easy and stress free for the children as possible.

- Let your grandchild(ren) know that it is OK for them to enjoy being with their parents. Even if it's difficult for you, children should realize that their feelings don't have to be a secret.

- Respect the privacy of your grandchild's relationship with his or her parents. Try your best not to pry, even though it may be difficult.

- Be careful not to say negative things or "bad-mouth" your adult child in front of your grandchildren. Remember, regardless of what or who your adult child may be, she or he is still this child's parents. Saying bad things about their parents makes children uncomfortable.

- Try to make your interactions with your adult child as positive as possible (e.g., don't shout, argue, lose control).

- Develop a welcome-home ritual. After your grandchildren have had time to bounce off the walls or relax, you could do something special. For example, you might have a dish of ice cream or a snack of cookies and milk together. The more rituals you can construct, the better it is for the children.

- As much as possible, try to help your grandchild(ren) to maintain a close, warm relationship with as many relatives as possible on both sides of the family. The more connections children have, the better.

- Do not compete for your grandchild's affection. He or she has enough love for both you and his or her parents.

## "What's in a Name?"
*By Madeleine Krebs, LCSW-C*

Shakespeare was onto something. While Juliette lamented that "a rose by any other name would smell as sweet," those of us in the adoption community know all too well the power of names. Terms like "real" or "natural" parent are terribly wounding to adoptive parents who feel compelled to fight for their authenticity. Kinship adopters face even more complex challenges because of their dual relationship to their child. Grandparents become "mothers and fathers" as do siblings, aunts, uncles, and cousins. Whether the adoption occurs in early or late childhood, helping family members, as well as outsiders understand and respect the significance of "what's in a name" is critical to the adopted child's well-being.

## Enlisting Family Support

In kinship adoption, when children do not have significant memories of other caregivers other than their current parents, their understanding of what adoption means is not much different than in any adoptive family. Children will grow into an understanding of who their birth parents are in much the same way as children in open adoption do, only they will also have to make sense of their birth parents' relationship to their "adoptive" parents. Equally important, the children will grow into the understanding of the dual relationship they share with their adoptive parents. For example, *"Mom and Dad are by relationship also my grandparents. Biologically, Dad is also my uncle."* Kinship adoptees may need to help to understand that this "secondary" relationship does not diminish the primary relationship of "mom and dad" in any way.

If extended family can refer to the child's adoptive parents as the child's parents and be supportive to that parent's role in the child's presence, then the child will have less confusion about the multiple names family members have. If all family members present the duality as their family's "normal," then the child will also experience it as such. Saying to a child, "Go ask your mom/dad" confirms the parents' roles in adoption, and it is especially supportive to both parents and child when the birth parent can do this.

Challenges to this goal may come from family members who persist in referring to the "adoptive" parents by the secondary relationship — "Grandma" "Aunt Betty," etc. This can be confusing to the child, of course. That is why it is important for parents to explain to their family members how upsetting and confusing this will be for the child and enlist everyone's support in preventing this from occurring. In many instances, family members may be conflicted with either loyalty issues to birth parents and/or causing pain to the birth parents. When birth parents are present, it can feel uncomfortable or awkward for them to refer to the kinship parents as "Mom" or "Dad." Family members may fear hurting the birth parent and triggering the birth parents' feelings of loss around not being the everyday parent. As opposed to avoiding this predicament, family members can be sensitive to the reality that the birth parents may need assistance to work through these feelings. Relatives also need to know that if they speak in a manner that the child experiences as unsupportive or critical of the adoptive parents, the child can become anxious and worried. Some children ask themselves, should I call them Mom or Dad, if others don't?

## Children Need Time

When children are adopted at older ages, it is natural for them to face difficulty in making the transition to calling their relative "Mom" and "Dad." The shift in familial relationships can make this transition even more daunting in kinship adoption. Children need permission to take their time in making this transition despite the natural inclination for parents to immediately want to be referred to as Mom and Dad, having claimed the child as their "son" or "daughter." As parents often tell us, "I do all the parenting, why can't I expect my child to call me Mom/Dad?" Parents who are relatively new parents to the child have to earn this title and one must be patient with a child who may have called many others Mom or Dad. Changes in relationships and titles take time, similar to changing one's name after marriage or divorce. It is new and it takes time to fit.

It is not uncommon for kinship adopted teens to continue to call their new parents by their other title. Teens have told us they know who is parenting them and they respect the commitment the adoptive parents have made to them. However, especially when they are with their peers, they sometimes want to shortcut the question, "who's that?" by referring to their adoptive parents by the original role. Teens often want to protect their privacy and become more selective around whom they share their adoption story.

## Dealing With School And Outsiders

Many adoptive and biological parents are older today, and are often subjected to the confusion of outsiders who automatically view them as the "grandparents." While annoying and sometimes embarrassing to both parents and children, families often laugh it off. Kinship families may not find this funny as it is one more reminder of the failure of others in the community to respect the dignity of how their family was formed.

We always recommend that adoptive parents inform the school that their family has been formed by adoption. We encourage adoptive parents to take the opportunity to educate school personnel to understand their child's unique needs related to adoption. For example, kinship adopters need to educate the school around the significance of relationships in kinship families so they are prepared to support their child should questions arise, such as "They're too old to be your parents — you mean they're your grandparents?"

As with all transracial adoptions, if the child is bi-racial and the adoptive relative is not, this can result in even more questions being asked of the child by classmates, teachers, and friends. School personnel need to know that the adopted child's "story" is private, but they can explain that families formed by adoption include relatives adopting children when birth parents are unable to be parents. C.A.S.E. has a publication, *SAFE at Schools: Support for Adoptive Families by Educators,* to assist adoptive parents in helping to ensure that their child is "safe" at school.

## The Power of Loss

The struggle around names as a way to acknowledge relationships in kinship adoptions is obviously a reflection of loss inherent in kinship adoption. The changed names change family dynamics forever. Children and birth parents lose the parent/child relationship. Relatives report feeling that becoming parents to their relative's child means putting the children's needs first — which can create distance in their relationship with the birth parent. Sometimes the need to set boundaries with their relative to protect the adopted child feels harsh and punitive when they might wish they could be more of a helper to their struggling relative instead. Likewise, the birth parent not only has to deal with feelings around losing the parenting relationship with his or her child, but also the feeling of loss when the adoptive parent sets new rules and boundaries because the child he or she has adopted becomes the first priority.

In kinship adoption, other relatives may experience loss as well and figuring out names and terms of relationships can be challenging. For example, will grandparents whose grandchild is adopted by a niece or nephew still be referred to as "Aunt or Uncle" or "Grandma or Grandpa?" Even though they remain in the child's life, it is a mistake not to acknowledge the loss they may feel as their son or daughter signs away his or her parental rights. Likewise, emotions are complex when the adopter is the birth parents' sibling. The child's grandparents are still grandparents, but they must cope with the reality that their one child's "gain" is their other child 's loss.

With all these complexities, kinship adopters may need the support of adoption-competent professionals who can help everybody navigate the normal challenges inherent in kinship relationships.

*Madeleine Krebs, a licensed clinical social worker, is the clinical director at the Center for Adoption Support and Education, (C.A.S.E.), an independent, non-profit organization providing pre and post adoption services to individuals and families. Krebs has more than 34 years of experience providing psychotherapy to children, adolescents, adults and their families in the Washington, D.C. metropolitan area. She has worked extensively with foster and adopted children, and their parents as well as prospective parents.*

*Prior to joining C.A.S.E., Krebs worked in both the domestic and international adoption fields. She provides training to foster and adoptive parents, as well as mental health and child welfare professionals. Krebs was awarded the 2005 Nancy Dworkin Award for outstanding service to youth and child advocacy. Additionally, Krebs received the Angels in Adoption award in 2008 sponsored by the Congressional Coalition Adoption Institute.*

# Grandmother to Michael

*By Donna M. Oxford*

Michael was almost three months old when I received the call that his mother had been arrested and was in jail because a positive drug test had violated the terms of her probation. At the time, his father was also incarcerated, so the only options were me or foster care.

At the age of 51, I became a full-time mother to an infant who had been neglected and projectile vomited after every feeding. His head was so flat on one side that he was unable to turn it and he would not make eye contact or smile. His five-year-old sister had changed his diapers and fed him. I played classical music, sang to him, talked to him, read to him, exercised him, and fed him anything I could find, which included DHA, an omega-3 fatty acid. He is now a happy, healthy, bright five-year-old.

*That being said, I wouldn't change my decision; Michael is a joy.*

He has limited contact with his father, my son, because of his lifestyle and drug use and has not seen his mother since he was 19 months old. In fact, he calls me Mom and isn't aware of his birth mother. I've discussed this issue with two child psychologists who have told me the same thing — I've been in the mother role since his infancy and he's too young to understand biological vs. non-biological until the age of five or six years old. His birth mother is unstable and has been in jail for most of his life, so I feel it is in his best interest to leave things as they are.

It is challenging to raise a child at my age. I often feel guilty about my lack of patience and energy that a younger person might have, but I'm also wiser and more experienced than I was when I raised my children. I consider myself lucky because I'm younger than a lot of grandparents who are raising grandchildren. It is also difficult financially. If I was a foster parent, I'd be entitled to a monthly stipend and various benefits, but since I'm his grandparent, I'm on my own. I have not received child support from either parent and recently lost my home of 27 years.

While many believe a child is best to live with his or her parents, that thought is changing when the parents struggle to meet their children's needs appropriately. For example, Michael's birth mother was cited for child abuse/neglect for the neglect he experienced while in her care for the first few months of his life. She was court-ordered into rehab, which she did not complete. Yet when I filed for custody, the female lawyers at my local Legal Aid office refused to help me stating, "we're not going to help a grandparent take a child away from his mother." They defended her for being in rehab as she was "trying to help herself." Even when I explained the neglect and the court order, they resisted. After Michael's maternal grandmother convinced his birth mother to sign the custody papers, my attorneys tried to contact her in rehab to ensure that she was fully aware of her parental rights. Custodial grandparents often express frustration that Children and Youth Services' goal is to reunite their grandchild with his or her parent.

Since taking custody of Michael, every aspect of my life has changed. Pre-custody, I enjoyed a fulfilling life as a single person. I spent time at my friend's beach house or at one of my other friends' houses, but once I became a mom, all of that changed. None of them had children and certainly didn't want a visitor who projectile vomited all over their beautiful homes. After Hillary Clinton conceded in the Presidential race, I was offered a position on the Obama campaign, which had been a dream of mine.

Unfortunately, Michael was a sickly infant who required round-the-clock care and the position was from 11 a.m. until 7 p.m., so I had to decline. I no longer apply for challenging, interesting jobs because I don't feel I can take on any additional stress. And, I have virtually no social life because I'm tired, broke, and have limited babysitting options.

That being said, I wouldn't change my decision; Michael is a joy.

I am able to offer him a relationship with his extended family that he wouldn't necessarily experience if he lived with a foster family. Also, I share our family history, especially pictures and stories of his father as a child. Michael spends time with his maternal family and his three half sisters. Most importantly, he has love and security.

*Donna Oxford is a mother of two adult children and grandmother of six. She earned a bachelor's degree in organizational dynamics and is employed as a university administrator for an association management company in King of Prussia, Pennsylvania. Oxford is a Democratic Township Committee Person who enjoys spending time with her family, reading, baking, and trips to the beach.*

# Begin with Kin but Honor the Bond

*By James Kenny, PhD, and Lori Groves, MS*

Once upon a time, fathers had an absolute right over the well-being and even the life of their children. No more. Time and an elemental democracy have seen the shift from authoritarian family politics to the equality of rights for all family members. In the past, children were the least protected and the most vulnerable parties. Now culture and law have progressed to protect those rights. The child's rights are paramount declares the Adoption and Safe Families Act. Every child has the right to a safe and permanent home.

Unfortunately, some judges and courts have moved more slowly to protect the child. They will give the birth parents chance after chance, sometimes even year after year to redeem themselves and reclaim the child of their flesh. In practice, the rights of the birth parents have continued to be seen to supersede the rights of the minor child, even proclaimed to be in the child's best interests. As one judge said in a case where the foster/adopt parents had raised a five-year-old since birth: "I put that child back where he belonged, with his real parents."

What kind of home is the best preparation for adulthood? Obviously, the home must be safe and secure. The parents must be relatively free of physical, mental, and criminal problems which would impede good parenting. Yet a critical factor, perhaps the most important one, has often been overlooked. That factor is bonding, the significant relationships that develop between the child and specific adults. Safety, security, and a stable parent all are mediated through the parent-child interaction.

Relationships are central to growth and development, the medium through which all else flows. A bonded relationship is critical, and the interruption of bonding leaves a gaping hole, one which doubles and triples the likelihood that the child will suffer mental illness, homelessness or problems with the law. We define bonding as "a significant attachment which both parties want and expect to continue and which is interrupted at peril to the parties involved." Bonding develops naturally in a family setting where people eat, sleep and play together.

Bonding is likely after three months, probable after six, and almost certain after 12 months. ASFA recognizes the critical importance of bonding by entrenching these timelines in law. One must do everything possible to preserve and improve the birth home. If, however, a child must be removed, we must work diligently to reunify. Should things move too slowly after six months? ASFA suggests a concurrent plan be prepared for an alternative home.

If reunification has not occurred after 12 months (or 15 of the past 22 months), the state is required to terminate the rights of the birth parents. Unfortunately, the Adoption and Safe Families Act has sometimes been referred to as "the law least followed."

The choice between the family of origin and the psychological or bonded parents is not a simple one. It is best answered in a context, along a time sequence. When charges of abuse or neglect are substantiated against birth parents, the state has five consecutive choices or options.

The first choice should be to maintain the birth home when possible. Bonding is important and the child, even in an unsafe and insecure home, is probably bonded to his or her parents. Disrupting this bond causes a trauma of its own. The key analysis is to consider a cost/benefit ratio. Does the cost of separation outweigh the risk to safety and security? If the child can remain with his or her birth parents, in-home support and services can be offered with regular monitoring. Parent training can be best accomplished by keeping parent and child together.

The second choice or step is to reunify. Time is a critical factor. Caseworkers should provide birth parents with an immediate "to-do" list of factors to remedy before the child can be returned. As the three-, six- and 12-month deadlines pass, the child is becoming bonded to another set of caretakers. The clock is ticking. Motivated birth parents will work diligently and with speed to get their child back.

Too often the process of reunification is delayed. Perhaps the birth parents are having trouble changing their lifestyle. Perhaps the caseworker does not monitor progress weekly or set deadlines. In any case, several studies have shown that reunified children fare more poorly than those who are adopted.

The third choice is kin care. The caseworker must undertake an immediate inventory of extended family members. If responsible blood relatives who want the child can be found, the child should be placed first with them. This has the major advantage of allowing the child to continue close ties with his or her extended family.

The disadvantage is that kin are sometimes seen as the easy answer by the state and an excuse to keep birth parents and child together despite safety concerns. Statistics have shown that between 20 and 40 percent of those who are in kin care, or reunified with the birth parents, re-entered the foster care system. These studies also suggest that kin care and reunification have more negative emotional and psychological outcomes than children who find other permanent placements. The remedy may be for interested kin to undergo the same thorough homestudy required for licensing foster parents.

The fourth choice is adoption by the psychological parent. As time passes, the child inevitably bonds with his or her new parents or caretakers. As has been seen, bonding is a significant attachment, one that develops naturally, but becomes vital. Bonding is reciprocal, between specific people, long-lasting and involves a forever commitment. In a case of dispute between kin and the psychological parent, or any disputed adoption, a bonding evaluation should be accomplished.

Bonding takes precedence over un-bonded kinship. In fact, bonding is a form of fashioned kinship, a vital relationship. Genes are not the only embedded trait. The habits learned over time in a stable home last a lifetime as well, and are passed on to future generations. When the choice is between kin-come-lately, a heretofore unknown blood relative, and a bonded foster/adopt parent, the child's right to a permanent home should outweigh the blood claim of the newly discovered adult.

*Lori Groves recently earned a master's degree in psychology. She is a birth mother, foster mother, and adoptive mother.*

*James Kenny, PhD, is a retired psychologist with more than 50 years of clinical experience. He has doctorate degrees in both psychology and anthropology and a master's degree in social work and the author of 13 books on family and child care. More personally, he is the father of 12 biological and adopted children, and the foster parent of many more.*

## Sometimes I Miss My Mom
*By Jan Wagner*

"Grandma, sometimes I miss my mom." This popped out casually while my grandson, who I adopted, was playing on his Nintendo DS.

"Well, sometimes I miss her too," I replied.

"Do you really?" he asked. "Awe, that's really nice of you."

"Do you feel bad when you miss her?" I asked.

"No, that's why I have you," he said. "So I don't have to feel bad. I just miss her, that's all."

# Kinship Families and Kids
# May Pay High Price If Allegations Happen

*By Jodee Kulp*

Caring for other people's children can become high risk with the complexity of children, their losses, and previous trauma contributing to high states of emotion. Many children entering kinship care arrive due to previous neglect or abuse. Often times these children's lives have been complicated by chemical use from their parents or other caregivers. One-third to two-thirds of child maltreatment cases involve substance use to some degree. And, children whose parents abuse alcohol and other drugs are three times more likely to be abused and more than four times more likely to be neglected than children from non-abusing families, according to information from www.childwelfare.gov/can/factors/parentcaregiver/substance.cfm.

All 50 states, the District of Columbia, and the U.S. territories have child abuse and neglect reporting laws that mandate certain professionals and institutions to report suspected maltreatment to a child protective services (CPS) agency. Each state has its own definitions of child abuse and neglect based on standards set by federal law. Federal legislation provides a foundation for states by identifying a set of acts or behaviors that define child abuse and neglect. The Child Abuse Prevention and Treatment Act (CAPTA), (42 U.S.C. §5101), as amended by the CAPTA Reauthorization Act of 2010, retained the existing definition of child abuse and neglect as, at a minimum:

> *Any recent act or failure to act on the part of a parent or caretaker which results in death, serious physical or emotional harm, sexual abuse or exploitation; or an act or failure to act, which presents an imminent risk of serious harm.*

Most states recognize four major types of maltreatment: neglect, physical abuse, psychological maltreatment and sexual abuse. Although any of the forms of child maltreatment may be found separately, they can occur in combination.

According to The Children's Bureau's most recent report on Child Maltreatment 2012 published February 2014, FFY 2012 had an estimated 3.4 million referrals received by CPS agencies. The national estimate of 3.4 million referrals were estimated to include 6.3 million children with more than 80 percent of the abuse reported perpetrated by the biological parents. Thirteen percent was by other individuals involved in a child's life and six percent was unknown. In addition, during FFY 2012, half of (unique count) victims did not have a prior history of victimization, according to the Children's Bureau. Of these allegations, 20-30 percent were substantiated and of these, 60-70 percent received services.

Child abuse occurs at every socioeconomic level, across ethnic and cultural lines, within all religions and at all levels of education. We cannot deny that abuse happens to our children; the United States has one of the worst records in the industrialized nations, according to the U.S. Government Accountability Office.

## In substantiated cases, children's lives are saved.

But in unsubstantiated cases, families are traumatized, marriages and jobs threatened, tax money wasted. And worst of all, kids are hurt. The victims of false allegations are not statistics. They are kids. And protecting them — as well as the great majority of the caring American families who share a deep commitment to healthy parenting, requires us to understand two points often missing or de-emphasized.

1. **Every kinship child and family finds themselves in an uncharted territory of new experiences and old secrets.**
   Not all kids enter kinship care as victims of abuse and neglect. Some come from loving families in the midst of medical or financial hardship. Others have physical or emotional problems that simply can't be handled at home. But in every case, children carry their past — often including deep feelings of loss, grief, lack of trust and confusion — into their new family situation. No adult experience quite compares with the challenges kids face in a new family. Sights, sounds, smells, languages, traditions, rules of behavior and family dynamics are all different. The resulting problems — many predictable and natural enough — are all the tougher to diagnose and solve because rules of confidentiality may prohibit social services from offering straightforward explanations even to relatives about kids' past life experiences.

2. **Allegations of abuse in kinship families should be expected. Even the best and most experienced parents are vulnerable to reports of suspected maltreatment.**
   That's partly because the rules of discipline may change when you are parenting someone else's child. Many loving biological parents, for example, find it perfectly acceptable to slap the hand or bottom of a child who is about to dart into the street or reach for a hot stove burner. Under most state laws for licensed providers, doing the same is abuse. Corporal punishment of any kind is prohibited; it is recommended you check with your local support services to find out your state regulations regarding kinship caregiving.

## The task of separating real from perceived child abuse can be tricky.

Make no mistake. If you are concerned about a behavior, reach out to your state kinship care association, a qualified therapist or the child's caseworker.

## Several common misunderstood behaviors include:

- A grieving child may appear withdrawn — not from abuse, but from sadness.
- An undiagnosed child with learning disabilities or medical condition may appear violent and angry due to frustration and inabilities to cope, not abuse from his or her home.
- A previously neglected child who has learned to beg, steal, or forage for food in neighborhood trash cans may continue that behavior in kinship care.
- A child prenatally exposed to alcohol, referred to as fetal alcohol spectrum disorders (FASD), may appear to be a chronic liar due to the organic brain damage suffered in the womb, yet the reality may be a memory issue or inability to process thought. In addition, people living with the challenges of FASD may have limited or no cause-and-effect thinking, limited impulse control and unprovoked rages. A person unfamiliar with fetal alcohol issues could point fingers directly at a kinship family working feverishly to keep this child healthy and safe.
- A previously sexually abused or exploited child, hungry for attention and affection, may behave provocatively in public, abuse other children at home or at school, or inappro-

priately touch others. If the child's primary family is under investigation, confidentiality laws may prohibit social services from telling kinship parents that sexual abuse may have occurred.

- A previously physically abused child may believe that attention comes only from hurting others. Bullying, arson, vandalism, and cruelty to animals are common among these children and sometimes defeat even the most patient kinship parents while the root cause remains a deeply repressed secret.

## What should I do if I am contacted by child protection?

- Keep a factual journal in a stitched student notebook (where the pages cannot be ripped out without noticing) of behaviors or situations that concern you. This is also where you can keep appointment information.
- Write the name and number of any social worker or professional who contacts you about the child and date it.
- Keep copies of all papers from Child Protection. If the worker finds there is not abuse or neglect, they will send you a letter saying so. It will also say that you can choose to have the whole file destroyed. Many times it is better to ask the worker to **keep** the file, so if there is ever a question about what happened, you have the records.
- If the worker finds that there is abuse or neglect, then you need to appeal that decision right away. To appeal, you must write a letter addressed to the sender of the findings (Dear —————,  I appeal the decision of ————- dated ——- Sincerely, —————-) It is not complicated to write that letter, but you must do it immediately and within the time frame stated.
- Keep notes of all meetings with workers, include the date, who was there, and what was said.
- Be cooperative and honest, but careful, when talking to workers. **Be honest!**
- Tell the worker what things will help your family fix the problems to develop a quality case plan. **Then follow the case plan.** If you do not, the worker will go to court.
- **Remember, your comments can be used in court.** Legally, they cannot force you to talk to them. But if you do not talk to them they may find that suspicious.
- Go to all meetings and court hearings. Bring a friend, advocate, or lawyer to meetings.

For those families who reach out in love to help a child, the investment you make is great. Keep yourself and the children healthy and safe. Thank you for caring.

*Jodee Kulp is an award-winning author, producer, and advocate who works tirelessly to serve children, adults, and families of Fetal Alcohol Spectrum Disorders (FASD). Hers is a mission of education, compassion, and growth. Through www.BetterEndings.org, she knows that only through communication do we learn about stories that "inspire, build hope and provide wisdom to change the world one person at a time." Jodee Kulp is the author of **Families at Risk**.*

# Guilt, Shame, & Love

"*Even though we were the ones petitioning to have her rights terminated, that final day was so hard. I think that a lot of the saddness came from the fact that she never cared enough to appear at any but one of the hearings we had over the period of 4 years leading up to our adoption. I just could not imagine what had happened to her that she would not want to fight for her child.*"

## Emotional Rollercoaster

*By Betty Hanway*

*Hello!*
*I'm 59, my husband is 67, and we are raising our eight-year-old grandson in Texas...*

After years and years of dealing with our youngest daughter's bad behavior and poor choices, she got pregnant. We thought this would be the turning point in her life, and it was for a while. She had a good job, car, and her own apartment, but drugs never left her lifestyle. After her life derailed one more time, we finally had to step in and take legal action against our daughter to get custody of our grandson. This was the hardest thing I have ever had to do. She was so resentful, even though deep down she knew it was best for her son. She was homeless, jobless, carless, and strung out on drugs. She and some loser boyfriend were stealing and pawning everything in sight. It was only a matter of time before she ended up in prison, which is where she is now.

Our grandson, we'll call him "T," was really happy to have his own room, clean clothes, and a schedule! I'll never forget him being so excited to have a sock drawer. He lined up all of his little socks in perfect little rows. He quit pooping in his pants within two days of being with us. He was happy and I think he was relieved. I know "T" loves his mom and misses her, but he is thriving with us and I believe he is thankful for us being here for him. This makes it so much easier on my husband and I since our lives have turned upside down.

We worked hard, saved money, planned our retirement years, and now that is all out the window. The last thing I wanted to do was raise another kid. Now I am back to making lunches, monitoring homework, attending parent-teacher conferences, finding a babysitter, scheduling doctor's visits, making playdates, arranging sleepovers, and planning birthday parties? I would rather go to the dentist!

What's hard for me is the dynamics of it all. On the positive side, I have another daughter who is successful in every facet of her life and has two sons of her own. She is a teacher and is wonderful in giving me advice on my parenting skills and suggestions with helping with his homework. It feels awkward talking to her about these things, as now she sees me as a peer and a parent of a student.

I just want to be grandma to all three of my grandsons. But I am grandma to two and grandma/mom to one and it's not fair to any of them. "T" gets jealous if I spend too much time with the other two and acts out against them. I don't know if it is because he resents them because he doesn't have a "real" mom and home right now, and they have a mom and dad, a nice house, every toy a kid could dream of and so much more. Or if it's something else.

So I don't spend as much time spoiling my other two grandsons like I would like to because of "T," plus I'm tired. I feel like I am in "little kid overload." I feel bad for several reasons. For years, my "good" daughter suffered while we were busy dealing with our "bad" daughter. And now her own children don't get as much attention from me because I am raising the "bad" daughter's kid. The balancing act is exhausting for me. I try my best to get to every activity they have so my "good" daughter never feels slighted, but I know deep down inside, it is a deep rooted pain that never seems to go away. I have it in me and I know she has it, too.

Men seem to have it easier. They just aren't the emotional beings us women are. My husband just rolls with the punches and tells me I overthink things. He's probably right. He is delighted to have a boy in the house. He never got to raise a boy and now he is getting that chance. He bought a race kart for "T" and got him into racing. "T" is pretty good at it and it has done wonders for his self-esteem. It is an event that brings our new little family together. My husband is living vicariously through "T" and has a "purpose," if that makes sense.

We were lucky enough to have already had our house paid off before we both retired and invested wisely all those years. We are not rich by any means, but we are comfortable. We certainly never planned for the expenses that come with being a parent again though. We can't put "T" on our insurance because we didn't have parental rights completely taken away. We were able to get him on Medicaid. Thank goodness! The caseworkers at the local office said they would take our income into consideration and there were no provisions for grandparents raising grandchildren. I asked that she get a supervisor to talk to me, and that person told me the same thing. When leaving, the receptionist whispered to me that I needed to go home and file online because all of these people in the local office were just clerks and didn't know anything anyway. The "real" caseworkers will help me. I guess the real caseworkers never talk to anyone face-to-face and are protected from the public? Anyway, I did as she suggested, and within a week, we had Medicaid. Woohoo!

All of these arrangements are complicated because we have "Joint Managing Conservatorship" with both biological parents. Our attorney said this was the easiest way to get both parents to sign voluntarily and avoid additional court costs. He was right. By giving the parents the option of being able to get their son back someday if they were able to prove to the court that either one or both can provide a safe, drug-free, violence-free, stable home environment, they willingly signed the documents. Plus, this gives us an out as well. If for some reason, "T" starts the same juvenile delinquent behavior both his parents did, we can petition the court to sever this arrangement. I will do everything in my power to keep him from repeating the same mistakes, but I already know that it will kill me if I have to go through that hell again. So I refuse to do it. Once was enough and unfortunately, it's still not over. My juvenile delinquent daughter is now 30 years old and still a part of my life.

My next step is to apply for a child only grant under TANF. I only haven't done it yet because I was concerned the state would go after the biological parents for reimbursement. I am not sure why I struggle with that because they brought a child into this world and didn't have the forethought to provide for him, and now we are left to pick up the pieces and completely change our life because of their poor choices, but I do struggle with it. I suppose I hope (even though I don't really hope anymore) that once prison is over, that somehow they can get their lives on track and this would be one less debt to have to repay.

Like I said, my biggest challenge is the emotional rollercoaster. I love both of my daughters. I celebrate in the successes of one and wallow in the muck created by the other. We know we are doing the right thing for our grandson and that helps to level things out a bit.

*Betty Hanway is a young grandmother raising her energetic grandson while trying to navigate the system.*

## Letting Go

*Taken from a blog post by Jan Wagner*

I am realizing I have been letting go of his mother. It is a process for both of us. Even in her absence, she is with us. But in order to move on in this new family, we have to find a place for her that is less painful and less in the forefront of our lives. After having him for more than four years, I didn't see how an adoption would change things, other than the legalities, but it has. There are no more questions about what would we do if or when she ever decided to take him back. She can't now. We are his parents. We are his forever family.

As much as I love my daughter, and as much as I pray for her safety, and hope that she one day will turn her life around, H., Papa, and I couldn't wait any longer. We all needed some closure. We needed to heal and to go on with our lives. And we are. She will always be a part of us, she is my child too, and she was his mother in the beginning of his life.

In letting her go myself, I am helping H. to let go. I am allowing her to follow her own path, but that doesn't mean I have given up the hope that one day it will lead her back to us because we are her forever family, too.

# What To Do When You Are Mom To Your Child's Mom

*By Jan Wagner*

If you have spent any time at all looking for information about how to juggle the relationship between the child you are raising and his or her biological parent, who just happens to be your own child, then you know there isn't much available. A friend and I decided to do a workshop titled, "It's all in the family" about this subject. We quickly realized we were going to have to rely on experience and self-knowledge. I believe the reason for this is that every family has its own set of dynamics and this type of situation can bring out the worst of behaviors, thus, not a high success rate to write about. What we found when we opened the workshop was that we didn't need any preparation of materials because everyone just wanted to have a chance to talk about the various situations and ask questions. I firmly believe in the uncharted area of kinship, it is about sharing our own experiences, strengths and hopes about what has and hasn't worked for us.

I am not going to claim that I have the perfect solution to the problems of how to maintain a healthy relationship with the biological parent and the extended families involved because some of the people involved are unhealthy to begin with. What I do have is 10 years of experience with two separate grandchildren, their paternal families, and my daughter.

The first time my youngest daughter abandoned a child she was married. My granddaughter was two and they were living on our property. Her husband stayed so that I could take care of her while he worked. None of us thought it was permanent. I will readily admit that if there was a way to do everything wrong, I did it. I wanted to be responsible for my daughter's actions because then I could also be responsible to fix her. I was consumed by denial, grief, and anger. I hated her, mourned for her, and just thought if she would come back, we could somehow make it right again. It wasn't to happen. My ex son-in-law eventually remarried, I was no longer the "mother" figure for my granddaughter, and he moved on. It took much work, but I can honestly say that I respect him, I love his wife, and their other children call me "The Grandma." I see my granddaughter as much as possible for being a busy, active pre-teen.

At the same time her ex was moving on, my daughter became pregnant again by a much older man in an unstable relationship. We convinced her to come home, but I was determined not to get attached to another of her children. We all know how well that works. When my grandson reached the age of two, she was ready to move on again. We obtained guardianship and after four years we filed for adoption. This time, contact and visitation was up to her. I would not make it happen and I would not watch another child mourn for a mother who was not there. There were periods of time when we did not hear from her for months or even more than a year.

When we filed for adoption, we had not seen our daughter for 18 months. She came to one out of five hearings. It was difficult to testify against her when she was less than five feet from me. The adoption was finalized in September of 2012. I have since sent her school pictures, lost teeth and every week or so an e-mail asking if she is well. Around Christmas we opened up contact and last week we had a visit. I have to say that, since the adoption, I do not feel threatened by her, and I think, neither does she by us. The visit went well, and my grandson/son handled it better than we did. But a DSi 3D helped.

Besides the relationship with his sister, who I am close too, and her family, my grandson has another sister who is 17 by his biological father. Her mother made the first move to contact us, and we have had some good visits with that family. We keep in touch and it is helpful to have medical history. We tried to have a relationship with the paternal grandmother, but that did not work out well at all. He does not know his biological father, who willingly relinquished his rights to him, but, we know who he is, and if there is ever a desire for contact with him when my grandson is old enough to understand, I have no objections to that.

The greatest impact of raising my grandson has been with my own biological children and their children. I desperately love my other grandkids, but my focus is on the one we are raising and we are not as available as we or they would like. We spend as much time as possible together so my grandson has a younger family influence and a relationship with his cousins the same age, but it is still strained. My adult children have real issues with their younger sister that I can't help.

I guess what I want to convey is that in spite of what has transpired, she is still my daughter. There is nothing worse than not knowing if she is safe or even alive, and we have gone through extended periods of time wondering that. Boundaries need to be set. But also realize, that the biological parent is going to try to cross those boundaries whenever possible. Nothing is carved in stone. No one is going to hold you to your boundaries but yourself. Consistency helps, but it's not always going to work. Just as I would have never allowed anyone near my own children if they were a threat or had the capacity to hurt them, I need to hold true for my grandson/son. The saving grace for me is acceptance. This is who she is now. This is what the situation is now. It can change in an hour. But he deserves the right to know her. I need to keep in touch with her. She needs to know that family is here. I have told her over and over — we haven't gone anywhere. We are still here. I need to allow and accept her for who she is and where she is today.

I am my grandson's parent. I am his advocate and his voice until he is old enough to make his own choices. I am responsible for his health, safety, and welfare. I will not knowingly allow him to be harmed. But, I also have to realize that unless I deal with my own "stuff" I, too, have the potential to hurt him emotionally. It is a fine line to walk, but I do it one day at a time, one step at a time.

*After raising three children, 37 years of marriage, and at the age of 57, Jan Wagner started ed raising her then two-year-old grandson, H. Jan Wagner is now an advocate for kinship families and is involved on a state and national level. You can follow her blog Raising H at jdwags.blogspot.com. She is also available to speak or give workshops on Kinship/Grandparenting issues.*

# "Grand" Parenting
*By Noelle Hause, EdD, LPC*

Kinship care occurs when a child cannot stay at home with his or her parents and is placed with, physically cared for, and emotionally supported by a relative or close family friend. Circumstances resulting in the need for kinship placement include death of a parent, substance use, mental illness, domestic violence, incarceration, abandonment, unplanned pregnancies, poverty, abuse, neglect, military leave, and chronic illness.

Kinship placements help to maintain family cultural practices and the feelings of "belongingness" for young children and frequently provide stability by allowing children to live with their siblings and family members with whom they have established relationships. Additionally, this arrangement can decrease the child's stress and trauma of separating from parents overall.

Temporary and sometimes long-term assistance resources are available to support these arrangements through a variety of ways, including financial assistance benefits for basic needs such as food, clothing, housing, medical and behavioral health care, legal services, public education, and child care. While kinship care seeks to promote stability within loving relationships for children, family members often struggle with a variety of emotions and lifestyle changes, many of which can impact their ability to be emotionally available and responsive to a child.

The needs of a kinship caregiver, especially a grandparent who must face the inability of his or her own child to parent, can appear confusing. They may feel loss, grief, guilt, responsibility, embarrassment, overwhelmed, anxiety, isolated, disappointment, fear, resentment, and even anger toward the adult child who is unable to parent. This is often coupled with little preparation or warning that the child will move in and while it may begin as a temporary placement, it could grow into a permanent one. They may feel judged by other family members, friends, and service providers, for their own perceived "failed parenting." Additionally, their plans for retirement or other leisure activities and their perceived traditional role of "grandparenting" can be derailed causing additional stress. As a result, grandparents may present to others as conflicted, i.e., while happy to care for their grandchild they could also appear hostile, pushy, disorganized, protective, defensive, unhappy, and/or desperate, as they attempt to meet the child's needs and still hold out hope for their adult child.

While many efforts are spent on providing services to children, consideration should be given to the adults caring for them. Because young children rely on their caregivers for basic care, guidance, support, modeling, nurturing, and teaching, it is essential that their caregivers have the capacity to meet these needs. This can be difficult unless they are simultaneously able to get their own immediate basic and emotional needs met. Including caregivers in all decisions made and services provided can assist grandparents in understanding the importance of their role and strengthen the bond with their grandchild.

In their new role, grandparents need to set their own limits around their time, energy, expenditures, previous social expectations, and reach out to their support systems and community resources. However, they should not feel alone in this new endeavor. With the growing recognition of "grand" parenting needs, family and friends can embrace grandparents and their new family compilation, decreasing their feelings of isolation and loss. From a service provider aspect, support groups, individual counseling/therapy, parent education, case management, systems navigation, and advocacy may be necessary to help grandparents chart this new territory, problem solve solutions and envision a new way of living for their family.

*Noelle Hause, Ed.D, LPC, is an early mental health specialist for North Range Behavioral Health, director of community health resources for the North Colorado Medical Center Foundation, adjunct faculty at the University of Northern Colorado and author of The Early Years column for Fostering Families Today magazine.*

**Resources:**

**American Association for Retired Persons:** www.aarp.org – GrandFacts State Fact Sheets

**Casey Family Programs:** www.casey.org

**Generations United:** www.gu.org

*"Very sad and emotional day. Our daughter's parental rights were severed in court this morning. I knew it was coming, as we were sure she wouldn't show up to court today, but I had no idea it would affect me the way it has."*

# I Cannot Give Away That Which Is Not Mine To Give

I cannot provide peace, tranquility, and calm to a wounded child,
if I am not at peace and calm.

I cannot provide safety to a child, if I do not feel safe inside.

I must remember my child's eyes, before they were far away eyes,
before they looked right through me, before they were vacant.

I must remember that my child has seen what no child should have ever seen;
that my child has heard what no child should have ever heard;
that my child has felt what no child has ever felt.

I must remember that the lens through which my child sees life, love,
family, and relationship is not the same lens through which
I see life, love, family, and relationship.

My child comes from a land of hurt, shame, abuse, and neglect.
My land is foreign to her.

My child comes from a home of anger. My home is foreign to her.

My child comes from a life of fear. My love is foreign to her.

We simply cannot expect our children to move into our worlds
when we cannot spare a few moments to join them in theirs.

We simply cannot expect our children to trust us,
because we say so. Many before us have said many things.

We simply cannot expect our children to obey us, because we are right.
They have been wronged too many times prior to our right.

If we are to become the conduit to healing such pain
in wounded children, we must first heal ourselves.

**We simply cannot give away that which is not ours to begin with.**

Peace,
Juli Alvarado, Foster Mom
www.coaching-forlife.com

*Juli Alvarado is the founder of Coaching for Life and an international speaker,
consultant and expert in the area of relationships, foster care, and adoption. Reprinted
with permission from **The Foster Parenting Toolbox***

# Kinship Care: A Journey through Sorrow

*By Amy Radtke, MA*

October 31 marked another anniversary of raising my now six-year-old grandson. I have slowly come to realize this is not a temporary situation. When asked what I personally feel are the biggest challenges raising a relative, I have to say it is the difficult emotions I find myself dealing with, especially the feelings of sadness and resentment. I remember asking my mom how she was doing when she was sick with cancer and dying. She always replied, "Some days are good and some days not so good." My life as a kinship caregiver is much the same — some days are good and some days not so good.

My grandson came to live with me because I filed an order for protection on his behalf against his mother, my daughter. For nine months I pleaded with the county child protection social worker to help my grandson. I knew my daughter was deep in her drug addiction, leaving my grandson with strangers. The social worker continually told me she did not have enough evidence to remove my grandson from his mother. However, she also informed me any adult can file an order for protection on behalf of a minor. Making the decision to file the paperwork against my daughter was heart wrenching. When the judge reviewed the paperwork, he was one of the few people who took action to help protect my grandson. He approved the order and I was able to legally get my grandson and bring him home. This was the beginning of my kinship care journey.

During that first year raising my grandson, I felt incredibly sad and also alone. I was a broken-hearted kinship caregiver, trying to provide care and nurturing, when my heart felt shattered. It took every ounce of energy to get through each day. I was grieving the loss of my daughter to meth addiction. Granted, she is alive, but she is gone. I cannot tell you where she is today. She has no known phone number to call her. She has no known address. She is homeless and envisioning my daughter homeless is incredibly sad.

During the first week my grandson was with me, he was diagnosed with several developmental delays. He was neglected by his parents for the first two years of his life. His pediatrician stated his developmental delays were likely due to the neglect he experienced. Each week for two years he received therapies for speech, fine motor skills, and gross motor skills. He was behind in all his inoculations so those first few months he was also going to the doctor to get caught up on his inoculations. I was grieving that my sweet grandson was so neglected and didn't receive the love and nurturing all children should have.

I was grieving my life. I had earned a bachelor's degree at age 40, was starting an actual "career" instead of a "job," and was making plans and setting personal goals. Suddenly, overnight, my plans changed. My dreams had to be revised. Giving up my life for a life of changing diapers, dealing with temper tantrums and meltdowns, bedtimes, baths, bottles, and having many more expenses was difficult to accept and made me sad.

Mixed with the feelings of grieving was the difficult feeling of resentment. I was angry with my grandson's parents. I was angry with the other grandparents and relatives. I was angry with my friends. I was angry with the government. I was angry with the court system. I was angry for the lack of financial support. I was angry that life was not being fair to me.

Slowly I came to realize pain and loss are a part of everyone's life. The circumstances may be different, but the feelings of loss and sadness are universal. The more alone or unique I think I am with my pain and loss, the longer I stay stuck.

Finding other relatives raising relatives is perhaps the single most important step a kinship caregiver can take to deal with grieving and loss. During the first year, I did not reach out for help. I slowly started to isolate myself. I didn't have money for a sitter, so attending support groups seemed too hard, especially trying to attend a group meeting in the evening, when I was too exhausted to leave my home. I also felt ashamed to be raising my grandson. Inside I had a deep insecurity that had I been a better parent, then perhaps my daughter would not be an addict and would be able to raise her son.

Eventually I stumbled upon a closed Facebook group of kinship caregivers. A closed group means only members who are kinship caregivers are granted access. There are privacy policies, similar to many 12-step support groups. At first, I was a "lurker," just reading the posts of other members, and frequently finding myself crying because I understood the challenges and feelings the members described. In time, I started to share my feelings and experiences as a kinship caregiver. This was a turning point. I felt I had finally "come home" to a group of people who understood 100 percent what I was feeling. I was no longer alone.

Acceptance is the key to living a happy life. Living with fear and resentment in my heart does nothing healthy for me or those I love and who love me. Yet, it can be incredibly difficult to embrace acceptance. I have learned it is not a one-time event. I have to constantly remind myself sick people do sick things and to let go of judging others and their behavior. My daughter is sick. If she could do better, she would. She can't. If I have any expectations of how I believe my grandson's parents "should" behave or judge other family members for their lack of support, I set myself up for future disappointment.

The best thing I did was reach out for support and offer my support, which helps me to stop focusing on my situation and to focus on providing support to other kinship caregivers. It is important to know there are other kinship caregivers who have experienced many of the same feelings. They have walked this difficult path of raising a relative. They helped to get me out of the darkness of isolation. It is my hope sharing my experience will help you to see you are not alone.

If you are grieving, give yourself time, and know that you will come through the grieving. The tight grip of sadness on your heart will ease up. You will laugh again. Likely, it will be the very person you are caring for who will put the smile on your face and laughter in your heart.

I am a grandma raising my grandson. It's all good.

*Amy Radtke, MA, is a grandmother and kinship caregiver in Minneapolis, Minnesota. Her website, RaisingKin (www.raisingkin.org), tells her personal stories of raising her grandson and includes resources for kinship caregivers. Her primary goal is to bring greater social awareness to the complex issues relatives raising relatives live with daily. She encourages guest blog submissions to help kinship caregivers feel connected by sharing their stories. Amy believes storytelling is one method to remove the isolation kinship caregivers often experience. You can email amyr@raisingkin.com to share your short story or to invite her to speak at your next fundraising event. Reprinted with permission from **Adoption Today** magazine.*

# Life With Charles

*By Lynda Hickok*

There was a time before I turned 60 that my life was relatively free, I worked full time and spent time at a friend's ranch. I could attend social functions and go out for evenings. I saw my daughters and their children often. I visited another daughter in Hawaii or Arkansas each year. I had my retirement planned. I would pursue several hobbies and, if finances allowed would travel a little. But life has a way of ignoring scripts we write. Instead of my happy plans, I became the custodian of a special needs grandson, Charles. My life was changed forever.

Life with this amazing young man is frustrating and rewarding, funny and sad, exhausting and uplifting, joyful and sad. In other words, life with Charles is an adventure in contradiction with surprises all along the way, but mostly life with Charles is about love and commitment by both of us.

Charles was born in 1992. There were serious health and developmental problems from the beginning. He had no sucking reflex and was fed via a tube. He cried a lot with a deep guttural cry that broke your heart. His mother was uninterested in his daily care and his father took on most of the feeding and other care. Charles would be dirty, smelly, and inappropriately dressed when they came to family functions. His aunts and I felt so sorry for this little guy and tried to find ways to help him. We would bathe him when we babysat him, but that upset his parents. They seemed to love him but had no idea how to care for a child with his limitations. His only stimulation was the television. Any suggestions that might be helpful for his development were met with anger and denial that there was anything wrong with him.

Charles has never had a diagnosis for his disabilities, though he appears to have symptoms of several conditions. He is mentally delayed with a development at age 17 of age seven. He has ADHD, Obsessive Compulsive Disorder, some symptoms of Autism, poor impulse control, and is physically delayed. Though he can walk, climb stairs, and even ride a bike, his coordination is poor and in many ways he is weak. His hands especially are weak and uncoordinated.

For reasons known only to God, Charles bonded with me as an infant, though he seemed to have no interest in most other people with the possible exception of a half-sister 15 months older than him. Whenever I saw him he attempted a smile and hugged me hard. A hug from Charles could leave me smiling for days. His parents divorced when he was four years old and he lived with his father for nearly the next four years. During those years it was obvious to everyone that, while his father loved him, he was neither able nor knowledgeable enough to care for him adequately. I often tried to talk to his father about keeping him appropriately and adequately bathed, clothed, and fed. Those conversations were met with anger and excuses.

Charles had almost chronic ear infections and a cough. However, they were rarely treated. Though the pediatrician's office was nearby and medical coupons took care of the expense, Charles' father just couldn't seem to find the time or interest to see that he had medical attention. When I asked his father if he had taken Charles to the doctor I was told either that he had taken him, or given a relatively reasonable excuse why he hadn't. As a matter of fact, I learned that Charles was rarely seen by either the pediatrician or the dentist. The lack of medical care for his ear infections resulted in a partial hearing loss. Three ear surgeries managed to reduce or eliminate the infections, but could not completely revive his hearing.

In 1999 Charles' father asked me to take custody in an effort to reduce his mother's unsuitable influence. The plan was that Charles would still live with his father, but disagreements concerning his care would be solved by me. His mother was unstable and often used Charles as a pawn to get what she wanted from his father.

Charles' mother was inappropriate with punishment for the disabled child. She would have him kneel in a corner and place a glass of water on his shoulder. If the water spilled, the punishment would be much more harsh. Charles' speech was poor and if his mother couldn't understand him she would put hot sauce on his tongue.

Though Charles lived with his father most of the time, he spent every other weekend with me. During those weekends we played in the yard, took walks and watched television. He loved his baths and ate anything I placed before him. Those weekends were both heartbreaking and joyful. When Charles saw me he would laugh and call out to me. I, too, would laugh with joy and my heart would soar just to see him. However, seeing Charles' filthy body and clothes was painful. But at least for those weekends he would be safe and well cared for.

After two years of weekends with Charles, it became obvious that his home situation was not going to change for the better. In fact, it had gotten worse. His father had a job for a short time and worked nights outside at a warehouse. It was wintertime and cold outside. He would take Charles with him and the child would sleep wherever he could find a corner. I was shocked to discover that his father had moved a family of five into their small apartment. All the adults smoked heavily and took drugs. No fresh air was provided in the apartment and the smells were overpowering. Mold grew on the walls. Charles no longer had a bed to sleep in.

During this time I told Charles' father that if things didn't improve drastically I would take Charles full time. That was not an idle threat as I already had custody. His father didn't believe I would do it. But I couldn't let Charles continue to live in such deplorable conditions.

Making the decision to seek full-time custody was difficult. My partner, Jim, was apprehensive and I was afraid I would likely lose him. My siblings were also against it, but didn't stand in my way. I knew I had to do something. After a lot of prayer and soul searching there didn't seem to be any alternative.

As I applied to gain full-time custody of Charles, an event took place that about broke my heart. I had visited the court facilitator and received a stack of paperwork that I had to complete. When I was finished I took the paperwork back to the facilitator's office. When I entered the outer office I saw a small bundle of clothing on a chair. As I walked by the bundle, it moaned "Oh Meema," (Charles' name for me at the time), I realized then that his mother was there attempting to gain custody. It was all I could do to continue my errand without just grabbing Charles up and running.

I knew when I took Charles that his father would be beyond angry and devastated at losing his son. He did, after all, love the boy. About three days after the court hearing granting me full-time custody, his father called asking when he would get Charles back. It was difficult to tell him that getting Charles back was not going to happen. He was, however, welcome to visit whenever he wanted. That offer was flatly refused. He has not seen Charles since I took him.

Charles adjusted easily to being with me full time. He asked about his father only a couple of times. I told him that his father had some problems he had to take care of. When I picked him up from school he would say we were going to "your house." I explained that it was now "our house" and he picked up on that quickly. After a few weeks Charles told me that his father was "fired," a term he was familiar with as his father had been fired from any job he ever had. Those first few months were an adjustment period for both of us, but we were happy together.

Charles had been called Buddy since he was a baby. After a few weeks living with me, he told me that he wasn't Buddy any more. He was Charles, the name he was given at birth. That seemed to be his way of separating one period of his life from another.

Charles had difficulty controlling his temper during the first several months he was with me. I attributed this to his confusion about his place in life. He would scream and stomp his feet when frustrated or lost in a strange situation. I quickly learned that if I would put my arms around him and hold him tight he would calm down. He seemed to know that in my arms he was safe.

Medically Charles had, and still has, several issues. His teachers thought that possibly he needed glasses and that he didn't hear well. Trips to various doctors confirmed that, and he began wearing glasses in the fourth grade and is never without them. The first thing he does in the morning is put them on. It was determined that he has pre-glaucoma and takes medication to lessen the possibility he will develop full glaucoma.

He was given hearing aids about the same time he began wearing glasses. But he had suffered so many untreated ear infections before he came to live with me that the aids were creating additional infections. After ear tubes to drain his ears did nothing to prevent infections he had three ear surgeries. The last surgery seems to have cleared up the constant ear infections, but it also made hearing aids impossible for him. He will always have some hearing loss. Of course, he also has "selective hearing," the same as all children.

Thankfully, Charles has been cooperative about any challenges I have placed before him. When he was 11 it was discovered that he needed back surgery for scoliosis as his spine was not only twisting sideways, it was also twisting forward putting pressure on his heart and lungs. He came through the surgery well and bounced back quickly. He was back in school within two weeks.

Another issue with Charles during the first year or two was toilet training. He was not toilet trained when I got him. He tried to comply with my insistance that he use a toilet and fairly quickly learned to use the toilet during the day, night wetting continued for more than a year.

Pulling a child from a home he knows and placing him in another home can create serious psychological abandonment issues. In order to address these potential issues I attempted to find counseling for Charles; that proved difficult. In general, when I found a counselor who would agree to see a special needs child he or she would spend the time with us speaking only to me without even looking at Charles. When I could find no real help for him I finally realized that there simply isn't any therapy available for a special needs child in our area. I was frustrated and prayed daily for guidance dealing with whatever issues arose. So we muddle through and somehow Charles has become a well-adjusted, surprisingly happy child.

*Linda Hickock is the grandmother to Charles whom she raised as a single grandparent. While she didn't have any books or other guidance to help raise him, she had a lot of determination and a lot of encouragement from a Grandparents Raising Grandchildren group which she recommends that you find and join in your local area.*

*"How could I have raised a child who can't take care of her own kids? Not just take care of them, but she abused them, too. My other children have been able to raise their own children but she prefered drugs and partying. What did I do wrong to make her want to do this?"*

# The Safety Net of Kinship Care
*By Amy Radtke, MA*

I read a research report stating, "Custodial grandparents can provide love, security, encouragement, and structure for grandchildren who might otherwise be in a foster care home. A grandparent can act as a 'safety net' for children whose families have been damaged or broken by death, drug abuse, family violence and abuse, incarceration, or divorce," according to a 2005 report in *The Gerontologist.*

I believe kinship caregivers do indeed offer a safety net for our relative children. Perhaps that is the single most important distinction between kinship caregivers and non-relative foster families. I am my grandson's link to his mom, my daughter. Based only on my life experiences, it seems no matter how "bad" a parent is, most kids will hold their mom and dad in high esteem. My grandson is too little to understand drugs. However, he does understand that his family loves him and families can be made in all kinds of ways.

I recall a conversation with my grandson after the 2011 holidays passed. We never heard from his mother. Not even a phone call. He didn't talk about his mom being gone during the holidays. It wasn't until after Christmas was over and the tree was down when he mentioned her. He said, "Grandma, my mom doesn't want to see me."

My heart ached for him. What could I say?

I tried once again to tell him that when people take drugs, they forget about their family because that is what drugs do. I said, "I know your mom does miss you. I know your mom loves you. In fact, your mom knew she might not be able to take care of you and that's why you live with me. She picked me to take care of you! When you were just a baby your mom called ME to come get you because she wanted you to be with her mom. She knew I would love you and she wants me to love you while she is gone."

He thought about that.

"You are my mom?" he asked, trying to follow along with his little five-year-old reasoning.

"Well, I am your mom's mom and I am sort of your mom because I am your GRAND mom." I replied. That ended the conversation and we moved on to more important topics, like whether the Hulk is stronger than Iron Man.

I know this conversation will come up again — maybe soon, maybe not. But it will come up again. What I can do is let him know how much ALL of his family loves him and families are made in all kinds of ways.

I am the safety net for him. That's what kinship caregivers do. We fill that void of the missing parent. We make sure they know they have family who loves them. Many will, like me, try to let their child relative know that although they are not with the parent(s), they are with family. I believe that is important and I also think that is why we do what we do. There is no financial incentive to be the safety net. In fact, most kinship caregivers take a huge financial setback to raise their relative. But we are family and families are made in all kinds of ways. And relative caregivers love their families and are committed to them.

I continue to think about the difference kinship caregivers make in the lives of the relatives we are raising. The other night my grandson and I were reading a bedtime book that mentioned a parade. I said, "Remember when you and your mom had a parade? Wasn't that fun!" and his face lit up remembering how his mom made a "flag" from a big tree branch and taped paper to it to make a flag. They then stomped around the driveway pretending they were in a parade, my grandson loudly blowing "music" on his harmonica. A foster family wouldn't have been able to remind him of that priceless memory. I could see the memory made him smile.

I tell him stories about when he was born and how happy his mom and dad were to see him. He likes that story. I tell him how they picked out his name. My grandson loves to draw and enjoys music. These are the same qualities his mom has. I know this and I can pass along this information to him. He never has to wonder about his mother, who she is, and what she was like growing up. I am here to fill in the gaps for him. Again, I offer him the safety net for his heart to take in the information.

I don't think a non-relative foster family could tell him these things and have it carry the same weight and meaning as a grandparent or other relative can. He knows I love his mom and miss her too. He knows I really do understand his little heart hurts and misses his mom.

In the late 1990s I was a foster parent. My last group of siblings was adopted. A few years ago I spoke with the oldest, now married. She told me how she wished someone in her biological family would have taken her and her siblings in. Hearing that lets me know how much it means to our relative children that we did not look away. There is comfort in that.

Although kinship care certainly comes with many challenges, it does carry certain joys. Every night my grandson and I have a special bedtime routine. We read three books, and then I tell him a made up story. He will usually tell me a made up story, often based on the one I just told. Then he will turn onto his side and drift off to sleep. These are priceless moments.

I won't have the same level of closeness to my other grandchildren because I am not as intimately involved in their day-to-day lives. But with this grandson, he hears the stories of my childhood and the stories of his great grandparents. When I tell him a story about being bullied growing up, he tells me how he is going to "beat up" those kids. Bless his little heart how much he loves me.

I can't say for sure how many other kinship caregivers feel this way, but I personally carry certain regrets for how I parented my daughter. We all know hindsight is 20/20. I like the saying Oprah often says: "when we know better, we do better." I am a better "parent" to my grandson than I was to his mother. There is a certain sweetness to having a "do over." As a grandparent, I have more patience. I place less importance on making beds. I am more emotionally available. For these things, I am so grateful.

I am a grandma raising my grandson. It's all good.

*Amy Radtke, MA, is a grandmother and kinship caregiver in Minneapolis, Minnesota. Her website, RaisingKin (www.raisingkin.org), tells her personal stories of raising her grandson and includes resources for kinship caregivers. Her primary goal is to bring greater social awareness to the complex issues relatives raising relatives live with daily. She encourages guest blog submissions to help kinship caregivers feel connected by sharing their stories. Amy believes storytelling is one method to remove the isolation kinship caregivers often experience. You can email amyr@raisingkin.org to share your short story or to invite her to speak at your next fundraising event.*

## Reference:

Hayslip Jr., B. & Kaminski, P. L. (2005). Grandparents raising their grandchildren: A review of the literature and suggestions for practice. *The Gerontologist, (45)*2, pp. 262-269.

# Perspective Of the Child

"*I wanted to leave home all the time but I couldn't because I had to keep my younger brother safe. Now he lives with me and my family hates me. I follow what CPS tells me to do and now my Aunt is not speaking to me. But I did what I had to. I couldn't think of a stranger taking care of my brother.*"

## From a Child's View

*By Lee Sperduti*

"What did I do wrong? What is happening to me? Do my parents hate me? Is there a secret that they are hiding from me? Why don't they want me with them? Is it always going to be like this?" These were the thoughts that constantly swept through my mind for many years while my grandparents raised my younger brother and me. Too afraid to ask these questions out loud, I suffered silently and began to create my own immediate family using television characters. I remember choosing Chuck Connors from *The Rifleman* as my father and Chip and Sandy from *Flipper* were my siblings. Strangely enough, I was unable to stretch my imagination far enough to identify a loving mother, so I grew up without one.

My grandparents did the best that they possibly could with us while working full-time jobs. Upon the birth of my youngest sibling, however, my grandmother informed my mother that she did not have the energy to raise another grandchild. My mother was then forced to assume full responsibility for all of her three children. Life for me quickly went downhill from that point, but by the grace of God, I was able to survive my childhood.

What would have helped me through those tumultuous years can be applied to assist today's foster children and youth. I needed someone to tell me that my situation was not my fault, that I was not responsible for getting myself out of my parents' care and that I was not responsible for getting myself back. Much of the guilt that I had shouldered for way too many years may have been relieved had I been told that my parents' problems were among themselves and had nothing to do with my brother and me. Knowing that they were working on these issues so that we could have a healthy family life would have freed me from self-condemnation and punishment. Occasional interventions by professionals may have also given me validation to my thoughts and feelings, as well as served to evaluate the progress of my parents and the family as a whole.

People seem to generally believe that everyone was taught and understands basic life and social skills. This is usually not the case, especially where foster children are concerned. Each move or living situation seemed to steal from the normalcy of learning these skills. I became increasingly aware of my lack in these areas while temporarily living with the intact family of my college roommate. "What's wrong with her," my roommate's mother asked. "Didn't anyone teach her about...or how to...?" My past had automatically exposed itself and I remember feeling raw in my soul.

Now having a family of my own, I am keenly aware of my deficits. With both age and therapy I am able to verbalize and counteract most of my issues. It took a long time to get to the point of openly sharing my childhood. I am thankful for resources such as the **Teen Toolbox** (www.facebook.com/theteentoolbox) that provide knowledge and strength to those in need. I hope the best for all foster children and those who care for them.

*Lee Sperduti is an administrator at the Thomas C. Slater Training School operated by the Rhode Island Department for Children, Youth and Families. She is in her twenty-fifth year with the department. Lee is a tireless advocate for children and their families. She and her husband and two children have provided respite foster care to Rhode Island foster children.*

# A Traumatized Child's Hierarchy of Needs

*By Beth Powell, LCSW*

I was blessed to have had my grandparents, my great grandmother, my aunts and my uncles to help raise me and my little sister. They saved our lives and certainly their love, strength, values and integrity helped us to grow into the people we are today.

"Mother" was a paranoid schizophrenic with severe borderline personality disorder and certainly had her share of old, archaic, brutal shock treatments in the late 1950's before powerful antipsychotics, like Thorazine, were on the market. I was her first born and she started drinking with me when she was about four months pregnant, undoubtedly helping to create the learning disabilities I still have and the regulatory problems I had back then. In other words, I looked pretty ADHD as a kid.

It was up to me, before it ever should have been, to keep me and my little sister alive and safe from Mother, the person who was supposed to have been responsible for our survival as small children.

My mother's sister and her family stepped in and virtually "kidnapped" us when I was two-and-a-half years old and my baby sister was just a few months old. They slipped us into their car and sped away back to Arkansas before my father got home from work. My aunt wanted us gone before he got home because she was afraid he wouldn't have let us go. My aunt said my mother had always been crazy and having babies had just made her worse, so they took us away.

As many times as relatives came and took us home with them, then that was as many times as we had to go back. They always intervened, either on their own, or because my father acknowledged he needed help when Mother was too violent and my sister and I were in danger. There was no Children's Protective Services in Mississippi in the late 1950's and early 1960's; the relatives just got there before the police did.

Thank God we had extended family members who wanted us. They stopped taking us in when I was about seven years old. It was thought that I was probably strong enough then to run away from Mother...and take my little sister with me. At least that's what my mother's sister said my father probably thought. Now that I think about that...maybe my aunt and uncle were just mad at him for not letting us live with them permanently? I'll never know, the elders who were involved in our care back then are now gone.

I used to wonder why my father didn't heed the relatives' advice about taking his girls and leaving Mother. I used to spend hours back then playing "Sodom and Gomorrah" with Barbie dolls, having Lot, over and over again, leave the mother of his two daughters, with his girls in tow, because "Mother" had disobeyed God and as a result was turned to stone. As an adult I figured out why my own play therapy as a child was a way that helped me get through those times and helped me make sense of my world. It also provided me with a weird sense of security where there was none: Mothers who are turned to stone can't harm their daughters.

I came to understand that my father believed that when "one digs their own grave; they should lie in it." And lie in it he did. One of his sisters told me, when I was an adult, that my grandfather, a Baptist Biblical scholar had given my father permission to leave Mother in the early years of their marriage, but my father found out she was pregnant with me. It is from him that I get my sense of duty, responsibility, and commitment...sometimes, like him, to a fault, I might add.

The combination of my life experience, my experience in helping heal traumatized kids and adults, as well as my educational background, has called me to modify Maslow's Hierarchy of Needs to fit the needs, as I see it, in order, of the traumatized child who frequently, like I did, lives with relatives.

## A "Modified" Maslow's Heirarchy of Human Needs:
### The Sequential Path to Successful Adulthood

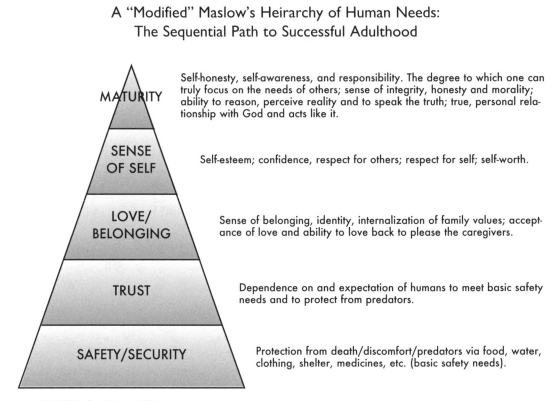

**MATURITY** — Self-honesty, self-awareness, and responsibility. The degree to which one can truly focus on the needs of others; sense of integrity, honesty and morality; ability to reason, perceive reality and to speak the truth; true, personal relationship with God and acts like it.

**SENSE OF SELF** — Self-esteem; confidence, respect for others; respect for self; self-worth.

**LOVE/ BELONGING** — Sense of belonging, identity, internalization of family values; acceptance of love and ability to love back to please the caregivers.

**TRUST** — Dependence on and expectation of humans to meet basic safety needs and to protect from predators.

**SAFETY/SECURITY** — Protection from death/discomfort/predators via food, water, clothing, shelter, medicines, etc. (basic safety needs).

© Beth Powell, LCSW, In-Family Services 2012

Look at the above graphic, from the bottom to the top, as the slow development of character. Character develops as one's needs are met, from basic to more complex. And safety-security needs are overridingly the most important and most basic of needs. No child should be abused, nor should they be spoiled or felt sorry for. Pity makes people weak. Letting kids run the household because they come from a hard place creates even more insecurity for them, along with lack of trust...not to mention anger, resentment and entitlement. If an adult is physically and emotionally run over by a child, then the adult is proving to the child that he or she isn't strong enough to protect the child from harm; and the hurting child may be the one who is causing the "harm." Sometimes we have to protect children from themselves.

An individual's safety-security needs require care-giving adults to be mature, responsible, emotionally stable, available, and consistent in their care-giving in order to provide children with a sense of dependable structure and a hierarchy of benevolent authority.

If self-esteem and confidence is the intended target before safety-security needs or the rhythm of reciprocal relationships has been established, then narcissism, self-destructive tendencies, or lack of confidence and true self-esteem could indeed be the end result. True self-love isn't possible until one has loved and been loved back by another. Self-esteem isn't given; it's earned by one's own accomplishments.

The top rung of the modified hierarchy above is that of Maturity. This is when the child-in-care becomes like the benevolent, mature, responsible, reliable relatives who are raising him or her. The child has absorbed the values, the integrity, the degree of responsibility and commitment. This is where, truly, the child can give back, to others, what was given to him or her. So, this is what I have done, am still doing, and will continue to do until I take my last breath. And I have my "people" to thank for who and what I have become.

*Conroe, Texas-based psychotherapist and neuro-behavioral educator, Beth Powell, LCSW, specializes in helping traumatized children and the families who raise them heal. She understands the importance that relatives and kin have on a traumatized child's life from her own personal growing-up experience and acknowledges she wouldn't have the insight and ability that she has today to help others if she hadn't "walked a mile in the shoes" of the people who seek her assistance.*

*Powell is also a CEU training provider, a social work supervisor of interns and externs as well as an adjunct instructor at Lone Star College's Montgomery Campus. She has created a unique systems-based child-in-family approach that includes the child's caregivers as part of the treatment team. For more information, visit www.infamilyservices.net.*

> **"Raising my grandchildren not knowing where their parents are has been one of the hardest things I have done. We don't even know if they are alive.  Every holiday raises questions from my grands that I can't answer. It makes me so sad."**

# Kinship Adoption:
# Family Provides Vital Information
*By Carol Lozier, LCSW*

## Kinship Care: A Growing Trend

In the United States, children who are placed by the state, cared for, or adopted by a relative, commonly referred to as kinship adoption, is on the rise. The U.S. Department of Health and Human Services estimates that one-third of children in the foster care system live with a relative, according to the Child Welfare League of America's Kinship Factsheet. American Association of Retired Persons (AARP) states that 7.8 million of our nation's households are headed by grandparents or other relatives providing care for one or more children.

According to the U.S. Department of Health and Human Services Social Security Act, relatives are given first consideration for child placements. Section 471, number 19 of the Social Security Act requires that the states should give "preference to an adult relative over a non-related caregiver when determining a placement for a child, provided that the relative caregiver meets all relevant state child protection standards."

*In a kinship adoption, unlike other adoptions, families often possess information that children yearn to know.*

## What Children Want to Know

Have you ever spent hours putting together a puzzle only to be left speechless when you realize several of the pieces are gone? Distressed, you search for them. You look in the bottom of the box or on the floor, but they are nowhere to be found. Even though you can discern the picture, somehow it feels incomplete without the lost pieces. This is a simplified version of the gnawing angst that so many adopted children face...they want the missing pieces about their birth family, and hence, about themselves.

In a kinship adoption, unlike other adoptions, families often possess information that children yearn to know. Typically, they have pictures, stories, and information that authenticates the child's early life story — the essential pieces to their identity puzzle.

Furthermore, as children head into adolescence their natural desire to know about their background increases. For many children, this developmental task becomes an agonizing experience when they do not have information about their biological heritage.

In therapy, children frequently disclose that their most significant emotional pain is the absence of information about their birth parents. Most children want information about their birth parents even if they were abusive to them. We all have an innate desire to know our history, and in particular, about the mother who carried and gave birth to us. Overall, children reveal similar nagging questions; they ask:

*What does she look like?*

*Do I have siblings?*

*Why did she give me up?*

*Why didn't she take care of me?*

*What happened to me when I was a baby, toddler, child?*

*Is she alive?*

*Where does she live?*

*Does she like to _____ (swim, draw, sing, and so on) like I do?*

In addition, children want discreet information that oftentimes a family member may be privy to, such as causes for the adoption, and the child's early life stories.

It is painful when children realize that their birth parents originally had the option to keep them. This can remain agonizing even if the child comprehends that the parent had no resources such as a lack of money, shelter, or food. The question of why their birth parent did not keep them remains a burning topic in their mind.

Children love to hear stories about their early life: how they came into the world, funny things they did as an infant or said as a young child, vacations, holidays, and how their family interacted with them. Hearing about a past event allows the account to come alive in the present, enabling children to own a piece of their personal history.

## A Closer Look: Grace S. and Maya D.*

Let's look at two examples of children who have gained from the connection of a kinship adoption: Grace and Maya.

## Grace

Grace is six years old. She is a stunning girl with a combination of features from her Hispanic mother and her Irish father. Grace was adopted at 16 months of age by her paternal aunt and uncle, Karen and Mike, due to her biological mother's (Alicia) incarceration. Karen and Mike maintain contact with both sides of Grace's extended birth family, including her half sisters and brother. While they deal with sadness and irritability after most visits, Karen and Mike feel the benefits for their daughter are far greater than the challenges.

In a recent session, Karen and Grace show a picture they were given by Grace's maternal birth grandmother. Karen says, "Grace, tell Ms. Carol about the picture we got from Grandma Jo at our visit last weekend." Grace looks up from coloring her paper with a glowing smile. "Ms. Carol. I got a picture. I got a picture of Alicia!"

Karen continues, "Yep. Alicia was about your age right now in the picture. She was looking right at the camera and smiling real big! And who looks like her, Grace?"

"She looks like ME!" Grace sings as she points to her chest.

## Maya

Sandi and Jay are adoptive parents to nine-year-old, Maya. Sandi's first cousin, Holly, is Maya's birth mother. When Sandi and Jay heard the news of Holly's pregnancy, they eagerly offered to raise the baby as the entire family was leery about Holly's long-standing drug problem and intermittent homelessness. Holly declined them.

For the first-year-and-a-half of Maya's life she and Holly traveled from place to place, and also lived in a shelter on two occasions. During this time, Sandi along with other family members were able to see Maya numerous times.

This cycle continued until one day, out of the blue, Holly called Sandi and said, "If you want her, come and get her."

"Of course I wanted her!" cried Sandi. "I only wish I could have gotten her home sooner."

In a therapy session, Maya talks about her desire to be in charge, instead of allowing Mom and Dad to take care of her. Maya and I sit on the floor; we examine her timeline and use a "Connect Back" worksheet to aid our process. Together, we search for the original traumas that created her negative self-belief, "I can't trust adults to take care of me."

As we work on this negative belief, Sandi tells Maya detailed information about past times when she or another family member were present. Maya quietly listens as Sandi shares accounts of Maya's neglect from the time she was a young baby: Holly handed seven-week-old Maya a bottle that she had to feed to herself, Maya was filthy and wore dirty clothing, each time they saw Maya her diaper needed to be changed and she was hungry. This information was immensely valuable in Maya's counseling and healing process.

Sandi told Maya joyful stories too. She told her about Holly's pregnancy and delivery, and Maya's first birthday party. Of prime interest to Maya was, "How did I eat my birthday cake?" and "Did I like it?" Additionally, Sandi has been able to show Maya pictures of her birth mother spanning from the time she was a young girl through her adulthood.

In an adoption formed through kinship, parents have the advantage of knowing inherent information about their child. Usually, parents know general, as well as exclusive information that will prove helpful to the child throughout his or her lifetime. These crucial pieces of information are healing to a child's loss or trauma, and can fill in the gaps to finally make the picture of their past — clear.

*Carol Lozier, LCSW, is a psychotherapist in private practice; she specializes in helping foster and adopted children and families. She graduated from Florida State University in 1989 with a masters degree in social work. Her website is www.forever-families.com*

*All identifying information has been changed to protect the confidentiality of the children and their families.

# Tara's Story
*By Anonymous*

My mother was just 17 years old when I was born. My mother was living in a foster home, where they made sure my mother received prenatal care and I had well-child checkups as an infant. That foster home was the last chance for my mom. She had run away from many homes, since the state removed her from her own mother's care, a victim of abuse and neglect. As soon as my mother turned 18, she took me and left the foster home. She decided she didn't want any rules, she thought she could manage on her own.

After moving from one friend's couch to another, my mommy and I ended up living on the streets of Olympia. She went to DSHS and asked for help. That's when she was told she needed to tell them who my daddy was. I had never seen my daddy — and his name was not on my birth certificate. It wasn't too long after this that my life changed — a lot.

I found out that the people at the office my mommy went to decided to look for my daddy. They gave him some papers and asked him to have a test done to see if I was really his child. Daddy came to visit me one day — and mommy let him take me with him to his parent's house. That was the first time I saw my grandma and grandpa. They took my picture and said how much I looked like my cousins. I stayed at their house with my daddy for several days, then went back to stay with my mom. Grandma and Grandpa babysat me a lot after that. They put medicine on the spot where I was burned by a cigarette, and on my head where it was cut when someone shaved all my hair. My mommy said they were trying to get rid of the bugs in my hair.

On my first birthday my grandma and grandpa took me to meet some of my cousins. They had a little party for me at McDonald's and I got to eat a whole cupcake!

It wasn't long before Grandma and Grandpa thought I should live with them all the time. They were both working full-time, but my aunt Valerie watched me while they worked. They took me with them to meet a lawyer and talked about going to court, to ask a judge if I could stay with them for always. My mommy wasn't happy about that, but my daddy decided that he thought it was a good idea. The judge ended up thinking it was a good idea also, and Grandma and Grandpa got something called "custody" — so I have been living with them for eight years now.

Grandma stopped working so she could stay home and be with me. I got to know a lot of cousins and made friends with children in our neighborhood. When I was four and five I got to go to Head Start and now I am in elementary school — I just began third grade.

My daddy doesn't come to see me often. He has been in jail a few times, but he's out now and still doesn't come to visit me.

My mommy used to come almost every week. She had another baby, so now I have a little brother. I don't think my brother lives with mommy anymore either. Mommy had to go to jail after a policeman found some drugs in her purse. My grandma said my mommy needs some time to work on getting healthy again. It has been more than a year since I have seen her. My daddy has two other children, I only get to see them every once in a while. His children don't live with him — he usually lives in a tent in the woods.

Last summer my mommy told my grandparents that she was going to let them adopt me. Nothing really changed after the adoption, because I had lived with them so long already — but now we will be a family forever. I know that my grandpa and grandma would let me see my mommy, but she never calls and we don't know where she is living. Sometimes I get sad when I think about her, and I cry for her.

My grandma and grandpa took me to a meeting called Kinship Support. I met a lot of children being raised by grandmas and aunties and even great grandmas and grandpas! I met a new friend there — Jasmin and her little brother live with their nana and papa. Now we get to go to Girls Scouts while the adults have their meeting. It's a lot of fun.

Grandma now works as a Kinship Navigator to help other families like mine. She told me I am just one of more than 40,000 children living with grandparents or other relatives in the State of Washington. Most of the children are not living with their parents because the parents abuse drugs and alcohol. Some have parents who are in jail, and a few have parents who have died. We all wish we could live with our mommies and daddies, but they just can't take care of us and keep us safe. We still love our parents, but we are grateful that our relatives decided to take care of us.

*"On particularly rough days when I am sure I can't possibly keep going, I like to remind myself that my track record for getting through bad days so far is 100%...and that is pretty good."*

# The Good, the Bad, and the Ugly
# of Kinship Parenting
*By Rhonda Sciortino*

In the summer of 1940, my grandmother met a tall, handsome lifeguard at Santa Monica Beach. She fell head over heels for this black-haired, blue-eyed Irishman who won every dance contest he ever entered. Within a few weeks they were married, and almost immediately the fairy tale began to fade.

That tall, handsome man had a violent temper. He had been left homeless by his mother at the age of 12, responsible for his little brother and sister. He raised his siblings by stealing clothes off clothes lines and vegetables out of gardens. There were scars on his head and back where he'd been beaten and burned. The details of those stories were the influence for the ever-present anger that flared for any reason or no reason at all.

Within two years my grandmother had two babies and a husband who, because of his violent outbursts, depression, and lack of ambition, had a hard time holding a job. For a time they lived in a post WWII government work program housing project. For several years that family of four lived in a 16-foot travel trailer in a campground. Finally, they moved into my grandmother's parents' home, where they lived out the rest of their volatile relationship. Both of their children were eager to get away from the chaos and abuse. Their son signed up for the Navy on his 18th birthday, and their daughter, my mother, exited the abuse by running away with the first boy who would marry her. She was 17.

My mother wasn't married long before the excitement of it all wore off. Her friends were going to dances and parties, and she was home taking care of a baby who kept her from having fun. So she packed her clothes, loaded her car, left me with a neighbor on the pretext of going shopping, and moved away with a young man she had only recently met. He made her feel wanted and promised her a new life — the life she'd longed to have. She didn't know if that opportunity would ever happen again, so she seized it.

In the 1960's, if the child welfare people could find a family member to take a child, their work was done. So I was left in the care of my mentally ill grandfather and my alcoholic grandmother in a dilapidated shack the size of a garage. The plumbing didn't work, the electricity was off half the time, and we frequently had nothing to eat.

I think my grandparents did the best they knew how to do, but their best was dismal. The fact that they took me in somehow satisfied their sense of obligation, but they made it clear that they didn't want me and hadn't planned for taking on the responsibility of raising another child.

I have a fairly good idea of how they felt and what they thought because they screamed it out daily. Normal conversations didn't take place in that shack. There was either screaming or cowering or both. There was sarcasm and flying objects hurled in rage in the general vicinity of one's opponent. And then there were the rage-inspired beatings.

A social worker rarely showed up. So with no oversight or concern of being caught, I was burned with cigarettes, stripped naked and beaten, and suffered second- and third-degree burns after my grandmother threw a skillet of hot oil on me. On one occasion, a social worker did come to the door to find that I had two black eyes. One could be explained away, but two...not so easily. So, I wound up in the care of a wonderful foster family for a brief period of time. It was brief because those people did the dastardly deed of taking me to church, which was frowned upon in the years just after the Supreme Court decision to remove prayer from schools.

My grandfather filed a complaint against the county, and I was removed from that clean, safe foster home and placed back into that filthy shack with the people who made it clear that they wished I'd never been born. You might wonder why in the world they'd go to such lengths if they didn't want me. The answer is because I was accompanied by a monthly welfare check, a $60 per month child support check from my biological father, food stamps, and free "government" cheese and powdered milk.

Having told this story, I have to interject that there are wonderful people raising their grandchildren throughout the United States. There are people who, when they thought they were all through raising children, took on the heavy responsibility of raising another. Many wonder if they have what it takes — the stamina, the patience, the money, and all the rest of what's needed to raise good people in a world that has normalized what used to be wrong and that uses words like "dope" and "bad" to mean "terrific." I applaud all grandparents who have stepped up to raise their children's children.

The point I want to make here is that in some cases the people who neglect, abuse, or abandon their children were victims of abuse themselves, so placing their children back into that dysfunctional or abusive environment is only going to serve to perpetuate the generational cycle of abuse.

It's been demonstrated time and again that abuse is generational. In these cases, placing a child who's been abused into a completely unrelated foster home can be the best thing that could happen in the life of that child. It certainly was with me. The foster family whom I stayed with for that brief time showed me in their living that there were people who didn't raise their voices to one another and didn't hit each other. They showed me that there were people who lived in a clean house and had enough to eat. They seemed to enjoy one another. And they had faith, hope, and love — three things I had never seen before. Prior to being exposed to those people, I had no idea that there was a different way to live. Without exposure to them, I could easily have gone the way of my mother, my grandfather, and unnamed generations before them.

Instead of someone delighting in my grandfather and gently teaching him right from wrong, his mother showed clearly that she valued her new boyfriend more than she did her children. Leaving them homeless and hungry showed indisputably that she considered my grandfather and his siblings worthless. Consequently, my grandfather went through life feeling worthless. He made choices that a person who felt hopeless and worthless would make. His hurt, anger, and depression influenced the way he treated his wife and children, and the result was that he raised up another generation of abusers. My mother abandoned me, and her brother was accused of molesting his children.

Here's my point: **If a social worker had taken a closer look at my grandparents and the way they lived, he or she would have seen that they were not fit to raise a child. He or she would have seen that the shack was uninhabitable. Had the social worker checked up on me regularly, he or she would have seen the obvious signs of abuse** that many of my grammar school teachers saw. Unfortunately, they were not mandatory reporters in those days. And the school system, as well as our culture, didn't support "interfering" in what was considered the private family affairs of others. Additionally, knowing that a social worker could show up at any time may have prevented some of the abuse.

Thankfully, things are much different today. Biological family members are not automatically considered qualified to parent because of some bloodline connection. And counseling and therapy is available to the child and family. Social workers remain involved for support and oversight. And strong efforts are made to reunify parents with their children. Given my circumstances, I always wonder, though, about the efficacy of trying to reunify parents with children they cannot care for or simply do not want.

I would be remiss if I didn't include a few words about the positives of kinship placement. Living with my maternal grandparents, I had access to pictures of family. My mother sent pictures to her mother of her and the children she kept and the life she lived. So, although I didn't see my mother or hear from her, I felt connected to her through the pictures she sent. I knew what she looked like. I heard stories about her — not all good, but they helped create a sense of connection nonetheless. Although it may sound odd, there was comfort in knowing what she looked like and seeing the pictures of where she lived. Because of those pictures, she seemed real to me. I knew my great-grandmother (yes, the one who left her children). She wasn't a nice old lady, but there was a sense of roots and stability in knowing her. Being connected, even loosely, to these "vertical generations" gave me a slight sense of belonging to a family. I say "slight" because I looked different and my name was different. The family was not a solid, supportive family, but I suppose there was some value in that connection.

An indirect benefit of my placement with grandparents was that, as a result of not moving around a lot, I was able to finish high school in the same school district where I started kindergarten. Having consistent education contributed to a sense of stability that I desperately needed. I found solace in education. I was safe at school, so I threw myself into school work.

In conclusion, I want to thank the family members who take a deep breath, up their vitamin intake, and step up to the responsibility of raising another generation. I know you feel like you didn't sign up for this, yet you do it anyway. I thank the social workers, psychologists, and teachers who invest in the lives of children who experience the pain of abandonment long after the placement is settled. I thank the volunteer mentors, coaches, and CASAs who stay involved and help provide a sense of stability, consistency, worth, and value to children who have been abandoned and abused. And I thank the churches and ministries that provide respite care and support to kids and families who so desperately need it.

*Rhonda Sciortino overcame abandonment, abuse, poverty, filth, and hunger, and built a life of affluence, order, fulfillment, and excellent relationships. Her desire is to help others mine the lessons out of their pain and apply them to their future to create their own success. She has written several books, including* **Succeed Because of What You've Been Through** *and the first in the* **Emerge Successfully** *series of gift books,* **The Prayer That Covers It All**. *Sciortino is the host of* **Rhonda's Radio Show** *on am590 The Answer in Southern California, where she interviews people who have overcome adversity as well as those who help others overcome.*

# Family Finding Fulfilling Our Promise
*By Matt V. Anderson, MSW*

Late last year I was visiting Pennsylvania on behalf of Children's Home Society of North Carolina. I was there to learn about Pennsylvania's efforts to integrate Family Finding practice into their child welfare system and how we might replicate some of their successes in North Carolina. Children's Home Society has been a leading agency in the implementation of Family Finding practice, and in the last few years we launched an effort to significantly expand and sustain the practice across North Carolina. Family Finding is an innovative practice that uses techniques and technology to search, discover, and engage extended biological family members and other caring adults in the care and placement of children living in out-of-home care. Our goal is to identify safe, caring adults who will provide a child with a lifetime network of support and the opportunity to be adopted into a forever family. We believe that children do best when raised in a family and the promise of family membership is possible for every child.

While in Pennsylvania I met Ashley, a bright and talented 20-year-old college student. She was about to graduate and embark on her next great adventure. It's generally a time when we celebrate our achievements and imagine that anything is possible. However, in just two short months Ashley was going to become a former foster youth. She was going to age out without a family to call her own.

Ashley came into foster care as an infant. She was adopted at age five but the adoption lasted for only four years. At age nine, she re-entered foster care where she spent the rest of her childhood. The foster care system had been her sole source of support. On her 21st birthday, however, her support system would vanish and she would be left alone in the world with her two-year-old son.

There are more than 400,000 children living in foster care, 100,000 of them are waiting for a family to call their own. As a public child welfare system we make a promise to each and every one of these children that we can keep them safe, find them a permanent family and help them succeed in life. Every year we fail to fulfill that promise to the 23,000 children who age-out, according to the 2013 AFCARS Report. These children suffer adult outcomes such as homelessness, incarceration and unplanned pregnancy at rates that far exceed those of their peers who have not been in foster care, according to the report "Midwest Evaluation of the Adult Functioning of Former Foster Youth: Outcomes at Age 23."

Last year, Ashley was included in that number. But as I have come to know Ashley, and so many young people just like her, I am convinced that this does not have to be the fate for 23,000 children every year. These children have families, large families. We can provide services that ensure children have lifelong relationships with their family that provide safety and stability, unconditional support and a foundation from which they can develop into healthy, loved, and productive adults. Our Family Finding program at Children's Home Society is being implemented with these principles in mind.

When I met Ashley she shared her experience of growing up in foster care and being on the precipice of aging out. She also said she and her son were going to spend Thanksgiving alone. Through choked back tears she lamented this reality; wishing that something had been done to help her find her family. The truth of the matter is that Ashley, like all of the kids we work with, has a family and does not have to spend holidays alone. This is reinforced for me every day as we deliver Family Finding services in North Carolina.

Now that she is an adult, Ashley, with the help of a Family Finder, decided to contact her first social worker to find information about her mother. As it turned out, her mother was contacting the social worker at the same time. Ashley gave the woman her address and asked her to share it with her mother. The next time I spoke to Ashley on the phone the mailman arrived to deliver a letter, the first communication with her mother. Ashley has since been to visit her mother, aunts and uncles, cousins and spoke with her grandfather over the phone. Through these encounters she has learned invaluable things about herself, her family and why she was in foster care. She could finally answer those burning questions that have weighed so heavily on her for the past 20 years.

When I asked her what it was like the first time she met her family, she said, "As I was standing in my great aunt's living room surrounded by happy faces and listening to tears of joy, I looked at my auntie and thought to myself, 'wow, blood family.' If you've ever known the feeling of loving someone without ever meeting them; that's how I felt. I love my family and I am ecstatic to begin our journey together."

Ashley has only just begun the path toward family membership, but is showing great promise. The last time we spoke she said she and her son spent Thanksgiving with her family last year. The question that remains is why did she have to wait 20 years to reunite with her family? Family Finding provides our foster care system with the tools and strategies to fulfill our promise of family membership to every child.

In 2011, Children's Home Society was awarded funding from The Duke Endowment, Edna McConnell Clark Foundation, and the Social Innovation Fund to expand Family Finding services in North Carolina and develop plans to sustain the practice. This funding was made possible because of the success of Children's Home Society's pilot project, which ran from 2008-2011 and is being evaluated by Child Trends, an independent, non-partisan research center. During the pilot project, Children's Home Society served 88 youth. The average number of known family connections at the start of those cases was only three. Our Family Finders were able to discover an average of 59 family members per child. Among the youth served, 86 percent of them had at least five relatives commit to being part of their lifetime network of support and 52 percent had at least one relative commit to adoption or guardianship. The success of the pilot project indicated that Family Finding could improve our ability to achieve both relational and legal permanency with children in foster care, even those thought to be the hardest to place. To read Child Trends' articles on their Family Finding evaluation, visit www.childtrends.org.

During the last year, Children's Home Society has hired 25 Family Finders and five program supervisors to serve 21 County Department of Social Services agencies across North Carolina. We are delivering services in rural and urban counties. We are doing Family Finding with children new to out-of-home care, those lingering in foster care and even those who have aged out but are receiving services voluntarily.

Family Finding is a six step process, which includes; Discovery, Engagement, Planning, Decision Making, Evaluation, and Follow-up on Supports. Our goal with every case is to discover a minimum of 70 relatives and other caring adults who were previously unknown to the case. This starts by talking with the youth about who has been important in their lives and to whom they want to be connected. Inviting them to participate in this process helps them to feel valued, supported and gives them some control over the decisions that affect their lives. By casting such a wide net we are able to engage a large number of adults who can provide safe, supportive, and unconditional relationships. With family members engaged, our Family Finders conduct a planning meeting with the family to identify the needs of the child and begin to consider how the family can come together to meet those needs. The decision-making meeting is conducted to formalize plans and define the different roles that family members are going to play. These roles can range from sending a birthday card to regular visitation or being a permanent placement. But a permanent placement alone is not the ultimate outcome. Family Finding also provides children with critical knowledge about their family of origin — information that will help them to answer questions like who am I, where did I come from and when am I going to belong to a family?

Children must belong to a well-supported family and network of caring adults, which have the resources and capabilities to help them heal, reach developmental milestones, and ultimately to succeed. As we continue to grow our practice and serve more children across North Carolina, this is the vision that we bring to our Family Finding practice. We are fulfilling our promise to children and youth so that they, like Ashley, can receive the benefits of family membership.

For more information about the program, contact Matt Anderson at mvanderson@chsnc.org or visit www.chsnc.org.

*Matt Anderson, MSW, is originally from Pittsburgh, Pennsylvania and currently resides in Greensboro, North Carolina. He earned a master's in social work from the University of Montana and has extensive experience in the youth services field with a focus on child welfare, youth engagement, and the creative use of media as a catalyst for change. Anderson works for Children's Home Society of North Carolina and is a director of planning of sustainability. Anderson's responsibilities include business development and public policy work related to expanding and sustaining the Family Finding practice in North Carolina. As a partner in Porch Productions, he also produced the feature documentary, "From Place to Place," about three foster care alumni who set out to change the system that raised them. Anderson serves on the National Association of Social Workers Communications Network Advisory Committee.*

# Kinship — Finding Our Place in the Circle
*An Adoptee's Perspective of Kinship*
By Sandy White Hawk

I was born on the Rosebud Reservation in South Dakota in 1953, the third child born to my Indian mother, Nina Lulu White Hawk Garneaux. It was during the time when Indian children were systematically being removed from their families and communities through adoption and foster care. During this time nearly 35 percent of all Indian children were adopted out, put in foster care, placed in orphanages, or indentured as farm laborers. I have been calling this period of time up to the passage of the Indian Child Welfare Act — The Adoption Era.

My adoptive mother was an only child whose mother died when she was two. I met her Uncle Ben and Aunt Maggie, cousin Bessie and Russell. I saw them about three or four times in my life. My adoptive father's family was from South Dakota and lived close to the Rosebud Reservation. I have only one memory of visiting my adoptive father's family after he died when I was six.

Aside from Uncle Ben and Aunt Maggie I don't recall saying uncle, auntie, grandma, grandpa, or ever playing with a cousin.

My life consisted of me, my brother (also adopted) and my adoptive mother. Life was difficult. My adoptive mother suffered mood swings that led to violent rages. She had to be tormented by loneliness as she had no relatives to look to for reprieve. She had a few friends but it seems they kept a distance. I had years of hurt, resentment, and anger toward her for the abuse and neglect. With the help of our Lakota ceremonies and understanding of our values I began to have compassion for my adoptive mother and no longer hold those negative, resentful feelings.

In 1988 I found the courage and strength to return to my homeland — the Rosebud Reservation, land of the Sicangu Oyate. My mother Nina had passed just two years before I made it home. As I met my uncles and aunts I began to heal from all the years of separation, isolation, grief, and loss. I met my brother Leonard. He was raised on the reservation by our grandpas so he learned our beautiful Lakota language and learned much of the old ways. He also suffered years of brutality at the Boarding School in Mission, S.D. He survived and has a beautiful family and was there on my first trip home telling me that he knew of me, that he wondered about me, where I was, if I had a good life and was so happy I made it back home.

I noticed that as the years went by it was hard for me to call my uncles and the one aunt I met, by Uncle Manfred, Uncle

Terry, Uncle Clifford and Aunt Cecilia. I had never had an uncle or aunt. Since I had never been a niece I didn't understand that it was disrespectful to refer to them by only their first name. It felt strange that my brother's children called me Auntie, almost uncomfortable. I didn't know how to be one. I had no reference point for kinship — relatives.

The loss of our Indian kinship relationships began in boarding schools when generations of children were raised away from their families. Many lost the ability to remember their language. They grew up without rites of passage from childhood to adulthood leaving them with no understanding of what it meant to be a man or woman. They did not receive their Indian names, or spirit names, as they are often called. A spirit name is given so that the spirit world will recognize the child, as we are instructed to use that name when we pray. We say our name so we are recognized. Indian names gives us our identity — over our lifetime it helps them understand who they are.

They would not have held a newborn baby — were not taught their roles of son, daughter, sister, brother, grandchild, niece, nephew, or cousin. They learned to exist — survive. It was a complete loss of sense of self, being part of family — kin. Kinship roles were stripped away and left them without the learned familial roles.

Adoption and foster care of Indian children has also impacted the loss of kinship roles. When an adoptee returns to his or her Indian family — kinship relationships and identity have been disrupted. The adoptee that grew up without any cultural connection learns and behaves in the culture he or she was raised — yet the Indian family left behind often forgets the adoptive relative will not know how to be a daughter, sister, niece, etc., in the Indian way. For example, white culture is more assertive, competitive, and focused on the individual and also has a different relationship with money. Indian people often see assertiveness as aggressive and even offensive. Money and resources are shared freely among relatives and friends of the family and community. The focus is more the family and community rather than the individual.

Our language speakers and knowledge keepers tell us that our communities had such a strong system of taking care of one another that there was no word for orphan because orphans did not exist. If all the adults of a family perished, the children were then taken into families in the village. If there were still extended relatives, the kinship structure of the tribe would determine if they went with the mother's side of the family or the father's side of the family. The care of children — the next generation —

was always a priority. The kinship system was so strong there was never an orphan. The state of being an orphan — alone without any relative or extended family simply did not exist. It wasn't until the many massacres and children forcibly taken from their families that orphans came into existence and the word created.

## Restoring Kinship Roles

In Lakota culture the grandparents are the teachers to the family and the young parents. Grandparents offer encouragement, suggestions, warn about certain decisions that may bring harm in the long run. Grandparents have already made all the mistakes and can share their life lessons. If the parent-adult child relationship is a trusted one, young parents can avoid any pitfalls in their relationship and in the relationship with their children.

I raised my children as a single mother in Madison, Wisconsin. After I went home and found my Indian family I found the Indian community in Madison. My children, then 7 and 13, were fortunate to experience the love and support of this community. The Madison Indian community gathered every Sunday for feast, drumming, and outfit making. Speakers traveling through the area were often our guests. It was how my children learned their role in the community and observed how to create community by watching the adults. They learned to greet adults, especially elders with a handshake and hello. My daughter learned to serve elders without being asked and learned to bead. My son sat on a drum and learned songs and drum etiquette. When my son had his first kill he shared the deer meat for a stew with the community. He gave meat to the women who did not have a relative who hunted for them. All this served to show them they are a vital part of a community — that the community is their extended family.

My granddaughter, Nina, received her Indian name — Maka aka mani winyan — Woman Who Walks on the Earth — when she was six. The spiritual leader who named her said that over time Nina would develop a relationship with Unci Maka — grandmother earth. No one told Nina this. After she received her name we heard her playing in the dirt of the campground repeating her name over and over.

We would occasionally just ask her, "What's your Indian name?" and she would repeat it. She began asking questions about death. Seeing pictures of her Navajo great grandmother she wanted to know where she was now. Her parents told her that her spirit was in the spirit world and that her body was in the ground. Something clicked for Nina and she began to see the earth as Unci Maka, something that was alive and that she had a relationship with her. We noticed it when she said "It really makes me mad when people throw garbage on the ground. That's my grandmother!" She was sincerely hurt and now that she is ten, she still remarks about garbage and how people who throw garbage on the ground are "disrespecting" her grandmother.

Aunts and uncles often offer the disciplinary role. When our grandsons are being difficult their mother will say, "I'm going to call Uncle." They usually cry, "No!" and pull themselves together rather than face their uncle's disapproval. Our granddaughter who was exceptionally energetic would stop in her tracks if her leksi (uncle) used that certain tone in his voice. All of this provides balance and sends the message to the children that their actions affect everyone and that they are loved by the entire family who will set boundaries for them.

My daughter, Nina's mother, is an artist who is a yearly art vendor at Sante Fe Indian Art Market. This last summer Nina, a budding artist, set up some of her artwork in her mother's booth. Her first painting that sold was "Woman Who Walks on the Earth." She drew herself walking on the globe. We all were so excited to see her expression of self — in her spirit name.

When an adoptee finds his or her Indian family there are so many emotions swirling from the lived experience of being raised away from his or her identity. It is not the absence or presence of adoptive parental love that is the most devastating. It is the years of being isolated in their adoption experience — not having anyone who can understand what he or she has to navigate daily — often being the only person of color in the family and community. This leaves the adoptee emotionally fatigued, full of fear and insecurity.

The Indian family may or may not know how to bring their relative back into the family. There could be years of guilt and often surprise that the adopted relative even exists. The collision of these wounded experiences can initially be tumultuous but if care is taken can be healing for everyone.

## Indian Families *Make Relatives* Formally And Informally

All tribes have a ceremony that adopts someone into a family or into a tribe. The Hunka Ceremony — Making Relatives — is one of the Seven Sacred Rites of the Lakota people. The elders tell us that Hunka happened in many different ways. If a child was lost to disease early in life a family may Hunka another child offered by another family. Adults would make relatives after their family member died so the family would Hunka a young man or young woman to take his place. This helped in a couple of ways. The young man or young woman who was adopted would assume the role of the missing family member. That meant contributing by hunting, preparing food, taking care of the children or the old ones; it preserved the family system and strengthened the extended family. The Lakota people have never stopped making relatives in the traditional Hunka ceremony. It is common to hear someone say, "This is my Hunka Uncle or Hunka Sister."

Indian families often take someone informally as their relative. As we socialize in pow wows or other social gatherings and develop relationships we often develop a familial affection for someone. It is then we start referring to that individual as niece or nephew or grandchild or the younger person begins to refer to a beloved elder as grandpa or grandma. This kind of kinship serves as the structure to instruct, nurture, and encourage. It strengthens our communities and contributes to community healing.

Indian families also have blended families although I have to say I have never heard any Indian family say that they are a blended family. Family is family and we bring our families together and with our Indian values as the guide strive for family unity. After divorcing, I married George McCauley. Together we have four children and five grandchildren. Once again I was challenged with learning to refer to my family without the larger societal labels like; step-daughter. And what is a step grandchild? Aren't they just grandchildren? Kinship ways of the Indian family are much more relaxed and to me it is healing. We are also blessed to have young people call my husband Uncle or Grandpa and I have many who refer to me as Auntie. These informal kinship bonds are healing to our individuals, family, and community.

## Healing Does Not Have A Timeline

Recently, I visited an elder friend on the Cheyenne River Reservation in South Dakota. He was a good friend to my eldest Uncle Manfred who is now in the spirit world. They met on the Ft. Benning, Georgia Army base in 1953. Today my uncle would be 79, his friend Harry is now 84. He misses his good friend, my uncle. When we visit he likes to tell me stories about Uncle Manfred — it helps me know who he was. As we visited this last time it struck me to be called "Manfred's niece." I'm 59 and have only been called niece a handful of times. It made me feel young, even little. It made me realize that while I have much healing I have a hole that will never be filled. But I can nurture that hole by making sure our grandchildren understand kinship. By being the best aunt to my nieces and nephews, those by blood and those who have chosen to call me Auntie brings healing to me and fills up that hole.

Today, as a people we are restoring our kinship roles and are healing from the intergenerational trauma caused from the Boarding School Era and the Adoption Era. It seems everyone, not just those who were raised away, are learning about their place in the circle — the circle being our families and communities. More and more Indian communities provide womanhood and manhood ceremonies, parents are making sure that their children are receiving their Indian names. Other healing ceremonies are being offered and much healing is moving through Indian country.

This loss of understanding and sense of kinship is why it is so important for me to give what I can to my children and grandchildren, nieces, and nephews. The cycle of loss has to stop with me.

As Indian communities bring their adoptees and those who grew up in foster care home, adoptees and those who grew up in foster care will be able to heal their disrupted kinship roles and heal and find their place in the circle.

*Sandra White Hawk is a Sicangu Lakota adoptee from the Rosebud Reservation, South Dakota. She is the founder and director of First Nations Repatriation Institute (formerly First Nations Orphan Association). Sandra serves as a Truth and Reconciliation Commissioner on the Maine Wabenaki Truth and Reconciliation Commission.*

## Two Worlds

Torn between
Two worlds
Torn between
wrong and right
Feeling
Abandoned, hurt, and sad
Kindness is a knife
Fear a constant companion
One world full of
Insecurity,
Another full of light
Fear makes me wonder
How long
Till they don't like me
How long
Till they leave
Their kindness is a knife
Slowly, ever so slowly
Their kindness cuts less
Slowly, ever so slowly
Fear begins to fade
Becoming secure
I belong
In the light

*the person who penned this poem*
*requested to remain anonymous*

# Finding Support

*We either make ourselves strong or we make ourselves miserable. The work is the same.*
*~ Carlos Castenada*

# United We Stand . . . Divided We Fall
*Keeping Successful Partnerships*
*When Sharing Others' Children*
*By Jodee Kulp*

Thirty-five years ago Karl and I met in a parking lot over a discussion about fishing. Much water has passed under the bridge we built that day. Storms have raised their ugly heads and we have cleaned up enormous debris scattered by children from hard places. But the bridge we chose to build has remained firm. We have kept our individuality on the banks of this torrential flowing river. We still have our strong personalities, ideals and opinions separate from each other, but on the bridge we unite. And because we come together in unity in our parenting, this old bridge has provided safety for young people as they crossed over into determination of who they will become.

It has been the children birthed to others who refined our connections and wisdom. These children diligently tested our patience and wore smooth our rough edges. They humbled us with the challenge of not judging the people they love in their lives. Most importantly they taught us not to judge each other as we hung over the edges of the bridge to pull another youngster back into safety.

Karl and I believe in possibilities for each person beginning or living life in a hard place. We believed we could make a difference in the course of a child's life — and these children changed us.

## We Let Go Of Dreams For New Possibilities

We discovered that our dreams and plans were filled with potholes. We could not repair the neurological and physical damage of prenatal alcohol exposure to our precious adopted daughter. We could, however, learn everything possible about Fetal Alcohol Spectrum Disorder, help her become the best person she can be and advocate for public awareness. We had to adjust our parenting to recognize her defiance was fear and she lived in a world experience vastly different from the one we understood. We learned that on our daughter's "off" days it is enough to be together as a family and simply love each other regardless if a scheduled event needs to be abandoned. During these times, if Karl or I are stressed we encourage time alone off the bridge embracing our individuality to restore our souls and spirits.

## The Bridge Stays Open During A Storm

It didn't take long for us to realize that two independent people were going to have two different opinions. We agreed to disagree. We also agreed that each of us had the right to safe and healthy anger and we would take turns being angry instead of defensive or offensive toward one another. Only twice in our relationship have we locked horns on individual issues — each time over a matter of life and death. Once we were both wrong and the truth lay between us on the bridge. The other time, well, he was right.

Choosing to take turns in being angry has paved our bridge with the strength of deep understanding. It has forced us to walk in the other's shoes and hear the other person when we are trying to listen, or not. It has meant that we have had to take turns to temporarily lay our own lives down (our personal agendas and opinions) for the advancement, safety and health of each other or our family team. It means that we show in our actions and words regard for our significant other's emotions, experiences, time, and ideas.

Standing hand-in-hand in the center of our bridge, Karl and I begin the last quarter of our life game. We know that time is a process that runs on different speeds for different people. When we reach out past our individuality and embrace the differences of others we are allowed the freedom to embrace many. Our bridge widens and strengthens to safely guide a child or an adult between its rails. We understand that complexities in life happen to all and guide others to safety. We celebrate successes and we encourage others as we learn to stand through crisis. Learning becomes a journey of many steps as we braid others into our life partnership.

## We Are But Partners For The Moment

My dear friend lost her husband to cancer. Their bridge wasn't going to go down, just because of a little old storm, even though at the time of his death they had ten children born under other mothers' hearts. The bridge they so strongly built did not crumble and not a child fell. Partners for the moment — friends, family, other caregivers, service providers — joined forces. Each partner took a small piece of the burden and we laughed and added the light of joy in that darkness. Friends offered respite services, retired foster care providers became a surrogate parenting team, social workers bought groceries, and their church brought hot meals. The partner community rallied upon the bridge the couple had so strongly built. On the strength of their bridge there was room for everyone.

In times of trouble and difficulty we become one unit without words, our thoughts and messages reach out beyond the current situation and our actions speak louder than our words. My husband's eyes shine as beacons for my encouragement and it is my hope that my smile and eyes do the same for him. We have partners for a moment. We understand in our hearts the meaning of — united we stand, divided we fall. We challenge you to build your bridge and be a partner.

*"There are few pioneers who must not only pave the path for others to follow...but also must define the landscape to illustrate its existence. Jodee Kulp has written and published more books about Fetal Alcohol Spectrum Disorders than any other parent advocate in our time. Her work has provided assistance to thousands of families and individuals living with FASDs." — Donnie Kanter Winokur*

*Jodee Kulp is an award-winning author, producer, and advocate who works tirelessly to serve children, adults, and families of Fetal Alcohol Spectrum Disorders (FASD). Hers is a mission of education, compassion, and growth. Through www.BetterEndings.org, she knows that only through communication do we learn about stories that "inspire, build hope and provide wisdom to change the world one person at a time."*

# Kinship in California

*By Juline Aguilar, MS*

I sat with my chin resting on my hand, the other hand cradling the phone. How can I help this grandmother? She received information on the class we were offering titled, "Relatives Raising Relatives," but as a senior on a fixed income she didn't have the money needed for gas to make a 30-mile round trip from her home to the class. Plus, the class was going to be in the evening and she was caring for a seven-year-old grandson who needed to do homework and get to bed, not attend a class for adults.

## Different Challenges

Clearly, kinship, or relative caregivers, have different challenges than traditional foster parents who are not related to a child placed in their home. Many feel they do not have a choice as to whether they accept the responsibility of raising their kin. They do it because that is what family does. The role of being a grandmother, brother, sister, or auntie goes through many changes when becoming the "parent." Many grandparents are on fixed incomes and dreaming of retirement, not starting over again with a young family. These relatives often feel isolated, not only in the community, but in their own families, where there may be tension and disagreement about the care of a young family member. In California, caregivers can find information and support with the Foster and Kinship Care Education Program provided by 62 California Community Colleges.

## Training Programs

The Foster and Kinship Care Education program was established in 1984 with the passage of Senate Bill 2003, and provided funding for education and training for potential and existing foster parents through the Community College Chancellor's Office. Additional funding in 2000 allowed for an expansion to include kinship care provider training. The Chancellor's Office of the California Community Colleges administers the statewide program with state and federal support in collaboration with the California Department of Social Services, the colleges, and the counties. The mission of FKCE is to provide quality education and support opportunities for caregivers of children and youth in out-of-home care so these providers may meet the educational, emotional, behavioral, and developmental needs of children and youth. The program offerings have grown to more than 30,000 hours of training annually. Nearly 6,000 kinship and non-relative extended family member caregivers participate each year at minimum.

The FKCE training is available to kinship caregivers and foster parents at no cost. Though the colleges vary in size and location, the curriculum that covers such topics as the role, rights, and responsibilities of a relative care provider caring for a relative child in foster care; an overview of the child protective system; relationship and safety issues regarding contact with one or both of the birth parents; and permanency options including legal guardianship, the Kinship Guardianship Assistance Payment Program and kin adoption. Many other resources and topics are discussed in the trainings and each local program is designed to fit the unique needs of each community.

The program at Folsom Lake College primarily serves rural El Dorado County which sits between Sacramento and Lake Tahoe in the foothills. Its trainings are offered both mornings and evenings so caregivers who work have options. We have a quarterly newsletter that provides information on trainings, as well as community resources. Last year, we collaborated on a kinship event with a local agency, Lilliput Children's Services, that offers the Kinship Support Services Program, a program funded by the California Department of Social Services to assist relative caregivers more broadly. By working together, kinship caregivers were offered a morning of training at a local church conveniently located near a preschool and elementary school. The morning began with a grandparent caregiver sharing her experiences of raising her grandson for more than ten years. The next speaker was from the local school district. As the foster youth services liaison she provided a wealth of information about the local schools and educational issues. A children's attorney then shared information on permanency options and how relative caregivers can navigate the court system. Finally, a clinical therapist addressed the many emotional issues that caregivers experience when caring for relatives. Caregivers left the training armed with new information and a feeling of connection to other caregivers.

The FKCE program at Woodland Community College serves Yolo County, a diverse blend of agricultural and suburban land and home to the University of California at Davis, a bedroom community to the state capitol in Sacramento. Attendance at the kinship program offered by Woodland Community College has been mandated by the local department of Child Welfare Services for all relative care providers. Under the leadership of Cherie Schroeder and Heidi Andersen, relative care providers are treated to two, three-hour classes, first focusing on supports and services and then the juvenile court process and permanency options, titled, "Kinship 101." Caregivers learn the basics about accessing health care, therapy, school resources, financial assistance, and most importantly, how to navigate the court system.

In the year before the Yolo County policy for training kinship caregivers was instituted, the county documented 16 children who had been removed from placement with these caregivers. In the year following the initiation of this kinship program only one child had been removed from the care of relatives. Schroeder recruited Andersen as a trainer, after meeting her for the second time as a relative caregiver. The first time the two met, Anderson was herself in foster care. She is now successfully raising two nieces and, along with her husband, has become a licensed foster and adoptive parent.

"Kinship care is so much harder than foster parenting," Andersen said. "As a kinship caregiver, you have no time to prepare, you get the call and they show up. Your role never ends. The child ages out and you continue to rework the relationship. Other parents just don't know what it is like. Until you've walked in these shoes, you don't even know how to tie them!" Schroeder and Andersen's program for Woodland Community College is obviously serving local kinship care providers well.

The FKCE programs in the 17 Los Angeles area community colleges offer orientation for new kinship caregivers covering kinship curriculum topics such as working with Child Protective Services, dealing with grief and loss, and educational issues. At Los Angeles Mission Community College the FKCE program collaborates with the program, Grandparents as Parents, which is a free community-based program in the greater Los Angeles area. Through the efforts of FKCE and GAP, the program provides caregivers up to 52 weeks of training and support. Grandparents, aunts, uncles, siblings, and extended family members discuss how to deal with issues such as having a biological parent in and out of a child's life, the child moving in and out of the caregiver's home, age related illnesses of caregivers, finances, and legal issues such as wills and care of the child after the caregiver's death.

Also in southern California, the San Gabriel Consortium, serving Mt. San Antonio, Chaffey and Citrus Community College Districts, serves kinship care providers with kinship orientation, kinship learning groups, and the Traditions of Caring curriculum. Relative care providers in these communities are mostly grandparents who gather regularly to learn and gain support from one another.

## Meeting the Challenge

Though the challenges of kinship caregiving are numerous, most relative caregivers would not trade the opportunity to provide a loving home for their relative children for anything. With opportunities for training and support, such as those provided by the Foster and Kinship Care Education programs through the community college system in California, caregivers can meet those challenges head on.

For more information about the Foster and Kinship Care Education Program in California, visit https://fkce.cccco.edu.

*Juline Aguilar, MS is a curriculum specialist for the Foster and Kinship Care Education Program at Folsom Lake College. She has a master's degree in educational psychology and lives in Northern California with her husband and two children. Reprinted with permission from* **Fostering Families Today** *magazine.*

*"Be strong enough to stand alone, smart enough to know when you need help, and brave enough to ask for it." Ziad K. Abdelnour*

# Understanding Respite
*By Stacey Leidner*

What is respite? Respite is a temporary break, given to caretakers, that provides a period of rest and renewal. The Respite Guide, *"Taking a Break: Creating Foster, Adoptive and Kinship Respite in Your Community,"* is intended to help parent support group leaders develop and provide respite programs to the families in their communities, or to partner with public agencies in their program development and implementation.

Respite care is a much needed service for all families, especially foster, adoptive, and kinship families. Scheduling time for respite allows primary caregivers an opportunity to plan activities and most importantly, it helps to keep families from becoming overwhelmed by their many ongoing responsibilities. It is imperative for all families to take time to refuel and re-energize.

Parents can utilize different respite providers as caretakers for their children. However, for children in foster care, finding respite caretakers can sometimes be challenging. All respite caretakers must have thorough background checks completed, which includes finger printing, to provide respite for foster children.

Some of the children in foster care have emotional, behavioral, or medical challenges. Respite caretakers for these children need extra training to work with the many challenges these children may have.

Respite is not only a great opportunity for primary caregivers, but it is just as important for the children in foster care. Often when the children are in respite, they are able to build healthy relationships with other children in foster care, pursue a special interest, or have fun doing an activity they enjoy. They get the opportunity to build onto their social skills and self-esteem. This allows them to learn to trust others and to trust that the caregiver is going to come back to pick them up. This is often important for children who are in foster care because many have often been abandoned by people earlier in life and they fear they will be left again. Ultimately, respite leads to healthier families and less placement disruptions.

The Respite Guide has three major sections. The first section is devoted to exploring the benefits of respite. These include: (1) allowing the caregiver to get some much needed free time, (2) a decrease in child abuse and neglect, and (3) a decrease in disrupted placements. One adoptive parent quotes, "Now, ten years later and after adopting six more children, we know when we keep ourselves healthy we can help our children heal and bond to our family. If we let ourselves get so drained we have nothing to give our children, we are in fact letting them down. Our health and the health of our marriage have to be intact so we can be a good parent to our children."

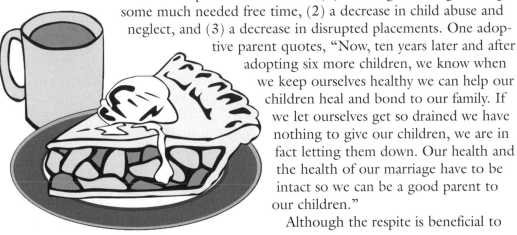

Although the respite is beneficial to

families and children it is not always available. First of all, one must also find a provider who can properly and safely care for the child. It is important for the family and the child to feel comfortable with the provider, so the experience does not feel like punishment for the child, and that it is a wholesome and positive experience for all.

The second section of the guide explores the various respite care options that might be developed for families. There are several model respite programs around the country. The models are designed to inform parent support group leaders about the programs that are available and helps them develop a program that is right for their families. What works in one area may not work in another area. There is also an emphasis placed on the parent groups conducting a needs assessment. This allows the parent group leaders to receive feedback from the families regarding the types of respite the families need.

The Continuum of Respite Care is based on the needs of the families. Respite can include in-home care which allows the child to stay in his or her own home and have a trusted adult come to the home. Group child care is another option and it allows the child to go to a daycare center with other children while the parent is at a parent group meeting.

Special interest and mentor relationship experiences are also a great option. These include the child being involved in an activity that they enjoy such as sports, music or Girl Scouts. Camps can also provide a planned form of respite care. Camps can be day-long, overnight, weekend, or week-long. It is up to the family and what the family needs are to determine what type of program would be best.

Therapeutic care is another option available to families. This is a much more restrictive type of respite care that is provided by trained professionals or experienced caregivers. Again, it is all based on the needs of the child and the family.

The final section of the guide shows the applicant how to develop a plan. Using the parent assessment tool, parent group leaders would design their respite program. Additionally, applicants are provided the guidance to ensure they have addressed all the legal requirements for a respite program.

Finally, this section emphasizes how important it is for the provider of respite care to form a good relationship with the public child welfare agencies in the jurisdiction of the program.

The group leaders must also determine the number of children to be served, the type of respite program desired, how often families can request the services, how many staff members are needed and where the program will be housed.

With the plan outlined, the budget can and must be developed. Last but not least, once a provider receives a grant, they will need to locate and train respite care providers.

Evaluations are a must. They are important for the group leader to gather information from the group to find out if the program met their expectations and needs, and to determine if the program should continue.

The evaluation is also a good way for people to share their ideas and discuss any changes they would like to see in the program. The evaluation can be done by survey, interview or just general conversation.

Finally, the Respite Guide also provides forms that groups can use for their program. Medical history, billing information, authorization forms, and child information forms are a few examples of the forms that are included in the guide.

Additionally, there are also several organizations and websites listed that can provide additional resources to the respite groups. For more information about the Respite Guide, "*Taking a Break: Creating Foster, Adoptive and Kinship Respite in Your Community,*"contact Diane Martin-Hushman at hushman@nacac.org or 866-622-2249. You can also download a copy of the Respite Guide at www.nrcdr.org/_assets/files/NRCRRFAP/resources/taking-a-break-respite-guide.pdf

*Stacey Leidner began her career in child welfare more than ten years ago. After graduating from college, she worked at a group home for children with severe emotional disabilities for four years.*

*There she gained significant experience with and knowledge of the children in foster care. There she met a child who she adored so much she brought him home to provide him with a family. Although he no longer lives with her, she is his family and he is her son. For the past seven years she has worked at AdoptUsKids. Her work with the families and the children is quite rewarding and it has been a learning experience. She has been a mentor for another child for the last four years and she is a foster mother to two little boys. Reprinted with permission from* **Fostering Families Today** *magazine.*

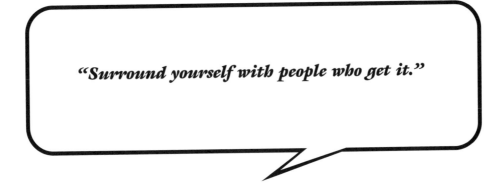

"*Surround yourself with people who get it.*"

# Kinship Support Groups

*By Debbie Willett*

About three years ago a group of adoptive moms, who are now grandparents raising grandchildren, expressed a need for support for other grandparents in similar situations. In my line of work I saw several grandparents who were either raising, or were the main care-taker, for their grandchildren. These events started a collaborative effort between our County Department of Children, Youth, and Families, the County Department of Aging, the County Department of Mental Health/Intellectual and Developmental Disabilities, and Child and Family Focus, Inc., a faith-based mental health provider for children and adolescents.

We developed a survey to determine the needs of grandparents raising their grandchildren. The questions were designed to determine what services these caregivers were aware of, the services or support they felt they needed, and whether they would be willing and able to attend a support group. In addition, the questions included what day of the week and time would be most convenient for them to attend a support group and whether or not they would need child care in order to be able to attend. The first informational meeting we hosted had a great turnout. We then met to discuss details such as location, day and time, child care, agenda, and other items necessary to establish a support group.

Since a post-adoption support group is already established in our county and run by the Department of Children, Youth and Families, we decided to meet during the same time. This gave us clearance approved workers to provide the child care. The adoption support group is divided into two groups for the parents based on the ages of their children, and into age appropriate groups for the children. We decided on a separate group for the Grand Families, the name we have given ourselves as some of the parents that attend are raising nieces and/or nephews and not grandchildren. The children of the Grand Families would be a part of the same age appropriate groups as the children of the adoptive parents. We felt that children being raised by other relatives face many of the same issues as children who were adopted; loss of birth parents, identity issues, split loyalties; and many other issues.

We have been meeting for about three years now. We meet for six weeks in the spring and six weeks in the fall. The support group has been a wonderful support for many families, and some of the friendships that have been formed through the group meet outside of the group also. In the past we have had a Respite Day where the Grand Families have been able to drop off the children and enjoy a few hours doing whatever they wanted to do without the responsibility of having the children with them.

We recently participated in a focus group that was done to gather information for our county to see what services the parents feel are working; what services do not work, and what new services may need to be put in place. I will list the concerns/issues of the group here:

1. There is a need for peer advocacy for the grandparents. They do not know where to turn for services or support. They said they were so thankful for the support group so we can share what we individually have found to be helpful. One of the grandmothers said she would love to be a peer advocate to help the grandparents. I

asked where they thought a position like that should be housed. They did not feel it should be in the Department of Aging because they won't work with you until you are of a certain age, and most of us would not qualify for their assistance. (I met a grandfather of a one-year-old who is 37). They felt it would be best housed in the Department of Children, Youth and Families.

2. The topic of legal representation was also discussed. The idea of being able to have access to the attorneys who work with the families involved with the Department of Children, Youth and Families was brought up. Also the idea of being able to have an attorney present to represent the best interest of the child was shared.

3. There was some discussion about seeing if there was a way of getting some legal changes made, and possibly having someone like a state representative attend a grandparent's meeting. They would like to know how in situations where the grandparents have been raising their grandchildren for years there could be some kind of permanent custody or guardianship, without having to go the adoption route, so there would be some permanency and security for the children.

4. They also discussed some financial assistance. The topic of subsidized daycare was a big topic. The financial assistance would be for families where there was proof that if the grandparents did not take the grandchildren that the children would have gone into the foster care system.

As a personal testimony of how the support group has helped my own granddaughter that I am raising, let me share an example. My granddaughter just turned five. She came to live with me at the age of 22 months. She loves attending the support group meeting in the preschool group. When she was four years old, she came to me and said; "I have two mommies. I have mommy Stacey, who I came out of her belly, and I have you. You are my MeMe, but I call you mommy." I was so impressed how clearly she understands her situation. Also recently while she was on the speaker phone with my daughter, my granddaughter wanted to ask me something and she said, "Mommy" and my daughter on the phone thought she was talking to her, so she replied "what?" My granddaughter looked at the phone and said, "No, not you, I am talking to my mommy that takes me to school every day." Again, I was so impressed at her understanding and confidence in her situation.

*Debbie Willett is the mother of 11 and grandmother to 4 amazing children. Ten of her children were adopted. She has been raising her 7 year-old granddaughter for the past 5 years. Debbie works for a faith based mental health provider as the Family Support Partner for families in her county who have youth involved in the juvenile justice system. One of Debbie's own son was involved in the juvenile justice system, as she serves as a peer support to help the families navigate the system. Along with a few other grandmothers, Debbie was instrumental in starting a support group for Grand Families. Grand Families are families who are raising grandchildren or nieces and nephews. Debbie continues to co-facilitate the group that has continually grown over the past 5 years. Debbie has been a single parent for the past 10 years.*

# Self-Care for Kinship Caregivers
*By Carol Lozier, LCSW*

*"Stressed souls need the reassuring rhythm of self-nurturing rituals."*

— *Sarah Ban Breathnach*

The daily caretaking of children is exhausting; this may be especially true in a kinship adoption. In fact, according to the American Association of Retired Persons, or AARP, there are more than 5.8 million children living in their grandparents' homes.* In retirement years, most grandparents are planning to slow down and have less responsibility as opposed to more.

Ongoing financial, health, housing, work, and family pressures can cause stress to our behavior, body, thoughts, and feelings. Many of us become accustomed to the symptoms of stress, and over time do not even notice them or consider them to be out of the ordinary. An article written by Mayo Clinic staff, *"Stress symptoms: Effects on your body, feelings and behavior*,"* points out some common symptoms:

• **Body:** Headache, back pain, heart palpitations, high blood pressure, sleep problems, and stomach aches.

• **Thoughts and Feelings:** Anxiety, irritability, depression, anger, insecurity, and forgetfulness.

• **Behavior:** Overeating or undereating, angry outbursts, crying spells, and relationship problems.

When children have trauma or loss, their healing journey is akin to a marathon as opposed to a sprint. As a result, it is essential for parents to practice self-care and to keep their stress at a healthy level. In this article, I will attempt to offer new strategies instead of recycling the same suggestions we usually read (proper nutrition, exercise, meditate, yoga).

- **Practice saying, "No, thank you."** Pay attention to how many volunteer and extra curricular activities you and your children are involved in. Of course, it is important to volunteer and participate, but too many activities deplete your energy. Practice saying, "No, thanks for asking," when you have reached your limit.

- **Laugh:** Laughter relaxes your whole body and keeps your outlook positive. As a family, watch funny movies or TV shows (we find *"America's Funniest Home Videos"* provides a good belly laugh) or buy a good joke book and take turns reading them.

- **Maintain a detached viewpoint:** Detaching with love is a strategy to practice when others initiate stress. Next time you feel aggravated, try this imagery: Imagine a protective glass wall around you so that your love can go out to this person, but their negativity cannot come back to you.

- **Reduce the amount of time you spend with technology:** Electronics, gadgets, computers, games and cellphones all require an inordinate amount of our attention. Reduce the amount of time you spend with technology outside of work.

- **Create a priorities list and stick to it:** Create a list of priorities for work, home, family, and spirituality. Which priorities are a daily must for your serenity? Postpone activities that create more stress than tranquility.

- **Find inspiration:** When we feel inspired it improves our mood and energy level. Take time each day to quietly focus on your personal source of inspiration whether it is antique cars, nature, knitting, dogs, gardening, or another favored activity.

- **Faith:** Relieve your stress by relying on your faith in times of trouble or uncertainty, and make your practice a consistent part of your life.

- **Make Your Dreams Come True:** Do something you have dreamed about but have not done yet. Maybe you have talked about learning a foreign language or a new hobby; do not put it off any longer.

- **Schedule free time in your day:** Yes, I said free time. Free time to do fun, carefree activities like go to the park, meet a friend for coffee, rest or relax...you have earned it.

*Carol Lozier, LCSW, is a psychotherapist in private practice; she specializes in helping foster and adopted children and families. She graduated from Florida State University in 1989 with a masters degree in social work. Visit her blog at www.fosteradoptchildtherapist.com.*

\* http://www.aarp.org/relationships/friends-family/grandfacts-sheets/
\* http://www.mayoclinic.com/health/stress-symptoms/SR00008_D

*"The first to apologize is the bravest. The first to forgive is the strongest. The first to forget is the happiest."*

*~ unknown*

# Making Time to Take Care of You
*By Sue Badeau*

> *I am on an airplane.*
> *Again.*
> *And the flight attendant has just finished giving us the safety instructions, including the ever important reminder to "put your own oxygen mask on first" when traveling with a child or anyone who might need your help.*

What a wealth of wisdom in those few words. Put your own oxygen mask on first.

You can't be there to care for others if you can't even breathe yourself. Simple. Profound. Not necessarily intuitive. And oh, so difficult to do.

Caregivers always want to reach out and help others first. It's in our blood. As kinship caregivers to children who have already experienced many losses and come to us vulnerable and needy — we see, hear and feel their needs acutely and being the "first responders" comes more naturally to us than breathing.

Taking time for "self-care" seems indulgent, unnecessary, or simply impossible.

> *Until the day we find we cannot breathe.*

In the world of trauma-informed care, I have learned that caregivers often experience what is known as "secondary traumatic stress." As we daily see and hear the grief, loss, trauma, and pain of the children in our home we can become overwhelmed, numbed out, drained.

Taking time for "self-care" is not indulgent, it is essential. How, then do we make it a priority? I suggest we all need to develop our own "stress-busters" and our own "self-care toolkit."

## Stress-Busters

Stress-busters are things that you can do daily, weekly, or "as needed" to renew, refresh, and revive yourself so that you will be better equipped and prepared to care for others.

### Daily

I find that little mini-breaks on a daily basis are a good first step. What are a few things you can do every day to renew and refresh your own spirit? For me, this list includes such things as my morning devotional and prayer time, listening to the music that re-charges my soul at the end of the day, doing a crossword puzzle, indulging in at least a teeny tiny bite of chocolate, and taking a walk. What are your daily "stress-busters?"

### Weekly or Monthly

While such daily moments are invaluable, sometimes they are insufficient to hold the stresses at bay. Sometimes we need a bigger break. We need something to do every week, something to look forward to. A weekly date with my husband, a Sunday afternoon nap after church, spending three hours in the kitchen cooking, lunch with a friend, book club with college friends, or cuddle time with a baby grandchild all work for me — what about you? What are things you can do every week or month for your own well-being?

## As Needed

Even the weekly breaks aren't quite enough — sometimes it takes more — that is where the spa day, the weekend retreat, or the romantic getaway — *unplugged from all technology* — come into play. Maybe I can only do these things a couple of times a year, but they are so restorative! Do you have special "big" treats on your calendar?

## Self-Care Toolkit

In addition to the stress-busters, I find I am better able to care for children if I am equipped with a state-of-the-art toolkit. When I go on a road-trip, I want to know that the toolkit in the trunk will get me through any travel challenge that might come my way, and likewise, my "self-care toolkit" gives me confidence that I will be able to get through any (or at least most) of the challenges caregiving creates. Here are a few of the tools in my toolkit — maybe they will help you as well:

- **KNOWLEDGE:** The more I learn and know about trauma, about the "system," about resources in my community, about legal rights for myself and my children, the less stressed I feel.

- **RELATIONSHIPS & INTIMACY:** Taking care of my own adult relationships — my marriage and my friends — gives me a secure foundation for successful parenting. If you are a single parent, you still need to nurture at least one or two close friendships where your own needs are nurtured.

- **ANGER MANAGEMENT:** Portable anger management tools like a pocket wrist exerciser or hacky-sack, stress-ball to squeeze, a pocket size journal and pen, or a pocket size book of favorite meditations, prayers, readings, or a particular piece of music on my iPhone that helps calm me when I get angry are essential, because guess what? Anger happens!

- **CREATIVE THINKING:** The brain is like a muscle in that it can be exercised, developed and trained. Just as you build your muscles by weight-lifting, running, or aerobics, you can build your creative thinking muscles by doing regular creative thinking exercises — I subscribe to a service that gives me at least one brain teaser a day in my email box as an example.

- **ROOM FOR GRIEF:** There is often a lot of loss and grief in kinship families. Find ways that are comfortable to you and fit within your values and culture to acknowledge and express grief. We have a special corner in our home with a bench, photos, candles, and other items that help us to reflect, pray, and grieve when we need that moment.

- **LAUGH, PLAY, BREATHE, RELAX:** I cannot overemphasize the value of laughter and play in reducing stress, building attachment and healing from trauma.

Do something silly every day. Wear your pajamas for dinner. Have a water balloon fight. Blow bubbles. Make faces. Laugh, giggle, chuckle, smile.

- **REACH UP and REACH OUT:** Don't do this alone — find your support system — whether it is your community of faith, a support group of other kinship caregivers, or another outlet, be sure you have a group of people in your corner and be willing to reach out to them when you need support. This not only helps you, but it is great role-modeling for your children. For me, it is my church, the other adoptive moms, kinship-caring grandmoms, and my online circle of writing friends. Do you have a circle of support?

All of these ideas are part of a healthy personal "wellness" strategy — tools that help me to process, learn from, vent at times, de-brief, and integrate the traumatic experiences I am emerged in every day with the ebbs and flows of daily life.

Sometimes we all need a little help putting that oxygen mask on and just taking a deep breath.

## Today, promise yourself a moment to breathe.

*Sue Badeau is a nationally known speaker, writer, and consultant. She has worked for many years in child welfare, juvenile justice, children's mental health, and education and serves on several national boards. Badeau writes and speaks extensively on topics related to permanency, trauma, children with special needs, and family engagement. Badeau and her husband, Hector, are the lifetime parents of 22 children, two by birth and 20 adopted (three, with terminal illnesses, are now deceased). They have also served as foster parents for more than 50 children in three states. They have authored a book about their family's parenting journey,* **Are We There Yet: The Ultimate Road Trip Adopting and Raising 22 Kids,** *which can be found on Amazon.com or on Badeau's website — www.suebadeau.com. She may be reached by email at sue@suebadeau.com.*

# How Two Determined Texas Moms Created a Non-Profit Organization to Help Relatives and Kin Who Are Raising Children

*By Beth Powell, LCSW*

Angel Reach, Inc. (www.angelreach.org) is a 501(c) organization that helps support relatives and kin who are raising children who came to live with them. Some of the children are placed by Texas Children's Protective Services and some have come voluntarily to these caregivers via the birth parents themselves who could not care for them.

In 2005, in Conroe, Texas, a town just north of Houston, Sandra Carpenter and Debbie Zempel, both of whom had fostered and adopted a number of children through Child Protective Services began to notice a shift in the foster care system: More and more children who could no longer live at home were going into relative/kinship care instead of professional foster care. There was essentially no system in place to help educate and support the families who were taking in these traumatized children and at that time, because of the lack of support, at least half of all relative-kinship placements were failing. Kids were ending up back in the system, looking for a new place to live.

In 2005, these special ladies began to help these parents raising children, with no funds, no 501(c) in place, but with huge hearts and a desire to serve and do their part to help make the world a better place. They provided advice, training, support groups, clothing, beds, food, and other household items out of a cottage that Sandra had on her property — all items donated by other people who just had a heart to help.

In the beginning I came in to help, too. I provided free parent training in that cottage, for the years 2005-2006 and saw families there who were lucky enough to have traditional Medicaid to reimburse me for my services. I believed in what these two ladies were trying to do, and eventually, in 2007, I paid the fees to help Angel Reach get its 501(c) and found and employed the non-profit specialist to make that happen. In 2007, Angel Reach, Inc. was born.

The official non-profit status of Angel Reach opened the door for larger tax-deductible donations and greater support, especially from the local churches. Debbie and Sandra always considered Angel Reach to be a Christian ministry and the local churches agreed with them. Angel Reach is now a prototype for the rest of Texas as to how determined normal people with a desire to serve can help create a successful, viable organization to help children who are living in alternate family care and how churches and other financially supportive sources can aid that endeavor.

Angel Reach has grown in a short time. It now also helps relatives habilitate their houses in order to pass homestudies so they can officially offer permanency to the children in their care. It provides referrals to attorneys and works with other legal and advocacy organizations to help children in care get their needs met. Angel Reach works in cooperation with other agencies to help improve the Texas foster care system and it now has a transitional living program for foster youth who have aged out of the system with no home to return to.

On the home page of Angel Reach's website is a Biblical scripture that is embraced by the tireless workers and volunteers who give of their time and hearts to serve others. It is a motto and a mantra to remind us all of what we, as Christians, are called to do in the realm of selfless service.

*"Along unfamiliar paths I will guide you; I will turn the darkness into light before you and make the rough places smooth. These are the things I will do; I will not forsake you."*

*Isaiah 42:16*

*Conroe, Texas-based psychotherapist and neuro-behavioral educator, Beth Powell, LCSW, specializes in helping traumatized children and the families who raise them heal. She understands the importance that relatives and kin have on a traumatized child's life from her own personal growing-up experience and acknowledges she wouldn't have the insight and ability that she has today to help others if she hadn't "walked a mile in the shoes" of the people who seek her assistance.*

*Powell is also a CEU training provider, a social work supervisor of interns and externs as well as an adjunct instructor at Lone Star College's Montgomery Campus. She has created a unique systems-based child-in-family approach that includes the child's caregivers as part of the treatment team. For more information, visit www.infamilyservices.net.*

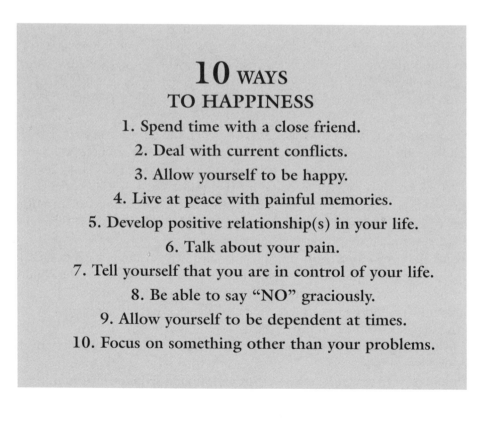

# 10 WAYS
## TO HAPPINESS
1. Spend time with a close friend.
2. Deal with current conflicts.
3. Allow yourself to be happy.
4. Live at peace with painful memories.
5. Develop positive relationship(s) in your life.
6. Talk about your pain.
7. Tell yourself that you are in control of your life.
8. Be able to say "NO" graciously.
9. Allow yourself to be dependent at times.
10. Focus on something other than your problems.

# Foster Care and Kinship Family Transitions
*By John DeGarmo, PhD, EdD*

More and more children each year are being placed with relatives instead of in foster homes. Indeed, there has been a rise in this during the past 15 years. Kinship homes have, for some, replaced foster homes due to two main reasons. First, there is a growing shortage of foster homes throughout the United States. Second, recent years have also seen a shift in federal policy toward kinship homes as appropriate placements for children in need. Indeed, many times, foster children have been moved from a foster home into a kinship home. Though there are benefits for this, it can be rather difficult, emotionally, for all involved, as relationships have been built between foster parents and the child; relationships that are important and meaningful for the child in regard to his or her growth, needs, and emotional well-being.

For those children coming from a foster home and being placed into a kinship home, it is important for kinship families to understand and appreciate what a foster family does, and the important role they play. Indeed, foster families have not only provided a safe and stable home and environment for the child, these families have also just been that, a family. Foster families and the children who stay with them form relationships of love and understanding, relationships that cannot only be healthy, but can last a lifetime, if nurtured. To be sure, when a child returns home or into a kinship home, it is often a time of much happiness and celebration. Yet, it may also be a time of grief and sadness, as well, as the child misses the relationships built in the foster home, as well as the family the child has left behind.

Your child will certainly be full of questions about where he or she will soon move to. It may have been some time when he or she last lived with the biological family. If the child is moving to a kinship home, it may be with a family he or she had not met, or has not formed strong relationships with. Either way, it can be a time of great uncertainty and uneasiness for the child. One way to help make this transition easier is to include the foster family with planning the move prior to actually moving. Work together to determine when the best time for the transition from one home to another would be — after school, on a weekend, in the morning, evenings, or another convenient time. Schedule visits to the foster home, if possible, allowing the child to see the two families working together in a positive relationship before the move takes place.

During these visits, discuss any parenting practices you might have in common, as well as any differences in house rules you might have. After all, the foster parents may have had much experience with parenting children through the years, as foster parents. Indeed, it could be valuable insight and wisdom that they can share with you, information and insight that you can use with your own child. Diet and eating habits, sleep patterns, and day-to-day skills are areas that the foster parents will have significant information on, information that will help make the transition easier in your own home. Along with this, your child may have picked up some useful and important skills while living in the foster home, skills that could benefit the child later in life.

If the child is in school, the foster parents will have knowledge of his or her academic progress, abilities and any concerns. It is important for the child's well-being that you not only know of these skills and information, but fully understand and appreciate them. After all, you may wish for the child to continue using these skills and information learned when he or she returns to your own home, and the information about his or her academic progress and abilities is essential to the child's success in school when returning to your home.

By sharing information with the foster family beforehand, you will help prepare your child for returning home, or to a new home, as it might help to answer some questions, thus easing the transition a little. Afterward, you may even find that the caseworker arranges for overnight and weekend visitations with the foster family, allowing for your child the occasion for a smoother transition from their home to yours, as well as give you a break from parenting for a short time.

After your child has moved back home, he or she will probably have feelings of anxiety. It is normal to miss the foster family, perhaps even grieve for them. Do not take this personally, as it is a normal process for children who leave a home where they have been cared for, provided for, and loved. To help the child in this time of transition, allow the child to contact the foster family on occasion. Call them on the phone and allow your child to tell them all about his or her new home and biological family. Encourage your own children to write letters to them and send pictures of your family and family events from time to time. Remember birthdays and other important events in their lives, such as holidays and school events. If you live nearby, let the former foster family know when they can attend the child's school functions and extra-curricular activities or programs of his. If possible, arrange visits for them to come to your house.

Saying goodbye is never easy for anyone, and may be especially difficult for your child. After your child leaves the foster home, he or she may have a difficult time adjusting to your home, rules, and expectations. The child may act out and be disobedient. On the other hand, he or she may become withdrawn and even remote. The grief the child feels may be overwhelming and it may be a while before he or she adjusts. Whatever the circumstance, there will be emotions involved. With the right preparation, and with working with the foster family, this time of transition can be a little bit easier for all involved.

*Dr. John DeGarmo has been a foster parent for 11 years now, and he and his wife have had more than 30 children come through their home. He is a speaker and trainer on many topics about the foster care system, and travels around the nation delivering passionate, dynamic, energetic, and informative presentations. DeGarmo is the author of the highly inspirational and bestselling book,* **Fostering Love: One Foster Parent's Story,** *and* **The Foster Parenting Manual: A Practical Guide to Creating a Loving, Safe and Stable Home.** *He also writes for a number of publications and newsletters, both in the United States, and overseas. DeGarmo can be contacted at drjohndegarmo@gmail.com, through his Facebook page, Dr. John DeGarmo, or at his website, www.drejohndegarmo.com.*

# HALOS Kinship Care Program
*By Kim Clifton, MSW*

HALOS is a small nonprofit organization based in North Charleston, South Carolina. It began in 1997 as a volunteer-led project that served as a "link" between the county Department of Social Service agency and faith groups that sought to provide resources for specific children who were victims of abuse and neglect. In 2004, after becoming a 501(c)(3) organization and hiring two full-time staff members, HALOS established its office at the Charleston County Department of Social Services (CCDSS).

## How Can We Help?

After the move into CCDSS offices, HALOS services began to evolve. The first sign that what HALOS had identified as needs of abused children differed from DSS identified needs occurred early on. I was the first full-time executive director and visited DSS supervisors to discuss HALOS' programs, how they were working and what else they thought would help children involved in the "system." I was immediately confronted with the issue of kinship care. The supervisor of the Family Independence Program (Temporary Aid or Needy Families) asked point blank, "what could I do for all of these kinship families?" The issue was raised again by the director of Human Services. She said one of their biggest issues involved grandparents or other relatives who took children in as infants or toddlers and called DSS when the children grew into hard-to-manage tweens or teens. She told me, "they say come get them." Without support, kinship caregivers, particularly older adults, were finding it difficult to parent older children.

## Critical Goods Resource

The second step toward the evolution into a direct service kinship program occurred when CCDSS caseworkers began to view HALOS as a resource for items critically needed to place children when they had to be removed from their homes for their own safety. DSS could not place a child without certain items in place, beds and cribs for appropriate sleeping arrangements, car seats for safety and other basic household essentials. HALOS began appealing to its network of supporters for these items and helping DSS place children safely.

During this time, a request was received from DSS to help a family consisting of a grandmother, "Mrs. Jones" and her two grandsons. DSS had been ordered to do a homestudy by the Department of Juvenile Justice because the older of the two grandsons had been getting into trouble at school. After she conducted the homestudy, the caseworker came to DSS in tears and explained the situation, asking for help. Mrs. Jones had been raising her two grandsons, ages 13 and 15, since they were toddlers because their mother was a drug addict and their father was mentally ill. They had been living in her daughter's home but that fell through and they had moved to a small, two bedroom subsidized apartment. There was no furniture in the home, except for a mattress on the floor and Mrs. Jones explained that the boys used the mattress and she was happy to sleep on the floor. The boys had no clothing beyond what they were wearing. Mrs. Jones, who the boys called

"Granny," begged the caseworkers not to take the boys, who she called "her life." Mrs. Jones was older than 60, partially blind and had a sixth grade education. She had never applied for disability and received limited public assistance. The caseworker was put in the position of potentially having to recommend removing the boys from a home in which they were loved and cared for because "Granny" was not able to provide for their care.

HALOS was able to collect donations to fully furnish their apartment and purchase new clothing for the boys, but this family really brought to light much larger issues and forced HALOS to confront questions — how many more families are barely existing like this? What are the long-term outcomes after providing crisis assistance? Where do they turn for help?

After routinely taking requests for "Critical Goods" as they are called by HALOS, it became clear that items were requested most often for situations in which CCDSS was working to place a child(ren) into a home with a relative, rather than on behalf of foster or biological families. This was obvious to everyone in the DSS "system" but for lay people it is much less clear. In South Carolina, while caseworkers are tasked with seeking relatives to take children so they will not have to enter foster care, and relatives are given preference in placements, they do not receive a stipend to off-set the cost of caring for the child(ren) or other resources. So in order to make a placement, often a DSS caseworker must work to secure items required for safety, which most often a grandparent or other relative is not prepared to provide, so they can place the child with the relative.

## Defining A Need

Recognizing that most requests from DSS were on behalf of kinship families, HALOS, as an organization, began to prioritize the needs of kinship families over those of foster or biological families in the distribution of services. As awareness of the need grew, so did awareness that there is a lack of services or support for kinship families in the community. It was clear in talking with other service providers that in their sphere of work they confronted issues when working with kinship families. Yet there was no open dialogue about this as an issue and no effort to work together as a community to mitigate the obstacles faced by kinship caregivers and to support them in providing safe homes to the children in their care.

A great deal of research was conducted prior to developing the HALOS Kinship Care Program. We could not look for examples of effective services in South Carolina, so we looked at programs operating in other states and at national research on the needs and demographics of the kinship population. We found that resources and programs for kinship caregivers differed greatly from state to state and that South Carolina was not alone in not offering a formal kinship program. Research examining kinship caregiving from a broad perspective shed light on how a program could be developed to effectively provide support and improve the likelihood of better outcomes for the children in these situations. We learned through this research that kinship caregivers are statistically more likely to be low-income and need cash (we did not have any); to feel isolated and lack emotional support; and to have less access to resources and services than foster or biological parents, even when those services were available. We found that demographically, caregivers tend to be older, lower-income, lower educational attainment, and African American. This provided a lot of insight into how a successful program must be developed in order to be effective and successful.

While we knew we could not offer a cash assistance program, we felt we could link caregivers to available services and provide support and connection to other caregivers through support group meetings. A staff person was hired to implement the program and a local church identified to host the meetings. The first obstacle encountered was getting referrals for the program. DSS staff believed that caregivers would not be interested if there was not a financial incentive. Other service providers seemed skeptical as well. It seemed that many providers, although they recognized that they faced challenges in working with kinship families, had not thought of them as a unique population to be served by a special or separate program. It took a great deal of community education, both in the general population and among service providers, for the issue to be understood and be recognized.

## Support and Connection

The support group meetings have evolved to two meetings per month, hosted in two different locations. They have grown from no participants at the first meeting, swelled to 20-30 participants, and have settled into a comfortable 8–15 adults at each meeting. We knew that we would have to provide child care in order for adults to attend. This became a large issue when there were eventually up to 60 children brought to meetings. We had to step back and think more critically about how we could implement the program and ensure the safety of children and maintain order. We began asking caregivers to reserve space for each meeting to ensure that we could plan appropriately. To accommodate child care we developed a volunteer program in which volunteers are recruited, trained and have background checks conducted. We reach out to community groups to provide a light meal to adults and children.

HALOS receives referrals to the program from other agencies, including the local child advocacy center, the local agency on aging, individual schools, as well as the Department of Social Services. Recently, relatives are making self-referrals with more frequency.

Once a referral is received, the HALOS Family Advocate contacts the caregiver and sets a date to visit the home and conduct an assessment of the family situation. Following that, the Family Advocate will make referrals for community services as necessary. We have found that the needs and strengths of families vary greatly. Some families really benefit from hands-on case management to get them past the point of crisis and into self-sufficiency. Most referrals are made when a family comes into contact with another agency; however, some families have adapted quite well, taken advantage of services when needed and are not interested in support groups or more intensive assistance that can be offered through HALOS. Most families require more help than a one-time visit and referral for services. Support groups are available, but those that commit to the support groups tend to be those that are already engaged in seeking assistance and resources — they are self-selected. There is a gap for those families that need more in-home support that is currently not being offered.

HALOS assists kinship families that are both formal and informal, i.e. situations in which children were placed with the family member by the local DSS agency or its equivalent, the court system, or some other legal entity that established custody with the family member or kin. In addition, we work with families that are in informal situations in which the child(ren) was left with the relative by a parent(s) and legal custody was not established. In South Carolina, when the kinship situation is set up through DSS, caregivers are not encouraged to become foster parents.

## Tips For Developing A Kinship Care Program:

- **DO RESEARCH** (nationally, regionally, and locally)

  *Questions to consider:*

  What is already happening in the community? Talk to caregivers and other service providers, including DSS or its equivalent and the local school system.

  What does the state offer as support for kinship caregivers?

  Will you offer a program only to DSS involved families or any kinship family?

  Are kinship caregivers who adopt to be included?

  Where are the biggest gaps?

  Will you address specific issues with caregivers or offer broad support?

  Most important — what are your goals?

- **Community Education**

  Make presentations, talk to groups, educate the general population about kinship caregiving and know your statistics and understand the issue as it relates to your community.

- **Provide Child Care**

  It sounds simple, but it is often overlooked. Caregivers cannot participate if they have to leave their children at home. Provide child care if you host meetings or trainings.

*Kim Clifton, MSW, is originally from Savannah, Ga., and a graduate of the College of Charleston. She currently is the executive director at HALOS, an organization that provides advocacy and support to abused and neglected children and kinship caregivers. Clifton earned a master of social work degree from Boston University with a concentration in program planning and development, community organizing, and nonprofit administration. She has also served as an AmeriCorps\*VISTA member on Whidbey Island, Wash., the director of development for a community center in inner-city Boston, and fundraising specialist in Guatemala. The HALOS website can be found here www.charlestonhalos.org*

# Parenting Children from Tough Starts

> *"The children who need love the most will ask for it in the most unloving of ways."*
>
> **Russell A. Barkley**

# "Smart Enough" Parenting
*By Sue Badeau*

When children come into kinship care households, they generally know the relatives who are now caring for them, and have a history with them. This is one of the strengths and protective factors that set kinship care apart from other types of foster care. Nevertheless, the child is still likely to carry a certain amount of baggage as a result of the separation from his or her birth parents (and often siblings), and possibly some time and multiple placements in foster care before joining the kinship family. Some of the items in this baggage may include rejection, loss, grief, trauma, identity issues, and more. As the child "settles" into the family, some of these issues will be best worked through within the family throughout the years, while others will require additional, outside help. How can you know when such help is needed?

When I went to an all-women's college in the 1970's, we were not encouraged to pursue "traditionally female" careers such as teaching, but rather to stretch ourselves toward the more "traditionally male" fields of law, medicine, engineering, or business. So, as our senior year approached, nearly all of my friends were busy scheduling their Medical College Admission Test (MCAT) or Law School Admission Test (LSAT) exams, and, knowing that I didn't really want to go to graduate school, I too decided to take these tests.

I scored well on both. So well, that my advisor was shocked when I decided not to apply to either law school or medical school like so many of my friends were doing. "Why not?" he asked, "Surely you can see that you are smart enough."

**"Surely you can see that you are smart enough."** At the time, those words gave me a boost of confidence and added to my self-esteem. However, throughout the years, the words almost seemed to become a taunting refrain echoing in my mind every time I faced a challenging and troubling situation as a parent (through birth, foster care, adoption, and kinship care). "How could it be?" I would often ask myself, "that I am smart enough to be a doctor or a lawyer, but not smart enough to be a mom?"

Not smart enough to know what to do when my bright son with the high IQ scores was failing in school. Not smart enough to figure out how to stop my talented son with the promising future ahead from descending into the pits of drug addiction. Not smart enough to prevent two of my young daughters from becoming pregnant within three months of each other. Not smart enough to help my handsome African American son avoid the stinging pain of racism and rejection when he got turned down for a prom date because of the color of his skin. Not smart enough to see the warning signs before a teen daughter's suicide attempt, or a teen son's runaway episodes. Not smart enough to help my granddaughter avoid a relationship with an abusive boyfriend. Yes, I have faced these and many more challenges in my years as a foster, adoptive parent, and kinship caregiver. And there were many, many times when I just did not feel smart enough to conquer the challenges confronting me. At times I was sheepish or even ashamed when I had to reach out to others for help, resources, and supports raising my own children.

And then one day, I had my proverbial "aha" moment. I was sitting in the driveway, in the car, about to drop off my young adult daughter and her two-year-old child. He had been giving her more than the usual run for her money that day and they were both exhausted. She turned to me with tears in her eyes and asked, "Do you think I will ever be smart enough to be a good parent?"

"Of course you are smart enough," I quickly reassured her, but added, "even smart people need help from time to time." I then thought of my professor all those years ago in college and I asked my daughter, "Do you think that I am smart enough to be a doctor — or maybe a lawyer?"

"Oh yes, Mom, you definitely could be a great doctor or lawyer."

"So, then, if you needed surgery today, would you trust me to wield the scalpel?"

She panicked for a moment, not knowing what to say. Finally, she quietly said, "Well, no, not really."

"Why not?" I asked, "I thought you just told me I was smart enough to be a doctor."

"True," she said "but you have never been trained as a doctor. You never went to medical school or learned all that stuff."

*Bingo.* Being smart enough doesn't mean you have all the knowledge, training, equipment, or tools needed to handle every situation in life. If I could easily acknowledge that I, while smart enough to be a doctor, could not actually practice medicine without further education, experience, coaching, and support, why couldn't I also acknowledge that as a parent or caregiver, especially of children with a range of special needs and early life exposure to trauma, I would also need further education, experience, coaching, and support to do a good job?

There is no shame in seeking help. Once we overcome that mental hurdle and are willing to seek help, the challenges become knowing when to seek help, and how to find the right kind of help for the situation.

When many of my children were elementary school age, one of them broke his arm at school. The school nurse called and I knew immediately that this was not simply a sore arm, but that he needed medical attention beyond the nurse's office and I promptly drove him to the hospital where his injury was diagnosed and a cast was set. But this did not mean that every time a child fell down on the playground, they needed to be rushed to the hospital. Nor that every sore spot could be fixed with a cast. Understanding this when it comes to the physical bumps, bruises, and ailments our children experience is pretty easy, but the challenge is harder when the injuries are less visible and more in the psychological and emotional realm.

When will a good pep talk, or going out for ice cream be enough to soothe an injured spirit, and when is professional help required? And even when we know that professional help is needed, how do we find the right kind? Certainly I wouldn't have taken my son with the broken arm to the eye doctor's office we passed en route to the hospital on the theory that expediency was essential so I had to get to the first, closest doctor I could find. Or the related theory that any doctor would do the trick. Yet, in the world of mental health and trauma-related care, this is often what happens — we are referred to the closest therapist, or the one who takes our insurance and assured that "any therapy" will do. And yet, it does not work out so well when we take that approach.

So after many years stumbling along as a "smart enough," but not always "prepared enough" parent, I have concluded that parents and caregivers who take the following four steps are not only "smart enough," but also equipped to handle even the most daunting challenges:

- **Learn, and keep learning, about normal child development.** So many times, simply knowing what behaviors or developmental milestones are to be expected of a two-year-old, nine-year-old or 15-year-old will help us assess our own child's behavior and development more appropriately. While it is not reasonable to expect a two-year-old to sit still for an entire two-hour movie or church service, it is reasonable to expect a two-year-old to walk and begin to form thoughts into sentences. So the parent of a child who can't sit still doesn't need professional support, but the parent of the child who is not yet walking or talking probably does. We can apply this same principle to school age children and adolescents.

**When many of us become kinship caregivers, it is "second-time-around" parenting. We have already raised our children when our grandchildren, nieces, or nephews join our family. By the time my 15-year-old granddaughter came to stay, I had a lot of experience raising children and teens. And yet, the world is always changing and the impact on child development is also changing. So it is important to continue to learn about child development and get the most current information if we are going to be the best caregiver to the children we love.**

- **Learn about the impact of trauma on children's development — and develop a tool-kit of trauma-informed parenting strategies.** Most children who come to us through kinship care have experienced early life traumatic experiences. Perhaps one or both of their parents became addicted to drugs, suffers from a mental illness, or is incarcerated. Perhaps there was domestic violence in the home. All of these situations can create trauma for the child. In recent years there has been an explosion of new science-based information about the impact of this exposure to trauma on the developing brain, and on the child's emotional regulation, behaviors, and social development. We also now know that typical parenting strategies, such as time-out, that work well with non-traumatized children — and worked well in the past with children we raised years ago — not only do not work well with these children, but can often serve to trigger trauma reminders, increasing the child's vulnerability and undermining their opportunity to heal. Yet, we also know that children can heal from trauma and that dedicated grandparents or other relative caregivers can be the most important conduits for that healing. Not all trauma-exposed children need professional therapeutic interventions, just like not every playground tumble requires a trip to the emergency room. Sometimes they just need a different style of care at home. I have listed a few excellent resources at the end of this article for caregivers who want to learn more about trauma. Advocate with your agency to provide trauma-informed training for all foster, kin, and adoptive parents.

- **Learn to recognize the warning signs of when a child needs more than the support of home and family.**
I have provided a list of possible "red flags" that may indicate a need for outside resources. All children are likely to display some of these indicators at various times. The need for intervention is more likely if the child displays several at once, or some over longer periods of time. If you see these signs don't hesitate to seek help, just as I

## RED FLAGS LIST

### Things that happened to the child:

- Severe illness or forced separation from primary caregivers in the first three years of life.
- Neglect of physical needs, especially during the first two years of life, physical abuse at any time, but especially during the first two years.
- Sexual encounters of any kind during childhood.
- Child witnessed traumatic events, domestic violence, alcoholic or drug-addicted parents, a parental death, a sibling death, a destructive fire, or other events.
- Child is forced to participate in a group that practices frightening rituals, animal sacrifices, or other rituals.
- Child is left alone for long periods or child is locked up.

### Behaviors a child may exhibit:

- Indiscriminately (physically) affectionate
- Refusal or fear of appropriate affection with parents or caregivers, excessive clinging on, need for physical affection, or attention.
- Pre-occupation with bodily functions, especially vomit, bleeding, urination and defecation, or sexual functions.
- Destructive to self, others, animals, material things. Lack of impulse controls, short attention span, hyperactivity beyond normal developmental stage.
- Difficulty and/or obsession with food, overeating, binging, refusal to eat, abnormal eating patterns, etc.
- Preoccupation with images of death, violence, and gory, graphic details.
- Inability to discriminate between lies and realities and/or telling of crazy, obvious, or outrageous lies.
- Extreme difficulty with forming peer friendships.
- Frequent bursts of seemingly unexplained anger, or outbursts of anger, fear, or anxiety that is triggered by specific smells, foods, colors, people, sounds, situations or activities.
- Difficulty regulating emotions, inability or difficulty expressing a range of emotions.

did not hesitate to seek medical help for my child's broken arm. Join a support group of other grandparents raising grandchildren with similar challenges. Peer support is one of the most effective and valuable ways to help caregivers know when some of the challenges they face are within the range of "normal development" or when extra help and support are needed.

- **Know how to ask the right questions to get appropriate services and interventions for the child you care for.** Never be shy at Individualized Education Plan meetings, doctor appointments or with your medical/mental health insurance provider. Ask probing questions about how and why the particular intervention they are proposing is appropriate for this child. Never settle for an eye doctor when your child has a broken arm. But when your child needs an eye doctor, make sure you get the best one in town!

*Sue Badeau is a nationally known speaker, writer, and consultant. She has worked for many years in child welfare, juvenile justice, children's mental health, and education and serves on several national boards. Badeau writes and speaks extensively on topics related to permanency, trauma, children with special needs, and family engagement. She and her husband, Hector, are the lifetime parents of 22 children, two by birth and 20 adopted (three, with terminal illnesses, are now deceased). They have also served as foster parents for more than 50 children in three states. They have authored a book about their family's parenting journey, **Are We There Yet: The Ultimate Road Trip Adopting and Raising 22 Kids,** which can be found on Amazon.com or on Badeau's website — www.suebadeau.com. She may be reached by email at sue@suebadeau.com.*

## Resources for Kinship Caregivers to Learn about Trauma:

- www.nctsn.org/resources/audiences/parents-caregivers
- www.attachmenttraumanetwork.com
- www.risemagazine.org/PDF/Rise_issue_11.pdf
- www.projectabc-la.org/parents/
- www.multiplyingconnections.org

# Sensory Integration: What it Is and How to Help
*By Barbara Elleman, OTR/L, BCP*

Have you ever wondered why the fast, spinning rides that you repeatedly enjoyed as a child, now make your head spin and your stomach turn? As we mature, our brain's ability to organize and interpret information from our senses (touch, taste, smell, movement, sight, sound, and body awareness) improves. This is a process called sensory integration. For most children, sensory integration occurs automatically. These children naturally seek out the sensory information they need to grow and mature. Some children do not. Some children experience **Dysfunction of Sensory Integration** (DSI).

Children, who have had a tough start in life may be at risk for Dysfunction of Sensory Integration. This may be due to early environmental circumstances, prenata, or medical factors that predispose a child to altered sensory input during the first year of life. A large amount of sensory integration occurs during the first year of life. The integration of simple sensory information becomes the basis for more complex tasks as a child develops. For example, an infant integrates information from vision, touch, and body awareness to locate and reach for a brightly colored toy held above her. Sensory information comes to the brain as input from sights, sounds, taste, smell, touch, movement, and body position.

The touch (**tactile**) system is highly responsive during the first years of life. It allows us to determine if we are being touched and to locate that touch (such as when a fly lands on our leg). The tactile system also provides us with the ability to react when the touch input is harmful (such as a hot or sharp surface). When a touch sensation is provided, our brain registers the sensation and determines a reaction (such as withdrawing a hand from hot water or swatting away a fly).

The movement (**vestibular**) system is also highly responsive during the first years of life. It informs our brain about the direction and position we are holding/moving in space and provides the foundation for coordination, balance, eye movements, and posture.

**Proprioception** is the term used for the sense of body position. It provides information about the position of our body in space. It allows us to perform tasks such as turning on a light switch in the middle of the night.

Dysfunction of Sensory Integration occurs when sensory integration does not develop as efficiently as it should. It may result in problems with learning, behavior, or development.

## Older children with Dysfunction of Sensory Integration usually exhibit more than one of the following symptoms:

- Over or under-reactive to touch, movement, sights, sounds, food textures, or tastes
- Easily distracted
- Unusually high or low activity level
- Clumsiness or difficulty with coordination

- Difficulty making transitions or accepting change in routine

- Inability to unwind or calm self

- Poor self-concept

- Difficulty with academic achievement

- Social and/or emotional problems

- Speech, language or motor delays

## Younger children with Dysfunction of Sensory Integration usually exhibit more than one of the following symptoms:

- Poor muscle tone

- Slow to achieve developmental milestones

- Unusually fussy, difficult to console

- Failure to explore the environment

- Difficulty tolerating changes in position

- Resistance to being held or cuddled

- Difficulty with sleep

- Difficulty with sucking

Not all children who have experienced less than ideal early years will have Dysfunction of Sensory Integration. Often, symptoms may be present right after placement, during the transition to a new environment. Dysfunction of Sensory Integration usually presents as a pattern of symptoms that persist well beyond the initial period of transition.

Immediately following placement, kincare providers can begin to provide activities to promote a sensory rich environment. A variety of sensory experiences should be incorporated into the child's everyday routine, introducing new activities slowly. Provide an opportunity and encourage participation, but do not force the child to perform. A list of suggested activities appears on the next page.

If you suspect your child may have Dysfunction of Sensory Integration, an evaluation may be beneficial. Occupational therapists with training in sensory integration can provide evaluations and develop individualized treatment programs to help children who struggle with the world around them.

*Barbara Elleman, OTR/L, BCP, works in the occupational and physical therapy department at the International Adoption Center located at Children's Hospital Medical Center, Cincinnati, Ohio. This article originally was printed in **Adoption Parenting Creating a Toolbox, Building Connections.***

# SUGGESTIONS FOR ACTIVITIES

## for Children with Dysfunction of Sensory Integration

*Caution should be used regarding the child's age and ability when choosing activities.*

## Touch Activities

- Finding small toys in sand or a container filled with macaroni or beads
- Rubbing with lotions, powders or towels
- Finger-painting, playing in pudding
- Dress up activities
- Building forts with blankets, towels, or sheets

## Movement Activities

- Playgrounds or backyard equipment — swing sets, slides, tire swings
- Gym programs
- Riding toys
- Sit 'n spin or spinning activities and games
- Gentle bouncing on an old mattress, cushions, lap, or when held securely on a ball.

## Proprioceptive (Body Awareness) Activities

- Crawling and climbing
- Wheelbarrow walking, jumping, hop-scotch
- Tug of war or obstacle courses
- Pushing or pulling weighted objects such as a wagon, laundry baskets, filled buckets
- Position games such as Twister or Simon Says Visual Activities
- Punching bags, balls, balloons, and bubbles
- Target games such as tee ball, tennis, or soccer
- Puzzles, tracing, dot to dot, mazes
- Scissor activities
- Mobiles

## Sound Activities

- Whistles, bells, and horns
- Listening to stories, tapes, and songs
- Repeating sequence of sounds
- Naming sounds for animals
- Rhythmic games and activities

# Healing Loss in the Traumatized Child
*By Ellen Singer, LCSW-C*

Thomas moved on and off between his birth mother and paternal aunt for the first seven years of his life. He was removed from that unstable situation after his aunt threw him down a flight of stairs, breaking his leg.

Now 10, Thomas has been in his pre-adoptive home for one year. As finalization nears, Thomas seems to be changing from a child who is eager to please, to one who is contradictory and noncompliant. He ignores many of his parents' directives and becomes anxious when reprimanded in any way. In addition, his school work is suffering, a turn of events that is particularly upsetting to his parents. His parents are wondering...Who is this child?

Many of the stories of children who enter the foster care system involve abuse — physical, sexual, or emotional — neglect or abandonment. Care-giving adults may be drug or alcohol addicted or mentally ill, unable to care for themselves, let alone children. In some instances, children have witnessed violence, even murder against loved ones. A large proportion of children lose connections with birth family members; others remain in contact with family members with whom they have ambivalent, conflicted, and difficult relationships. For some children, placement occurs because a caregiver has died.

Unfortunately, multiple caregivers and moves both prior to and subsequent to placement in foster care compound the experience of trauma and loss.

Amazingly, adults often expect children to move into adoptive placements smoothly, settling into their new lives with relief and minimal disruption. It is hoped that children can understand how the old and the new are separate worlds, and despite the considerable efforts of many people, those two worlds are permanently apart. These expectations, combined with the fact that adoptive parents may have had little knowledge of how prior trauma can cause depression, anxiety, or acting out behavior, may be a recipe for disaster.

Fortunately, much has been learned about the long-term impact of trauma on both children and adults. However, not all foster and adoptive parents are informed, and some mental health practitioners are unaware of the powerful, unique complexities of loss for children in foster care and adoption. It is critical that social workers learn how unresolved grief about previous losses can manifest itself in new home environments, and that information must be shared. Fears and worries grounded in former experiences must be recognized and addressed to diminish difficult or puzzling behaviors that challenge new families where safety and nurturing are present.

Last year, Thomas was referred to The Center for Adoption Support and Education, Inc., or C.A.S.E., in Silver Spring, Md.D, with his foster soon-to-be adoptive parents. Their therapist, Madeleine Krebs, was not surprised by the route that Thomas had taken to reflect his anxiety and insecurity. She began by asking Thomas, "How did you get to this family?" She created a trusting relationship and a safe place where he could share his understanding of what had happened in his life and process his feelings related to his experiences and the losses he incurred.

Over time, through the use of activities designed to help him express his sadness and confusion, Thomas shared his anger. He made balls out of clay and threw them at the couch in Krebs' office, expressing fury at his aunt who had hurt him. Sometimes he would get angry at Krebs, who used the opportunity to help Thomas see that it was all right for him to get angry — healing his sense of trust in adults. He talked about his concern about the fate of a cat that had lived with him at his birth mother's home, eventually letting Krebs know that he was worried about his birth mother and wondered where she was.

Krebs also worked with Thomas' parents, coaching them to provide Thomas with what he needed, as well as how to respond appropriately to his difficult behavior. Krebs notes, "I needed to help his parents understand how his traumatic past resulted in a lack of trust which translated into anxiety, insecurity, and a hyper-vigilant stance in the world."

Thomas was testing his parents, and needed reassurance that he would be accepted and loved despite his misbehavior. In addition, Krebs helped Thomas' parents understand how his emotional challenges may have been interfering with his ability to learn and that throughout time, this might improve as well. In the meantime, she emphasized the importance of providing Thomas with support. The C.A.S.E. model of therapeutic support incorporates understanding of the impact of trauma, grief, and loss in foster care and adoption as it relates to attachment. The concept of ambiguous loss, as described by Pauline Boss in *Ambiguous Loss: Learning to Live with Unresolved Grief*, and the good grief model developed by Maria Trozzi in *Talking with Children about Loss*, are important theories for treating children who continue to have contact with birth parents, as well as those who do not.

Ambiguous loss refers to loss which is uncertain and often unrecognized by others because it does not follow traditional patterns leading to closure. Unlike the finality of death, for example, ambiguous loss blocks the coping and grieving process because the loss situation may change. Children may believe they will reunite with birth families. Without more absolutes, the "family relationship freezes in place," Boss states in her book, complicating children's ability to move on and form new attachments, despite their need to do so.

The "good grief" model outlines the stages of grief for children and teens, and emphasizes that "grief shared is grief diminished," as stated in Boss' book. Trozzi believes that grief cannot be rushed, and that children need to be in trusting relationships to work through the pain of their losses.

## Phases of "Good Grief"

**The first of the four stages identified by Trozzi is understanding.** At C.A.S.E., therapists help children to verbalize their perception of the situation that caused the loss. Sometimes information can be added or corrected, or different perspectives can be provided to help children comprehend why events occurred. Sometimes loss is not of a person, but of innocence, trust, or safety.

Lifebooks are helpful tools for concretizing the past for children. At C.A.S.E., therapists also help children identify "lifelines" that provided support to them at critical points in their young lives.

Lifelines are clues for effective coping skills that can be useful again. They may be people, or activities such as playing sports, reading, phoning a friend, or they may simply be thoughts that were comforting or encouraging at a difficult time.

**The second phase is grieving.** Krebs notes that children can be helped to understand that painful feelings are normal, they can be expressed in healthy ways, and that they do not go on forever. "We need to help them keep faith and hope for the future."

**The third phase, commemorating,** helps children believe that there is value to their loss and that others will acknowledge the loss. Krebs emphasizes the importance of helping children keep and treasure photos of people and places. In addition, foster parents can maintain respect for children's losses through language. An example, "I was thinking about your birth father today, and I wonder if he had a good throwing arm when he was young — just like you!" Or, "I know your sister's birthday is this month. Would you like to make a card that we can send to her?"

**Finally, the fourth phase is, going on, or moving forward with life** by accepting and integrating the loss psychologically and emotionally within. However, children are likely to move back and forth through these phases; it is not unusual for them to return to intense grief when it has appeared previously that their sadness had waned.

The nature of loss for children in foster care is deep and often effects their self-worth. Many lose not only their birth families but possibly friends, teachers, and pets. Often they have moved from school to school and are unable to keep mementos or schoolwork that made them proud. They may lose things along the way, such as clothing, books, and photos. Grieving these losses is no quick or easy task.

### The importance of grief work cannot be overstated.

When children are not given the opportunity and assistance to effectively communicate their grief, as well as the feelings related to other traumatic experiences, the result can be a serious erosion of self-trust as well as trust in others. The result can be feelings of incompetence, and a belief that the world is unfair, unsafe, and unmanageable. These powerful emotions, if not recognized and alleviated, can have a serious negative impact on a child's ability to attach to a new caregiver.

Shana, 15, was removed from her biological family at age 10 after her mother failed to retrieve her and her eight-year-old brother from a babysitter's home. After living in several foster homes, she was placed for adoption at age 11. She entered therapy four years after adoption because she felt unattached to her adoptive parents and was asking to be removed from their home. Shana's parents had reached the point where they wondered, "She is so insistent about this, is there nothing we can do but let her go?"

Treating traumatized teens can be especially challenging because, according to Debbie Riley, executive director of C.A.S.E., teens frequently deny that they need the help of a therapist and that problems exist. Instead, teens may present self-injurious behaviors, depression, anxiety, anger-management issues, substance abuse, and relationship problems that stem from previous trauma. She notes that frequently, the situation is complicated because little information is available about the trauma the teen may have experienced in his or her early life. To heal, the essential components for recovery include the emotional support of the family as well as the therapeutic relationship. The adopted teen may have lived in environments where adults harmed and betrayed him or her, but helping build safe connections with others so that he or she may successfully attach to adoptive parents is crucial.

Riley describes the process of helping Shana share her story and express her emotions to be complicated. Although Shana tried to push her away, Riley remained steadfast and worked to slowly build the trusting relationship which helped her describe the sexual abuse she suffered at the hands of her stepfather. Riley sat with Shana as she poured out her pain, rage and fear that she was unlovable. The experience of sharing her memories led to Shana's ability to recognize and grieve the loss of the friend and other people she missed from her previous life.

Riley's work with Shana's parents centered on helping them understand Shana's traumatic past and the impact of the past on her ability to trust and attach to adults. Her parents had been unaware of the extent of Shana's experiences. Her rejection of her parents was an attempt to protect herself from future harm. Shana's parents were warm, loving people who did not want to lose her but had been hurt themselves by her behavior. They agreed to "hang in there with her" as long as she agreed to continue with them and her therapy.

"How kids work through the mourning process and grow from it is up to us," Trozzi notes. Children who are separated from birth parents and those who have been involved with the foster care system have experienced disruptions and losses that affect their ability to adapt to a family environment. It is up to adults — parents, social workers, nurses, doctors, and teachers — to anticipate, accommodate, and support these children as they grieve. Many children cannot maneuver through the complexities of their significant losses and their life stories without support that is enhanced by deep appreciation for the unique nature and challenge of those losses.

*Ellen Singer, LCSW-C, is a therapist/educator for The Center for Adoption Support and Education (C.A.S.E.) in Burtonsville/Silver Spring, Md. She provides clinical services for prospective parents considering adoption/third party reproduction, foster and adoptive parents, adult adopted persons and their families, and expectant/birth parents and their families. Singer facilitates adoptive parent support groups and provides training to parents, community groups, educators, and other professionals. She is the editor of C.A.S.E.'s monthly e-newsletter and contributes articles to parent/professional publications. Singer has served on the Board of Directors for RESOLVE of the Mid-Atlantic, and the Professional Advisory Council for RESOLVE. Singer and her husband are parents to two children, by adoption and by birth.*

# Chronological Age vs. Developmental Age
*By Kate Oliver, MSW, LCSW-C*

When you have a child in your home who has experienced a change in primary caregivers, even within the same family, you may notice that they may act younger than their age. Many kinship care providers have reported to me that the child or children in their care can seem to switch from being much older than their years to much younger than they actually are in an instant. One moment a 10-year-old says something profound about family dynamics, the next the child has a complete meltdown when you say he or she has to wait 10 minutes for dinner to be ready.

When figuring out how to best meet the needs of children, it is important to understand their developmental age. For many children this can be the same age as the chronological age, the age we typically think of when we talk about our children, however, if you care for a child who, among other possibilities:

- has a history of trauma or neglect,

- came into kinship care at an older age (18 months or more),

- has a developmental disability,

- has experienced the death or loss of a primary caregiver,

- has experienced a major change in family structure,

- or has a parent with a serious illness or addiction,

you may have a child who has a "stuck" part of his or her development. If you care for a child like this, typically you might notice that there are times when he or she acts much younger than you would expect for his or her chronological age. What makes this confusing is that the same child may be able to do things that are appropriate for his or her chronological age. For example, you may have a child who works at or even above grade level in reading and/or math, but in some emotional areas may be developmentally younger than his or her chronological age.

Let's look at an example everyone can relate to, think for a moment about a time when you have been triggered into a younger developmental age, say, when you go to your parent's house for the weekend. Even as an adult, you may find that you act differently toward them or your siblings than you would in your day-to-day life. You may feel younger, angrier, more docile, or more or less confrontational. What that signifies is that there is a part of you that has not left or resolved some of the struggles from your own childhood. Most of us have something like this. Our children are no different.

## Some important questions about an area where a child seems stuck in a younger developmental age are:

1. Is this child capable of meeting the demands of this developmental stage? Developmental delays, learning issues, issues related to physical abilities and early

childhood exposure can all add to a child's difficulty in meeting a developmental milestone.

2. Has this child ever been properly taught how to meet this developmental milestone? For example, if you are a kinship care provider for your niece who came to live with you at age five, she may not ever have been properly potty trained and taught to clean herself appropriately after using the bathroom. It may be that while we expect that to be a skill children learn between ages two and four, this child may require instruction now, as she has not received it before.

3. Did something prevent this child from being able to learn this skill at the appropriate time? Perhaps the child in your care has or had medical issues, experienced a traumatic situation or something else. At the time when other children were learning to make friends and play nicely with other children, the child you are caring for now was busy managing an internal or external stressor that demanded all of his or her attention that he or she would otherwise have been able to focus on meeting a developmental milestone.

4. Does the child have a traumatic trigger that remains unresolved which prevents him or her from moving through a developmental stage? My specialty is in working with children who have experienced trauma. Many of them have memories associated with trauma that prevent them from focusing on a task. Children (and adults) with unresolved trauma have what we call triggers, which remind them of the traumatic incident. Depending on what happened, a trigger could be a bathroom, a car, candy, really anything that reminds them of the trauma. What this means for parents with children who have experienced trauma is that the simple act of making a snack for your child could result in a child acting much younger until the traumatic triggers have been identified and resolved so that the apple you cut is just an apple again, instead of a reminder of a difficult past.

Why is it important to know where your child might have a developmental lag or stuck place? Knowing that there are areas where your child is developmentally behind his or her chronological age allows you to make decisions about how to handle his or her behavior appropriately.

## What to do about a child acting developmentally younger:

After considering the reasons behind the developmental delay, it is easier to figure out how to address the issue. Sometimes it may just be a matter of time, or finding appropriate school or therapeutic support to allow a child's brain to develop. For children who are delayed due to an external factor, in addition to school and therapeutic support, consider attempting to change your response to match his or her emotional/developmental age for the issue you are addressing. What would you do for a two-year-old who needs to brush her teeth? Would you tell her to go brush her teeth and expect that she was going to easily and happy get right over to the toothbrush and begin throughly cleaning her teeth after applying just the right amount of toothpaste to the toothbrush? Of course not! Ideally, you would go with her (even if she is grumbling), you might remind her of why tooth-brushing is so important (if you have a child who came into kinship care at an older age, please remember it may be that no one ever taught him or her the importance), you would make brushing fun by singing a silly song to say how long you need to brush your teeth.

I know many care providers reading this might say that a 12-year-old, who acts like a two-year-old at brushing time is not going to stand for you hovering over her while she is brushing her teeth, and you are not going to talk to her like you would talk to a two-year-old. You are right, I am not recommending that you use the tone you would for a two-year-old because you might get the death stare or worse, escalate a tense situation. No, I am saying to use what you would do with a two-year-old as a guideline for figuring out something with a child who acts developmentally two during tooth-brushing time, but is residing in a 12-year-old body. To me that would look something like playfully having a contest to see who can get just the right amount of toothpaste on the toothbrush or offering to get the child started by putting the toothpaste on the toothbrush, then saying a silly poem or singing a silly 12-year-old song, or reading a page out of a joke book to a child while he or she brushes so the child can get an idea of how long to brush. Only read or sing when the child is brushing, stop if the child stops and starts when the child starts again, and stay playful. Yes, the child may look at you like you are crazy, but is the child brushing while doing it?

Yes, I can hear protesting caregivers, now saying that you do not want to put toothpaste on your 12-year-old's toothbrush because he or she is old enough to do it! I know the child is chronologically old enough, however, we are talking about something that the child experiences at a developmentally younger age. And, here's the good news, if you speak to a child's developmental age for a while, his or her need for that developmental stage will get met, and the child moves on to the next stage of development for that issue.

*Kate Oliver, LCSW-C, is co-owner of A Healing Place, a private practice in Columbia, Md. Before opening her private practice, Ms. Oliver worked first at the Sexual Trauma, Treatment, Advocacy and Recovery Center (STTAR) in Columbia, Md. for five years. During her time with the STTAR Center, Oliver completed a year-long program where she earned a certificate in working with children and adolescents with attachment disorders. After learning more about attachment, Oliver went to work with incarcerated, pregnant mothers in Baltimore City as the clinical director for the program, Tamar's Children. Tamar's Children worked with an attachment protocol, The Circle of Security, which taught adults with a history of trauma and neglect to bond with their infants. She used this method with the residents and added an additional group for women already in the program who were going to be reunited with older children in foster and kinship care. In 2007, Oliver opened A Healing Place, where she now specializes in working with children with trauma and attachment related issues. Additionally, she has a blog, Help4YourFamily.com, where she writes about ways to help children and parents feel happier and healthier.*

# Hidden Differences Shout Loudly
*Understanding a Child Prenatally Exposed to Alcohol*
*By Jodee Kulp*

Chemical dependency is often the reason children enter into a kinship care-giving arrangement and the likelihood of a child living with the challenges of fetal alcohol spectrum disorders (FASD) is great.

Children with this permanent brain injury need:
1. Non-judgmental, loving friends and relatives, who accept them as they are,
2. Playful and healthy encouragement but not a demand for growth, and
3. Celebration in strengths and accomplishments no matter how small.

This sounds so simple until you spend 24 hours a day, seven days a week trying to help understand this personal bundle of energy. So much of our learning came through heartache. It is my desire that the information I share below benefits your family and the children you love.

## What every child with FASD needs

- Someone who believes they are capable
- Unconditional love
- Structure and environmental controls
- Wisdom
- Patience and understanding
- Redirection
- Acceptance
- Supervision
- Attention
- Help to slow down when getting out of control (de-escalation)

*"You can only buy something under $10."*

An armload of new clothes later, the teen assumes you will purchase all she has found, as long as each is under $10.

## Poor impulse control is a brain injury issue and frustrating behaviors are most likely not intentional.

The child is more than likely not misbehaving. View behavior problems as a disability that can be dealt with, rather than disobedience. Keep your cool and refrain from yelling. Put on your detective hat to get to the bottom of the behavior. The child may not be able to do two things at once. If you are eating or playing a game the child may not be able to talk. Or the child may not be able to use his or her feet and hands at the same time. Think stretched toddler, the child may look like other children that age, but will need more supervision when it comes to responsibility and amount of freedom. It is for your protection and the child's safety.

## Communication is a two way process.
## Here are tips on communicating with a child with FASD.

Find a quiet place to talk. Hang a do not disturb sign so you are not interrupted. Large, noisy, and busy areas are hard to communicate and function well in. Turn off the radio or TV. Move to a quieter area. Begin talking with simple topics. How is your dog? What did you eat for lunch? Talk about things the child likes. Stay on one topic and state one sentence at a time. Keep information simple but don't talk down to the child or use baby talk. Allow more processing time to answer. Keep sentences short and allow time for the child to respond, refrain from hurrying the child. If the child cannot get the right word, don't fill in, give clues, descriptions, or ask the child to point. Wait it out. Make it easy for the child to participate in a conversation by asking yes and no questions. Or repeat a point using different words. Why? Instead of asking why, use words like where, how, what, who, or when. Why will send their brain in a house of mirrors.

- How we look at or understand something may be totally different from how they understand something.
- Watch *Forrest Gump* with Tom Hanks to get an idea of concrete thinking. For example if you tell the child to handle it, he or she will physically place something in his or her hand.
- Share with us and others if you learn better ways to talk with the child so all can benefit.
- Avoid behavior which winds our child up, such as tickling, wrestling, and pillow fighting.
- In a group, make sure the child is placed so conversation can be around him or her.
- The child may not be able to express needs such as thirst, hunger, going to the toilet and may fidget instead.

Remain still or walk at the same speed as the child when talking. Be an active listener. Give frequent eye contact. Look for gestures. Give choices to ease decision-making, but still allow independence of choice. If understanding is unclear, take a guess (are you talking about...Oh, now I get it.) Look through the child's eyes.

## Provide opportunities for your child to succeed.

Change your idea of event success. New people or visitors in your home are a change in routine and may be difficult for the child. Spend only short periods of time at an event and then leave to integrate the child in regular community life — find out what the first act at the circus is and if it is lions — go and see the lions and then go home. Go to church for the singing. Watch a marching band at the parade and not the whole parade. Go grocery shopping for 10 items — get in and get out. Go to the carnival and play a game every child wins. Visit the amusement park on Mother's Day when other mothers are doing something else and there are no crowds. Go to the museum to see one dinosaur or the library to get one book. Enjoy dessert at the restaurant — we didn't do dinners. Keep it small, keep it short, and keep it fun. You may have to avoid family holidays and birthdays, you may have to only attend community sporting events or miss the movies. These events may be too much for the child to handle.

**Think different for birthdays.** Consider letting the child pick out his or her own presents and don't wrap them. The energy of the surprise may be hard for the child to handle. Unwrapping a present may be confusing. Start the day with a special breakfast and a few tiny presents in a bag. If you have a party, keep it organized and simple. Have the child pick a favorite dinner. Make it a pajama day. Stay home, goof off and do things together.

**Think different for holidays.** Wear matching family T-shirts on holidays, community events, and birthdays. Sponsor a family for a holiday; visit a shelter to deliver presents. Have a holiday tea party with the family — tea, cookies, or just appetizers. Make a paper chain that the child can rip off a chain per day to countdown to the holiday or write a number count down on a calendar and cross off days.

- Have a New Year's Party on the child's time zone while still awake. Make a time capsule using a can with a lid, include a picture of the child, favorite toy, food, color or story. Write a New Year's wish. Open the capsule next New Year to see how much the child has changed.
- For Valentine's Day have everyone in the family write or say three nice things about every other family member.
- Create Thanksgiving trees from Nov. 1-31 and secretly place paper leaves with notes of thanksgiving on a bare twig tree.
- Develop a bedtime and wake up ritual.

## Break learning something new down into small steps.

Set an attainable goal and break into small steps and show progress to a larger goal on a posted chart with stickers. The first gift we are sharing came from an untrained and wild-eyed dog that before his death was a certified Canine Good Citizen and Dog Scout. His name was Mac and he proceeded to teach us the steps to reach out and teach our daughter. This out-of-control dog gave us hope.

1. REVIEW. Review the options of how to teach so you have a backup plan. Make the initial calls, visit the site and discover the details.
2. WATCH. Tell the child what he or she is going to learn and take him or her through the process to accomplish the task. In this first step the child is simply watching, there is NO PRESSURE to learn and we do not require learning.
3. WATCH — EXPERIENCE. Repeat the experience with the child contributing pieces of the learned task.
4. EXPERIENCE — WATCH. Repeat the experience with the child contributing more pieces of the learned task and begin to step away.
5. EXPERIENCE — SHOW. The child now tells you and teaches you. Laugh and enjoying being a partner in the child's learning.
6. SHOW — LET GO. The child shows you. Watch and continue to let go.
7. I CAN. The child begins to skillfully and a bit fearfully complete the process, while you sit near or close to a phone to guide but not do. This "I did it! I can do it," may take a few more steps of three through five. There is no hurry in solid learning. When learning is mastered we move on to the next step in our adult journey. Remember if the child is tired, stressed, overwhelmed, or hungry these things need to be handled first.

*"Why does the counselor want me to ride in a wagon when I am mad?"*

An anger management specialist had recently described that emotions ebb and flow like waves. You need to ride them up and then ride the wave back down.

Being from the Midwest and not used to wave action, the conversation was understood as a wagon.

The changing weather and movement of clouds would have been a better visual.

### Chores are great "I Did Its."

Teach the child the best way you know how to do the chore. First learning is important to children with FASD, but be patient in your tiny step successes. Focus on the positives "Wow, I see you did… that really helps our family." Realize the child may not be able to cross midline so sometimes ability may be not yet possible. Use small steps, separate modalities — show without telling as explained above. Yes, yes, and yes you do have to teach everything. Sit or squat next to your child, do not stand over. Show the child exactly how you expect the chore to be done. Make a checklist of steps (use pictures or short words). Have fun — the more fun you are having, the more solid the learning. Start on the last step or in the middle of the chore first to keep it informal and not so overwhelming. Build from that point backward or forward. Set up playful inspection checkpoints: "Inspect what you expect."

### We plan in some controlled safe failures.

We allow the child to fail at times so that he or she safely learns the consequences. We offer Plan A and Plan B. Plan A allows the child to do it the way he chooses and Plan B provides another way to handle a situation. We role-play both plans. We discovered "real life" experiences provided better opportunity to make a permanent memory, so sometimes we allow her to try her way first even when we know it will fail. Once the choice is made, we provide the supports to help her learn from her choice.

### We need the help of friends and extended family.

It is exhausting to raise a child who has a prenatal brain injury. Consider learning how to provide respite for yourself. Please understand this is a brain injury, not an issue of "bad" parenting and our child is not a "bad" child. Here are some ways others can help your child grow.
- Praise their strengths.
- Acknowledge their expression of frustration.
- Respect their fears and difficulty with change.
- Understand that behaviors may be a "can't do it," not a "won't do it."
- Talk to them as a person — not someone who is stupid.
- Keep from comparing them with others.
- Keep from joking, teasing, or putting them down.
- Keep yourself from telling them, "you will grow out of this."
- Get involved in their interests.

- Find out what they are trying to learn and think of fun ways to join.

**And last, now that our daughter is an adult, what would we have changed if we could have a "do-over" in parenting?**

- Get a diagnosis earlier and begin brain reorganization and sensory integration work before age five.
- Realize in the beginning we are raising an adult and regardless of differences, build a skill base for adult living.
- Create more healthy adult relationships for her as a youth that would braid into her adulthood and provide wholesome activities.
- Give her time to process as she is learning, realizing that the way she experiences the world is vastly different from the world in which I work, live, and participate.
- Utilize her learning strengths of being shown versus being told. Provide experience in step-by-step skills and time to practice — one step at a time — until confidence is gained.
- Understand and accept it is a brain-based injury and day-to-day life is complex and gets more complex in adulthood.
- Develop a safety plan with skills training beginning by 10 years old for managing money, making decisions, remaining safe, seeking help, cooking, cleaning, and other daily life skills.
- Seek support services before she was a teen to offer skill building and friendship.
- Volunteer more with her in the community to build relationships, experience, and skills.

*Jodee Kulp is an award-winning author, producer, and advocate who works tirelessly to serve children, adults, and families of Fetal Alcohol Spectrum Disorders (FASD). Hers is a mission of education, compassion, and growth. Through www.BetterEndings.org, she knows that only through communication do we learn about stories that "inspire, build hope and provide wisdom to change the world one person at a time."*

*"There are few pioneers who must not only pave the path for others to follow...but also must define the landscape to illustrate its existence. Jodee Kulp has written and published more books about Fetal Alcohol Spectrum Disorders than any other parent advocate in our time. Her work has provided assistance to thousands of families and individuals living with FASDs." —* **Donnie Kanter Winokur**

## LIFE LINKS: Transitioning Children with Less Trauma

*By Jennifer Winkelmann, MA, LPC, NCC*

You've welcomed a child who wasn't born to you, but rather, was born into your family. For reasons that range from mental health challenges to problems with substance abuse, you have stepped into the role of "parent." Sometimes with kinship placements, a child's move into the home is such a whirlwind that the whole process is more like whiplash than moving day.

When I did agency work, one of the most significant facets of my job was supporting families as they transitioned children from one home to another. These moves are necessary when children are unable to live in the care of their birth parents, but each time it happens, I grieve again for what our children must endure.

According to Miriam Webster's online dictionary, a "transition" is "passage from one state, stage, subject, or place to another." Not so bad, right? But "transition's" synonyms give a better glimpse of what our children face when they move: **change**, conversion, **flux**, shift, **switch**, turn, **upheaval**.

During a child's move from one home to another, their lives are turned upside down — even if positive feelings are expressed associated with the change. Transitions, even in the best of circumstances for our children, are also traumas. They are usually sudden or unexpected and confusing. The meaning our children assign to their moves often contributes to a negative sense of self and poor self-esteem. And none of this weighs the impact of the losses children face when they move — birth parents, other caregivers, pets, siblings, teachers, playmates, the familiarity of their school/daycare, the blanket that smelled "just so," the "right kind" of milk, and (no matter how traumatic) the rhyme and rhythm of their family... Each time they move, there is an infinite list of losses along with a shuffle into an inconsistent and unpredictable world.

From my experience in child welfare, here are some all too common circumstances when children are moved through the system:

- Moves usually happen on an emergency basis, where the child has little, if any, notice.

- The child is often moved with little or no explanation, with no understanding about what is happening and why.

- At times, these moves are also surrounded by frightening stimuli, such as the presence of law enforcement and/or human service workers. Intervention sometimes happens in the middle of the night or while the child is sleeping.

- Children are often removed from the care of their parents by a person who is a stranger.

- A child's belongings are often left behind or lost in transit.

These things happen on the watch of well-meaning adults who lead the charge, but have lost sight of their highest priority: the souls of the children in our care. We must take greater care with the part we play in the midst of these traumas called "transitions."

It is easy to assign the burden to caseworkers, who are sometimes, tragically, one of the most consistent adults in a child's life. For those youngsters who come to you with clinical support, there could be convenience in relying on the child's therapist to provide guidance and call the shots. Or is it your job, as the family member welcoming a child to your home, to know what the child needs? The tension is this: No one party should bear full responsibility for something so significant in a child's life. And at the same time, each party should feel the full weight of advocating for the child's best interest. But what do we advocate for? There is no single recipe or prescription to fit the unique needs of each child when it comes time to move. While we can't tackle transitions with a cookie-cutter approach, there are some principles that apply across the board for children in transition. Being mindful of these things, you can champion efforts to help kids transition with less trauma.

## Opt for what is familiar to the child.

Just before, during, and after transition is the worst time for the players to change. Every time a child meets a new worker or family member, this too, is another transition. So, the person who directly facilitates the transition should be someone with whom the child is familiar… someone in whom the child finds comfort, who is available on both ends, and all the way through. If you have an existing relationship with the child, that facilitator might be you. But sometimes, even extended family members are basically strangers to the child being welcomed. In those cases, if from the child's perspective you are (as the caregiver) a stranger, yield to others with whom the child might be more familiar. Felt safety for the child during this process is essential.

In some cases, a child will come to you after first being placed in foster care. These transitions have the potential to go more smoothly because it's possible they can happen on a non-emergent basis. Some children are placed in foster care for a matter of days or weeks while a caseworker searches for family members. Others may live with a foster family for an extended period of time before coming into kinship care. At times, a foster family will even look toward adoption, and at the eleventh hour — just before the adoption is finalized — a family member is located and plans to move the child are put into place.

As a family member welcoming a child, it is important to understand that he or she may have developed connections with a foster family. Losing them in order to come to you will add to the list of things the child has to grieve. Remember: If a child is in foster care, there are other losses before this one. Whether the child's stay in foster care was short or extended, if the relationship between the child and the foster parents is positive, the foster family can be a bridge between their home and yours for the child. Know that while you may be biologically connected to the child, the foster family (as the child's most recent caregiver) may be a wealth of information that uniquely equips you to successfully welcome the child into your home and the rhythm of your family.

## Cast the net wide.

If a child comes to you with positive relationships in his or her life, work hard to help the child maintain those connections. For children who have been separated from their birth families or first caregivers, a lack of trust about a caregiver's ability to stay, to remain in the child's life, is compromised. So, if anyone has a positive connection with the child — a foster parent, teacher, other extended family member, family friend — make every effort to keep that person connected. These relationships increase a child's sense of felt safety and communicate that you, as the new primary caregiver, are "on the same page" with other people the child knows and loves. Research shows that any positive, connected, healthy, stable relationship in the life of a child will go toward building the child's resiliency in the future. Our youngsters who have suffered great losses need every support available. Cast the net wide, and see those other adults who are willing to come alongside the child and your family as assets.

## Answer questions, tell the story.

When it comes time for a child to move, we may wrestle with how to present it. While it is important to be mindful about how a child will internalize what is shared with him or her, it is equally important to tell the truth — gently. Often, the reasons for a child's move from the care of his or her parents has to do with some difficult truths about the child's mother and/or father. To transition children with less trauma, we must be truthful *and* gentle. Work with a therapist during this phase if you have questions. There are many gifted clinicians who can offer support or consult about how information should be shared with a child. Remember, even young children have a certain level of "knowing" about their experiences. The child is, after all, the central player in his or her own life. So, even if a child is unable to express what he or she has witnessed with his or her parents, it is important to understand that the child fully experienced these circumstances, and so if nothing else — the child "knows" on an experiential level and may need your help to make sense of what the child "knows."

Before, after, and during the transition, it is important to answer the child's questions, even if they aren't asked aloud. As you tell the story, help the child to understand what has happened and what will happen next, weaving in answers to: "Where is my mom or dad?" and "Why aren't I with him or her?" Understand that there will likely be some grieving associated with these abrupt changes and that a child's grief often looks different from an adult's. When you are intentional about telling the story, you provide a forum for the grief process. It gives the child an opportunity to create meaning and make sense (with your healthy and grounded influence) of the changes he or she is experiencing. In the hustle and bustle of all of it, we must connect with the child's experience, giving the implicit message that what is happening to him or her matters. Telling the child's story communicates, "Kiddo, you matter!"

## Provide consistent sensory input.

I get a much better night's sleep in a hotel room if I bring a pillow from home. There's a reason for that — I'm bathing myself in sensory input consistent with my home environment, and it regulates my system. The same is true for our kids. It may sound silly, but exploit the senses to minimize trauma; the sense of smell is especially linked to memory storage, and emotional state, so maintain sensory input, in whatever ways you can. If you are the receiving family, find out what detergent the child's parent used, the brand of the child's toothpaste, which is his or her favorite cereal… If you're able to bring some things from the child's home with his or her parents, opt for things that give sensory input that bring comfort, such as a blanket, favorite stuffed animal, or the child's bed sheets. If the child is of an age where he or she can communicate what it is he or she wants to bring, yield — no matter how small or insignificant the item may seem to you. By giving the child some power in a situation in which he or she already feels powerless, you can minimize the effects of the helplessness the child feels.

### Exercise awareness x 2.

I will never forget a late night drive across town to move two little boys from their foster home. I felt sick, fretting about what elements of our nighttime emergency would be triggers for them as they got older. Would they always have a fear of women with brown curly hair? Would the sight of a white Honda always bring them waves of anxiety? I knew what I had to do because of the unavoidable circumstances, but with everything in me, I didn't want to do it this way. During the drive, I talked with a co-worker, who reminded me how terrified the children would be about what was happening. The high levels of adult stress I was experiencing due to our "emergency" would have meant a lack of attunement to the boys' experiences with the move, making me emotionally unavailable to them. She coached me to "feel" as calm and safe as possible, for their sake. She nudged me to take care of my own business. We must assess where we are and tell the truth (to a partner, friend, or even yourself) about our own levels of stress. If we can't dial into ourselves, it will be impossible for us to attune to the child and **authentically** meet his or her needs. And we have to make sure we do some processing with another person about the experience for ourselves as we're making our way through the process of helping a child move. We want kids to be able to discuss their challenges, and this is one way for us to "walk the talk." Plus, it's a way to keep ourselves healthy, and the healthier we are, the healthier transitions we'll facilitate.

### Give — and tap into roots.

When children are shuffled around, often many details of their lives are lost along the way. When you have a child in your care, consider yourself a biographer and historian. Make the most of lifebooks and photos. Write letters to the child as an adult about what is happening in his or her life as a youngster. Keep a journal as a record you will send on with the child. These efforts bear witness to the child's life today, and give a springboard for tomorrow, when children will work to integrate all the pieces of their puzzle (making sense of where they lived, with whom, why, and for how long).

If you know stories about the child's life, have previous experiences with him or her, have your own mementos and photos from an earlier time and use them to communicate, they help the child build a sense of belonging in your home. Every child deserves to live with someone who loves him or her enough to have a photograph on the mantle and his or her artwork on the refrigerator.

### Give dignity.

This is "Transitions 101," so it should go without saying: Kids deserve to be moved with their dignity intact. Their belongings should not be packed in trash bags. Consider, for a moment, the message we send our youngsters when their possessions are transported by the same vessels we use for what we send to the city dump. If you are responsible for helping a child pack his or her things, use duffle bags, suitcases, or backpacks. It is a small price to pay for dignity.

As you turn the page into the next chapter, when you think about transitions, commit to one thing that you will change and/or be aware of the next time you participate in a child's move. Ask yourself, "If it were me having to move today, how would I want it to go?" Remember, moves go best when we are flexible, creative, adaptable, collaborative, and mindful of a child's individual needs. It's in the details, and a minute action on your part may make all the difference in trauma reduction for the child.

*Jennifer Winkelmann, MA, LPC, NCC, is the founder and clinical director of Inward Bound, LLC. As a psychotherapist for individuals, couples, and families, her primary clinical focus is adoption and foster care issues, including the impact of early trauma and the spectrum of relationship difficulties that result from disrupted attachments. In addition to her private practice, Winkelmann serves as the consulting clinician for Catholic Charities Child Welfare programs and frequently partners with Coaching for Life and the National Institute for Trauma Informed Care. While she specializes in work with children who have suffered attachment trauma, she also offers services for couples addressing marital issues and to adult individuals seeking help with depression, anxiety, relationship difficulties, stress, and grief/loss. Her website is www.inwardboundco.com.*

## In the Beginning
*Taken from a blog by Jan Wagner*

Looking back on those early times with H, I wonder how I kept it together. I am sure those closest to me would dispute that I did. He was so young, barely two, not eating solid foods, not sleeping more than an hour at a time, not able to be alone in a crib, and not talking. It wasn't as if I was completely out of practice because the other five grandchildren had come before him in rapid succession during a five-year period and I was involved in their lives. But full time, sleepless nights and all day neediness was difficult to say the least. We have come so far since those early months and years, H, Papa and I, yet some of the effects of early trauma and separation issues remain. He still cannot sleep alone for an entire night, he struggles with being separated from us, and needs constant reassurance that we are coming back. School was a nightmare the first year.

*After raising three children, 37 years of marriage, and at the age of 57, Jan Wagner started raising her then two-year-old grandson. Jan Wagner is now an advocate for kinship families and is involved on a state and national level. You can follow her blog Raising H at jdwags.blogspot.com. She is also available to speak or give workshops on Kinship/Grandparenting issues.*

# Sexual Abuse: How to Get (and Give) Help!

*By Amy Lang, MA*

Sadly, children *in* foster care are four times as likely to be sexually abused than children not in the system.[1] Some children are abused by their foster parent, another familiar adult who has access to them, or by other children in the family. Often the abuser is the child's parent, step-parent, or sibling, which can make things more complex because the offender may be related to you. Regardless, the good news is that children who receive treatment can and do recover and go on to lead healthy and happy lives.

The following are some simple steps you can take to help a child in your care. Remember, a child's safety is an adult's responsibility and if you know a child is being abused, it is your responsibility to get him or her help and report the offender.

## If a child discloses sexual abuse to you:

1. Remain calm and go to a private place to talk. If you get upset about the situation or offender, the child may believe you are upset with him or her.

2. Believe the child. Only two percent of disclosure of sexual abuse is false. Kids don't lie about this.[2]

3. Treat the child like a crime scene and don't cross examine the child. Ask simple questions — Where? When? Who? Has someone touched you in a way that hurts you or feels uncomfortable? The interview specialist will investigate fully. This isn't your responsibility. Less questioning is better.

4. Tell him or her you will need to tell other people and the number one priority is to make sure the child is safe.

5. Don't congratulate the child or chastise him or her for confiding in you.

6. Quickly report what you've been told and call Child Protective Services (in home molestation) or the police (out of home). If they aren't responding fast enough, complain.

7. Write down what the child said and describe his or her attitude and behavior.

8. Get support for everyone — the child, yourself, and anyone else in the family who may need it.

If you suspect a child has been sexually abused, but he or she hasn't disclosed it, it's better for the child to be interviewed by a professional, rather than by you. This is called a "forensic interview" and it is not traumatic for the child. The folks who do these interviews are amazing, kind, gentle, and know just what to say and do to draw a child out.

## Some sexual behaviors that would be considered "concerning" and worthy of at least a phone consultation are:

- Adult-like sexual activity — anything that seems like adult sex in any way. This can

## Resources from Amy Lang

My Facebook:
www.facebook.com/
birdsbeeskids

My TWITTER:
www.twitter.com/
birdsandbees

My BOOK:
**Birds + Bee + YOUR Kids –
A Guide To Sharing Your
Beliefs About Sexuality,
Love + Relationships,**
Peanut Butter Press, 2009

## Other Web Resources:

www.stopitnow.org

www.d2l.org

www.savvyparentssafekids.com

## Other Books:

**Protecting the Gift: Keeping
Children and Teenagers Safe
(and Parents Sane),**
Gavin de Becker

**It's So Amazing!: A Book
about Eggs, Sperm, Birth,
Babies, and Families,**
Robie Harris and Michael
Emberley

**It's Perfectly Normal:
Changing Bodies, Growing
Up, Sex, and Sexual Health,**
Robie Harris and Michael
Emberley

be "humping" another child or adult repeatedly, oral contact, attempted penetration, explicit language, too much knowledge for their age, etc.

- Your gut or intuition tells you — in a loud voice — that there is something off, unusual, or wrong about the child's behavior.

- The sexual behavior is with a child who is not a regular playmate, is much younger or older, is more powerful (smarter, bigger, etc.), or involves aggression, violence, threats, or bribery.

- The behavior happens a lot — over and over again and the child doesn't respond to correction.

- The behavior is directed at an adult.

## Other behaviors that can be considered warning signs that abuse may have occurred:[3]

- Nightmares, trouble sleeping, fear of the dark, or other sleeping problems.

- Extreme fear of "monsters."

- Spacing out at odd times.

- Loss of appetite, or trouble eating or swallowing.

- Sudden mood swings: rage, fear, anger, or withdrawal.

- Fear of certain people or places, for example, a child may not want to be left alone with a baby-sitter, friend, relative, or some other child or adult; or a child who is usually talkative and cheery may become quiet and distant when around a certain person.

- Stomach illness all of the time with no identifiable reason.

- An older child behaving like a younger child, such as bed-wetting or thumb sucking.

- Sexual activities with toys or other children, such as simulating sex with dolls or asking other children/siblings to behave sexually.

- New words for private body parts.

- Refusing to talk about a "secret" he or she has with an adult or older child.

- Talking about a new older friend.

- Suddenly having money.

- Cutting or burning herself or himself as an adolescent.

## Physical warning signs a child may have been sexually abused:

- Unexplained bruises, redness, or bleeding of the child's genitals, anus, or mouth.

- Pain at the genitals, anus, or mouth.

- Genital sores or milky fluids in the genital area.

Sexual abuse is something no one wants to deal with, but for many children (and adults) it is an enormous problem. Being a supportive, open, and askable parent is the best thing you can do for any child. And if you were sexually abused yourself, imagine what your life would be like if just one adult in your life stepped in to protect you and offer help and support.

## For more help contact any of the following resources. You can usually call anonymously.

Stop it NOW! 1-888-PREVENT or StopItNow.org

Rape Incest Abuse National Network — RAINN.org

Darkness to Light — 1-866-FOR-LIGHT or D2L.org

Birds + Bees + Kids — BirdsAndBeesAndKids.com

*A sexual health educator for more than 20 years, Amy Lang teaches parents and other folks how to talk to kids of any age about the birds and the bees. She is the author of the Mom's Choice Award® winning* **Birds + Bees + YOUR Kids – A Guide to Sharing Your Beliefs About Sexuality, Love, and Relationships** *and* **The Ask ANYTHING Journal***. She created the lively and engaging video* **Birds + Bees + Kids: The Basics** *so parents can learn how to talk to their kids about sex and values without leaving the couch! She can be reached at www.birdsandbeesandkids.com or www.bbkvideo.com.*

[1] http://www.cfrc.illinois.edu/pubs/Pdf.files/childmalretro.pdf
[2] www.sidran.org/pdf/Falsereportsbychildren.pdf
[3] http://www.stopitnow.org/warnings

# To Be Concerned? or Not To Be Concerned? That is The Question!

*By Noelle Hause, EdD, LPC*

> *I remember when my husband and I moved to a new home twelve years ago. Our 11-month-old son was just on the verge of walking and talking prior to our move. However, due to the delay in the construction of our new home and the prompt sale of our old home, a two-week hotel stay was required while all of our personal belongings went into storage. My son's development appeared to, well... just "stop." No words, no walking for the next three months. It was at that point that I realized how difficult it is for young children to adjust to change in their routines, caregivers, homes, families, and support systems.*

Such disruptions can result in development delays and negative behaviors as the child attempts to adapt to these changes. This does not mean that the child will be delayed or display challenging behaviors forever. With the right supports, understanding and relationships, young children can make those developmental adjustments. It is important to sort out typical development and responses to change from more serious mental health or social-emotional/behavioral issues.

If you have concerns related to your child's behaviors, start by asking yourself the following questions.
- Has there been a change in my child's routine?
- Has there been a change in relationships such as a caregiver or child care provider?
- Has my child been ill?
- Is my child's behavior developmentally appropriate?
- Have I been emotionally available to my child?
- Does my child have delays in any area of development, such as speech-language, motor or cognitive development?
- Does my child lack the appropriate skills to be successful?
- Has my child's behavior been reinforced by someone or something in the environment?
- Does this behavior happen across all settings or just in certain settings such as school or home?

If you answered "yes" to any of these questions, were unable to answer any of these questions or are just interested in learning more about your child's behavior, try the following:

*1. Keep a regular schedule and routine.*

*2. Keep a log or journal of concerns related to development and behavior.*

*3. Don't assume that your child knows how to behave. It takes years to teach young children basic social skills.*

*4. Expect a change in behavior or delay in development when major life changes occur.*

*5. Visit with your child care provider and observe your child in other settings.*

*6. Ask yourself: Who does this behavior bother? Me? My child? His or her teacher? Other children?*

Know your developmental stages. (Figure in a 3-4 month plus or minus factor, i.e. some children will master them early, some later).

1. Typically developing babies are eager to relate and explore the world around them — including other people.

### End of 3 months

- Develops social smile
- Benefits from short, frequent interactions when alert
- Appears to recognize and is comforted by primary caregivers
- Is interested in and enjoys playing with others
- Responds positively to touch
- Communicates more with face and body
- Imitates some movements/facial expressions
- Becomes aware of body parts and realizes they are attached; i.e. observes hand
- Can latch onto bottle or breast

### End of 6 months

- Enjoys and imitates social play, i.e. begins to play peek-a-boo
- Interested in mirror images, responds to others expressions
- Shy or anxious with strangers
- Body typically relaxed
- Can calm within a half hour, i.e. sucks on hand or pacifier, responds to blanket
- Likes to be picked up/held and mealtimes
- Communicates hunger/illness through different cries
- Can eat within 30 minutes without gagging or vomiting
- Stays awake for an hour or longer and falls asleep easily
- Normal bowel movements

### End of 12 months

- Prefers familiar people
- Expresses several emotions: joy/pleasure, distress, interest, disgust, displeasure, and discomfort
- Communicates hunger, pain, or tiredness
- Responds actively to language
- Shows displeasure when a toy is taken away/dropped
- Shows anxiety when separated from caregiver.
- Feeds self using fingers, holds cup, and drinks with help
- Babbles sounds; blows "raspberries"
- Will assist caregiver in getting dressed by holding out arms and legs
- Laughs

2. When you think of a two-year-old does the word "NO!" come to mind? Prior to this stage, infants have limited knowledge of themselves being separate from their caregivers.

They are simply part of the adult who cares for them. As they are increasingly able to physically move to and from their caregiver, toddlers begin to realize their separateness. This recognition of being separate leads to "individuation" or the development of the infant's ego and sense of identity. So what should the social-emotional development of a toddler look like?

### End of 24 months

#### Social

- Imitates behavior of others
- Shows concern by looking when another child cries
- More aware of herself as separate from others
- More excited about company of other children
- Can be helpful i.e. put a toy on a shelf
- Shows intense feelings for parents and others
- Likes praise
- May be aggressive if unable to communicate needs (biting)

#### Emotional

- Increasing independence
- Self-conscious emotions emerge: shame, guilt, pride, and embarrassment
- Shows defiance; uses the word "no"
- Begins to use basic emotion words: "happy" and "sad"
- Recognizes/smiles at self
- Initiate and play by themselves
- Self-regulation involving ability to inhibit behavior
- Curious about body/toileting behaviors
- Trust in caregiver increases
- Separation anxiety may result in nightmares

3. Toddlers approaching 36 months are trying to figure out where and how they fit into the world around them. While a toddler's use of "NO!" is annoying and inconvenient, it is an important developmental stage. If a child has been recently separated from a primary caregiver, distress may result and separation anxiety may be heightened. A child may even show signs of bereavement if the separation is an extended one.

### End of 36 months

#### Social

- Imitates others
- Will spontaneously show affection for familiar people
- Can take turns with another
- Understands concept of "mine" and "his/hers"

- Eager to please and look for approval from others
- Wants to feel needed/included
- Notices how he impacts others as well as how others affect him.

### Emotional
- Expresses a wide range of emotions
- Identifies mad, scared, happy, and sad in self
- Uses emotion language in pretend play
- Talks about causes and consequences of some emotions
- Talks about emotions in the:
    - Past — "He lost his dog, he was sad."
    - Present — "I am happy. This is my birthday party."
    - Future — "I am going to grandma's house, that makes me happy."
- Separates easily from parents
- Objects to major changes in routine

4. "That's not fair!", "Why don't I get to go?", "Did I do it better?", "Let's pretend that...", "Can I play with my friend?", "I want the same shoes as her", "I will help you if you give me some candy." Sound familiar? Fairness, belongingness, competition, pretend play, friendships, likenesses and differences, awareness of gender and negotiation all characterize the fourth and fifth year of social-emotional development in young children.

### End of 48 months

#### Social
- Interested in new experiences
- Cooperates with peers
- Plays "Mom" or "Dad"
- Develops friendships
- Creativity in fantasy play
- Dresses and undresses self
- Negotiates solutions to conflicts
- More independent
- Shows interest in gender differences

#### Emotional
- Unfamiliar images may be "monsters"
- Views self as a whole person involving body, mind, and feelings
- Often cannot distinguish between fantasy and reality

### End of 60 months

#### Social
- Wants to please and be like her friends

- Likes to sing, dance, and act
- More independence
- Some understanding of moral reasoning (fairness and good/bad)
- Compares self to others
- Tries to assimilate others rules into what has already been learned
- More likely to agree to rules and is interested in fairness but may not be fair

### Emotional
- Aware of gender and gender differences
- Able to distinguish fantasy from reality
- Sometimes demanding and/or eagerly cooperative
- Realizes that the same event can cause different emotions in different people (one person can win a game and another person can lose)
- Understands that one's feelings can persist after the event that caused them

Be reasonable with your expectations of developmental milestones. A child with cerebral palsy may have a more difficult time calming than a child without cerebral palsy.

Contact your local child find organization, pediatrician, or mental health center for access to a full developmental screen and/or evaluation with an emphasis on social-emotional development.

Young children who are competent in social-emotional development have the ability to: tolerate frustration better, persist in tasks, follow directions, problem solve and manage conflict with peers, develop good relationships overall, identify, understand and communicate their own feelings, regulate their emotions and behaviors, and develop empathy. In addition they are physically healthier, less impulsive, more focused, have greater academic achievement, and experience a sense of confidence and competence. In short, children who are competent in social-emotional development have increased school readiness and the ability to maintain long-lasting relationships. Healthy, normal social/emotional development is an essential foundation for all other learning.

*Noelle Hause, Ed.D, LPC, is an early mental health specialist for North Range Behavioral Health, director of community health resources for the North Colorado Medical Center Foundation, adjunct faculty at the University of Northern Colorado and author of* **The Early Years** *column for* **Fostering Families Today** *magazine.*

# Understanding Attachment

"*A normal, healthy child obeys Mom and Dad because she wants to please them. A child with an attachment impairment doesn't have any interest in pleasing her parents, because she doesn't trust them. Attachment therapy is designed to increase the level of trust. But in the meantime, consequences are necessary so the child can start to learn from her own experiences, until she is able to learn from Mom and Dad. In addition, children with attachment impairment have a deficit in cause-and-effect thinking. They don't understand that if they break their brother's toy, it will cause upset feelings and further disrupt an already poor relationship. Children with attachment impairment also have toxic shame — the feeling that "I am bad" — not just that I feel guilty because they did a bad thing. Consequences allow a child to fix their mistake, which allows healing from the toxic shame.*" ~Lynne Lyon, MSW

# Attachment 101

*By Arthur Becker-Weidman, PhD*

After you read this article you should have a basic understanding of how normal and healthy attachments develop, why this is important, and how to help wounded children come closer to developing healthier patterns of attachment. In preparing this summary for you I am drawing on material from several of my books (in particular, **Attachment Parenting,** edited by Arthur Becker-Weidman & Deborah Shell, Jason Aronson, Lanham, MD, 2010).

## What is Attachment?

Attachment is a process involving a caregiver and child. It does not reside in the child, but is reflective of the relationship between caregiver and child. In simplest terms, the attachment system is a "proximity-seeking" system. It operates like a thermostat; if everything is comfortable, you don't know if your heating and cooling system is operating, it only comes on when the temperature is outside some pre-set range. Attachment behavior is proximity seeking behavior and is activated when a person feels some threat. In those instances, the person seeks the security and comfort of a preferred other person. For children this preferred other person will usually be a parent; for you this preferred other person may be your partner; the person you turn to when things get difficult.

The attachment system and attachment behaviors are activated when the person experiences some threat, fear, or discomfort. What normally occurs and what is supposed to occur in infancy, is that the parent responds to the child's distress, providing comfort and soothing the child. In the toddler years, the parent provides a safe base from which the child can begin to explore the world and learn. Without a sense of safety and security, learning can be difficult; but more about that later.

## Why is Attachment So Important?

As the child grows and develops, attachment security provides the basis for learning, developing healthy relationships, positive self-esteem, effectively managing stress, learning cause-effect thinking, and many other important things. When a child is raised by a "good enough" parent who is committed to the child, sensitive to the child's emotional and physical states, largely responsive to the child's needs, and able to be insightful and reflective regarding their own mental states and how those affect the child, then that child is likely to develop a secure and healthy pattern of attachment. Once that pattern is formed, then future relationships will be based on that secure pattern of attachment. If the parent is less than "good enough," lacking sensitivity, commitment, and responsiveness, being harsh and punitive, or caught up in their own difficulties, then the child is likely to develop an insecure or disorganized pattern of attachment. In these instances, the child will show a variety of difficulties, more on this later.

Another important and biologically based system is the fight-flight-freeze-appeasement system that is activated when a person experiences some threat. When faced with some threat, we may fight, flee, freeze, or engage in appeasement behavior. So, what happens if the source of threat, which activates both the attachment and threat-response systems is the source of comfort and security; the parent? In those instances, the child's psychological and mental processes will become quite disorganized. The child who experiences early, chronic maltreatment within a caregiving relationship, also known as Complex Trauma or Developmental Trauma Disorder, will develop a variety of difficulties and dysfunctions that the child will not grow out of and that require specialized and therapeutic parenting.

## What Happens When it Doesn't Work?

Children who have Complex Trauma and disorders of attachment will show low self-esteem. Their early experiences have "taught" them that they are unlovable, unwanted, defective, and bad. They will have problems with cause-effect thinking. Children learn, experientially, about cause-effect thinking because in early childhood their parents responded to their needs in a relatively consistent manner. The child "learned," "if I cry this way I get fed, if I cry that way I get picked up." The child learns cause-effect. In addition, the development of motivation and persistence comes from these early experiences. Why bother "trying" if your early life experiences have "taught" you that nothing you do matters? The stress of living in a chronically maltreating and threatening home causes real changes to the brain. Chronic high levels of stress hormones make it hard to learn and cause problems moving information from short-term to long-term memory. School and learning problems result. This high level of stress then becomes the normal "set point" for the child, who is now always on high alert. A child in a chronic state of high alert will have a much harder time managing stress and little will be necessary for the child to become overwhelmed and dysregulated: temper tantrums, and low frustration tolerance are what you will see.

So, the child in your home has likely experienced chronic early maltreatment within a caregiving relationship and the resulting damage to this child's pattern of attachment; then the child's capacity to form trusting and healthy relationship with adults, capacity to form positive peer relationships, capacity to learn, ability to regulate behavior and emotions, and physical functioning will all be impaired. It is as if the lenses through which the child views the world and relationships have been distorted so that the child's experience and your experience of the same event may be vastly different. "Normal parenting," what you may have used on your birth children with great success will probably not be helpful with this child. That is not your fault. Your "normal" way of parenting may have worked just fine with the children you raised from birth; because you had them from birth. The child now in your home has a different history that causes that child to experience the world and act differently. Think of it this way. A child is like a house. When you raise a child from birth you build the house from the foundation up. When a child is placed in your home, the foundation and some of the other structures may already be set. If the foundation is shaky, then no matter how lovely what you try to build on top of that, what you try to build will likely be unstable and fragile, and may likely crack and crumble.

## Attachment Facilitating Parenting

So what is a parent to do? We know that the four most important factors in placement stability are:
- The foster parent's own pattern of attachment, based on their early relationships with the people who raised him or her.
- The foster parent's commitment to this child.
- The foster parent's ability to be insightful and reflect on the child's experience as different from his or her own.
- The foster parent's ability to be sensitive and responsive to the child.

**What these children need is a home that is stable, secure, free of physical and emotional threats, shame, or harsh and punitive methods.**

A few principles for you to use are the following:
- It's about connections, not compliance.
- Behavior has meaning.
- Fear is often the basis for much of what is problematic.
- Avoid saying "no."
- Keep the child close.

It's about connections, not compliance. But it does NOT mean that compliance is not important. Being respectful, considerate, and obedient are certainly traits that any parent would want in their child. But, how do you get that? Instilling fear, being punitive and harsh do not engender true compliance. When a child internalizes you, your values, beliefs, and approach, then you achieve true compliance; and this is achieved by creating a deep and meaningful relationship or connection with the child. Think of the story of Pinocchio. He only behaved if Jiminey Cricket was on his shoulder; when Jiminey was gone, Pinocchio got into trouble. Pinocchio only became a real flesh and blood boy when he and his foster father Gepetto developed a connection and an emotionally meaningful relationship; when Pinocchio went to rescue Gepetto from the whale. Gepetto was always there for Pinocchio. Gepetto was accepting, loving, and provided unconditional love and acceptance of the person.

All behavior is adaptive and has meaning. As a therapeutic parent you want to dig down below the surface to figure out for the child what is driving the behavior. Responding to the surface behavior of symptoms will not be helpful; what helps is figuring out the cause of the problem behavior, and addressing that. Most often, what will be at the root of problem behavior will be fear and the child's difficult early experiences. Does the child take things that do not belong to the child? Well, that may be a good example of the child just not experiencing adults as helpful and of chronic early neglect. The child may be "help-blind" and not see the help that is right in front of the child. So, when the child needs something, the child takes what the child needs. It does not even occur to the child to ask for that dollar for lunch or whatever it is the child takes. So, why doesn't the child learn when you tell the child to "just ask me?" Although the child will say that the child "knows" that and although in the calm of discussion the child does recall that, probably when under stress, the child is not thinking. Chronic stress can result in the child becoming easily dysregulated and not being able to access information in memory; a real cognitive impairment.

Keeping the child close and interacting with the child is an important aspect of therapeutic parenting. By keeping the child close, you will become more able to perceive what the child is feeling and experiencing and put that into words for the child; because the child cannot do it, you must do it for the child. Remove obstacles to the relationship as a means to avoid saying, "NO." Most often WHAT the child is asking for is acceptable, it is the timing that is off; so you can say yes to most things.

*Child: Can I watch a movie? (Said at 8:30 p.m. on a school night)*
*Parent: Sure, this Friday we'll rent a DVD and pop some popcorn.*

*Child: Can I go to Mary's house? (Asked on a school night before homework is done.)*
*Parent: You bet, after you clean your room and finish your homework.*

*Child: Can I drive the car? (age 14)*
*Parent: As soon as you get your license!*

So, as a foster parent you are the most important adult in this child's life right at this moment. You can be a huge positive influence on this child, IF you understand the child and use the right parenting approaches. The child in your home has been the victim of awful things; you cannot make that go away, but you can go a long way toward fixing the foundation and helping the child build a better future.

*Arthur Becker-Weidman, PhD, has been treating the families of adoptive and foster children for more than three decades. As director of the Center For Family Development he consults with Governments, Departments of Social Services, Residential Treatment Centers, Mental Health Clinics, and professionals throughout the United States, Canada, Singapore, Finland, Australia, The Czech Republic, and Slovakia. Becker-Weidman's work has focused on the evaluation and treatment of adopted and foster children and their families, Complex-Post Traumatic Stress Disorder, and Alcohol Related Neurological Dysfunction. Becker-Weidman has published more than a dozen papers in peer-reviewed professional journals. He has written several books and has several DVDs available for parents and professionals. More information can be found at www.Center4FamilyDevelop.com. Reprinted with permission from **Fostering Families Today** magazine.*

# Ten Ways to Help Children Feel Less Anxious

*By Martha B. Straus, PhD, and Melanie Ernould, MA*

Children in foster care tend to be among the most anxious kids around. It's understandable, of course, but that doesn't make them any easier to live with and teach. In our research and clinical experience, almost every foster child we've met qualifies for at least one kind of anxiety disorder; most of them fit the descriptions for several, at least in some part. These kids have specific fears, phobias, and obsessions — and a more general "free-floating" anxiety, too. They fear separations, as well as being too close, being controlled, as well as being out of control. They're afraid both of change and boredom. Some need nearly constant reassurance; others chew their cuticles until they bleed. Most adults can't even imagine how these children get through the day trying to manage such a relentless level of anxiety.

These children can become better self-soothers and problem-solvers. But in order to help them we first have to understand a bit about their wiring — everyone has their own way of being comforted that's based on temperament, experience, and ability to self-regulate. One child may need to run around the outside of the house three times to calm down, while another would prefer a bubble bath. Some kids are so intense they can't self-soothe at all once they're upset, while others regroup quite quickly with a hug and a little encouragement. Some of the children we know are aggressive and get angry in the face of stress; others are so sensitive they seem to crumple under the pressure of their lives. As you get to know your foster children, and they get to know themselves, you will be able to notice their patterns of anxiety and discover the strategies that work best for them.

Keeping in mind the fact that you and your children are going to have to figure out what specifically works best given their unique style of living in the world, we offer these ten tried-and-true general anxiety-management techniques for you to expand upon:

## 1. Take the Worries Seriously.

Empathize with what your child is experiencing. It is hard for them, and that's important to acknowledge. Sometimes kids calm quickly when they "feel felt;" they can sense that you do understand. It makes them feel less crazy and out of control to hear that you know they are suffering. When you take their worries seriously, you're also getting onto the same team as them, and putting anxiety on the other team that you'll oppose together. By the same token, it is usually pretty futile to admonish someone to "stop worrying" or to offer empty reassurances that "there's nothing to worry about." It is not possible for most kids to turn off their anxiety like a switch, and this kind of approach is likely to make them feel worse anyway. Tell them, "I know you are feeling very worried and your stomach is in a knot." Or, "I'm sorry you're having such a hard time. I can try to help you feel better — may I?"

Together you might draw a "worry machine" based on how your child thinks his or her worry works. Then draw a "fear extinguisher" that includes a list of the strategies your child wants to use to calm down. Put it on the fridge to serve as a reminder.

## 2. Keep it Predictable.

All anxious children are sensitive to change and foster kids have particularly good reasons to yearn for a predictable and routine life. They need warnings of transitions and even of small variations in schedule, though not too far in advance which can make them worry more. They benefit also from practice for the big changes — rehearsing the steps they will take. For example, when children make the switch from elementary school to junior high or middle school, they'll manage better if they already know their way around the new building. Kids who have a hand in their routines also seem to feel more in control. Have them draw their own calendars, make decisions about the order of events when they can, and review what they know. Use the most predictable schedule you can devise, and try to maintain it every day. Come up with some simple language that explains what happens next, and use that predictably, too. For example, say, "After dinner, it will be bath, story, then bedtime." Plan with children instead of for them — this can also reduce their anxiety.

## 3. Help Them Manage Their Bodies.

Everything you've heard about exercise, a healthy diet, deep breathing and body awareness for reducing anxiety is probably true. It's a fact that kids who are in control of their bodies feel less anxious. Notably, children with physical trauma tend to be more anxious and cut off from their body signals. They will particularly benefit from strategies that get them to live more fully in their physical selves.

**Exercise:** All able-bodied children should be physically active. You and your child will have to figure out what kind of exercise is fun for them. They should also be aware that exercise is a great strategy for managing anxiety. Research shows that regular exercise releases endorphins, which are brain chemicals that help with relaxation. Exercise also improves sleep, which is frequently a casualty of anxiety. Eventually, exercise lowers the heart rate and blood pressure, builds muscles and stamina, and nurtures self-esteem. It has short- and long-term health benefits for both managing and decreasing anxiety. As an added benefit, exercise also exposes children to how it feels to have an increased heart rate during a typical circumstance. If you have a child who doesn't want to run around, dance, or get sweaty in a sporty way, you might also look at yoga or martial arts as alternative forms of exercise. For children who can handle team participation, group sports activities also help children develop confidence and social skills, reducing anxiety that way, too.

**Diet:** Foster parents frequently have their hands full dealing with food struggles and idiosyncrasies in their children. Food is often the symbolic and real family battleground where anxiety runs amok. To the extent possible, though, do avoid caffeine, which is shown to consistently increase anxiety and is found in soda, chocolate, tea, coffee, and some painkillers such as Excedrin and Anacin. Try to engage children in the discussion of why you are limiting treats and be prepared to offer enticing replacements.

**Feeling awareness:** Help children recognize and label their feelings, and know where they are located in the body. Use your language to aid them in pairing sensations with words, until they develop their own. Be prepared to guess and wonder, over and over again. "I wonder if you are feeling so worried that your tummy hurts?" "It seems like you are so mad that your head is hurting." The more they know how they are feeling, where it is located, and why they feel that way, the better your chances for helping them find self-soothing strategies. Your stance should be curious, not judgmental or dismissive.

Children can also learn to do "body scans," thinking about their feelings from head to toes, and trying to think about the messages their bodies are trying to give them. Do they feel like running away, freezing, fighting, or talking endlessly? Where is the trigger located and what does it seem to say?

It is also useful for children to know how much of a feeling they have. We ask, "On a 1 to 10 scale, with 10 being so anxious you could throw up, and 1 being totally cool and calm, how worried are you right now? What can we do to get the number one point lower?" Awareness of the intensity of a feeling, especially for kids who tend to be black and white thinkers opens the window to many useful techniques. Once children see they can reduce their anxiety even a little, they will start to feel much more in control of themselves.

**Breathing:** Deep breathing is essential for relaxation; shallow breathing makes anxiety much worse. When we're upset, it takes most of us about 10 minutes to get reasonably relaxed when we consciously start breathing more slowly and deeply. Children need to learn how to breathe deeply when they're anxious, following these general guidelines: First practice this when everyone is calm. Tell them to put their hand on their belly where a belt would sit, and push out while inhaling. They should try to only breathe nine times in a minute with long, deep breaths. They can do this by counting to four while breathing in. Then, they should exhale slowly. Make sure your child has relaxed shoulders while doing this exercise. Younger children can pretend they are blowing up a balloon and watching it float up into the sky. Be sure to notice and praise your children when they are breathing well so they can become conscious of what it feels like physically to be less anxious.

## 4. Practice Mindful Awareness.

Parents and children can work together to stay in the present. Anxiety diminishes when we remain focused in the here and now, and in our bodies. Practice several times focusing internally and externally: alternating attention inward by saying "notice your breathing" and outward by commenting "now notice the chair you are sitting on," inward by saying "listen to your heart beating" and outward by saying "hear my voice speaking to you."

Some children become so anxious they seem to forget where they are. Keep children attuned to the present by orienting them: "You are safe here in the living room, I am here with you." Give them permission to replace anxious thoughts with relaxing images that you've discussed before. "Remember the happy, safe place we talked about? Well let's go there in our minds. Imagine you're all wrapped in a cozy towel after a swim in the ocean, and the sun is warm, and I remembered to bring that beach chair with the cup holder you like so you can sit in it, and we're about to have a yummy picnic." When children learn they can remain present and have some control over what they think about, they become less anxious.

## 5. Don't Listen When Worries Come.

Although this is a difficult technique for many children to master, it can be helpful for kids who tend to be obsessive worriers. First, children have to recognize when they are worrying. Then they can name it. It is helpful to give the worry its own name, for example some children we know have called it Mr. Anxiety, Worry Worm, Hornet, the Nudge, and Peanut Butter. The point here is that it isn't the child who is anxious and is a problem — it's anxiety that's "visiting" the child who has a problem. This strategy externalizes anxiety and lets kids see themselves as functionally independent of it. They can even cope with it by making choices to relax and have fun instead of letting worry take over. They can draw pictures of "Hornet," or make a puppet of him. Help your child think about ways to challenge and defeat worry: "Oh, Hornet is not going to let you enjoy going bowling even though you've been looking forward to it. What can you say to him so he'll go away for a while?"

## 6. Worry Well But Only Once.

Some children and adults get on worrying jags, with one worry leading to the next. Anxiety can be a runaway train. It is helpful, therefore, to allot time for worry saying, "We'll talk all about it, and then be done." Some children even benefit from a designated worry time set aside each day for them to share everything on their minds. We can note and appreciate that the child has a big worry, but then after about 10 minutes we need to get them to agree that, "The worry department is closed for the day." When the worry returns, offer reassurance and reiterate that this is already a done deal. Try to get the child to focus on what's next: "We already talked about that and it's settled for the time being. Now I need you to count out five forks and five knives and put them on the table."

## 7. Tell Stories.

Stories help children feel less isolated and defended, and they add logic and pattern to events. Tell them stories about people you know, other children, yourself as a child and now, and about themselves when they were younger. "I know a boy who..." "I sometimes feel..." "Last year when you..." "When Sammy was at the baseball game he..." Talk with them about the characters they learn about in books and movies, about how these fictional people cope with worries and triumphs, too. One of the sources of anxiety in foster children is their difficulty developing coherent narratives — they struggle to tell stories of their lives that seem logical and linear. The lack of coherence provides fertile ground for worry. These kids need the chance to develop this cause-and-effect thinking to help them feel more in control. Thus, storytelling is a critical component of anxiety management for them. The more they see the narrative logic of events, the less fearful they'll be about what is going to happen next.

## 8. Have a Little Fun.

Most foster children have had less happiness in their lives than they should have so they benefit all the more from increased opportunities for joy and pleasure on a daily basis. Be silly by crawling on the floor, making faces, and telling jokes. Help put laughter on the daily menu for your children. Make fun of yourself. Sadly, you may have to teach them to have fun. Are there television characters that hit a funny bone? What makes you laugh so hard that milk comes out of your nose? Anxiety and laughter are incompatible; children who are giggling are usually not too anxious. And the more time children spend having fun, the less they'll have for fretting.

## 9. Don't Overprotect.

Some parents see the worlds of their children get smaller because the stress of transitions and novelty causes too many melt downs and conflict. Well-intended, these parents have gotten into the habit of protecting their children and themselves from the feared situations. It is important to gradually attack anxiety head on and not let it win over family life, either. Exposure to a fear is necessary for your child to begin to overcome it. Additionally, children need to learn that often the anticipation is worse than the actual experience. The exposure doesn't have to be drastic — it's more like slowly entering cold water a little bit at a time.

Begin by role-playing with your child through a feared situation, backing it up to the most comfortable starting point. For example, if a child is afraid of dogs, he or she might be able to role-play with a stuffed animal, or a picture of a dog to begin. You will need to figure out a ladder of steps, gradually ending with exposure to the feared object such as touching a safe dog. When a step becomes easy, move to the next.

Take your time, and never proceed until the child is completely successful and confident along the way. You may have to break a step into even smaller steps to make it successful. Don't push too hard, and make sure you're engaging in other, less stressful activities, too. At the same time that you're helping your child to face his or her fears, you'll want to build his or her confidence and competence elsewhere. Sometimes a little boost of self-esteem can make a worry get smaller all by itself.

## 10. Reward Brave Behavior.

Many of the children we live and work with are heroes and survivors of frightening and tough lives. It is therefore important that we recognize their efforts, however small, to stay in control of themselves and their worries. Notice and praise brave behavior, being specific: "You got right in the car when I asked even though you were a little worried about seeing the doctor. Great job!" Keep your praise immediate and succinct. Over-praising and vague praising tend to backfire and make kids feel worse about themselves because they can't connect the words with their actual behaviors. If you use rewards such as money, points, activities, and stars to get children to stay bravely on track, make sure you're clear and consistent about the behavior, and why you're reinforcing it.

These 10 strategies will help your kids become less anxious over time. Keep in mind that even after many successes, anxiety is likely to rear its ugly head again, especially in times of increased stress. We need to let our children know that when they feel overwhelmed by fear and doubt, it's time to revisit the strategies that worked in the past. Remind them with a hug. There's no need to worry about the worry, and there are many effective ways to manage and defeat it.

*Martha Straus, PhD, is a professor in the Department of Clinical Psychology at Antioch University New England Graduate School in Keene, NH, and adjunct instructor in psychiatry at Dartmouth Medical School. Straus is the author of numerous articles and four books, including "No-Talk Therapy for Children and Adolescents," and more recently, "Adolescent Girls in Crisis: Intervention and Hope."*

*Melanie Ernould, MA, is a doctoral student in the Department of Clinical Psychology at Antioch University New England Graduate School. Ernould is currently working at Advocates Community Mental Health Center in Marlborough, Mass.*

# LOVE is Spelled T-I-M-E

*by Andrea B. Smith, PhD, and Linda L. Dannison, PhD*

*pause with your grandchild...*
*when others are hurrying by*

*walk with your grandchild...*
*when others find themselves running*

*talk with your grandchild...*
*when others prefer shouting*

*listen to your grandchild...*
*when others can find only frowns*

*play with your grandchild...*
*when others prefer to be entertained*

*praise your grandchild...*
*when others can only find fault*

*read with your grandchild...*
*when others prefer watching television*

*learn from your grandchild...*
*when others have given up their own curiosity*

*study with your grandchild...*
*when others have little interest in schoolwork*

*forgive your grandchild...*
*when others expect them to be perfect*

*hug your grandchild...*
*when others fail to sense the power of touch*

# PLACE Parenting
*By Kate Oliver, MSW, LCSW-C*

**PLACE Parenting**

**P**LAYFUL

**L**OVING

**A**CCEPTING

**C**URIOUS

**E**MPATHY

When you are caring for a child with any sort of attachment disturbance, you also have a child who is good at making you feel like you don't know what you are doing. In one training I went to on attachment disturbance, the presenter, Art Becker-Weidman, said one of the parents he worked with described it something like this: "It's like you, as the parent, are the control room for a radio station, then the kids come up and play with all the buttons until they find one that gets the response they are looking for. When they find that button that gets them what they want, they just keep flipping the switch over and over again." I have used this description with the parents and caregivers that come through my own practice and find it resonates deeply with them as well. What do you do when you are the caretaker for a child who is constantly pushing your buttons and finding creative ways to make you feel like you don't have a clue what you are doing?

Daniel Hughes and Art Becker-Weidman are working to popularize a parenting attitude that can work wonders if parents are able to maintain it when they have an attachment disordered child (or any child for that matter). It is called the PLACE mentality; it stands for: Playful, Loving, Accepting, Curious, Empathic. I find that while the words are familiar it can be easy to misinterpret the meanings of those words in this particular context so it helps to look at each word to see what we are talking about when it comes to parenting children using the PLACE mentality.

## PLAYFUL:

The most common misinterpretation of this quality that I hear from kinship care providers is that they believe I want them to throw a parade in their child's honor every time they do something desirable to the caregiver. What I really mean by being playful is just finding an approach that has a less authoritarian tone. Instead of telling kids where to go to find their glasses, encourage them to play a little game with you where they have to look at your face so you can give them a hint using your eyes about where the glasses are. Another example is when they look into your face and lie, come up with a playful response, "That's a good one. I've always known you were creative. Tell me another!" Often being playful can help everyone tone it down a notch. If you have a child with a history of abuse or neglect, it can also keep him or her from getting triggered into believing that he or she is in huge trouble and helps prevent the child from going into fight or flight mode so that you have some chance of the child hearing some of the words you are saying. A way to really get playful is to learn from a parent who really gets this stuff. Christine Moers is a mom raising adopted children with attachment issues. She posts vlogs on YouTube to help other parents (and to keep herself sane). Her video blog at *http://www.youtube.com/watch?v=HDAALaVG27k&feature=fvwrel* is a wonderful example of how to discipline in a playful way. I would recommend you look at her videos when you need help staying sane.

## LOVING:

When I think of saying things in a loving way to children, what helps me to stay in that place is remembering my purpose for saying the words in the first place. Yes, ultimately I may ask my child to do a task because I want it done. But the bigger picture reason for asking children to do a task is to teach them so that they know how to do it, to give them a system for tackling problems, to get them into the routine of caring for themselves and planning how to fit everything into a schedule, or something else like that. In the end, our job as guardians is to make it so children no longer need us in order to make it through the day. When we remember that we are asking children in our care to do something because we love them and want them to be happy, healthy adults, we can state requests in a more loving way. By remembering this, I believe the primary change is our tone of voice, which makes a world of difference to children who are used to being treated harshly and/or ignored altogether in the past.

## ACCEPTING:

One trap I see so many parents walk into is the argument with their child(ren) about whether their child is having a reasonable feeling or not. Both the child and care provider find this is a way to feel crazy pretty quickly and I would like to present an alternative... acceptance. Here is how it goes, maybe it sounds familiar:

> **Child comes down to breakfast dressed in a completely inappropriate outfit for school.**
>
> **Kinship care provider (being curious):** *Wow, is there something going on at school today? That's an interesting outfit.*
>
> **Child:** *I knew you wouldn't let me wear it. You never let me wear anything I want! You're such a witch! You want me to be the ugliest girl in school!*
>
> **Kinship care provider (accepting):** *That made you mad. I can see how you would be mad if you thought I wanted you to be the ugliest girl in school.*

It's that simple — do not engage in an argument about whether you want her to be the ugliest girl in school! If that is her belief in that moment, accept that her feeling is appropriate for the interpretation.

## CURIOUS:

In my office, I often frame this curiosity as being a "feelings detective." I tell kids I ask a lot of questions because I am a curious person and sometimes it takes me a while to understand things. Get curious about the children in your care. In the above example, rather than arguing about who wants whom to look ugly, you might get curious about it. "I wonder what made you think I wanted you to look ugly when I asked about your outfit." Another way to help with getting kids to understand you are curious (not judgmental) is to say something along the lines of, "I'm curious what got you so mad because I don't want you to feel that way again." When they tell you what got them mad, again make sure you avoid arguing about whether that is really what happened (accepting) and then...empathize.

## EMPATHY:

Empathy looks like this, "If I thought someone felt that way about me/said that to me/said that about me I can see how you would feel mad/sad/scared too." That's all empathy is...being able to see something from the viewpoint of another person. Empathy does not involve any discussion about whether someone is right or wrong for feeling the way they are feeling.

## So, why does this work?

It works because many children, especially children with a history of abuse or neglect, can find the things we need to do most often, educate, speak with authority, and parenting, to name a few, to be triggers to them of things that remind them of times they were hurt or neglected. When kids do not learn the typical role of parents early on, they easily misinterpret the actions of parental figures. Using the PLACE mentality is one way of reducing the number of triggers for a child, not to mention that it just makes caring for them more fun. I like it because it works with children without a traumatic history as well and I know that one of the many issues that can come up in a kinship care home is that of integrating children with greater emotional needs into the family setting without disturb-whothat are already there.

Of course, this is a quick overview of the PLACE mentality. It is important that if you feel you are in a position with a child where you need to utilize the PLACE attitude more and could use support in doing so, that you see a therapist who has an attachment informed practice.

*Kate Oliver, LCSW-C, is co-owner of A Healing Place, a private practice in Columbia, Md. Before opening her private practice, Oliver worked first at the Sexual Trauma, Treatment, Advocacy and Recovery Center (STTAR) in Columbia, Md. for five years. During her time with the STTAR Center, Oliver completed a year-long program where she earned a certificate in working with children and adolescents with attachment disorders. After learning more about attachment, Oliver went to work with incarcerated, pregnant mothers in Baltimore City as the clinical director for the program, Tamar's Children. Tamar's Children worked with an attachment protocol, The Circle of Security, which taught adults with a history of trauma and neglect to bond with their infants. She used this method with the residents and added an additional group for women already in the program who were going to be reunited with older children in foster and kinship care. In 2007, Ms. Oliver opened A Healing Place, where she now specializes in working with children with trauma and attachment related issues. Additionally, she has a blog, Help4YourFamily.com, where she writes about ways to help children and parents feel happier and healthier.*

# Behavior & Discipline

"*The kids who need the most love will ask for it in the most unloving of ways.*" *~Unknown*

# Why Doesn't Discipline Work the Way it Did in those 'Good Old Days'

*By Penny G. Davis, MA*

Many of us, who thought our days of parenting were over, and are now called upon to revisit this time of life for whatever reason, may find that it's a whole new ball game. Things have changed when it comes to raising kids, and the arena of discipline is often the most challenging. It just doesn't seem to work the way it did when we were kids...or even when we were parenting our own children. Most of us recall that if our parents said "jump," we jumped. We didn't say, "why do I have to jump?" or "how come I have to jump when my brother doesn't?" or whine "I don't LIKE jumping." We just did as we were told. It seemed to work fine for us...we turned out pretty OK. Or DID we? The point is this, "do what I say, when I say it, because I'm the adult," is the way most of us were raised, as were our parents before us and THEIR parents before them. It no longer appears to work quite so easily and many of us "older" adults wonder why this is, what has changed?

For generations this culture (and I will primarily speak of the North American culture) had a "top down" leadership style. Some led and others followed. This was true in government, the workplace, among races, between genders, and in the family. So, in the workplace the boss often ruled with an iron fist – workers did what they were told and had little input into how things ran, Caucasians held most of the positions of power and influence, men were perceived to be better and more powerful than women, and dads were the "boss of the family." So, for example, in the 1950's when I was growing up as part of the first generation of TV viewers, our family regularly watched "Father Knows Best," "Leave It To Beaver" and that "Nelson" family. Dads went to work, moms stayed at home, Dad did what he was told at work, Dad told Mom what to do at home, and Mom told kids what to do. On our TV sets, and in our culture in general, there were few people of color in positions of influence, and there were few, if any, women in the workplace. Almost all of our models of how the world worked were this 'top down' style of leadership. It makes sense that we would "do as we were told," because there were examples of this all around us. Our belief system told us some people make the rules and have the power and influence, and other people followed the rules and had no "say."

Things have changed (you've probably noticed this)! For those of us who are or have been in the "follower" role (and most of us have been), at some point we begin to feel that we have little or no control over our own lives or environment, we feel sad and hopeless; we might have difficulty standing up for ourselves (many of us have struggled with these feelings as adults as a result of being raised this way). When stuck in this role, eventually people begin to get mad. They begin to resist the "follower" role, they rebel, and some, eventually, band together with others and work toward changing things. We have had many, many examples of this in the past 50 years. We've had the minority rights movement spearheaded by Martin Luther King, whose message spoke of respect and dignity for ALL human beings, and the women's rights movement with a similar message. We've had changes in the workplace that now legislate the illegality of refusing to hire a person because of race, gender, age, sexual orientation, or other discriminatory reasons. Our culture is shifting from a "top down" model to a more horizontal one. When our children and grandchildren watch TV or absorb our culture in other ways, they no longer see those same messages of "do what I say, because I have the power." They see people of color and women both in the workplace, as well as in positions of power. A person of color, in fact, currently holds the MOST powerful position in our nation. They see workers having more control over how they do their jobs and sometimes even how companies are run. They see moms having equal status in the family. They see all people expecting to be treated with dignity and respect. This has filtered down into their lives in the family. Children now know, on some fundamental level, that they too are equal human beings and that they deserve to be treated with dignity and respect. Of course, our little ones are not lying in their crib holding a placard that says, "I deserve to be treated with dignity and respect," nor are they attending equal rights marches. What they ARE doing is making the same statement with their behavior. They are asking why, they are engaging us in power struggles, and they are "talking back." Does this mean we should abandon all discipline? No, absolutely not. Adults still need to be leaders as we teach our children how to be responsible and we need to model how to do the "right thing" even when no one is looking. We need to look for new tools that demonstrate firmness — guidelines, limits, and expectations — while also being kind and respectful of our children (grandchildren) and their intrinsic worth as human beings.

*"Children now know, on some fundamental level, that they too are equal human beings and that they deserve to be treated with dignity and respect."*

In early childhood, this might look like giving them limited choices, within safety guidelines. Saying, "would you like toast or cereal for breakfast? You choose" can be an easy way of showing respect, as well as helping to build a sense of personal power for this little one. With older kids, engaging them in a dialog that encourages them to think through a situation is often helpful... "What happened? How did it happen? What were you trying to accomplish? What might you do differently next time?" These are all powerful ways to be respectful of the child, to help him or her learn from mistakes and to figure out how to fix a situation. Aren't these questions helping to build the qualities of good decision-making and problem-solving we all want for our children/grandchildren, long-term?

## What about those kids we care for who have histories of trauma?

Discipline, and the use of new relationship-based tools, is even more important for children who have experienced abuse or neglect, or who have had multiple, inconsistent caregivers during their early years of life. These kids often operate from the "survival" part of their brain. As an infant or toddler, if the basics were not met (food, shelter, safety, love), THAT is where they are stuck. They may be 4 years old, 8 years old, or 16 years old, but the messages that they got about not being safe, not being cared for, not being protected, and other messages are still operating within their brains. This is not conscious, it is "out

## Recommended Reading:

*Positive Discipline:* Jane Nelsen, EdD

*Beyond Consequences, Logic and Control:* Heather Forbes, LCSW

*The Whole Brain Child:* Daniel J. Siegel, MD

of awareness." Anytime a child with a history of trauma feels threatened in any way, the survival part of the brain, which is primarily the "fight/freeze/flight" part kicks in. So, for example, we might say to our 10-year-old grandson, "Go clean your room," which to us feels like a pretty harmless directive. To our grandson something entirely different may be playing out...maybe he forgot to clean his room, or he doesn't know how, or he thinks he can't do it. Whatever is going on translates as "fear." His infant brain kicks in and he believes his survival might be at risk (again — totally out of awareness on his part). He doesn't know what might happen now. He might get hit, he might get sent away, you might not love him anymore, so his ONLY possible response in this moment is "flight/freeze/fight." He may come unglued and start screaming at you, he may run out of the room, he may look at you blankly, like he didn't hear a word you said. Any and all of these responses throw us into a tailspin. Yikes, we think...what is wrong with him...I only asked him to clean his room!

So, for kids with trauma histories it is extremely important to focus on the relationship, rather than "fixing the behavior." HOW we phrase things becomes important, such as, rather than saying, "go clean your room," it might be wise to say "How about you and I listen to some music together while you get that room tidied up?"

We need to begin to ask different questions when we live with children who have trauma in their backgrounds. Instead of "How can I control his behavior?" or "How can I get her to mind me?" or "How can I fix this?" we need to ask, "How can I build my relationship with him right now?" "What might be going on for her right now, and how can I help?" or "What can I do right now to help him feel safe and loved?"

One of powerful quotations that I often use when working with caregivers of children who have experienced trauma in their lives is, "We cannot fix the child, we can only provide the environment for the child to heal." I believe this healing environment is possible only with the tools of a more respectful, relationship-based model of parenting.

*Penny G. Davis has been a parenting educator, teacher trainer, and consultant for more than 30 years. She has held a number of professional positions in non-profit agencies, schools, and colleges working directly with parents, teachers, children, and early childhood staff, as well as foster/adoptive caregivers and social workers. She is a Certified Positive Discipline Associate and a Certified Lead Trainer with the Positive Discipline Association. Davis earned a bachelor's degree in sociology from the University of Alberta in Edmonton, Canada, and her MA in Human Development from Pacific Oaks College in Pasadena, Calif. Her graduate work was focused on attachment, brain development, and behavior of children, as related to those who have experienced chronic trauma (abuse and/or neglect). As a result of this work, she has extensive experience training social service staff and caregivers regarding behavior management of children with trauma histories.*

# Appropriate Boundaries in Parenting

*By Sue Laney*

## What do parents most want from children?

Is it obedience — for children to do what parents think is best whether for the benefit of the child or for the parent? Could it be love — that parents want their children to love them unconditionally as parents try to love their children unconditionally? What about becoming good citizens who are responsible, pleasant to be around, non-offensive to others, and working toward success and independence? And, does love equal respect? So, how do parents get what they most want from their children? The answer is setting appropriate boundaries. These boundaries look and feel different depending on the chosen parenting style. There are typically three styles of parenting with some parents jumping from one style to the other depending on what point or convenience they believe is important to make at the time.

## Lines in the Sand

The first boundary style is called "lines in the sand" as described here:

Four-year-old Jody and her mother are eating lunch at a local restaurant. Jody wants gum out of the gumball machine and asks her mom for some money. When Mom says, "Not now, sweetie," Jody continues to ask and Mom continues to deny the request. Mom decides to call a friend on her cell phone and while Mom is distracted Jody goes into her mom's wallet, gets a handful of change, puts the coins in the machine and comes back to the table with some gum in her mouth. After a bit, Mom finally notices Jody chewing gum and tells her friend the whole story as Jody listens. Mom expresses to her friend she just doesn't understand why Jody doesn't obey her. Jody is never personally scolded for her poor choice or instructed how to make a better choice.

Although many parents want to have fun with their children, when a parent draws a line in the sand as the boundary for the child to follow, the relentless waves of the tide come in and wash the line away each time it is drawn. Therefore, what did Jody learn? If this parenting style is used often, Jody will relentlessly test her mom and other authority figures just to see where the boundaries actually are. Often, foster parents are unsure of where to place boundaries on foster children and may be overly lenient to compensate for the hurt foster children have experienced. "Lines in the sand" parenting tells foster children that 1) they are not good enough to have set or standard boundaries and will need to set their own, 2) the parent is incapable of setting appropriate boundaries, or 3) they are special and don't need to follow the same boundaries as other family members. This parenting style leads birth and foster children toward rebellion, breeding chaos, fighting, disrespect, and a low sense of self-worth.

## The Brick Wall

The second style of parenting is described as a "brick wall." Picture it … a tall, thick, red brick wall. Does it signify protection, strength, a sense of durability; or could it be described as more cold, looming, harsh and impenetrable? Children need the protection and strength from parents but never do they need parents to be unwelcoming, forbidding, rigid, or unforgiving. Children also need the opportunity to learn to make good choices. A safe and comfortable home environment is where children can experience many opportunities to practice making choices. Being allowed to make choices encourages confidence.

If children find the answer to their requests always being "no," or a place where guilt and unforgiveness is the rule of the day, then those children will seek acceptance elsewhere and usually in unfavorable settings. This parenting style also leads children to rebellion, breeding chaos, fighting, disrespect, and a low sense of self-worth. Often children run from rigidity because their inherent sense of free will or freedom of choice is being squelched.

Foster children have often been reared in homes which have neglected their needs either through moving or non-existent boundaries, such as "lines in the sand;" or strict boundaries described as "brick wall" parenting.

## The Deep-Rooted Tree

The two extremes in parenting have been explained, leaving the third parenting style of the "deep-rooted tree." Picture a tall, sturdy tree whose branches spread out over the yard giving shelter, shade, beauty, freedom, creativity, recreation, and a feeling of being tested over time.

One of the benefits of this parenting style is the manner in which life's storms are weathered — with grace, flexibility, and wisdom. There's no room for arrogance, impatience, or pity. A quiet strength is rooted in good soil, rich with healthy nutrients expressing the importance of taking care of oneself and others. There are no inappropriate expectations nor judgement, but a joy when family members choose to spend time together under the tree. Delightful flowers and foliage often bring forth delicious fruit allowing others to share from the bounty and the beauty this style offers. When the storms come, deeply planted roots hold the tree upright with a strong trunk. The branches know just how far to bend without breaking from the wind. And so it is with this parenting style.

As children need strength and wisdom from their parents, they also need flexibility. "Deep-rooted" parenting has a strong foundation supporting children to learn from their personal experiences through proper guidance in making effective choices. These teaching moments become life lessons which mold children's character and prepare them to respond appropriately in future situations.

As foster parents, strength with flexibility offered to all children shows parents care about children as individuals, that parents believe in children and trust their ability to make good choices for their level of development. Children experience freedom and peace when acting within appropriate boundaries. In return, through time, parents will receive the love and respect that they demonstrate to others.

Although flexibility is the key element in appropriate boundaries, determining how far a parent is willing to go and being consistent in not going beyond the boundary limit is crucial.

A rubber band has several uses but is most used for holding things close or together. It can only be stretched so far before it pops. When the band does pop, it is no longer as useful; it stings anything near it; and if the ends are tied together again to resume its initial purpose, there is less room to perform its purpose inside the band. Therefore flexibility has its limits.

Appropriate parenting boundaries are defined as: the structure from which to operate, which is geared for protection and effective living, offering freedom to act within the limits, while encompassing positive and negative consequences for reinforcement of the structure.

## Without Boundaries We Have Chaos, Conflict, and Confusion.

When setting boundaries ask the question, "Is this boundary used for protection and teaching or is it for my comfort?" Keeping the child's best interest at heart will help to ensure boundaries remain appropriate. Use boundaries suitable for the appropriate age and stage of the child's development and use reasonable punishment to fit the crime. Pay attention to the behavior you want to see by using many more rewards than punishments.

The best rewards are praise, hugs, or a pat on the back, which don't cost any money. And if you want children to obey, they have to trust in you — not just trust you, but in you — trusting that you always have their best interests at heart.

*Sue Laney is the author of* "**Nurturing God's Way Parenting Program for Christian Families®**", "**Basic Home Visitation Skills™ Training Curriculum and Survival Kit for Parents™**" *and* "**Nurturing Your Home® Training Curriculum**." *She is the president and CEO of the Family Nurturing Center of Georgia and a national trainer/consultant for Nurturing Parenting Programs®. Currently she is the project director of Nurturing Georgia's Families® Project.*

*"Put aside your preconceived expectations about your child's behavior relative to his or her age. At-risk adopted children may appear to be a certain age physically, but inside they are playing catch-up-emotionally, behaviorally, and developmentally."*
*~ Dr. Karyn Purvis*

# Don't Use an Elephant Gun to Shoot a Mouse
*By Walt Piszchala*

I remember sitting in the office of my first supervisor as a young and inexperienced child care worker, in Warehouse Point, Connecticut, at the State Receiving Home. This is a facility run by the Connecticut Department of Children and Families, the year was 1975. Silas W. Davis, a man I would come to view as both a mentor and a father figure was speaking to me about his personal philosophy of disciplining children for inappropriate behavior. The words he spoke to me seemed strange and it was a while before it registered with me. He said, "I want you to remember this, *'Don't use an elephant gun to shoot a mouse...*"

Fast forward several months later, I was experiencing my first baptism under fire with an angry and oppositional 15-year-old boy who was telling me in plain English that would make any sailor or truck driver proud, what I could do with my rules. Enraged by this blatant lack of respect, both for myself and the rules of the cottage, I proceeded to operate on pure emotion and adrenaline and totally ignored what Davis had told me in his office. You see it is one thing to remain calm reviewing a programmatic rule and even possibly role playing a situation in training under controlled circumstances, but it is quite another experiencing it in real life. It didn't just affect the young man in question and me; it was in front of 17 other children and several of my co-workers.

Being young and inexperienced, I did what every parent since the dawn of time has done when their child goes into a meltdown, and does something either at home, school, or church to the embarrassment of both themselves as well as their family, I brought out my own personal elephant gun. Needless to say I turned a routine verbal intervention into an exasperating incident which damaged not only my relationship with this child, but everyone who was witness to it. I always want to remember my personal elephant gun story so I can help every person I train to never have to experience what I did.

I would like to share with the readers, one specific area of my own Verbal De-escalation Curriculum that I teach to foster and adoptive parents in local and national conferences. I offer a five-step approach to setting limits that can be adapted to any age, population, or functioning group.

## Step One: Use language that calms.

Tell your child in language that I refer to as "affect neutral" what it is that you are asking, not telling, them to either start, or stop, doing. An example of each would be:

A. *Your child gets into a heated argument with a sibling and becomes increasingly aggressive with both body language and verbal threats.* In this situation you are setting limits to have them "stop" engaging in an inappropriate behavior. It's not the argument that is our issue; it is the aggressive body language as well as the threats. If you start trying to intervene and stop your child from typical age appropriate behaviors, or sibling rivalries, you will never get anything accomplished. In addition to my "elephant gun" metaphor I always stress that in order to act in the best interest of the out-of-control individual we need to clearly be in control of our own feelings and emotions first. Have you had a bad day at work? Are there existing marital or financial problems in your relationship? These personal issues can exacerbate the situation and cause you to bring out your own personal elephant gun to try to settle a situation.

**B.** *The second example of asking them to, in this case, "start" doing something is at 7 p.m., dinner is finished, the table is cleared, and chores complete, it is now homework time. Tommy has seated himself in front of the TV and is about to play his favorite video game while everyone else has gone to their rooms and cracked open their books.* In this situation, an example of bringing out your own elephant gun would be to go over to the TV, take the remote, and "click." We all know it is not going to end there. A line in the sand has been drawn and someone is going to lose. And, the unfortunate reality is it is going to be you!

## Step Two: Tell them why...

You must clearly and concisely inform the child why you are asking, not telling, him or her to do something. The reason "why" should always go back to the common theme of "because the rules of the house" say that from 7 to 9 p.m. it is homework time and nothing else. Do not let the situation become personal, keep the focus on them, not you.

## Step Three: Review the consequences.
*(This can be a deadly minefield for a parent to navigate through.)*
The classic elephant gun, "negative consequence," is an empty threat. For instance, "if you don't go to your room right now you are going to lose TV for one month!" Now you know full well there has never been a parent in the history of the world who could stick to their guns for an entire month of no TV. Isn't the primary point of consequences — both positive and negative — to teach children a lesson? What lesson are you imparting to your child if you bring out the negative consequences first?

They begin thinking back on all of the times that the adults in their lives have yelled, screamed, and used negative reinforcements to try to change their behavior. Always try to remember, "in order to change a child's behavior you have to first fundamentally change the way they view their world." What are we doing if all we engage in are threatening, negative consequences using our own elephant guns?

So what else can we rely on instead of negative consequences? How about starting your intervention with a positive consequence for complying with your request, not demand, first? Sometimes the positive consequence will be a tangible reward, however other times the positive consequence may simply be not earning a negative consequence. Try it sometime; it may surprise you with its effect on your child.

*Now, once you've gone over the positive consequences for complying, you must then let them know what the negative consequences will be for failure to cooperate.*

## Step Four: Give them some time.

You have to give them a brief cooling off period, no more than a few minutes. Trying to coach an answer out of children after all of this is too overwhelming. They need a few minutes to process everything, to make the best possible choice for themselves as well as lose the least amount of face with their siblings.

## Step Five: Be prepared to enforce.

You need to be ready to do what you said would happen, both positively as well as negatively. The two biggest mistakes you can make at this stage are to not follow through with the positive consequence you said would happen, and being a parent that says, "This is it! No more chances! You better not do that again!" If this is your personal elephant gun, then I say give them your car keys, your Visa or MasterCard with directions to the nearest shopping mall, because at this point they own you. You have lost your credibility with the child as well as the rest of his or her siblings.

You all have a profound impact on your children's lives. You are welcoming children into your homes who in many cases have been damaged beyond our own imaginations and we are charged with the task of nurturing them into healthy and productive citizens of our society.

*The Connecticut Department of Children and Families employed Walt Piszchala for 33 years, working with children in a variety of capacities, in residential care. For 27 of those years Piszchala worked as a trainer in the field of Crisis Intervention and Health and Safety, teaching both verbal and physical intervention techniques and CPR, AED, First Aid, Blood Borne Pathogens. Piszchala retired from the Connecticut Juvenile Training School as a full-time training coordinator. His main focus had been in the development and implementation of a comprehensive behavior management and crisis intervention program. From 1997 to 2006 Piszchala was an adjunct staff trainer at the Department of Children and Families training academy. Since retiring in January 2007, Piszchala has become a member of the training faculty for the Connecticut Association of Foster and Adoptive Parents. He offers courses in verbal de-escalation and works with oppositional and defiant children. For more information, visit www.piszchala-associates.com. This article originally appeared in* **Fostering Families Today** *magazine.*

# Child Neglect and Hoarding Food

*By Charley Joyce, MSW, LICSW*

Food hoarding is a common issue displayed by children who have experienced early childhood abuse and neglect. Food hoarding can be central in a child's world and resistant to change. Additionally, hoarding food behavior can bedevil and bewilder parents. So why does a child hoard food? Often food hoarding is directly connected to significant neglect that the child has experienced in consistently having his or her basic needs for life sustaining food denied or inadequately met. As a result, the child is forced to become prematurely self-reliant in meeting his or her own basic needs. For example, in a situation where the parent is chemically dependent resulting in inconsistency in providing and having food available, it would be reasonable that when food is available that a child would view this as an opportunity. It would be logical that a "survival mentality" would be for the child to respond to the availability of food in self-reliant ways which could include over-eating and hoarding food in secretive ways. In neglectful situations, food hoarding is a wise alternative to ongoing food deprivation.

What can be confusing and frustrating to foster-adoptive parents is why food hoarding continues when the child is being properly cared for and has no apparent reason to continue to hoard food? Unfortunately, child neglect often leaves a child insecure, seeing him or herself as unworthy of care and lacking in a sense of partnership with kinship caregivers. They may not feel that their foster-adoptive parents are available and sensitive drawing this false conclusion from their previous "blueprint" of being victimized by negligent parenting.

When trying to positively impact food hoarding, we hope to move the child from solitary and secret self-parenting behavior to a world of meeting his or her needs within a healthy parent-child relationship. We want to avoid drawing battle lines around food. If we lock the pantry, the refrigerator, the kitchen, we create a "mine and yours" mentality, one the child is familiar with from the past. Designing family interventions should be preceded by a close look at the child's function of hoarding food which is, at all costs, to avoid food deprivation caused by neglect.

Several examples of interventions that are designed to focus on the function of neglect-based food hoarding include:

**Food baskets:** Provide food baskets in the home that incorporate the child's input in creation and consist of snacks that are healthy and appealing to the child. The child should be told the food baskets will be re-filled and are a "better alternative" than hoarding. If the child hoards the food basket, set limits but do not discontinue. Some schools will also cooperate with food baskets, especially if the child is prone to take other students' snacks.

**Backpacks:** When packing lunches for school or events, pack a "special container" of food that can be removed and is with the child. This provides a traveling sense of food security and food availability for the child.

**Coupling nurturing with food:** Always positively reinforce any progress the child makes on hoarding behavior. If the child utilizes a food basket, nurture the child when he or she seeks items from the food basket. Positively comment on how all family members are always fed. Weave this message into mealtimes and have this message commented on by various family members.

**Teach food regulation:** If the child has a tendency to gorge, set a "food time out" after a complete meal is consumed. Make certain this applies to all family members. The goal is to assist the child in learning to experience a sense of "fullness." The "food time out" should not be presented as denying food, but rather delaying additional eating for a prescribed period of time. Describe how the physical sensation of "fullness" feels. Fifteen minutes after the completion of a meal is an estimate of the time before fullness will be experienced.

As with all behavior and emotional challenges, a child's special needs and individual circumstances should be considered when designing interventions. Additionally, professional therapeutic assistance can offer help in the assessment and treatment of food issues. In an effort to understand the function of food hoarding, the following questions can assist in a parent's understanding of his or her child's food hoarding.

- Could there be psychiatric or biological issues contributing to the hoarding?

- Does the child's history reveal reasons for fixation on eating?

- Does the child substitute a food fixation for a loving relationship with parents?

- Are there things that trigger eating problems in the child?

- Is the child displaying an emotional neediness in the way he or she eats?

It is important to understand how the child's food issues impact you as a parent. Become aware of your own food issues and explore if they influence your ability or willingness to look at the child's problem with an open mind and creative flexibility. Also study yourself to determine if the child's food hoarding personally threatens your role as a provider/nurturer.

*Excerpts taken from "**Behavior with a Purpose**" Charley Joyce, LICSW, and Rick Delaney, PhD. Copyright 2009, TX ul-271-754; cannot be reproduced without permission*

*Charley Joyce, MSW, LICSW, has been a social worker for 35 years. He is the co-author of the book "**Behavior with a Purpose**" and a contributing author of the book "**Assessing Youth Behavior.**" He began his career as a VISTA volunteer and has worked as the clinical director of a psychiatric facility, as an outpatient therapist, supervisor of outpatient therapists, as a foster care caseworker, and as a clinical director of treatment foster care services. He is currently in private practice in Bismarck, ND. On a part time basis, he teaches in the social work program at the University of North Dakota and develops online trainings and training DVDs through the Foster Parent College, Eugene, Oregon. Annually he provides numerous trainings for foster-adopt parents and child welfare professionals. He earned a master of social work degree from the University of Iowa and he has completed post-graduate education in family therapy funded by the Bush Foundation. He has been married to the same person for 35 years and they have two adult daughters and a grandson.*

# Foster Children And Cruelty To Animals

*By Charley Joyce, MSW, LICSW*

## Innocent or Problematic?

A childhood behavior that deserves attention from parents, and others involved in the care of children, is childhood cruelty to animals. The initial step in assessing the serious- ness of a child's striking-out toward animals begins by reviewing the intent, frequency and pattern of the child's behavior. At times, children will innocently mistreat an animal. As an example, a young child may pull a cat's tail not understanding that it is hurtful to the cat. In this innocent example, the cat would generally react to the child, resulting in the child becoming startled and also causing the child to feel a sense of regret for hurting the cat. Ideally a parent would also explain to the child that this is hurtful to the cat, reinforcing that animals need to be treated with care. Generally, if the mistreatment was an innocent act by the child, the type of behavior described in the example will extinguish as a result of the child learning from the cat's response, coupled with parental input and the child's internal emotional response. Unfortunately, if a child consistently hurts animals, seeks ani- mals to hurt, and does not respond to parental interventions, a problem could exist.

## Why Would a Foster Child be Cruel to Animals?

We know that a common reason that children are in foster or kinship care is because of child abuse and neglect. The feelings of being abused physically, sexually, or neglected can cause a mixture of complex hurt and angry feelings in the child who has been victimized. These feelings often become overwhelming for the child and can be acted out through a combination of internalized and externalized behavior. As a result, a child who has been abused and is angry might displace anger onto a vulnerable animal. The cruelty can become a way to release internalized aggression that the child cannot express in appropriate ways. There might also be an emotional gratification for the child in being able to be in complete control and dominance of an animal's safety, pain, and life. Additionally, the psychological process of re-enactment can be a dynamic in cruelty to animals. For example, I once con- sulted in regard to a youth, who at a young age, was forced to be sexual with dogs. Past the point of her removal from her home where she was being sexually abused, she continued to display this behavior with dogs.

## What Can Be Done To Help Children Who Are Cruel to Animals?

Unfortunately, intentional childhood cruelty to animals can be linked to a lack of con- science development. It is essential that youth who display intentional cruelty to animals receive psychological assessment and treatment. A comprehensive treatment model should include:

- Establishing clear boundaries for the child's contact with animals. Adult supervi- sion is recommended whenever the child has contact with animals. In extreme cases, animals may need to be removed to a setting where the child does not have access to them.

- Within the limit of confidentiality, information should be provided to other settings where the child might have contact with animals such as day care, relative's homes, or other places.

- Observed, appropriate contact with animals should be positively reinforced.

- If the youth is a victim of abuse and/or neglect, the child should be involved in therapy that helps the youth heal from these experiences.

- Therapy that is focused on teaching skills for effective anger recognition and expression is an important component.

- A therapy component that focuses on empathy development is recommended.

- Parental consultation and/or involvement in the child's therapy is essential.

In closing, I want to return to the scenario of the youth who I mentioned earlier who would become sexual with dogs. That youth experienced a comprehensive treatment approach such as described above. She responded well to treatment and responded extremely well to the foster family's care and structure. When I discontinued my involvement, her sexualized behavior with dogs had discontinued and the foster family that she had been placed with was considering adoption on her behalf.

*Charley Joyce, MSW, LICSW, has been a social worker for 35 years. He is the co-author of the book "Behavior with a Purpose" and a contributing author of the book "Assessing Youth Behavior." He began his career as a VISTA volunteer and has worked as the clinical director of a psychiatric facility, as an outpatient therapist, supervisor of outpatient therapists, as a foster care caseworker, and as a clinical director of treatment foster care services. He is currently in private practice in Bismarck, ND. On a part time basis, he teaches in the social work program at the University of North Dakota and develops online trainings and training DVDs through the Foster Parent College, Eugene, Ore. Annually he provides numerous trainings for foster-adopt parents and child welfare professionals. He earned a masters in social work degree from the University of Iowa and he has completed post-graduate education in family therapy funded by the Bush Foundation. He has been married to the same person for 35 years and they have two adult daughters and a grandson. For more information visit www.charleyjoyce.com.*

# Lying: Why & What To Do About It.

*By Charley Joyce, MSW, LICSW*

If you have never told a lie, please quit reading this article now. If you are still reading, chances are you are like most people and have periodically told "little white lies." Most of us view being honest as a goal to shoot for, but we have probably been guilty of spinning the truth or omitting certain parts of the whole story. However, it seems that some youth, especially youth who have suffered from maltreatment, take lying to an extreme. So what are some of the purposes of lying for youth who have been maltreated and what can we do about it?

The following purposes of lying for youth who have been maltreated are drawn from my practice experiences and literature research on the topic of maltreatment, as well as thepractice experiences of others.

**Children lie out of a sense of fear.** Many youth who have been abused live their lives in fear of how adults might react to them. They are experts at "reading" situations and trying to predict if they might upset adults or others who could potentially harm them. They often develop a protective defense system that may over react to you, as a kinship caregiver. This predictive defense is especially activated when the youth sees you as angry, frustrated, or when he or she "predicts" you might become upset. Behaviorists refer to this as punishment-avoidance. Often, kinship caregivers don't realize the child is reacting in this manner, they just conclude the child is lying, seemingly without reason.

**Children who lie out of fear.** As with all children, it is important to learn as much as possible about the youth before they come to live with you. If you learn the child has a history of maltreatment and lies out of fear, be patient as this will not change quickly. Become aware of your voice tone and physical presence. Attempt to model using your personal characteristics in a manner that models safety and problem solving. Attempt to teach the child that negotiation, compromise, and listening all precede accusing.

**Children lie because it has become a pattern of behavior.** Some people refer to lying that has become a pattern of behavior as pathological lying. In these types of situations, lying has often been modeled by adults so the child learns lying as a way to meet his or her needs in multiple situations. In simple terms, lying has been presented to the child as normal. And since lying has been presented as normal, and has worked for the child, it will not change easily. Usually kinship caregivers will pickup if lying is a pattern. It's baffling to kinship caregivers because it seems that the child will lie about things where there is no reason to lie.

**How to support change with a youth who has a pattern of lying:** If a youth has lying as a pattern of behavior, it is important to see this as a treatment issue for the child in the home. A model for responding to this type of lying can be a consistent combination of teaching honesty, allowing for a change from a dishonest response to an honest response, applying consequences when necessary, and using "statements of facts." To illustrate this through an example, lets assume "Johnny" has told you an obvious lie. You might want to state: "Johnny, I don't think that's true, because this is what I know about the situation, why don't you try again?" A follow-up statement could be: "You know we don't consequence for telling the truth." Remember the boundary for this type of approach is that the lying won't be consequenced if the truth is told, but the behavior behind the lie may need to be consequenced based on the severity of the behavior. If the child continues to tell an obvious lie, restate your "statement of facts" and ignore his or her efforts to convince you to believe the lie.

**Lying as a way to feel important.** Children will often lie as a way to make themselves feel important. This often takes the form of exaggerating accomplishments and/or experiences. In a paradoxical way, there is a purpose to this type of lying that is positive. It often is a way for the youth to try and receive attention from the caregiver and to be recognized as important and worthwhile. Additionally, a twist on this type of lying is that a youth may lie over seemingly insignificant issues in order to "save face." Unfortunately, they have not learned, nor internalized, that we all make mistakes and they will not be harshly judged as a result. This type of lying is often present in youth who experience low self-esteem.

**How to support change with a youth who lies as a way to feel important.** Often this type of lying will lessen, or extinguish, with increased maturity and confidence. If the child you are caring for displays this type of lying, try to eliminate his or her need to do so. Place significant attention on building self-esteem, in a consistent, targeted way. Make it a point to recognize the youth's real accomplishments with interest. Talk about how mistakes and successes are the mixture of life. Amplify his or her strengths.

**Lying as a way to exploit others.** Hopefully you will not see this type of lying often and we should be careful about over diagnosing this type of lying. Lying to exploit has as its purpose victimizing others who are vulnerable for personal gain. A central theme is having power over others and controlling them through the threat of intimidation or harm. Some of the causes of this type of lying include a history with caregivers who were abusive, exploitative, unreliable, and unresponsive. It is generally seen in combination with other anti-social behaviors.

**How to respond, and to attempt to create change, with a youth who lies to exploit.** Generally the response to exploitative lying should be direct, clear and focus on holding the youth responsible for the lying. If the lying includes activity that is illegal, legal consequences should be applied. If you are fostering a youth with this type of lying, it is important that you work closely with other helping professionals in order to avoid being drawn into manipulative maneuvering.

*Excerpts taken from "Behavior with a Purpose: Thoughtful Solutions to Common Problems of Adoptive, Foster and Kinship Youth" By Charley Joyce, LICSW, & Richard Delaney, Ph.D. Cannot be reproduced without permission.*

*Charley Joyce, MSW, LICSW, has been a social worker for 35 years. He is the co-author of the book "Behavior with a Purpose" and a contributing author of the book "Assessing Youth Behavior." He began his career as a VISTA volunteer and has worked as the clinical director of a psychiatric facility, as an outpatient therapist, supervisor of outpatient therapists, as a foster care caseworker, and as a clinical director of treatment foster care services. He is currently in private practice in Bismarck, ND. Annually he provides numerous trainings for foster-adopt parents and child welfare professionals.*

# Helping Older Children With Bathroom Related Issues
*By Kate Oliver, MSW, LCSW-C*

No one wants to talk about it. It's a messy issue, and it stinks...literally. In my practice I see quite a few children who, at a much older age than usual, have bathroom issues, where either they wet themselves at night or during the day. Some even soil themselves. It is often a difficult issue for caregivers to bring up, and there are times I have seen a child for months before anyone is even willing to mention it, even though it is one of the questions I ask during my initial caregiver visit for children in foster or kinship care or pre-adoptive placements. Many of the caregivers whot come to me say it is the most embarrassing of all the issues the child in their care has. It is also the thing that can make adults angry the fastest. After all, if you have a 10-year-old who just wet themselves in your car, it is easy to forget that there might be more going on than lack of self-control. Instead, we tend to focus on the fact that your car smells like urine and a 10-year-old did it!

## To Fix It, You Must Know Where It Comes From

When a child has a behavior like enuresis (wetting during the night or daytime) or encopresis (soiling), I always look for the root cause. It is important to know where this problem starts because often by knowing where something starts, we can figure out how to fix it in the most loving way possible. In this article I am going to focus on daytime wetting and soiling, as I believe that bed-wetting is an easier issue to find information about and can have a different origin than daytime wetting and soiling which I see most often in children with a history of trauma and neglect.

The first step in tackling any issue the children in your care have is understanding the origin of the problem. As a wise professor of mine once said, "If you know where it started, you know how to fix it." With daytime wetting and soiling it is absolutely essential to start at the beginning. You can get help figuring out the origin of the problem by asking the following questions:

**1. Has the child seen a doctor about this issue?**
The first place to start with any problems involving the bladder is always with a child's doctor. Even if your child has not been complaining about a bladder issue. Even if you asked all the

questions that go along with having a bladder infection, still go to get tested. This is important, especially if the child in your care has a history of neglect, since he or she will be more likely to be out of touch with his or her body so may not be alert to discomfort until it is a major problem. Additionally, even when there is a mental health issue related to a child's enuresis or encopresis, some children require a medical intervention because, especially for a child that holds onto bowel movements, there can be a cycle of holding onto bowel movement's followed by a painful releasing that can require a doctor's help in order to stop the pain that reinforces the holding of the bowel movement's in the first place.

### 2. "Was this child properly potty-trained?"

This may seem like a strange question to ask if you have an 8-year-old, however, as a kinship care provider, you may have more insight than other caregivers into this issue. Was the child in your care potty trained by an abusive, or actively drug-using parent, child-care worker, grandparent, or someone else. during the time when people normally get potty-trained (anywhere from 2-4.5 years old)? If you even think the answer might be yes, knowing what you do about your family, then the child may not have been taught in the ways that he or she was able to understand. It may be that no one ever walked the child through proper wiping procedure after going to the bathroom. It may be that no one ever taught the child how to tell if he or she needed to go. A child may have a developmental lag in this area because he or she was not able to "master" the developmental milestones that go with being properly potty trained. Additionally, if a child was not properly trained, he or she may not have developed the muscles that we do not even think about which we use every day to control our bladder that keep us from our own embarrassing issues.

### 3. "Does this child have trauma associated with the bathroom?"

It may be that a child avoids the bathroom because some bad stuff happened in and/or related to a bathroom at some point, or, the child may have experienced trauma related to wetting or soiling. Potty training is reported to be the developmental step during which a child is most likely to experience abuse. If you have a child who has experienced trauma, ask yourself if he or she may be avoiding the bathroom because it reminds the child of something he or she would rather not think about. Maybe it was a place the child hid from someone. Maybe it was a place where the child or someone else he or she loved got hurt. Maybe the child was beaten or threatened with harm if he or she had an accident during potty-training. For children with severe trauma, it may be that they experience a "trigger" wherein they feel terrified, and/or they may experience a traumatic re-enactment, that is, they are re-experiencing a traumatic situation as their brain's way of making sense of it and the experience is so intense that they end up peeing on or soiling themselves. A quick example to explain the ways in which the brain can respond when triggered comes from when I was a kid myself:

*One night I woke up to a small fire in my room. No one was hurt and the house survived but it was scary. The fire truck came and it was pretty clear that things would have been way worse had I not woken up when I did.*

Many years later when my children were small, I remember taking my daughters out to play in the snow. It was a cold day and several people had made fires in their fireplaces. When I went to enter my own home (where we did not have a fire lit), I had a moment when the smell of smoke hit my nose, probably from a nearby chimney. I handed my youngest daughter to my husband and yelled, "Stay out of the house, there's a fire!" Then I proceeded to run into the house, looking for smoke so I could see where the fire was.

Because I am telling you this story, I'm sure you have figured out by now that there was no fire, however, I can tell you that at the moment I entered my home, I was 100% certain that there was. The smell of smoke was the trigger and I responded accordingly. While it did not involve a wetting or soiling incident (lucky me), I think it does describe how our brains can get tricked for a moment into thinking something is happening again, even when it is not. As I said before, this can sometimes happen with enuresis and encopresis in children of all ages. The trick is figuring out what the trigger is for the child. Is it the tile? Is it the memory of something that happened in a bathroom or remembered threats related to the bathroom? Is it being in an enclosed space? Or is it something else?

### 4. "Is this child pissed off?"

Well, what is the best way to show someone that you are pissed off? Some of the kids who come to see me, intentionally urinate or defecate either on themselves, the furniture, or even a prized photo album. If a child has not been given the tools to express feelings in a reasonable way, the child expresses them in whatever way occurs to him or her at the time.

Any survivor of abuse or neglect who has not had adequate opportunity or support to process the impact of the trauma often carries an intense level of anger or rage inside. When the anger is not addressed, it comes out in other ways. Even though I have had caregivers report to me that their child does not act angry when urinating on furniture, it is possible that a child with a history of abuse or neglect would seem relatively calm while seething with rage underneath. I liken it to the times when I have gone to the ocean and the lifeguards warned people not to go in the water because the undertow is too strong. The waves look the same to me but there is a pull underwater that you cannot see and that can carry you away from safety. Whether it is because they were not allowed to express feelings for fear of harm, or they gave up on expressing feelings because their feelings were not honored anyway, some children learn that the most effective way to express how they feel is by urinating or defecating intentionally.

### 5. "Is this a child who is fearful of connection to others?"

For children with a history of abuse or neglect, it is not uncommon for them to make themselves seem repellent. I hear a lot about children who refuse to bathe even though they smell terrible, or who have disgusting habits that repulse the people caring for them. If a child is fearful of connection, then feels connection despite that fear, they may do something to make themselves feel more comfortably distant. I see this sometimes when a child comes into my office and we have a moment when the child connects to a caregiver. Maybe she says something nice about her aunt, or they share a hug. For a child where connection is terrifying due to early abuse or neglect, he or she may subconsciously find a way to re-establish a distance by wetting or soiling.

Now that we are getting curious about the origins of daytime wetting and soiling, it is time to look at how to help children break the cycle of enuresis and encopresis. As I stated earlier, the first intervention is always to follow the suggestion of each child's physician as we do not want to fix a broken bone with a bandage and some medical intervention may be necessary.

## Motivating Children to accept the help you offer.

Before I give you suggestions, I want to give two important guidelines for all the interventions I use with children. My number one guideline is to follow the PLACE (playful, loving, accepting, curious, empathic) (See Page 208, PLACE Parenting article) parenting attitude as explained by Daniel Hughes, whether your child has attachment disturbance or not. The second is to make sure the child in your care is primed to receive help from you. What I mean by that is, ask the child if he or she wants help. If he or she says, "no," DO NOT OFFER IT. When you offer children help and they don't want it, you are only listening to yourself talk and asking to be frustrated. If you offer it, then back off. After the child has refused a couple of times and the refusal has been listened to and honored, curiosity begins to take over and eventually he or she asks you what help you have to offer. Then, and only then, is the child open to receiving and he or shey will be primed to listen to your advice.

## Ways to Help Children With Enuresis and Encopresis:

1. Especially if you recently accepted this child into kinship care, do not panic. You may have a child who is looking for buttons to push to get you upset or make you reject him or her. If you have an upset reaction, the child may see that it gets a rise out of you and will be more likely to continue. Without over-reacting, try to employ natural consequences, such as the child has to clean up the mess as appropriate for his or her developmental age. Remember to use your PLACE attitude, which means that humiliation and embarrassment of a child are not acceptable consequences. In fact, with a child who would purposefully wet or soil themselves, humiliation and embarrassment may actually reinforce the behavior in ways you did not anticipate.

2. My first suggestion for someone with a child with ongoing problems of this nature is therapy. While my sample is quite skewed, I have not seen any children with this issue that did not experience a feeling of fear about the problem, often accompanied by humiliation, even if the behavior is perceived to be intentional by their caregivers. While aunts, uncles, and grandparents can be helpful in navigating those feelings, therapists are trained to add an additional and necessary layer of help. Also, as you well know, children are often more motivated to do something someone else suggests over the suggestion of their care providers. You know all children do things for their teachers that they would not do for a parent figure and bringing the issue to the child's attention while in therapy often gives a child an extra bit of motivation to work on it. Additionally, if a child has a history of trauma that includes the bathroom in any way, it is important for him or her to be able to process this history with a trained professional. And, in case you are not already convinced, think about the possibility that the child in your care may be protecting you in some way from knowing about something his or her parent did. The child may worry that you will

no longer like his or her mom or dad, or that you will see the child was wrong, or a "bad kid." Children will not have these issues to the same degree with a therapist.

3. My most successful intervention in the area of helping older children with encopresis and enuresis is to reintroduce the idea of toilet training. Before you skip this idea because you think the child in your care is too old to re-potty train, let me tell you that I have used this with children in their early teens with success. The reintroduction is delicate and goes like this (think about using a tone similar to how Mr. Rogers would say it):

"I wonder if when you were younger and didn't always get what you needed, you might have missed out on some of the signs your body gives you when you need to go to the bathroom."

It may take a few times of gently suggesting this to a child for him or her to begin to get curious with you. Suggest you could help him or her to learn how his or her body knows it needs to go. Think about this. Your body knows it needs to go when your bladder feels full. I teach kids to playfully ask their bladders out loud in my office, "Bladder, do you have to go to the bathroom?" You would be amazed how many children have quickly realized by asking that question that they do, indeed need to go...right then...and we end up taking a quick restroom break.

You can also point out to a child that sometimes you have been able to tell when they need to go and that when kids are young and have parents who are making good choices, the parents often point out when a child is doing the potty dance. You can say that maybe this child's mom and/or dad missed that part about teaching kids about going to the bathroom. For some kids, we come up with a signal that a caregiver can make, rather than asking out loud in public whether a child needs to go. This works well with a child who has a history of being shamed or traumatized in relation to going to the bathroom, or who was never potty-trained appropriately.

4. An additional technique to use with children who were not properly potty-trained, is to teach children about controlling their bowels. One way I do this is to have children picture a balloon full of water. I tell them to picture the balloon turned over so that the opening of the balloon is on the bottom. If you are using your fingers to pinch the balloon, it is like the muscles around your bladder holding the pee or poop in. If you were to let go with your fingers, you would see the water come out of the balloon. For some balloons, you would have to give an extra squeeze from the top to empty it out. Bladders can be like this too. When I work with kids with issues controlling their bowels, I suggest to them that they picture the balloon as their bladder every time they need to go to the bathroom. Muscles hold the urine until you get to the toilet, then they let go and make sure your bladder is emptied completely. For kids with urinary issues that are feeling brave, I also suggest kegal exercises, where they start urinating, then try to stop the urine one or two times every time they go in order to build up the muscles (consult with a physician to make sure this is a good idea for your child).

Also, and many adults do not know this, there is a right way and a wrong way to empty your bowels. To most easily and completely empty your bowel, teach children to sit, leaning forward with their forearms resting on their thighs. Have a small stool near the toilet so children can put their feet on the stool making it so their knees are higher than their hips. This will help kids who hold onto stool and urine, to most easily and quickly relax and let go when they are going to the bathroom.

whothat hold it until it gets painful, I teach a quick exercise to help them control bowel functioning. This is good for relaxation as well. Lie on the floor and counting slowly to five while pulling your belly in. Picture your belly button touching your spine. Then, again to a slow count of five, push your belly out until your belly button is actually sticking up. See if you can make the pulling your belly in, equal in time to the pushing of your belly out. Ideally, kids who are learning to control their bowels will do this exercise for three minutes a day. The typical response I get from kids when I teach them this exercise and they actually do it in my office is a moment afterward when they start to get excited (like the potty dance) then a request to go to the bathroom. Success!

For children where this does not work, see about helping them find a Pilates class in your area. Many of the Pilates exercises, strengthen the core and pelvic muscles allowing for greater control.

6. I find the toughest kids with bathroom issues are typically the ones who are doing urinating and soiling on purpose, although often the times they do it are few and far between. It is important to figure out the why, but really the intervention for purposeful urinaters and soilers is to make sure they are in therapy with someone who works on teaching them to state their feelings. Often these kids need remedial learning in the expression of feelings, and, while caregivers can do some of this and are essential in reinforcing it, a child therapist will have the training to find ways that work for each child to teach them the proper expression of big feelings. Sometimes this means helping them to understand that they will not be harshly punished for the expression of their feelings, and for others it will mean having a therapist identify that your child may be experiencing a traumatic re-enactment.

*Kate Oliver, MSW, LCSW-C , is co-owner of A Healing Place, a private practice in Columbia, Md. Before opening her private practice, Oliver worked first at the Sexual Trauma, Treatment, Advocacy and Recovery Center (STTAR) in Columbia, Md for five years. During her time with the STTAR Center, Oliver completed a year-long program where she earned a certificate in working with children and adolescents with attachment disorders. After learning more about attachment, Oliver went to work with incarcerated, pregnant mothers in Baltimore City as the clinical director for the program, Tamar's Children. Tamar's Children worked with an attachment protocol, The Circle of Security, which taught adults with a history of trauma and neglect to bond with their infants. She used this method with the residents and added an additional group for women already in the program who were going to be reunited with older children in foster and kinship care. In 2007, Oliver opened A Healing Place, where she now specializes in working with children with trauma and attachment related issues. Additionally, she has a blog, Help4YourFamily.com, where she writes about ways to help children and parents feel happier and healthier.*

# Trying to Shift a Child's Negative Behavior Pattern
*By Cheryl A. Lieberman, PhD, and Rhea K. Bufferd, LICSW*

After 10-year-old Matthew was officially adopted by Darcy and Judah, it was time to set up a meeting with his birth parents (court-mandated open adoption). There had been visits with his biological brother in another foster home, and it was decided that the families would meet at a Department of Social Services office. The session was difficult for everyone. The finality of the moment was overwhelming for Matthew, who realized that he would never go back to live with his birth mother; and this visit where he said goodbye with no hope of returning was devastating. For people who do not understand why a child would want to go back to a house where abuse and neglect were rampant, the situation might be compared to the witness protection program. The government promises you safety. All you have to do is give up everything that has been part of your life so far. It must be difficult to accept that offer.

Matthew's upset continued and finally resulted in his being suspended from school and after-school programs. He expressed no remorse, and often said that he didn't care about anything. His adoptive parents were stumped, and when it was suggested they do a ceremony they decided that they had nothing to lose.

## Making Room For Good Messages

**Preparation:** Take several 3 X 5 index cards and put a bad message on each one. The messages should he based on knowledge of what had been said to the child in his or her past and what the child has said aloud about himself or herself.
- You are a rotten kid.
- You'll be the death of me yet.
- You'll never make it.
- You are unlovable.
- You are stupid.
- You are dumb.
- You are bad.
- You drive me crazy.
- You are a monster.
- You are clumsy.
- I hate you.
- Why can't you be good like (name)?
- It is your fault that you can't live here.

Then get another group of index cards. Cut each card into an interesting shape and put a colorful sticker on it. The messages used for Matthew were:
- You are good.
- You have a nice smile.
- You are unique.
- You try to do your best.
- You are super.

- You are huggable.
- You are lovable.
- You are smart.
- You are a terrific kid.
- You are kind.
- You have courage.
- You are special.
- You are brave.
- You are willing to try new things.
- You will be the best you can be.
- You are wonderful.
- You are helpful.
- You are clever.

The good messages should focus on basic characteristics, not on things the child did or did not do, such as, "You are good in math" or "You don't mess up your room." For Matthew's ceremony, two colorful folders were attached in such a way that the inside had three sections — enough to hold the good messages. The outside was decorated with colorful stickers and "Matthew's Good Messages" was printed on the front cover. Also at hand were Scotch tape and a glue stick (so Matthew would have a choice later) and a small, reclosable plastic bag.

## The Ceremony

Mama:        Everyone at some time will hear good messages and bad messages from people.

Papa:        Sometimes people say good things, such as, "You are a nice person." Sometimes people say bad things, such as, "You are a rotten person."

Matthew:     People might be kidding around and say things like, "Boy was that dumb," and you may feel like they said you were really dumb. That kind of kidding hurts. Sometimes people are angry or tired and they can say things like, "I could kill you" or "You are a monster." Children can take those messages and have them grow inside of them so that soon they believe that they are bad, rotten, or no good.

Papa:        What kids have to learn is that just because people say bad messages, that does not make them true. Because kids are small and growing, they may not have room for good messages unless we get rid of the bad messages from time to time.

Mama:        Today's ceremony will do just that — get rid of bad messages so that there can be room for more good ones. Matthew, are you ready to do that now?

Matthew:     (Says his answer. If Yes, go on; if No, stop for the time being and do this ceremony later.)

### If They Continue:

Mama:     We have written on cards bad messages that adults and other kids sometimes give kids. If you have ever had that bad message given to you, let us know and we will put that into a pile.

Papa:     If you can remember a time you heard it or a person who said it and want to share that, we will listen. If you have gotten messages that we have not written on cards, let us know and we will add them to the pile. After we do this, Mama will explain what happens to the bad messages.

(Matthew reads each message and puts some of them in a pile. When he is done, he decides to put all of them into a pile, just in case someone said one of these and he doesn't remember. Then Papa asks him to read each card out loud and then to tear each into tiny pieces and put all the pieces into the reclosable plastic bag. Papa closes the bag, has Matthew stomp on it, and then throws it into the trash. Since Matthew was having trouble with fire setting, they decided not to burn these messages. Matthew walks back, saying how much room he has for good messages.)

Mama:     Now that we have started to remove the bad messages and there is room for good messages, we need to fill that space. We have written on cards good messages that we think apply to you. If you agree, we will make a way to push them into the space you now have for them. After each message is chosen and absorbed, we will put them in a special folder so that you can look at them often and share them with others.

(Mama shows Matthew the cards and he reads each of them, stopping to enjoy the stickers, too. He says he likes the stickers and doesn't want to eat them to get them inside. Mama assures him that he does not have to. They decide that Matthew will pick up each card in turn and Mama and Papa will read it. Matthew will put it next to his body at his head, upper chest, or abdomen. Mama and Papa will read it together and pretend to push it into his body at one of the three places he chooses. Then Matthew puts each card aside. Halfway through, Matthew throws his arms wide open and with a big smile says, "I am being so filled up with good messages." Papa shows Matthew the folder and helps Matthew put his cards inside the folder — this is not rushed, but done at Matthew's pace.)

Matthew:     (Says how he feels now and what he thinks of the ceremony. Then he reads.) It is important for me to hold these good messages inside me. If I ever feel as though bad messages are trying to push them out, I will let you know that I need another ceremony to help me. I promise to try to believe the good messages people give me and to learn to manage the bad.

Papa:            We promise to help you hold onto good messages. If I ever give you bad messages that hurt you inside, please tell me so that I can change the messages right away.

Mama:            If I ever give you bad messages that hurt you inside, please tell me so that I can change those messages right away.

Papa:            We will end the ceremony by reading the good messages in your folder because we believe they are all true.

(Mama and Papa read each message in turn.)
Group hug.


## Afterward

At one point in the ceremony, Matthew threw his arms open and exclaimed, "I am really getting filled up with good messages!" His demeanor and behavior changed significantly after this ceremony. He stopped being oppositional and quieted down a lot. The ceremony had helped him cross a bridge from despair back to calm. It seemed to be one of the most behavior-changing events in this child's life.


*Cheryl A. Lieberman, PhD, is a single adoptive parent. Her sons, Eric and Christopher, both from the same birth family, came to live with her when they were seven-years-old and six-years-old respectively. They have an open adoption arrangement. Cheryl earned a master's degree in social services and city planning and a doctorate in organizational planning from the University of Pennsylvania. She is founder and president of Cornerstone Consulting Group, Cambridge, Mass., which provides strategic performance enhancement and change management services to numerous profit and nonprofit organizations.*

*Rhea K. Bufferd, LICSW, has been an adoption social worker since 1974, when she joined the Massachusetts Department of Social Services. She went on to work with Cambridge Family and Children's Services and is currently an adoption therapist. Rhea earned her master's in social work at Boston University School of Social Work and did postgraduate work in family therapy at The Institute at Newton, Mass.*

# Working With Schools

*"Students traumatized by exposure to violence have been shown to have lower grade point averages, more negative remarks in their cumulative records, and more reported absences from school than other students. They may have increased difficulties concentrating and learning at school and may engage in unusually reckless or aggressive behavior."*
*~ Sandra Kwesell, therapist, educator and creator of the SOS For Parents program  www.sosforparents.com*

# Supporting Kinship Care Children in the Classroom
*By Christine Mitchell*

## School Issues for Kinship Care Children

The school years play a critical role in shaping a child and his or her future. For many students growing up in kinship care families, emotional, behavioral, and learning difficulties can significantly affect their school experience. A child's issues may stem from prenatal substance exposure, abuse, neglect, institutional care, loss of birth parents, and multiple foster/kin care moves.

Schools can help students by being sensitive to the effects of trauma, as well as issues such as foster care, adoption, and diversity. Teachers can also broaden family-based assignments to accommodate non-traditional families, and help children cope with intrusive questions. Many parents choose to educate their schools about respectful kinship care and adoption language. Most importantly, caregivers can help teachers to understand the child's unique learning, social, emotional, and behavioral challenges.

## Before School Starts

When enrolling a child at a new school, kinship care parents need to have all the required paperwork for enrollment. This generally includes immunization records and/or a record of the child's last physical exam, prior school information, the child's social security number, emergency contacts, and doctor's contact information. Kinship caregivers will want to be sure the school understands exactly who is to receive information regarding the child (kinship caregivers, birth parents, social worker) and who is to participate in school conferences and Individualized Education Plan meetings, if applicable.

If a child has been recently placed, it is important to ensure that he or she knows the full name, address, and phone number of the caregiver. The child also needs to know the drop-off and pick-up routine, and the route to and from school or the bus stop.

It can be helpful to practice with a child how he or she might respond to difficult or intrusive questions from classmates. Caregivers should also help children **understand which information is appropriate to discuss with peers and which details are private.** The more personal details that classmates know, the more likely the child is to be teased or bullied.

## Talking with the Teacher

It is wise to schedule a conference with the child's teacher shortly before or after the start of school to discuss the child's unique needs. Parents and guardians should disclose only information which will help the school to meet the child's needs. Many details about the family's situation or the child's history are not relevant to the child's current issues, and thus should not be shared. Teachers can be reminded that information about the child's history should be kept confidential.

## Emotional and Behavioral Issues

A kinship care child may grieve the loss of his or her birth family and other prior caregivers. The child may have experienced neglect, abuse, separation from siblings, and multiple care moves. These factors can significantly influence his or her school behavior and perform-ance.

Students dealing with trauma and complex emotional issues often have less energy to pay attention in class and focus on lessons. They may have behavior issues such as low impulse control, defiance, wetting/soiling, stealing, lying, and destructiveness. When teachers understand that grief and loss are playing a role in a child's troubles they are in a better position to support the child.

Both at home and school adults need to establish clear rules, behavioral expectations, and consistent consequences. Additionally, if parents notice certain warning signs before a child erupts, or discovers a particular disciplinary, calming, or re-directing technique that works well, they can pass the information along to the teacher.

Children in kinship care may also lag behind in social skills. If a child is having trouble making or keeping friends at school, he or she may need help developing social skills. Perhaps the childe could benefit from some coaching about sharing, taking turns, and not hurting other children's feelings.

It is important to note that sometimes children who have been abused are confused about memories, and which caregiver (current or past parent) actually perpetrated the abuse. If a child has shown any tendency for confusing memories or caregiver names, it might be wise to inform the teacher of this before a serious misunderstanding occurs.

## Grief Triggers

Parents and teachers will want to look out for changes in a child's mood such as increased anger, sadness, or anxiety that may be tied to grief from past trauma and losses. Grief often resurfaces as children reach new developmental stages, and it can be triggered by various events.

Changes in routine, such as vacations, field trips, or substitute teachers can be difficult for a student with a history of instability. The child may also be more sensitive or likely to his birthdays or Mother's Day. Even holidays like Thanksgiving and Christmas can stir up feelings for kids who remember spending those holidays with their birth family. Parents should notify teachers of any new losses the child is experiencing (loss of a pet, changing therapists, etc.), which may remind him or her of the separation from birth family, trigger-ing grief reactions and behavioral changes.

In many classrooms students watch non-educational movies from time to time. Parents may want to ask teachers about plans to share movies or books that feature orphans, foster care, or adoption. Many children's movies involve themes of parental loss, which can trig-ger grief or anxiety in some children. The caregiver may wish to discuss the film with the child beforehand, or offer to supply an alternative movie for the class.

If parents and teachers recognize that emotional issues can be triggered by changes in routine, holidays, and other reminders of past losses, they can offer extra patience and support during these times.

## Transitions

Children who have experienced multiple moves and caregivers may have intense anxiety during transitions such as moving to a new school, and the beginning or end of the school year. As the end of the school year looms, children worry about losing what is familiar — both their friends and teacher. Children also worry about what their new teacher will be like and fear that the new teacher will be mean or scary. They may demonstrate increased anxiety and behavior problems, and have difficulty focusing on academics.

As with other issues, parents can talk to the child about his or her feelings and acknowledge that school transitions are tough for many children. These kids may also be reassured to some degree by being given information about their new teacher, and any friends whot will be in their class the following year. Ideally, the student should visit the new classroom and teacher before summer vacation. Keep in mind that children may be particularly apprehensive about the start of school if they have experienced difficulties in the classroom in the past.

## Special Education: Learning and Developmental Disabilities

Children in kinship care situations may be more likely to have speech and language delays, learning disabilities, developmental delays, and emotional or mental health issues. Therefore, it is important that parents and caregivers educate themselves on services that may be available to children as well as applicable laws and protections such as IDEA, ADA, IEPs, 504 Plans. The Individuals with Disabilities Education Act (IDEA) is the federal legislation behind most of the rights guaranteed to children with learning disabilities. It includes terms such as FAPE (free, appropriate, public education), IEP (Individualized Educational Plan), and (LRE) Least Restrictive Environment.

Wrightslaw.com is an outstanding source of information on special education rights, and a great place to start is with the book **Wrightslaw: From Emotions to Advocacy,** 2nd Edition, by Peter W. D. Wright, Esq. and Pamela Darr Wright.

## Parents and Schools Working Together

Because children spend a great deal of time at school, their school experience plays a significant role in their future and their self-worth. By making educators aware of the challenges faced by children in kinship care, parents and guardians can help schools become a source of support for these students rather than an additional hurdle. Schools can offer flexibility in challenging family-based assignments, encourage positive language, and be sensitive to grief triggers for traumatized children. Kinship caregivers can educate teachers about their child's unique issues and strategies that are effective with him or her. Open communication between caregivers and teachers will enable them to work as a team to meet the educational and emotional needs of kinship care children.

*Christine Mitchell is also the author of* **Welcome Home, Forever Child: A Celebration of Children Adopted as Toddlers, Preschoolers, and Beyond, Family Day: Celebrating Ethan's Adoption Anniversary,** *and* **A Foster-Adoption Story: Angela and Michael's Journey,** *co-authored with Regina M. Kupecky, MSW. This article originally appeared in* **The Foster Parenting Toolbox.**

# Making Sense of the Letters
*By Christine Mitchell*

Because adopted children may be more likely to have speech and language delays, learning disabilities, developmental delays, and emotional or mental health issues, it is important that parents educate themselves on services that may be available to their child as well as applicable laws such as IDEA, IEPs, 504s, and the ADA.

**IDEA:** The Individuals with Disabilities Education Act is the federal legislation behind most of the rights guaranteed to children with learning issues. It includes terms such as FAPE (free, appropriate, public education), IEP (Individualized Educational Program) and (LRE) Least Restrictive Environment.

**IEP:** The Individualized Education Plan is a document which spells out the components of a child's special education. It lists educational goals for the student and details the services and accommodations the child will receive to help him or her achieve those goals.

**ADA:** The Americans with Disabilities Act (ADA). Title II of the ADA prohibits discrimination on the basis of disability.

**504 Plan:** Section 504 of the Rehabilitation Act of 1973 is designed to protect individuals with "handicaps" from denial of benefits or discrimination from any program receiving federal funds which includes public schools. Students may qualify for accommodations under a 504 Plan if they have a health, mental, or emotional disability which does not qualify for an IEP.

**NCLB:** The No Child Left Behind Law of 2001 provides for testing accommodations for learning disabled students in regard to NCLB assessments:

- Presentation (example: repeat directions, read aloud, use larger bubbles, etc.)

- Response (example: mark answers in book, use reference aids, point, use computer, etc.)

- Setting (example: study carrel, special lighting, separate room, etc.)

- Timing/Scheduling (example: extended time, frequent breaks, etc.)

# How to Get the School to Work With You and Your Child

*By Jan Wagner*

It is commonly known that children who come into care are more likely to have developmental delays, learning disabilities, and a wide array of disorders which interfere with his or her ability to perform at the expected level in school. Just the fact that the child has been removed from home and placed in another family will compound the already existing trauma suffered from neglect and abuse. Because the child is now living with a relative in a safe, stable environment doesn't mean everything will resolve itself with time. There are some things you can't love away. Not only does the new family member need to be informed in how to parent a child with special needs, so does the school.

*Anyone with any trauma/attachment disorder training will know that isolating, restricting, or sending them to the principal's office for a stern talking to is not going to work for these children.*

Many of the more obvious physical and educational handicaps are being addressed through the Special Education Department. But what about the child who has emotional impairments? These children are most often viewed as being difficult to handle, or having bad behavior. Rather than looking for the basis of the problem, the children are disciplined the same way other children are in the classrooms. Anyone with any trauma/attachment disorder training will know that isolating, restricting, or sending them to the principal's office for a stern talking to is not going to work for these children. They need the positive reinforcement for what they are doing right, not on what they have done wrong.

We began our contact with special services when my grandson showed signs of delay when he came to us at two years of age. He was evaluated by our local Early On, 0 to 5 program and they helped us during that first summer. He had two mostly uneventful years of pre-school, but when he started all-day-every-day kindergarten the bottom fell out. Going to "real" school was a trigger for whatever it was that he experienced before he was able to talk. It wasn't just separation anxiety, but real fear and distrust. He could not be calmed down, and could not be touched without striking out. He had sensory disorders, showed signs of being on the autism spectrum, ADHD, social isolation, and a total inability to perform the simplest school tasks. I was at a loss. This was not the child who had adjusted so well to life with Grandma and Papa. We had not experienced these behaviors prior to this. We tried half days of school, me staying at school with him, dietary changes, quiet rooms at school, time outs at home, but everything resulted in an escalation of his behavior. Eventually, he chose to be an angry kitty cat, crawling out of his classroom into others, hissing, biting, and scratching. It was time to do something when the school called and said he had run from the social worker into the street where the principal caught him, carried him to his office, which he proceeded to trash.

About this same time I was taking a training in early childhood trauma and its effects on a child's behavior. It was my "aha" moment and I began to explain some of my grandson's story to the principal and asked him to contact our Intermediate School System and ask for a Review Existing Evaluation Data, or REED, as soon as possible. We also engaged a private therapist who had been trained in childhood trauma by Dr. James Henry. My grandson was observed, evaluated, and we were interviewed. The therapist also tested him and one of the results was that in spite of only a partial testing, his IQ was far beyond a five-year-old.

He was back in school full time, had an aid to shadow him, got sensory breaks and didn't receive the disciplinary slips. But it wasn't working. He was out of the classroom most of the day with breaks, walks, and quiet time and he was not doing regular classroom assignments. We still did not have an Individualized Education Plan in place, which meant there were no real goals for my child. I took a special education advocacy class. I got my hands on the "Big Book." You know, the three-ring binder that you put on the table between yourself and the school personnel. I found out they were in non-compliance and one phone call to politely inform them of that fact and a special education social worker was at my house that day. It took less than a week to have a meeting and to put an Individualized Education Plan (IEP) in place.

The most difficult part was that he had to have a diagnosis and he did not qualify for an "Otherwise Health Impaired." He had to have an EI, or "Emotionally Impaired." This was hard. He was only five years old. He wasn't mentally ill. He was just a scared little boy who had a rough start in life. I can remember when my daughter, his mother, was having emotional problems affecting her ability to learn. I was told at that time — whatever I do, do not go with an EI "label" as that was for kids with severe mental illness and she would be put in a category with the kid who sat under his desk and barked at people. Well, my grandson was hissing and scratching. His emotional state was causing learning impairment. We went with the EI label.

I cannot say enough about the wonderful team that has been put in place for my grandson. It consists of the support staff from the Intermediate School District Special Education, his teacher, his full time aid, the school special education teacher, social worker, and principal. We meet monthly for an hour. They are more in tune to his difficult days than I am. I consider each and every one of them an important factor in his ability to cope with school. How has this been able to work? I was open and forthcoming with information about his history. That is one of the real advantages of having guardianship. I know that non-relative foster parents cannot disclose a child's background, even if they did know all of it. His team has told me repeatedly how much this has helped them help him. We were also fortunate enough to have a team leader who is trauma informed. Not only am I able to talk openly about what has and is happening in his life, but he also is

*Denial is not going to help him, but asking for help just might. Educate yourself about the disabilities that can be caused by neglect and abuse and by exposure to drugs and alcohol prenatally.*

encouraged to talk with them.

I was in the school office and a father was irate with the secretary because the school had suggested his son be tested and he said he was pulling him out of there if they couldn't handle him. I wanted to take him aside and give him the benefit of my experience, but I don't think he was in a listening mood.

It is not particularly easy for me to have a child with "special needs," but when I see how far he has come in this year, I am grateful I followed my instincts. Be that child's advocate. Be honest and up front with the situation. Denial is not going to help him, but asking for help just might. Educate yourself about the disabilities that can be caused by neglect and abuse and by exposure to drugs and alcohol prenatally. Even stress in the mother can cause distress to the baby. You need to be the one to put that request in writing for an evaluation. And, unfortunately, it will be your responsibility to follow through with it. Take a special education advocacy training so you know your child's rights to an education. The earlier you start the interventive process, the more chance for success your child will have. Work with your child's team and don't be afraid to speak up. His entire future depends on what you do for him today.

*After raising three children, 37 years of marriage, and at the age of 57, Jan Wagner started raising her then two-year-old grandson, H. Wagner is now an advocate for kinship families and is involved on a state and national level. You can follow her blog Raising H at jdwags.blogspot.com. She is also available to speak or give workshops on Kinship/Grandparenting issues.*

# Bullying
*A Real Problem/Some Real Solutions*
*By Sherryll Kraizer, PhD*

Bullying is an integral part of our culture. It happens every day in classrooms, in bathrooms and hallways, on playgrounds and in the neighborhoods of all communities. It is insidious and it is hurtful. Children who are bullied, physically, emotionally, or socially, are deprived of their right to go to school and to live in communities where they feel safe.

Being bullied is linked to depression and low self-esteem. Many adopted and foster children suffer with these also — linked to loss, feelings of "not being good enough" to remain with birth family, and also feelings of being different to their (often white) adoptive or foster parents. Some adopted or foster children are vulnerable with regard to social skills. The baggage that being adopted or of living in foster care brings these children means that they are open to becoming bullied or bullies. Some children present as easy prey to classroom bullies, while others bully as a means of bolstering faltering esteem.

What can foster parents do to help things in the classroom change? Most adults easily remember a specific bullying incident from their past. If they were the victim, they remember the panic, the sick feeling, wondering why no one was helping. If they were the bully, they remember the feeling of power and perhaps the shame for what they did to others. Some were bystanders. They remember the anxiety of not wanting to be the next target and often guilt for failure to intervene, even though they didn't know how.

## Is Bullying Really That Harmful?

Bullying is the deliberate and repeated infliction of harm on another person. It takes many forms. It may involve one child bullying another, a group of children against a single child or groups against other groups. Bullying includes many behaviors. Common forms of physical, verbal, emotional, and social bullying are shown below:

| Physical | Verbal | Emotional | Social Bullying |
|---|---|---|---|
| Hitting | Name-calling | Exclusion | Peer pressure |
| Pushing | Teasing | Rumors | Exclusion |
| Kicking | Belittling | Acting superior | Making fun of |
| Shoving | Making fun | Being mean | Taunting/Baiting |
| Pinching | Bad language | Not caring | Set up to get in trouble |
| Violence | Verbal abuse | No conscience | Threats |
| Abusive | Mimicking | Thoughtlessness | Ganging up on someone |
| Destructive | Shouting | Gossip | Name-calling |
| Spitting | Taunting | Threatening | Pranks |
| Tripping | Cursing | Belittling | Internet harassment |

Whether the bullying is direct or indirect, perpetrated by an individual or a group, the key component of bullying is that the physical or psychological intimidation occurs repeatedly over time and is designed to hurt. Young people who are bullied are more likely to be depressed, to feel isolated, anxious, to have low self-esteem, and to think about suicide. Bullying, as most children know, starts early and it is devastating. And as we have seen, it impacts all the harder on adopted and foster children with their intrinsic vulnerability in regards to self-esteem, and damages these children all the more.

## What Is the Role of Adults?

All forms of bullying are opportunities to teach children how to get along, how to be considerate of all people, and how to be part of a community or group. But, children do not learn to solve conflicts and get along with others naturally. They have to learn specific skills that will prevent and thwart problems with bullying. As soon as children are old enough to interact with others, they can learn not to be bullies and not to be targets. This includes giving them the words to express their feelings, skills to monitor and change their behavior, and conflict resolution strategies.

When preschoolers begin to call people names or use unkind words, we should intervene immediately and consistently. In kindergarten, children learn the power of exclusion. We begin to hear things like, "She's not my friend and she can't come to my party." Respond with, "You don't have to be friends with her today, but it's not all right to make her feel bad by telling her she can't come to your party."

In the early elementary grades, cliques and little groups develop which can be quite exclusionary and cruel. Children need to hear clearly from adults, "It's not all right to treat other people this way. How do you think she feels being told she can't play with you?" Kids don't have to play with everyone or even like everyone, but they can't be cruel by excluding others. Children who are not bullies or victims have a powerful role to play in shaping the behavior of other children. We need to teach these children to speak up on behalf of other children being bullied. "Don't treat her that way, it's not nice."

## What Is Role-Play?

Role-play is the tool that turns theories about prevention into reality. It is the game parents and teachers can use to coach children to better life skills. It is the way to find out what children think about the social problems they encounter and how they actually handle them. It is the primary skill-builder for prevention of bullying. It's also a lot of fun!

Role-play is really just practice for life. It's a way of preparing for what we can anticipate. Everyone does it. If you are going to your child's school to discuss a significant problem with a teacher, you probably rehearse what you are going to say, or mentally practice how to approach the issue, thinking through how to respond if the teacher says this, or that. It is perhaps the most powerful way to prepare to be effective.

Learning to speak up is also a skill learned by doing. When a child is able to say, "Don't do that to me, I don't like it," in a tone of voice that is clear and assertive, while standing up tall and looking directly at the person, you will know that role-playing has worked.

## How Do I Get Started?

Initiating role-play is as simple as asking a "What if…" question or responding to a child's "What if…" question. For example, you might begin with, "I heard that there was a prob-

# Role Play
## *Some Good Ways To Respond To A Bully*

It is helpful to have a range of statements, behaviors, or actions in mind as children are role-playing. The following chart will help you get started.

| Statements | Behaviors |
|---|---|
| "That wasn't nice." | Walk away |
| "Don't do that." | Join another group |
| "I'm going to tell if you do that again." | Laugh and leave |
| "That really hurts my feelings." | Ignore them |
| "That's not a very nice thing to say." | Act like you don't care |
| "Give that back or I'll tell the teacher." | Avoid the bully |
| Make a joke — "Whatever," "No kidding" | Get away and tell |
| "Leave me alone." | Ask a friend to help |

Children should also develop action plans to get help. This might include:
- Go and tell a teacher.
- Tell a parent or another adult.
- If they are really afraid, run to someone who can help.

*Practice, Practice, Practice*
Role-play takes these concepts and makes them skills. Be sure to have fun putting an end to bullying with role-plays. Children love to role-play and will rapidly use it as a way to address other concerns they have. This is invaluable for parents and teachers. The "What if..." questions or scenarios kids suggest reflect their fears, concerns, anxieties, and curiosities. Children hear stories about things that have happened to other children, or they witness something in school or on the playground. They naturally think about what they would do. They want to role-play so they know how to handle a similar situation. By eliciting children's ideas through role-play, we discover how they think, how they solve problems, their concept of how the world and their social groups work, and what they know and don't know about solving interpersonal conflicts. Always look for the skills children are bringing to these problem-solving, "What if..." scenarios and acknowledge them. These are the building blocks for all future skills.

Role-play scenarios are easy to create and modify according to the situation or the skills and needs of an individual child or group. Always keep the experience positive, empowering, and fun! Remember that interpersonal skills are learned a little bit at a time, so each step a child takes in the direction of being a clear, powerful, and assertive communicator is important.

lem in the lunchroom with one of the boys taking other kids' desserts. What would you do if that happened to you?" When the child begins to tell you, suggest, "Show me what you would do, I'll be the kid trying to take your dessert." Play it out. See what resources the child already has.

If the child isn't particularly effective, suggest you switch roles. The child is now the bully. You should model standing up straight, looking the bully in the eye, and clearly saying, "Do not touch my lunch." Then change roles and let the child try it again. If he or she gets part way there, provide coaching. Whenever you role-play, remember, it is a process. You are learning what the child's skills are and helping to develop new ones. Avoid judging or making an issue over any part of the role-play or the value will be lost. Role-play is never a confrontation. It is an opportunity to share ideas, initiate discussion, and learn new strategies.

## The three key elements of role-play are:

1. **Speaking** — this includes deciding what you want to say and then saying it in an assertive manner, paying attention to tone of voice, volume, pitch, clarity, etc.
2. **Body language** — this includes posture, facial expressions, the distance between the people involved, use of hands, etc.
3. **Eye contact** — communication that is delivered face-to-face, eye-to-eye is more powerful.

Consistently combining all three of these elements takes time and practice. Children most often learn the skills one at a time and then integrate them. Practice and successive approximations is the key. Role-play teaches children how to communicate effectively and consistently so they can utilize the skills automatically.

## Family Ethos

Perhaps your child isn't being bullied or isn't a bully, but children are aware of it occurring. Ask any children from kindergarten through high school who is bullying whom. A teacher or parent may not know, but the children always know and they don't want to be next. They are also highly conflicted because they don't want to be marked as a "tattle tale." Okay — let them become **advocates.** Children like to speak up for others!

Advocates are those children who are neither bullies nor targets and they have the most powerful role to play in shaping the behavior of other children. They tend to have better social and conflict management skills. They are more willing to assert themselves without being aggressive or confronting. They suggest compromises and alternate solutions. They tend to be more aware of people's feelings and are the children who can be most helpful in resolving disputes and assisting other children to get help. Often adopted and foster children who have proactive parents will have already been discussing the key elements of bullying (difference, weakness) with their parents, because adoptive and foster parents are aware. Maybe they will have discussed the effects of difference and feelings of inability, loss and vulnerability.

Schools need a policy and an educational plan regarding bullying that targets the entire student body. It should include:

- A clear statement regarding bullying: that it is unacceptable.
- A plan for student and parent education about the policy.
- Adequate and active supervision, especially at times when students are moving about freely during recess, class breaks, lunchtime, and after school is dismissed.
- A policy of immediate and early intervention (always too early rather than too late).
- Training that makes every child an advocate for every other child.

We should scrutinize our schools for diversity and empathy for difference. And, we need to become advocates against bullying. If each of us is willing to speak up and to learn the skills to intervene effectively against bullying, this can no longer be a culture of meanness and violence.

*Sherryll Kraizer, PhD, is the founder and director of the Coalition for Children. This article originally appeared in **Adoption Parenting: Creating a Toolbox, Building Connections**.*

## What If a Child Wants To Disclose Bullying?

Children use "What if..." scenarios as a way to tell their parents and teachers things that have happened. It seems less like tattling to them and makes incidents easier to talk about. For example, "Mom, what would you say if some of my friends were making the little kids miss the bus and blaming it on someone else?"

To follow up, you would want to explain that telling about a problem is not tattling and that you would like to help without making the situation worse. You might role-play your child talking to someone at the school, with or without you. Or decide together that this is a situation you should handle with the school directly.

Always remember to thank your child for speaking up and for being an advocate for another child.

# Overcoming Difficult Comprehension Challenges

*By Lee Tobin McClain, PhD*

*"This is boring," mutters your teenaged foster son, slamming shut his science book.*
*"That quiz wasn't fair," whines your 10-year-old foster daughter.*
*"I read the chapter but I still flunked!"*

These are typical kid complaints, but be alert. Sometimes remarks like these reveal that your child is having trouble reading. "But he reads just fine," you may say, having seen your child spend hours perusing the TV guide. Her teacher may concur. If your child did well with reading in the early years, the school most likely concluded that no special help is needed. But as kids get older, their reading material becomes more challenging, and new strategies are needed to comprehend the harder stuff. That's when kids with smaller vocabularies and fewer background experiences — most foster kids — start to struggle. In addition to sharing your concerns with your child's teacher, there are ways you can help at home. Here are several:

**Share Your Reading Process.** When you're reading assembly instructions, talk yourself through them within hearing of your kids (omitting swear words!): "That doesn't make sense. Let me read it again" or "Now wait — this is just like that table we put together last month." By re-reading and using background knowledge, you're demonstrating important skills.

**Keep Highlighters Handy.** A major part of comprehension is figuring out what's most important and what can be safely skimmed. If you ever cut articles out of the paper or a magazine to show family members (a wonderful way to share reading enthusiasm), highlight two or three important sentences. Keep highlighters near the magazine piles in your home, and your kids may start to follow suit. For school textbooks, keep a jar of sharp pencils handy: kids can be coached in drawing a light line beside the most important text and erasing it later.

**Pre-read With Your Kids.** Pre-reading is what many of us do naturally, browsing through a book or article, skimming chapter titles and subheadings to get a sense of what it's all about. Kids who've been in the system may have missed out on this training, but you can casually replicate it at home. "Let's see what you're doing in science," you can offer. Then pick up the book and run a finger down the table of contents. When you reach an interesting-sounding chapter, flip to it and page through, reading aloud some subheadings and captions. Talk about what your child already knows about the topics. "Did you ever see a lemur at the zoo?" or "remember when we watched that hurricane on TV?" Since foster kids often lack experiences other kids have had, you may have to dig a little, or plan a quick trip to the natural history museum right before the class hits the archaeology chapter. That's a comprehension strategy too.

**Ask Questions.** This one requires some delicacy, especially with sullen teenagers; it helps if you have a real interest in what they're studying. Many people learn better by discussing a topic with others, so once your child has done a bit of reading on a topic, see if you can engage him or her in conversation about it. "What's going on in Africa these days, anyway?" or "I've always wondered why heat rises" might get the ball rolling. If your child knows a little bit more than you about something, his or her self-esteem mounts, and he or she might even get eager to learn more.

**Read Aloud and Get Him or Her to Read Aloud to You.** Reading out loud fosters fluency, an important aspect of reading comprehension. Set the example yourself by reading tidbits from your newspaper or magazine to whoever's around. Ask a kid to read you the assembly instructions while you're putting something together or the recipe while you are cooking. Have them re-read it a couple of times. Encourage doing homework at the kitchen table, and ask your kids to read the interesting parts to you while you're fixing dinner.

**Make Reading a Priority.** Comprehension strategies like these may seem obvious, but in the busy rush of family life, conversation about books and active engagement with reading can often get sidelined. Bring reading back to center stage and you'll give your children a boost in many areas of schoolwork and adult living.

## Stages of Reading

Learning to read isn't a one-time event. Instead, kids go through predictable stages in the journey to becoming an excellent reader. The trick is that, if one stage isn't mastered well — likely for children from troubled or chaotic homes — a reader can get stuck there, which affects his or her ability to understand and learn for years to come. Check out these brief descriptions of the stages to see where your foster child fits, and how you might nudge him or her onto the next stage. Descriptions of these stages were developed by pioneering Harvard researcher Jeanne Chall, who also attached ages and grade levels to the stages. Many children from disadvantaged backgrounds will lag behind the stated age and grade levels.

**Pre-reading: Birth-6** During this stage, children are learning about the world and sounds in language. Both are important to later reading skills. Children need to experience many people, places, things, and activities so when they start to read, they can link words on a page to something they know in real life. They also need to hear many words and sounds, so that when they run across the word "veranda" in text, they've sat on one — and talked about it — at Grandma's house. To support this developmental stage, talk to your children a lot and read them a lot of stories, running your finger along the text as you read to emphasize the link between those squiggles on the page and the words you're saying.

**Decoding Stage: Grades 1-2, Ages 6-7** This is the stage where kids "learn to read." Laboriously at first, they begin to connect letters to sounds and decode words. Kids at this stage need practice to remember vowel and consonant sounds. They may need to point at each word or use a straightedge to keep their focus on a line of text; reading researchers say they are "glued" to the text. Since they are working so hard to decode, they often lose the bigger thread of the story; illustrated texts or an adult's gentle summary of what's happened so far can help with comprehension. Show your kids how to sound out harder words and give them plenty of chances to practice. Also take the time to read to them; at this stage, their ability to read lags behind their ability to understand and enjoy, and listening to more complicated stories reminds them that becoming a better reader is worth all the time and hard work they're putting in.

**Fluency Stage: Grades 2-3, Ages 7-8** During this stage, kids start to recognize whole words automatically without sounding out each letter. Such automatic decoding allows a child to read fluidly without focusing on the act of reading itself. His or her mind now has space for higher-level concepts and more complicated stories. At this stage, young readers need to practice. Reading easy books for pleasure builds fluency and speed, so don't worry if your child wants to read every book in a silly series, or to read books that seem overly simple to you. Your job is to keep plenty of reading material at just the right level close at hand, a challenge when the "right level" is changing every month or two. This is the time to trade books with friends or make weekly visits to the library for stacks of Magic Tree House books or A-to-Z Mysteries.

**Reading: Grades 4-8, Ages 8-14** Now that the child is a fluent reader, things get more complicated. In the middle grades of school, children are no longer learning to read; now they read to learn. All the previous stages come into play: children must have ample background experiences so they can understand new information; they must be able to decode unfamiliar and complex words; and they must read fluently enough to focus on the meaning of a complicated text. It's at this stage that many foster kids run into trouble. Yes, they can read; but due to impoverished backgrounds, they may not have the life experience to put what they read into context. They may be poor decoders or less than fluent. And now, they're being tested on their ability to make sense of a textbook in social studies or health.

How can you help? Before your child starts reading a chapter in his or her science book, talk about what he or she already knows about the subject. Remind him or her of the television show on elephants or the way oil and water don't mix when baking a cake. Have him or her skim the subheadings in the chapter, and talk about learning expectations in the chapter. Look at the pictures. After the reading is complete, have him or her tell you some of the things learned.

## Stages of Reading for Teens

The following are the higher stages of reading useful for high school and older students — and how you can help your foster kids, who may have missed out on some stages, improve their skills.

**Reading To Learn** After your child has learned to read, he or she begins to read for information; vast percentages of what we end up knowing comes through the written word. Materials children read in middle school build vocabulary and add to background knowledge. Now they're reading about topics that don't come up in ordinary conversation — the characteristics of the solar system or the *War of the Roses* — so they must be able to use skills from all the other stages: discovering main ideas, decoding new words, and applying background knowledge. They may need help with strategies like pre-reading, skimming, and note-taking from texts. Frequent conversations about what they've read can promote comprehension and help them make links to prior knowledge.

**Multiple Viewpoints: High School Reading** As readers become comfortable with gaining information through reading, they are able to understand multiple viewpoints — reading several books and articles about Michael Jackson, for example, and realizing that some of the information and attitudes conflict. Such conflicts force them to analyze and critique what they read, rather than accept it all at face value. This "critical comprehension" stage is where students learn to deal with layers of facts and to correct their own previous ideas if new material proves them wrong.

**Constructive Reading: Age 18 & Older** In the most advanced stage of reading development, learners construct knowledge by taking information from various sources and skillfully interpreting and combining it. They create their own truth from the truth of others. They use texts for their own purposes, knowing what to read closely and what to skim. They form their own educated view based on various sources. Obviously, our culture benefits from having many readers at this stage who can make informed judgments about political candidates, serve on juries, decide on school curriculum, and evaluate and solve social problems.

Almost always, one part of the solution is to encourage pleasure reading. Find texts your child can read easily, preferably matching his or her interests, and encourage frequent stints of reading. How? Baskets of

## What Can Go Wrong

Effective reading at each stage depends on adequate knowledge of the previous stages, and herein lies the problem for many kids in the system. If they've missed out on decoding-stage skills, reading for information is laborious: instead of having the mental energy to learn new concepts and complex ideas, they're stuck trying to remember what sound goes with which letter. Reading becomes a frustrating experience, so they don't want to practice, which means they don't improve. Likewise, if teenagers haven't learned the vocabulary and background information of "read-to-learn" texts, it's harder for them to understand and analyze the multiple viewpoints encountered while researching for a high school paper.

## What You Can Do

If you notice your child is struggling with reading, schedule a meeting with his or her teacher right away. Sometimes, they'll suggest ways you can help at home: more practice reviewing the reading story each week, or a computer game that improves decoding skills. Teachers can start the ball rolling on intervention services or place the child in a more appropriate reading group. Though we often think of reading specialists as an elementary-school phenomenon, in fact, most middle and high schools offer reading support as well.

books in the bathroom and at the kitchen table; a good reading lamp and a couple of magazines on the nightstand; audiobooks in the car. All build vocabulary and fluency, and with these skills solidified, older kids have the mental space to wrestle with difficult concepts.

It can be a challenge to focus on a child's reading skills when the future is uncertain. Maybe he or she will go back to his or her birth family in a few months, or be moved to a different placement. And reading skills sometimes seem like the least of a troubled teen's problems. But reading can help teens do better in school, escape from home problems, and build self-esteem. Even a small boost may be enough to push kids to the next stage. Reading well will serve the kids we care about for their whole lives. It's worth all the effort we can put into it.

*Lee Tobin McClain, PhD, teaches writing and literature at Seton Hill University. She's the author of three novels featuring teens in foster care, "My Loco Life," "My Abnormal Life," and "My Alternate Life." For more information, visit www.leemcclain.com. This article originally appeared in* **Fostering Families Today** *magazine.*

# Troublesome Family-based School Assignments
*By Christine Mitchell*

Several common school assignments can make foster and adoptive children feel sad, left out, and uncomfortable. Children may lack the information for some projects like the "Family Tree," "Family History," and "Bring-a-Baby Picture." Basing lessons on a traditional family model not only excludes these students, but may also trigger strong grief reactions.

Teachers are generally not aware of the impact of these projects on foster and adoptive children, unless the subject is brought to their attention. Fortunately, these assignments can be easily modified to work for children in all different types of family configurations, by broadening the scope of the assignment and offering students wider choices.

Caregivers are advised to ask the teacher about any upcoming family-based projects at the start of the school year, or when a child starts a new school. The outline below lists some common assignments and the corresponding challenges they present, as well as solutions to make them more inclusive.

## "Bring a Baby/Family Picture" Assignments or "Bring Photos at Each Age from Birth"

*Problem:* An adopted or foster child may not have baby or family photos.
 a) This assignment emphasizes an issue that is already painful for children.
 b) It puts the child in the difficult position of explaining to other kids why he or she doesn't have baby or family pictures.

*Solution:* Present the assignment as a choice. Bring pictures of:
 a) The child as a baby or any younger age.
 b) Of the child on various holidays or doing various activities.
 c) Important people in the child's life.

## Family Tree Assignments

*Problem:* The standard format does not allow for foster, adoptive, birth, or step parents and siblings.

*Solution:* Rather than avoiding the family tree assignment, parents and educators can use it as a tool to teach children about the many varieties of family structures. Offer a choice of the following formats like:
 a) The Rooted Family Tree, where the roots represent the birth family, the child is the trunk, and the foster, adoptive, and/or step family members fill in the branches.
 b) The Caring (or Loving) Tree, where the child can fill the branches or leaves with all sorts of important people in his or her life.
 c) The Family Wheel Diagram, where the child is in the middle and the outer rings of the circle represent the birth, foster, adoptive, and step family relationships.
 d) The Family Houses Diagram, which uses houses instead of trees to show connections between birth, foster, adoptive, and step family members.

## Autobiographies and Family History Assignments

*Problem:* Many foster and adopted children lack information about their early years, or the information is painful and private.

*Solution:* Offer students a choice to write about:
a) My life.
b) When I was younger.
c) My summer vacation.
d) A special event or person in my life.

### Create a Timeline of the Student's Life

*Problem:* Some children have little or no information about their milestones. Other children may wonder if they need to include private information like foster care moves.
*Solution:* Do not require that the timeline begin from the child's birth, just that it cover a period of time. Alternatively, allow children to create a timeline for a historical or fictional character.

### Superstar, VIP, Student-of-the-Week Projects

*Problem:* Having students share information about themselves is intended to be a fun activity that helps students get acquainted. But it can be uncomfortable for children who have limited access to pictures and information about their early years. Some children may also have painful memories of their early childhood.
*Solution:* Instructors can provide students with a list of many alternatives for the information to be shared, including more innocuous choices such as interests, hobbies, sports, or pets.

### Tell About Your Name

*Problem:* Some children will not know why their birth parents chose their name, and may even have gone through a name change.
*Solution:* Call the assignment "What's in a Name?" and let students choose between writing about their own name or interviewing a friend or relative about their name.

### Write About Your Birth

*Problem:* This assignment can be fun for children being raised by their biological parents, who can interview their parents about and learn interesting details of their birth. This project is difficult or impossible for many foster and adopted children to complete.
*Solution:* Ideally, eliminate this assignment altogether, as the questions tend to be intrusive even for families formed by birth.

Assignments revolving around family and personal history can prove troublesome for many types of students. Increasing numbers of families differ from the "traditional" configuration in one or more ways: single-parent and step families, same-sex parents, transracial families, foster and adoptive families, and kinship caregivers. By modifying assignments, teachers will be exposing all of their students to positive messages about adoption, diversity, and respect for all types of people and families.

*Christine Mitchell is also the author of* **Welcome Home, Forever Child: A Celebration of Children Adopted as Toddlers, Preschoolers, and Beyond; Family Day: Celebrating Ethan's Adoption Anniversary; A Foster-Adoption Story: Angela and Michael's Journey,** *co-authored with Regina M. Kupecky, MSW. This article originally appeared in* **Fostering Families Today** *magazine.*

# Special Education 101
*The Basics for Fostering a Child with Special Education Needs*
*By June Bond, MEd, and Mary Eaddy*

Advocating for your children in the school system may be one of the most daunting tasks that a kinship caregiver undertakes. This is especially true for new kinship parents who may have a wealth of child rearing experience, but no experience in the world of accessing special education services. This article is designed to help parents understand the basic programs offered in special education and how their programs may benefit children in their care.

## What is Special Education?

Special education is instruction that is specially designed to meet the unique needs of children who have disabilities. This is done at no cost to the parents in the public school system. It should be noted that private or parochial school systems may not have a wide array of special education programs or may charge for added services. Special education can include special instruction in the classroom, at home, in hospitals or health-related institutions. It is estimated that more than five million children receive special education services each year in the United States. So, take heart, you and your child are not alone.

Many of the programs that are included in special education are related to the Individuals with Disabilities Education Act. This federal act is often referred to as IDEA. There are 13 general categories of disabilities listed in IDEA. These categories include autism, deafness, deaf-blindness, hearing impairment, mental retardation, multiple disabilities, orthopedic disabilities, emotional disturbance, speech and/or language impairments, traumatic brain injury, visual impairments, and "other health impairments," which can be defined as affecting a child's life functions, of which learning is one of life's functions.

The first initial steps to receiving special education services are: 1) to ascertain that your child has one or more of the disabilities that fall into one of the 13 designated categories AND 2) that this impairment affects the child's school performance. Sometimes children in kinship care may already have been evaluated and deemed eligible for special education services. However, a young child or a child who recently came into your care for the first time may not have been evaluated for special education services. Consequently, it is critical that families understand the evaluation system that leads to special education services. A good understanding of the evaluation system and rules relating to the evaluation of a child can open doors to access the services to the fullest extent and benefit for the child.

## Having the Child Evaluated

The first stepping stone to receiving special education is to ask the school to evaluate the child. The guidance counselor or director of special education can assist in the request and paperwork. Request in writing that the school evaluate your child as soon as possible. Remember to date and save everything that relates to your requests. A slow evaluation will lead to a slow implementation of extra help. In most cases, the school will evaluate your child at no cost to you. You should be aware, however, that the school does not have to evaluate your child if school officials do not think your child has a disability or needs special education. In times of budget crises, this can be a real issue. If the school refuses to evaluate your child, the school must outline its reasons in written form. A parent has two rapid fire responses to a denial for evaluation:

1. Request the school system's special education policies, as well as parent rights to disagree with decisions made by the school system. The stated policies should have added steps to take *and*

2. Get in touch with your state's Parent Training and Information Center, which is an excellent resource and advocacy for parents to learn more about special education, their rights and responsibilities, and the law. To locate your state's Parent Training and Information Center, go to www.parentcenternetwork.org.

**What happens during an evaluation for special education services?** The full evaluation team should look at a host of factors to ascertain how the child is affected by the disability. This evaluation should include assessing the child's health, vision, hearing, social and emotional well-being in addition to general intelligence, performance in school, and communication and physical skills. The evaluation must be complete enough to identify all of your child's needs for special education and related services.

> **Required Reading for Parents with Special Needs Children in School**
>
> *Wrightslaw: From Emotions to Advocacy The Special Education Survival Guide* by Peter W. D. Wright and Pamela Darr Wright
>
> *How To Compromise With Your School District Without Compromising Your Child: A Field Guide For Getting Effective Services For Children With Special Needs* by Gary Mayerson

Thoroughly evaluating the child can provide a great deal of information that can help decide if your child has a disability and how an Individualized Education Plan can be specifically designed for your child's needs.

You are one of the most significant people on the evaluation team. In addition to you, there should be at least one regular education teacher, a special education teacher, service providers, a school administrator who is familiar with all programs at the school for both regular and special education, a professional who can interpret the evaluation results and talk about what instruction may be necessary, as well as individuals who have knowledge about your child, such as the foster care worker. Do not forget about other qualified professionals who are familiar with your child's situation. These professionals may include a school psychologist, an occupational therapist, a speech and language pathologist, a physical therapist, or a medical specialist.

**What makes up a good evaluation?** Individual and group tests scores, observations of your child's teaching team — your observations and concerns can provide a starting point. Medical records, psychological reports, birth parent information, counseling observations can also provide a more global picture of the child's disabilities. The evaluation team, with your permission, should collect information about your child from many different people and in many different ways. Tests are an important part of an evaluation, but they are only a part.

Once the evaluation is completed, many foster parents are uncertain as to what should happen next. The evaluation team will determine if your foster child meets the definition of a child with a disability as determined from the IDEA and from the policies your state or district uses. If so, your child will be eligible for special education and related services. In most states, the caseworkers and the kinship parents have the right to receive a copy of the evaluation report. If the group decides that your kinship child is not eligible for special education services, the school system must tell you this in writing and explain why your child has been found "not eligible." Make certain that you know what policies the school district has for rebuttal to a contested decision for receiving special education.

## Developing an Individualized Education Plan

If your child is found eligible for special services, the next step is to develop an Individualized Education Plan to address the child's basic disabilities. Once eligibility is established, a meeting must be held within 30 days to develop the IEP, which is a written program statement of the educational program designed to meet a child's individual needs. Every child who receives special education services must have an IEP. The IEP will: (1) set learning goals for your child; and (2) state the services that the school district will provide for the child. Please bear in mind, that it is important that children with disabilities participate in the general curriculum as much as possible. In addition, participation in the mainstream extracurricular activities and other nonacademic activities is also important. Your child's IEP needs to be written with this in mind.

## A child's IEP will contain:

1. Present levels of achievement and educational performance. This statement describes how your child is currently doing in school. This includes how your child's disability affects his or her involvement and progress in the general curriculum.

2. The IEP must state annual goals for your child. Annual goals reflect what the team thinks he or she can reasonably accomplish in a year.

3. The IEP must also list the special education and related services to be provided to your child. Related services can include, but are not limited to transportation, speech-language pathology, audiology services, psychological services, physical therapy, occupational therapy, early identification and assessment, counseling services, orientation and mobility services, medical services for diagnostic or evaluation purposes, school health services, social work services in schools, and parent counseling and training.

4. The IEP must also define how much of the school day the child will be educated separately from nondisabled children or not participate in extracurricular or other nonacademic activities such as lunch or other activities.

5. The IEP should also address testing modifications or changes in how the tests are administered.

6. In addition, the IEP must state (a) when services and modifications will begin;

(b) how often they will be provided; (c) where they will be provided; and (d) how long they will last.

7 Finally, no later than when your child is 16, the IEP must include measurable post-secondary goals related to training, education, employment, or independent living skills.

A meeting must be scheduled with you to review your child's progress and develop your child's next IEP at least one time per year. The team will discuss your child's progress toward the goals in the current IEP and what new goals should be added. There can be changes if need dictates in the special education and related services. This annual IEP meeting allows you and the school to review your child's educational program and change it as necessary. Remember, you don't have to wait for this annual review. You may ask to have your child's IEP reviewed or revised at any time. Under the IDEA, your child must be re-evaluated at least every three years. The purpose of the re-evaluation is to find out if your child continues to be a "child with a disability."

Remember that you do have a role in this process. The law is clear that parents or guardians including kinship caregivers have the right to participate in developing the child's IEP. Your input is invaluable. You know the child well, and the school needs to know your insights and concerns. It's important that you attend these meetings and share your ideas about the child's needs and strengths.

*Mary Eaddy is executive director of PRO-Parents of South Carolina; the South Carolina PTI. She has been affiliated with PRO-Parents since its inception in 1990 when it became the parent training and information center for South Carolina. She serves on multiple task forces and committees with the South Carolina Department of Education, South Carolina Department of Mental Health, South Carolina Department of Social Services, South Carolina Developmental Disabilities Council as well as other state and local agencies. Eaddy's most relevant knowledge and passion for her work comes from parenting two children with learning disabilities and attention deficit disorder and being grandmother to a grandchild with developmental delays*

*June Bond, Med, earned a bachelor of arts in psychology and a master of education in early childhood education from Converse College. She is the executive director of Adoption Advocacy of South Carolina. She has published numerous articles that relate to adoption, education, and family issues and speaks nation-wide on adoption-related issues. She was South Carolina Adoption Advocate of the Year in 1995. She is also the 2006 Congressional Angel in Adoption recipient. She is the mother of six children. She resides in Spartanburg with Bill, her husband of 30 years. This article originally appeared in **Fostering Families Today** magazine.*

# The Teen Years

"*And every time I think of her story of having a child at 15 (who was me) and how we grew up basically together — I am reminded that teenagers are children.*"

# Parenting the Hormonally Challenged: Teens and Sexuality
*By Denise Goodman, PhD*

Many parents feel overwhelmed or tentative about the prospect of dealing with their teenager's emerging sexuality. For many kinship care families, this task is complicated by the fact that the youth may have been sexually abused as a younger child. The following provides a good foundation for parenting teens around sexuality issues:

1. **Be comfortable with your own sexuality and theirs, too.** Too often, adults are paralyzed when it comes to discussing sexuality with teens. Teens are sexual beings and since birth have been growing sexually as well as cognitively, physically, socially, morally, and emotionally. However, the influx of hormones and the onset of puberty put sexual growth in the forefront of the youth's developmental processes. While there are many "normal" behaviors during this stage — promiscuity, sexual aggression and gender identity issues may be signals that the youth is dealing with past abuse issues.

2. **Build trust:** Teens who have been sexually abused often lack basic trust in adults. They may be scared of the dark, the bathroom, the basement, or a medical examination. It is critical that parents be supportive by accompanying the teen to the doctor's office or by installing nightlights without drawing attention to the teen's fear. Teenagers need to know that they can count on consistency, honesty, and support from their parents to make them feel safe and secure.

3. **Set clear boundaries:** Sexually abused youth have had their basic physical boundaries violated. Kinship care parents must work to restore them. Clear boundaries that apply to all family members must be set for dress, privacy, and physical touch:

   *DRESS:* Examples for dress are that every family member must be covered when coming out of the bathroom or bedroom, no coming to breakfast in your underwear, and the youth can't see company without proper clothing. Encouragement during shopping trips can assist in more appropriate clothing selections.

   *PRIVACY:* Examples for re-establishing a sense of privacy are knocking or warning before entering bedrooms and bathrooms and making rules about when it's okay to close doors. Another rule of privacy is that no one listens to another's phone conversations or opens another's mail.

   *PHYSICAL TOUCH:* Parents must approach physical touch with caution, and caregivers should avoid any contact that could be misconstrued as abuse. The parent should gain the teen's permission to hug or touch him or her. Rules for touch should generally be that "okay" touches are above the shoulder and below the knee, and the youth should have the power to decline any physical affection or touch.

4. **Learn to talk with teens about sex:** To assist youth in dealing with their victimization or to support their normal development, use the correct language and not slang names or euphemisms. Parents who avoid conversations about sexuality force teens to learn from unreliable and inaccurate sources such as their peers, siblings, or

the media. Parents can think about the five toughest questions they could be asked and prepare answers so that if the opportunity presents itself, they'll be prepared.

5. **Educate the youth:** It is important to give teenagers accurate information about sex, sexuality, and human reproduction. This may be difficult for parents who may feel education will lead to sexual intercourse and experimentation. However, teens need information, not taboos. Sexually abused children need to learn about the emotional side of sex, as they have been prematurely exposed to the physical side of sex. Both boys and girls need to learn about birth control and sexually transmitted diseases. Parents can seek help from community agencies such as Planned Parenthood and Family Planning.

6. **Use the "3 C's" in an emergency:** It is not uncommon for a parent to encounter a "sexual situation" that involves their teen. Consequently, all parents must be prepared to handle these incidents as therapeutically as possible.

   *CALM:* Remain calm while confronting the situation, even if it requires getting calm or faking calm. When parents are in control of themselves, they are able to use more effective strategies to handle the situation.

   *CONFRONT:* Confront any unacceptable behaviors. This information should be given specifically and gently without threatening or shaming. Too many times parents say, "Don't do that" or "Stop it" without being specific. Teens can become confused or ashamed if they are not confronted directly and supportively.

   *CORRECT:* Since a teen's behavior is purposeful, offer the youth a substitute behavior to use when the need arises. Suggest more acceptable and appropriate alternatives. When the youth uses the alternative behavior, give positive reinforcement.

7. **Advocate:** Parents must advocate for the needs of their children. Teens who have been sexually victimized may need a variety of services; therefore, the parent should advocate with the social worker, agency, or the mental health center until the services are in place. This may mean that the parent calls every week or even every day and leaves messages. The parent may need to contact managers or administrators to obtain services for their teen. In other words, ask until you get what you need for your child.

## Conclusion

Sexuality is a normal part of human growth and development. Every teen, including you and me, struggled to figure out who we were as sexual beings. Today's teens are bombarded with sexual stimuli in music, on TV, in the movies, and on the radio. Coupled with a past history of sexual abuse, it can be a daunting task for a teen to come to terms with who they are sexually. Be supportive and understanding...and remember, a sense of humor goes a long way.

*Denise Goodman, PhD, is an adoption consultant and trainer with 25 years of experience in child welfare, protective services, and foster parenting. She currently conducts workshops and consultations throughout the United States on topics related to foster care and adoption.*

# Adolescence: Surviving and Thriving
*By Brenda McCreight, PhD, RSW*

## The Evolving Challenge

The teen years — we've only considered this time of life, carved out between childhood and adulthood, since the late 1890's. Prior to that, boys and girls matured later with menstruation rarely beginning before age 16. By that age, youths were considered to be young adults and they were expected to undertake the responsibilities of work and marriage. As the demands of the workforce changed with industrialization and the availability of food increased, puberty onset began earlier and entry into the workforce was delayed, thus creating a time in life that was not defined by economic need or biological function. So there we were, for the first time in recorded history, with a socially defined life stage that held no particular value beyond the emotional place the youth had in the family.

It may seem like we should have figured out what to do with this life stage by now, but 120 years is a pretty short length of time for people to develop a new set of social constructs and role definitions. And, to make it more complicated, this life stage isn't generalized throughout all societies; it's mainly evolved in North America and has been shaped by, and reflected back into, the values of Western society and culture. So, we stand almost alone in this historical journey, inventing and re-inventing adolescence with each generation.

Today, this stage of life has become negatively associated with rejection of parental values, drugs and alcohol, a separate set of music and cultural idols, and its own use and interpretation of language. Indeed, with the rapid expansion and dissemination of technology, the younger generation often knows how to use current communication devices before parents (i.e. Son, can you show me how to use my new phone?). That the young have access to more ways of communicating and defining how these are used is unprecedented in history.

With adolescence continuing to evolve, parenting has also had to change with each generation. Few of us parent the same way we were parented, and I doubt anyone does it the way our grandparents did. The demands and expectations we place on our children have also changed and increased. Today's children and youth are expected to learn more in school, to achieve highly, to participate in a myriad of after school activities, and to avoid peer pressure that might lead them astray. With the dangers of easily available drugs and alcohol, and the fear of other negative influences ( What do I do with a 16-year-old who has become the queen of Goths at school? and "How will I know if my son is beginning to experience annihilation type delusions brought on by overexposure to violent video games?") adolescence has become a time that creates fear and uncertainty in many parents and in society.

## The Adolescent Brain

Those of us who foster teens, or adopt older children and teens, often find that these fears are compounded by the fact that our teens' brains were negatively impacted and indeed, altered in structure and function, by the prenatal exposure to drugs, tobacco, and alcohol, and by their early experiences of neglect, abuse, and multiple caregivers. So, not only do we have the general problems of raising youth in a culture that doesn't know what to do with this life stage, we have the added factor of raising youth who may not have the capacity to respond and react in a healthy manner to the demands of today's world.

Some people question why we need to understand the adolescent brain. Isn't it enough, they ask, to simply deal with the behaviors? The answer is, no, it isn't enough. There isn't a technique or approach that is right for every single foster or adopted teen, or for every parent and every family. Different people use and respond to different things. In order to understand the foster or adopted teen, we first need a basic understanding of what makes them tick so that we can devise, in the moment it's needed, the best way to handle difficult situations and even reduce some of the potential problems.

The adolescent brain undergoes a massive change beginning at about 13 and finally finishes its work by age 25. During this time, the brain connections grow and interconnect in a way that selectively changes over time to meet the needs of the environment and to respond to the incoming stimuli — that is, the family, the peer scene, the school, the overall culture etc. For our teens, this also may include the additional emotional tasks of dealing with birth family, or with foster/identity issues, or with abandonment and lack of attachment as well as the almost overwhelming tasks of an altered brain undergoing basic change. At this stage, it begins with the grey matter volume increasing in the pre-teen stage, followed by sustained loss and thinning starting around puberty, which happens at the same time as advancing cognitive abilities. This process results in greater organization of the brain as it prunes useless or underused connections, and enhances the tissues that transmit brain messages.

At the same time, areas associated with fairly basic functions, including the motor and sensory areas, mature rather early in the process. Areas involved in planning and decision making and the cognitive or reasoning area of the brain (which are important for controlling impulses and emotions), seem to develop much later, more toward the end of the process. The part that leads to so much risky behavior and is the cause of so many grey hairs developing in parents, is rooted in the brain's reward center which becomes more active during adolescence, so the adolescent brain still is strengthening connections between its reasoning- and emotion-related regions.

## Parents Do Make the Difference

In a nutshell, the brain grows massively, and the parts that are underused are basically pruned off, while the parts that are regularly used and stimulated are allowed to grow and shape the personality of the youth. What does that mean for our teens? Well, to begin with, many of them are still stuck in behaviors that are rooted in trauma. The early traumas will have dug deeply into the youth's brain and are regularly stimulated by a life of uncertainty. For example, the worry, "Will I be moved from this foster home before the end of the school year?" is going to further entrench and activate the abandonment issues. So is, "Will my foster mom think I'm just like my birth mom if she finds out I smoked pot last weekend?" and "If I don't sleep with my new boyfriend will he leave me just like everyone else in my life has?" and "Is my foster dad going to yell at me again when he sees the make-up I'm wearing?" and "Will my foster parents dump me when they find out I've been stealing again?" The sexual and/or physical abuse traumas are triggered constantly by the sexual pressure placed on our teens by society and peers. As well, if the parents don't address the underlying trauma openly, then the teen's attempts to meet expectations while repressing the memories will also dig the trauma deeper and deeper into the maturing brain so that these memories become the foundation of the brain structure and the subsequent behaviors. The teen begins to experience what has been called "emotional self-mutilation" which is demonstrated by rages, running away, drug and alcohol abuse, and other forms of self-harm.

It often seems like our kids don't give any thought to how or what we parents are feeling. In reality though, they consider our behaviors constantly. And, what we have to realize that how we, the parents or caregivers, choose to interact with our teens will influence what genes and neurons are activated in our teens' brains. Our reactions to their behaviors will, to a large part, determine whether their brains are flushed with the destructive stress hormones which shut down reasoning and communication as well as destroy any potential for resolution; or, whether our own behaviors toward the teen will decrease the stress hormones and bring in the self soothing and calming hormones and chemicals which allow for attachment, communication and resolution — and most importantly, healthy relationships and positive behaviors. Maybe the situation can't be resolved as in "You aren't going to the party tonight even if every other teen in town is allowed" may have to stand, but the conflict and the emotional energy can be toned down and the relationship left intact so that there can be resolution tomorrow, or even a year from now, and the relationship remains strong.

## Key Parental Behaviors

Regardless of what parenting methods and behavioral approaches you decide to use in your family, they will only succeed if they are created from an emotional attitude on the part of the parent that allows for nurturing, calm, and provides a general feeling of wanting the best for the child or youth. That may seem impossible at times, and once again, the burden is on the parent to set the tone even in the face of a youth who is hurling the F-word around or a 10-year-old who is raging and throwing chairs against the window. However, if the parent follows some basic steps in emotional climate control, most of the more severe outbursts can be avoided.

To begin, as soon as there is any escalation on the part of the child or youth, the parent needs to do a quick mental survey of himself or herself and determine his or her own level of anger or bad mood. It's always going to be up to the parent to get to the right emotional space quickly and as much work as that feels like, it's what we all signed up for when we became kinship or adoptive parents. Taking some deep breaths, focusing on the child, clearing the area (no audience, please), and sitting down are first steps to sidetracking a raging youth. Follow that with a lowered voice tone, and a calm appearance. Most importantly, the adult has to remember that *this is about building and maintaining a relationship and changing an emotional state* — it's not about drug abuse or school failures or sexual acting out or any other topic that lead to this particular conflict. After all, consider what you would do with a screaming, kicking six-month-old — you wouldn't tell her to be quiet, or to stop it and you wouldn't challenge her feelings. Instead, you would stop what you were doing and walk her up and down the room, cuddling and cooing, until she was able to regulate her emotional state. Our children and teens are simply larger versions of an angry six-month-old, with the same inability to self-regulate. No matter how angry our teens are, no matter how foul mouthed, or aggressively dressed they are, they are victims of a rotten childhood that left them unable to self regulate and in as much need of the external regulation the parent provides as a six-month-old. If they could do better, they would. You can, you will.

It's always important to remember in times of escalating conflict, that if you change the youth's emotional state, the change in behaviors will follow. Once you have seated yourself, regulated your breathing, lowered your voice tone, and removed the audience, your mirror neurons will start to help. What are mirror neurons? These are neural circuits located in the frontal lobes that fire off in response to the people we are with. If you watch a football game, your pulse can get as high as that of your favorite player on the field. If you get into an argument with your teen, the emotional arousal of your teen will be "mirrored" in your own neurons and you will begin to escalate your own behavior. However, you are not at the beck and call of your teen's neurons — you have a mind that can exert control and so it becomes the parental responsibility to use his or her own mirror neurons to regulate those of the teens.

This takes considerable self-awareness on the part of the parent. It's not easy to withstand the anger and chaos that is launched from the angry and unreasoning teen. Still, it can be done. And, if the parent practices this state of mindful interaction and self-regulation on a daily basis, it sets a tone in the relationship that often prevents further angry escalation and confrontations. The teen needs to find the same stability in the foster or adoptive parent that he or she should have found in the birth parent. As the foster or adoptive parent becomes better at creating this positive relationship based connection with the teen, the brain of the adolescent can begin to change and resolve into the more mature version that is supposed to be developing.

*Brenda McCreight, PhD, RSW, is an adoptive parent, therapist, and the author of* **Recognizing and Managing Fetal Alcohol Syndrome/Effects: A Guidebook; Parenting Your Adopted Older Child** *and the children's book* **Eden's Secret Journal: The Story of An Older Child Adoption**. *Brenda is the mother of 14 children, 12 of whom are adopted and are considered to have special needs. Since 1982 Brenda has worked as a therapist with children and families facing issues such as sexual abuse and family violence as well as adoption and foster related concerns. Brenda is a writer and a sought after speaker in the area of behavior disorders. Her website is www.theadoptioncounselor.com.*

# Teenage Kincare
*By Sherry Howard*

Parenting a teenager was the last thing I expected to do in my sixties! When I said this to a psychologist I worked with years ago, he answered that few people lived out their older years as they expected to, especially if they had children. When I first flew solo with Hunter after his parents' bitter divorce, I expected to share the parenting, being there only as needed. However, both parents took so many detours that I often had complete responsibility for Hunter, with help from other family members. Even as it became clear that I would have Hunter with me for the long haul, I always expected that his parents would one day step up and want him to be more a part of their lives. Now, at nearly 15 years old, I expect that Hunter will always be with me full time since I now have sole custody of him. Hunter and I are both happy with this!

So here we are, Hunter and I, muddling our way through his teenage years together, with one night most weekends with his dad and daily calls from both parents. Our kinship arrangement would be challenging in general; it's especially challenging for us. I am disabled with a spinal cord injury sustained when I was a school principal. I am also a widow, with a new appreciation for single parents; I was abysmally ignorant about the special challenges facing single parents. Hunter has ADD and asthma, which has been in crisis several times, requiring EMS calls and hospitalizations. All families have their unique challenges and those are ours. We have many blessings which offset these challenges. I work hard to "normalize" our lives as much as possible.

> *Parenting a teenager was the last thing I expected to do in my sixties!*

In the early years of abandonment, it was extremely difficult. Almost every night at bedtime held special challenges. Hunter could neither understand, nor accept that his parents were not there for him any more. However, during those years, it was easier to distract with fancy footwork, excuses, and wildly imaginative play and storytelling. Hunter was not really aware how different it was to have neither parent caring for him and his world was pretty small, requiring no explanations to other people about our living arrangements. And, often, his mother would pop into his life, even living with us, although not providing his care. He more easily accepted any explanation, such as mommy and daddy being at work or just away without too many questions, just a lot of sadness.

Early, he learned not to share information from one home to another as he visited, always afraid of getting someone in trouble and having even his limited contact cut off. I learned much later of the many dangers he was exposed to and never told about. He suffered silently, yet with visible effects like thumb sucking, bedwetting, and eating issues. It really took a village; we had so much support from his aunt and uncle in those early years and he was integrated into their family activities as soon as they had their own children. Our large extended family has always provided huge love and support for Hunter, also. His occasional visits to his paternal grandparents were infrequent but a positive part of his life.

The elementary school years were challenging for me because he became more aware that *his* parent was a grandma. I volunteered at his schools and stayed involved and kept him busy with sports and activities; he saw that most people just assumed that I was an older parent. But he always wanted it known that I was not his mother. There was constant discord in our lives during those years because his parents stayed involved with him sporadically and sometimes in a negative way. Those were the years that Hunter developed the ability to "split" in three, being with a mother, a father and a caregiver in different ways and constantly transitioning to accommodate the changes. He always required time when returning from visits to assimilate the change of environment, needing to be left alone for a while until he was once again grounded at home. I feel that he has kept many secrets, some of which he eventually shared or which I discovered otherwise. Hunter always needed to hear the backup plan for his living arrangements; to lessen his fears of abandonment we often reviewed the list of all the people who "wanted" Hunter if anything happened to me. He needed constant reassurance that I was not going anywhere!

Then came the middle school, pre-teen, and early teen years. Add the roller coaster of puberty to the roller coaster of life with shared families and it's a sure mix for problems. And we had our share of problems. Our health scares during that time kept us focused on caring for Hunter's asthma carefully and football kept us grounded and busy. Hunter's wonderful best friend and his family became an important part of Hunter's life. Hunter and his friend were baptized together and spent all of their spare time together, a healthy part of adolescence you have to accommodate.

When I was a middle school principal, some of the most "at-risk" boys I saw were those who had been babied by older parents. Those boys were ill-prepared to survive in the real world, having been protected from harsh reality and those ups and downs of a normal childhood that teach children life's lessons. Those were the kids who were picked on unmercifully. Early on, I made a conscious decision that I could at least avoid that mistake with my grandson and not be overprotective. His middle school assistant principal thought the world of Hunter, complimenting what an awesome kid he is!

His early middle school years were probably the easiest from an emotional perspective, with his father gaining more stability and engagement with him and an overall excellent school experience for three years. At that age he understood more and questioned less, seeming to have a growing acceptance of the "limitations" of his own situation. He also at that time cared a lot more about peer interactions than family, getting a lot of his reinforcement from social interactions. He continued to stay involved in football, the sport he had preferred since the age of six. This is a wonderful sport for boys needing an identity; the bonding opportunities are tremendous! There were many struggles for me to just have him where he needed to be when he needed to be there. Often, my days were from 5:30 a.m. until midnight, doing high energy activities I did not really expect to do and sometimes hated to do. Who *wants* to get up at 5:30 a.m. to get someone ready for school when they finished doing that years ago?

Hunter's middle school years were also the years he really began to grapple with his mother's mental illness and abusive marriage. These things preoccupied a lot of his emotions. Eventually, I sought the guidance of a police officer, who spoke with Hunter frankly about the situations he encountered and taught him to self-protect and report. She was a wonderful influence in helping him adjust to the emotional discord that occurs when a parent places her child in danger. I also sought help from psychologists and talked with Hunter in detail about some of the issues I had tried to keep hidden from him. The psychologist advised that by the age of 11 or 12, one must begin to answer questions honestly to maintain a sense of trust. So, I did, and those were some hard conversations. However, after those conversations, Hunter seemed to have a greater ability to verbalize his fears and concerns for his mother without fear of consequences. During those years, because of the repeated dangers her behavior presented, I was awarded sole custody. This also helped Hunter's sense of stability and control. His mother lost the ability to use him as a weapon to get what she wanted, and he no longer was required by law to go with her when he was afraid to.

Then, this year, high school started. Hunter is nearly six feet tall with a football player's build. The physical dynamics of our relationship went crazy quickly, with Hunter looking down on me during his frequent bear hugs!

Expecting a hard transition as Hunter met new people and teachers and had greater independence, I was pleasantly surprised that he actually began to have conversations with other kids about the difficulties of their home lives. He began to learn that many children had less than ideal situations, learning about the many children with totally absent fathers and the parents who beat their children and the kids who had no home at all. In comparison, he began to count his blessings, I think, from a more mature perspective.

The teen years lessened the confusion about our arrangements but that clarity brings another set of problems. There are still huge challenges during these teen years: physical, emotional, social, educational, financial, and familial. I operate on the same principles I did as a school principal: never show your fears or insecurities and be in command at all times. This is often difficult to do in a time of crisis, but it is the only way for children to feel safe; they have to know that the adult can handle the situation.

The physical challenges are real. You don't have the energy or the enthusiasm you had for your own children and will regret the limits this places on the child you are raising. Your life with this child will likely be different from your earlier parenting for sheer lack of energy! It's hard, after you think you are finished, to be up at 6:00 a.m. and keep up with school, activities, sports, home maintenance, involvement with other grandchildren, and your own parents. It's unlikely you will have an expansive social life.

Social challenges include the judgments people can make about children whose parents are not raising them, categorizing them by the sins of their parents. Neither you nor your child fit well in social categories, at least not in our neck of the woods. I found no other parents in my area in the same situation and Hunter knew few kids who lived with no parent in the home. It does set you apart socially. We have great friends and a large family, so for us it has been okay, but I expect it could be isolating for some people.

Educational challenges are, of course, unique to each child. However, children with so much stress in their livese will experience distractions that affect them academically. I have been known to allow a mental health day for Hunter when extreme stress has given him a sleepless night after an unpleasant episode. Fortunately, Hunter has always tried hard and tutors have been within our budget when needed. Generally, share as little information as needed with school personnel; it seldom serves a purpose and will result in gossip sometimes, even though it shouldn't.

Financial burdens are different for each family. We have been blessed with just enough to meet our needs comfortably. However, the expenses I've incurred to try to help Hunter's mother have eliminated all savings I've ever had and exceed $100,000. There are no college savings for Hunter, although I was able to pay my children's undergraduate college expenses. I expect most people meet greater financial challenges than I do and access the limited funding that is available for kinship care. This funding is critical to these families and shouldn't be so difficult to get.

Familial problems are unexpected when they come. There is just an undercurrent of judgment from some family members and a lack of understanding or interest from many. My family has been my greatest support but there is loneliness about this which even close family can't address. It is difficult for my other grandchildren to understand why Hunter gets to live here and why I buy him everything. We talk openly about it. I actually started a small allowance for my nine-year-old grandchild so he would not feel so left out. It really worked to make him feel special, too. Because Hunter lives here, my other grandchildren stay here often, creating our own micro family much of the time. My four-year-old granddaughter recently drew a picture of all the people who lived in our house and included her and her brother in it.

The greatest challenge for me has been the "aloneness" of the journey. The emotional burden has been heavy. I don't really "fit" with my age peers and sure can't keep up with the younger parents. I enjoy my extended family and work at maintaining my closest friendships, but my life is about the PTA while theirs are about retirement travels. Support groups are nonexistent in my area and I don't have the time or energy anyway. Knowing that I will parent until such a late age is daunting. It is all worth it because every day I have a wonderful kid and we share a special bond!

## My advice to anyone parenting a teen in a kinship arrangement is:

- Normalize your home life as much as possible by permitting your child to be childlike with pets, other children, and chaos invading your home. It will be worth it.
- Seek professional advice when you are unsure from attorneys, counselors, psychologists, or other professionals.
- Develop a strong support system. It will work best if you include family members since they will best understand the uniqueness of your situation. Your support system will be fluid as your needs will change throughout the years.
- Enforce rules without guilt...your failure to do this will do much harm. Recognize that being a full-time parent limits your ability to be indulgent.
- Discuss the differences in your rules and expectations compared to other settings.
- Always express love, compassion, and respect for the parents no matter how unearned that is.
- Respect the need for quiet time to soothe the inner chaos. This child needs time to process a lot more information than most children deal with.
- Discuss honestly the problems he encounters with parents such as drug abuse, criminal behavior, neglect, financial issues, or mental illness in age appropriate ways. You may need to get professional guidance.
- Acknowledge and discuss weaknesses that your caregiving creates, try to be creative with solutions and always ask, "What can I do to make this situation better for you?"

- Be as involved as possible in school and activities for as long as you can; he will let you know when to back off.
- Be aware of the abandonment issues your child will face and the stronger need for parental love no matter how much he loves you...this is normal.
- Listen, listen, listen. Have sideways conversations instead of sit-downs. Find ways to talk without pressure, riding in the car, getting ready for dinner, passing through a room. Teens generally don't like to "sit down" and talk; save that for emergencies or when they approach you.
- Help them keep their expectations for their parents minimal, so they are not constantly disappointed. Emphasize the positive and praise the smallest positive things a parent does. If a child can feel his or her parent cares the child will be happier.
- Keep the communication open with the parents, and keep your home open to them if possible. Often that isn't possible, but it is ideal.
- Accept the emotional complexities that come with puberty. There will be more embarrassment about not having the involvement of parents. Don't be surprised to hear your child lie to cover up this lack of involvement.
- Be prepared for a broader life which includes needs for transportation and midnight pickups among other things.
- Be strong, steady, stable, and sure of yourself even when you don't feel that way...he needs your strength.
- Use your maturity to your advantage: you know better than to sweat the small stuff.

*Sherry Howard is a freelance writer and editor. Howard's advanced degree and experience as an award-winning school principal in one of the largest urban school districts in the United States provided her with a broad background on the growth and development of children. During her career in education, she authored and edited many professional publications and earned her black belt in understanding kids! Howard's other credentials include consulting with a major publisher, advocating for special needs children, and volunteer work in the schools she loves. Her kinship experiences with her grandson influenced her to share the challenges and joy of a kinship caregiver through writing. Her own kinship experiences taught her that parenting chosen children is an especially rewarding journey. Howard's current project is a mystery for adolescent readers inspired by her grandson and his friends.*

# Response Styles

*By Andrea B. Smith, PhD, and Linda L. Dannison, PhD*

**Example:** (Grandchild to grandparent) "Everyone else gets to go hang out at the mall. Why can't I go and stay there as late as I want to? I like to be with my friends."

1. **INFORMATION GIVING** — The mall is a place where people go to shop, not hang out.

2. **ADVICE GIVING/ORDERING** — Instead of hanging out at the mall you should spend more time working on your school work.

3. **RIDICULING/CRITICIZING** — You're always making a big deal out of nothing.

4. **THREATENING** — If you don't stop asking me that, I'll never let you go out with your friends again.

5. **IGNORING** — (Grandparent walks out of the room)

6. **LABELING/STEREOTYPING** — A kid like you is always making a little problem into a big deal.

7. **MORALIZING/LECTURING** — I have told you many times why I don't want you to go to the mall. All the kids there are up to no good. I'm not going to let you...

8. **QUESTIONING** — Why don't you think of something to do at home with your time?

9. **CHANGING THE TOPIC** — So, what did you do in school today?

10. **DISAGREEING/DENYING** — None of your friends get to go to the mall every time they want to. They all have curfews too.

11. **SHARING OWN EXPERIENCE** — You think this is unfair. When I was a child, no one ever went to the mall. We rarely saw our friends except during the school day.

12. **AGREEING/SUPPORTING** — You're right. A lot of your friends do go to the mall and hang out.

13. **REFLECTING/CLARIFYING** — You must feel that I am over-protective when I don't let you go to the mall or come home as late as you would like.

14. I **STATEMENT** — Although I am glad that you have friends you like to spend time with, I worry about your well-being. I want what is best for you.

# What's With Those Teenagers?

*By Penny G. Davis, MA*

Raising teenagers is no easy task. Most parents and other caregivers, past and present, have had challenges living and working with this age group. Never before have we had to raise teens amidst the onslaught of media influences and technology that we are faced with in today's culture.

The good news is, we have much more knowledge today about adolescent development and how the teenage brain works, both of which can help us understand and cope with some of the behaviors that we see, and find challenging.

## Identity vs. Confusion

Developmentally, according to Erik Erikson's social-emotional stages, teens are in the stage of "Identity vs. Confusion." By the end of their adolescence, young adults need to have a pretty good sense of who they are, what kind of career they might like to pursue (although this may change during their 20s), what values they hold dear, and other similar concepts. They also need to have some skills around decision-making and problem-solving — after all, most will be off to college or working and living on their own, and will assume at least some adult responsibilities. This explains why during their teen years, many of our children seem to question everything adults say and do, test our limits at every turn, and even reject the values we have taught them. We parents/caregivers who were once so smart in their eyes, have now become totally clueless about almost every subject. Try not to take it personally...it's not really about us — it's about them. Teens are trying to figure out who they are. Because they don't know or aren't sure who they are or want to be yet, they only know who they're NOT — us! Because teens know that we love them uncondi-tionally and they are safe with us, they are able to try out "new" attitudes and behaviors with us. Most often, once our teens have moved through this developmental phase, they come back around and embrace many of the values we helped instill.

## Under Construction

Another thing that's helpful to understand is the change occurring in the brain of the adolescent. Research now tells us that the teen brain functions quite a bit differently than the adult brain. There are many books on the subject, two of which are listed at the end of this article, so I won't discuss specifics here. Suffice it to say that the teen brain, and in particular, the prefrontal cortex (responsible for reasoning, understanding cause and effect, controlling emotions, and similar thought processes) is "under construction." As puberty hits, there is a huge upsurge of activity in the prefrontal cortex, similar to the activity of the new brain in infancy. How this "construction" phase of brain development during the teen years plays out in behavior, is that emotions tend to rule, quick rewards are valued over long-term ones, and spontaneous "this could be fun" decisions outweigh thinking about the consequences of said decision. Several other factors come into play. One of the first factors includes the importance of peers. Teens begin to spend much more time with others their own age than they do with parents. It's hard for us to not take this personally, but it's really a biological, survival mechanism. Teens need to bond with other teens because they are forming relationships that will help them leave the nest, so to speak, and learn how to survive in this new world they are about to enter called adulthood. Second, the adolescent sleep/wake cycles are slightly askew. The circadian rhythm, the biological/brain clock that, for adults, begins to slow our bodies and minds down in the evening in order to prepare for sleep, is pushed back a bit for teens. This makes it difficult for them to sleep at night. This was only a slight issue in bygone eras when teens had few distractions to keep them up...once the candle burned down, with no radio, TV computer or cell phone, they were forced into sleep. Not so today — our teens have all of this technology at their fingertips. Recently a grandparent shared with me that she discovered her granddaughter with her cell phone on vibrate, hidden under her pillow, so that if she got a call while she was sleeping, she could wake up and answer. Research on sleep tells us that teenagers need an average of a little more than nine hours of sleep each night to be fully rested and functional. Most of our teens are getting six or seven hours. So, to summarize, we are looking at young people who are often sleep-deprived, likely to make spontaneous decisions, and take risks, based on emotions and quick rewards, and to whom "fitting in" with peers is of great importance. No wonder they get into difficulty!

## History Of Trauma

Adolescents in our homes who have a history of trauma (abuse, neglect, etc) tend to struggle even more, primarily because of compromised attachment in their early years. Without secure, nurturing attachment in the early years, these teens may still struggle to attach (feel loved, connected, and safe) with their caregivers, at a time when developmentally they are supposed to individuate. They may already have a compromised ability to use the "causal thinking" part of the prefrontal cortex that allows them to understand cause and effect and thereby think through situations and make good decisions. They often have a lessened ability to regulate emotions, and a heightened "thrill-seeking" (feel good) desire. All of these factors make it even more challenging to live and/or work with these children when they become adolescents.

## Tools and Strategies

Here are some tools and strategies that are helpful with teens with trauma backgrounds.

**Focus on attachment first.** Look for ways to build the relationship and help them feel safe — understand and validate feelings without judging or moralizing; providing structure and regular routines, respond to "sense" needs they may have missed in their early years — for example, spending time outdoors, listening to music, dancing, baking, and other activities.

**Let teens get extra rest when they can** — it might be important to allow them to "catch up" by sleeping in on the weekends, or taking a nap after school when possible.

**Have clear rules, expectations, and limits**, but work to have as few "non-negotiable" rules as possible to ensure the safety and comfort of everyone in the family. As teens are finding out who they are, they need to feel they have some control or personal power in their lives. Negotiate and compromise on things that you can, in discussion with teens. If their curfew is 10:30, and they want to stay out until midnight, perhaps you can compromise on 11 or 11:15. If it's their responsibility to do dishes or mow the lawn, give them some choice about when it gets done.

**Ask "what and how" questions,** to show your interest in their lives, but to also give them the opportunity to practice problem-solving. For example, "what do you think you might want to do after high school?" "How are you going to accomplish that?" "What's your plan for getting a job?" An important piece here is to ask these in a spirit of curiosity, not blaming or with any hidden agenda.

**Practice problem-solving** in conversation WITH your teen taking into consideration his or her ideas and concerns, then making agreements.

**Focus on solutions.** Punishment only pushes them into resentment and revenge. Asking what happened, how it happened, and helping the teen figure out how to repair the situation or what he or she can do differently next time, is much more effective in building attachment and in growing the ability to problem-solve.

**Whenever possible, encourage and empower them** — let them know you have faith in them, that you love them no matter what.

## RECOMMENDED READING

**Positive Discipline for Teenagers.** Jane Nelsen, EdD, Lynn Lott, M.A, M.F.T

**Brainstorm: The Power and Purpose of the Teenage Brain,** Daniel J. Siegel, M.D

*Penny G. Davis, MA, is a certified Positive Discipline Lead Trainer and does relationship, parenting education, and teacher training consultation.*

## Family Talk: How to Handle Teen Lying
### By Drs. James and Mary Kenny

**Q: Dear Mary:** My husband and I are feeling betrayed and hopeless because our 16-year-old daughter lies to us. She seems sincere, but on several occasions we found out later that everything she said was untrue. I fear we cannot be close as a family if we cannot trust each other. Is this likely to pass? Is there anything we can do?

– **Pennsylvania**

**A: Dear Pennsylvania:** You describe well parents' feelings of dismay. Most often children lie to keep from getting in trouble. Another reason may be to get their way. As a teenager might put it: "If I told the truth, you wouldn't let me do what I want." These reasons do not excuse lying, but help to recognize why it may occur. Lying frustrates parents like no other misbehavior because lying is totally within the child's control. The usual suggestions about rewarding good behavior and disciplining misbehavior firmly and promptly do not work with lying. Often parents do not even know when the misbehavior is occurring. The parents' only recourse is to take away the payoff for lying. If lying works for the child it is likely to continue. To take away the payoff for deception a parent must verify everything from other sources. Is Lisa staying overnight with her girlfriend? Call the girlfriend's parent. Has Larry skipped school and lied when you questioned him? Contact the school counselor and set up a program to check on and discipline attendance. Call the counselor personally whenever your child is going to be absent. Does Tim come home after curfew with the excuse:"We had a flat tire?" Establish that curfew is curfew. If he is late because of a misfortune, sympathize but impose the penalty anyway. You will have taken away the reason to make up an excuse. Next, when some activity cannot be verified from another source ignore it. You ask: "Where were you?"And he or she responds: "We went to a movie." In most cases the parent cannot verify this. Of course, you could grill the child: "What time did the movie start? Tell me the plot?" Such questioning focuses time and attention on lying. Ideally, you want to ignore lying. Ignoring is an effective way to stop behavior. Suppose each morning on your way to work you meet your neighbor. Each morning you say,"Good morning." Your neighbor, however, never returns your greeting. Rather quickly, you will probably stop your greeting. Ignoring can have the same effect on lying. Will lying stop eventually? Some adolescents who lie grow into adults who are open and honest with their parents. While no one can predict the future, human behavior suggests that lying will stop most quickly when it proves useless and is ignored. Some parents try to "nail" a lying child by setting him or her up. They get evidence from outside sources, let the child lie, then confront him or her with the facts. While such a practice may give the parent a grim satisfaction, it destroys the child's self-respect. It is the cruelest of put-downs and leaves the child no way out. For these reasons it is not a good way to handle lying.

Verify your child's activities from outside sources. Disregard what cannot be verified. With no reason to lie, lies will likely stop.

*Drs. James and Mary Kenny host a regular column in **Fostering Families Today**.*

## Let's Talk About It

*Checklist of things to discuss when youth enters your home:*

⇨ What do you expect of them?

⇨ Where will they sleep and where can they put their things?

⇨ Where are things like shampoo, soap, towels, etc.?

⇨ Do you know anything about them visiting their family?

⇨ Is there anything "off limits" in the house?

⇨ Can they use the kitchen when they want?

⇨ Where are dishes and where do dirty dishes go?

⇨ What about the dirty laundry — do they have to do their own?

⇨ What school will they go to? How will they get there? When can they go and visit if it is a new school?

⇨ How can they get involved in extra-curricular activities? How would that work?

⇨ Can their friends come over? If close enough, can their brothers/sisters visit?

⇨ How much "freedom" do they have here? What can they do with free time?

⇨ What are the rules around TV, using the phone, using the computer, etc.?

⇨ When is bedtime? Do they have a curfew?

⇨ What happens if they don't follow the "rules" of the house?

⇨ What type of chores or "help" around the house is expected of them? How much allowance will they get?

⇨ If old enough can they get a job?

⇨ Will they be involved in family activities and family vacations?

⇨ What are they supposed to call you and how will they be introduced to people in the community?

⇨ Can they date?

**Created by the Iowa Youth Connections Council**

# It's Not "What You Do," it's "How You Be."

*By Mary-Jo Land, CPT, CDDP*

> *"What should I do when my grandson lies?"*
> *"What should we do when our niece steals?"*
> *"What should I do when my grandson hurts his brother?"*

These are questions the "parents," however you came to be a parent to this child, ask frequently. Before I learned about attachment disorder and the effects of early trauma and neglect, I would talk with kin-parents about antecedents, behaviors, and consequences. We would engage in conversations with the child about what the rules are and what will happen if they are broken. This dynamic is at play in most "Western" culture families, and is reflected in our society. Our legal systems focus on negative consequences for unwanted behavior. We use police to gather evidence, courts to examine it, and judges to decide the fate of the accused ne'er-do-well. As a kin-parent do you ever feel as though you have become the police, judg,e and jury when your children misbehave? When behavior is the focus, this is likely to occur.

This cognitive behavioral approach works well with typically-developing children; children who love and trust their parents and who strive to maintain concordance with them. This is the way most of us were raised. We didn't want to get into trouble because we didn't want to feel our parents' disappointment, or experience unwanted emotional distance. Our actions were governed by the internal motivation of feeling in the good graces of our parents. Any breach in that feeling of the positive, protective relationship was uncomfortable, if not painful. The rules that were broken were relatively minor, and correction came quickly with natural and logical consequences. The breach in the relationship was restored. This normal repair system worked because the child with secure attachment has an intact sense of self; she believes that she is good, worthy, and valued; that parents are trustworthy and well-intended; and the world is a safe and interesting place.

Children with early relational trauma begin life with a basic failure of the care-giving system. As a result, they do not develop a secure attachment characterized by trust in the benevolence of the adults in their lives. Rather than basking in the knowledge that they are loved and protected by their parents, they are uncertain about or fearful of parents. Benevolence is not assumed. Maltreatment is anticipated. Rather than an intrinsic motivation to remain emotionally close and harmonious, the motivation becomes survival of the self through independence from others. We see this as pathological or precocious self-reliance. In this way, children with attachment disorder have not had the opportunity to learn to want to be acceptable to the primary caregiver.

Another aspect of this dynamic is the child's need to avoid his or her own inner life. How can the child examine feeling scared, rejected, and shameful when he or she feels alone and without help to do that? Without the ability to reflect on his or her own inner life, the child struggles for any understanding of the inner life of others (Theory of Mind). Emotional and physiological dysregulation are common — and frightening — experiences. Children with traumatic relational experiences often feel out of control. When a behavioral consequence is administered to a child who is out of his or her own control, the child may feel unjustly and unfairly punished because he or she did not consciously intend nor premeditate the misdeed. For some children though, punishment may be sought out as a way to have the parent see the "bad child" that the child believes he or she is. If punishment is given while the parent is angry or upset (frightening), the child is reinforced in his or her belief that parents are malevolent; and the attachment disorder is supported.

One more reason why behavioral methods are not effective for children with disorders of attachment is that rewards and consequences are conditional on behavior. The positive regard from parent to child is felt by the child to be conditional. In other words, "I know I am bad. My parents reward me when I am good, but deep down I know I am bad and not really worthy of a reward. They don't love me when I am bad so that proves I am unloved/unlovable." Parenting children with relational trauma requires therapeutic parenting. Providing your child with unconditional positive regard (not just love) is essential to gradually growing the seeds of a positive sense of self. This is about accepting your child as he or she is (while not permitting your child to do as he or she likes). Consistent unconditional positive regard for your child in the face of obnoxious or violent behavior is one of the keys to reducing the deep shame the child feels. As you remain open, kind, and calm in the face of your child's dysregulation, he or she learns that no matter what, you accept the worst he or she has to give — the smeared feces, the broken lamps, the urine on the carpet, the terrorized dog and the disgruntled neighbors. As the child experiences your love of the "bad child" whom he or she knows he or she is, along with the good child you want him or her to be, the child can begin to trust that you won't leave, hurt, or shun him or her. Because you pay attention, care, understand, and accept the child, the shame has a place to heal.

So when parents ask, "What do I do?" I reply, "Create physical and emotional safety. Be calm. Be kind. Be accepting." Connect heart to heart with your child by staying close. Be wise and confident as you reflect his or her feelings so he or she can learn to understand them. Talk about what happened only when your child is calm and able to listen. Work out what to do (repair, give restitution, reconcile) only after your child's emotions and behavior have re-stabilized through your positive regard. Natural and logical consequences need to be short and occur when the child is calm and hopefully, willing. Parents of children with attachment disorders should not expect to change behavior, but to teach that limits can be safe and not shaming. The change in behavior will occur through the process of the development of attachment as the child's shame is reduced and self-regulation develops. Emphasis needs to be on relationship repair not punishment. Try to end the event with you and your child feeling as close as, or closer than, when it began. In fact, it isn't over until you are.

*Mary-Jo Land, CPT, CDDP, has been certified as a child psychotherapist and play therapist, dyadic developmental psychotherapist, sensorimotor psychotherapist level 1 and an attachment-focused therapist, consultant and trainer. She is a registered attachment clinician with ATTACh and currently president of ATTACh (www.attach.org). As a private practice therapist, she assists foster and adopt parents and children in their attachment and bonding while resolving early trauma and neglect. Land and her husband were therapeutic foster parents for twenty years. They have 5 children, one of whom is adopted and 2 grandchildren. She can be reached at www.maryjoland.ca or homeland@sympatico.ca.*

# Tying Up Loose Ends

"*I am the result of my life experiences good, bad, and everything in-between. The people and the places that are enmeshed in my memories and in my heart add to my wisdom and wonder of this world. The story I have shared with you, through this book, is only one square of the quilt that will someday be my life's story. I can only hope that it has, in some way, helped others to hear of our struggles and triumphs. Thank you for the opportunity to give back. God Bless all of those who are in the trenches and all of those who have helped others climb out!*" ~ Julie Carpenter

# Kinship Care is Complicated
*By Casey Mills*

When I was adopted by my mom's oldest sister at age 2½, my aunt became my mom, my mom became my aunt, my older brother and sisters became my cousins and my cousins became my siblings. It's always difficult for me to explain to others the interesting dynamics of my family make-up.

I don't really have a lot of feelings one way or another about whether kinship care is good or bad. Unfortunately, my birth parents were alcoholics and someone needed to step in to take care of me. While I was adopted by my aunt, my siblings all stayed with my birth mom until they were all placed into foster care several years later. We all faced different challenges and hardships, but I don't think those things really made us who we are, they were just small pieces in the puzzle of our lives.

Even though I was raised by my aunt, I don't really have a good understanding of what all happened when I was young. The pieces are still missing for me. And even though I reconnected with my biological father just before he died and I am in contact with my biological mother, we never really talked about what happened. My biological mother is no longer an alcoholic, but I think she struggles with the regrets of what happened to me and my siblings. I just don't bring it up, I'm just happy to know that she can have a small part in my life.

For me, being raised in kinship care was complicated. I don't feel really close to my cousins who became my siblings because they were quite a bit older than me. My aunt who became my mother just wasn't a very happy person and we're not close today. I was kept away from my biological parents and my siblings for a number of years, so really only in the last 10 years have I been able to create a new connection with them.

Today, I have a close relationship with my oldest sister, but I think it is something that we have created together as we got older. We have visited each other throughout the years and keep in close contact and for that I'm truly grateful. I think that's probably the biggest benefit of being raised in kinship care is knowing who my family is and our story. I don't have to question where I came from or where my brother and sisters are today. We are all connected and have relationships with each other.

My real family is the one I've created for myself. My husband and my children are who are important to me and I've worked to create a family life that is completely different from my early childhood and my adoptive family.

*Casey Mills lives in Gillette, Wyoming with her husband and two daughters. After growing up in a complicated kinship family, she focuses her energy on being a good mom. She has reconnected with her biological family and enjoys a quality long-distance relationship with them. She works in the construction industry as an administrative assistant.*

# Kinship Care: Look Before You Leap

*By June Bond, MEd*

In a perfect world, a child is born into a caring family with parents who have made a commitment to love, nurture, and "be there" through thick and thin for the child. In that same perfect world, there is an extended family that is also bonded to the child and is willing to play a significant role in the child's life, providing family values, experiences, love, and a safe haven in the event that the parents cannot care for the child due to illness, unforeseen circumstances, or death. It seems common sense in this perfect world that kinship care is the "care of choice" in the event that parents are no longer able to care for their offspring.

Unfortunately, there is no prefect world. Norman Rockwell is dead, although his idealized portraits still haunt many of us as adults, wondering why our holidays cannot live up to the paintings that grace his Christmas cards and calendars that are sold in the mall kiosk.

Those of us who work in the child welfare field or are foster or adoptive parents realize that there are many sides to the "whole story." Cases are different, families are different, support systems are different, and there is no one-size fits-all solution to the thousands of children who are abused and neglected each year. With that being said, I would like to make a few points about kinship care before leaping to the conclusion that kinship care is always the preferred solution to finding care for children who can no longer live with their birth parents.

### 1. Is DNA, or presumed DNA, the most vital connection to a person?

Just because a child shares DNA with another person does not make the connection the most important and vital consideration in the placement of a child. I have seen foster care workers spend inordinate amounts of time and energy trying to find relatives who may step forward to care for a child who has been taken from the birth parents. It seems common sense that if the family member has no contact to the child, there may be no vital connection, DNA or not. My question in review board sessions has been, "where was this relative when the family was in crisis?" While there are exceptions to the rule, it is a point worth considering.

Another point worth considering in today's non-Norman Rockwell world should be... is there really a DNA connection? For example, 15 years ago Annie Brown, whose name has been changed to protect her privacy, gave birth to a daughter, who tested positive for a variety of drugs due to her mother's habits. The baby was taken into custody and placed at 4 months old with the alleged birth father and his parents, the Jones family. Fifteen years later, Grandmother Jones was in the process of officially adopting the child in order to gain Social Security benefits for her. The birth mother's memory was much clearer without drugs, and she admitted that Mr. Jones was not the father of the child. DNA verified her revelation. Mr. Jones and his family was, however, the best option to care for her child at that time. The child was reared as a kinship care placement for 15 years, only to find out that there was no DNA connection, but a bond of love that held the child to the family. It is interesting to note that from the time of 4 months old the local social service workers never came back to the home, resting assured that the child was placed in the care of kin.

## 2. Is kinship care time effective?

As alluded to already, many caseworkers spend much time and energy trying to find kin to step forward. Could this time be better spent in helping treatment plans be accomplished or looking for permanency in the event that there is no suitable kinship care to be found. There should be a time limit on looking for kin, since there may be better options for the placement.

## 3. Is the kinship placement safe?

As a parent of grown children, I understand that families have a constant flow of visits. With visits, there is likelihood that the child in kinship care and the perpetrator of abuse can encounter each other. This can make the healing process incomplete, particularly in cases of sexual abuse.

## 4. Is long-term kinship care a path to permanency for a child?

The answer to this question can only be answered affirmatively if the kinship care results in an adoption. Permanency usually means that the child either returns home to a reunified and rehabilitated family or has been adopted. If long-term kinship care does not eventually result in an adoption, it is not considered a path to long-term permanency. As a foster care review board member, I have seen kinship care disrupt in the difficult teen years, thus leaving a child with little possibility of an adoptive "forever family." If kinship care is going to be long-term, shouldn't we strive for the forever home that adoption can provide?

## 5. Is kinship care consistent with the bonds that are already established for the child?

I am certain that the bonds that are established in foster care comes to everyone's mind in this factor. But, there is another significant dilemma of breaking emotional bonds and ties with kinship care placement — the bond of siblings. When a sibling group comes into care, there may be several paternal extended families involved. Paternal kinship may be offered to one sibling, thus separating the siblings who have been together throughout their lives.

Case in point, the Gray* children, a sibling group of three placed in a pre-adoptive home in South Carolina. James Gray, the 5-year-old is a half sibling to Jillian and Trevor, age 7 and 9. A paternal aunt came forward and wants to bring Jillian and Trevor into her home for kinship care. James was not included in the arrangement since he is not kin to the aunt. James has been adopted by the family in South Carolina. Fifteen months later, Jillian and Trevor are still waiting to find out if they will go to an aunt who they do not know and leave their brother, who has been a part of their lives since birth. Not to mention that Trevor and Jillian want to be adopted by the Granger* family, with whom they have lived for 16 months. A case for Solomon for certain.

The love of extended family can never be underestimated in the life of a child. However, there are legitimate factors that caseworkers, GALs, CASAs and family court judges must weigh in considering kinship care. We must resist the urge to leap before we look at all of the factors, making certain that long-term kinship care can lead to timely permanency, healing and consistency with the bonds that are already important in the life of the child.

\* The cases in point are actual, but the names have been altered for privacy.

*June Bond, BA, MEd earned a bachelor's degree in psychology and a master's degree in early childhood education from Converse College. She has published more than 40 articles that relate to adoption, education, and family issues and speaks nation-wide on adoption-related issues. She was South Carolina Adoption Advocate of the Year in 1995. In addition, she has worked with the Presbyterian Church of the United States to develop a portion of the nation-wide curriculum – Wee Believe. She is a 2006 Congressional Angel of Adoption recipient. She serves as chairman of the Spartanburg County foster care review board. Bond is currently the executive director of Adoption Advocacy of South Carolina. Adoption Advocacy is a not-for-profit agency that works with families that want to enlarge their families through adoption. The agency focuses on being the adopting family advocate and has a special grant program through the Dave Thomas Foundation and Adopt America Network to assist families who want to adopt children and sibling groups, age 8 and older, who are currently legally free and residing in foster care. This special grant program has assisted South Carolina families to welcome 576 children to their forever homes. Bond has been a certified adoption investigator for more than 25 years. She is the proud mother of six children, ranging in age from 21 to 34.*

# Full Protection under the Law
*Wills, Guardianship,and Life Insurance*
*By Tia Marsh with CJ Lyford, Esq.*

## Crash couple leave 2 kids

*"Avid motorcyclists who died Saturday when they collided with a pickup had given their 4-year-old daughter, Hailey, her first real birthday party just last week..."*
*From the Raleigh News and Observer*

When we bring children into our homes, we feel we are finally with caseworker involvement, tpr hearings and dealing with birth family (our own family, if we're taking in kin), and we want "just" to live our lives. But we owe it to our children to dot all the i's and cross all the t's to give them as much legal protection as possible, especially when we're raising our grandchildren, nieces or nephews or other kin at an older age.

Parents with children younger than 18-years-old need to make several estate planning decisions: how to provide income for the children in the event of the parent(s) death, how to manage those assets, and who to designate to care for the child(ren).

Wills, guardianship, and life insurance apply to all families with children, and are especially important for kinship families who may have messy familial relationships and may be parenting at an older age.

**Disclaimer: This article does not provide legal advice. It is not a substitute for the services of an attorney. Its purpose is to inform parents of issues they should consider to ensure their children are fully protected under the law.**

## Wills

Although it is not a required part of the adoption or guardianship of kin, creating a will is important. Upon death, your heirs will have many issues to consider: funeral, bills, personal property, insurance, income tax owed. Dying without a will, in legal terms intestate, means your property will be divided according to the rules of intestate succession in your state. Consequently, your property may or may not go to the person(s) you wish. In many states, the property is divided between a spouse and the children in equal shares.

## Trusts

Establishing a trust is another consideration when creating your will. If you die before your children are 18 years old, the court will appoint (or approve) a guardian for the care of the child and the management of their funds until age 18. If you execute a simple will, your child at 18 would receive full control of the assets of your estate. On the other hand, if you establish a trust, you can provide for distribution at a later date or in stages when the child might be more mature to handle the financial responsibility. With an establishment of a trust, you name a trustee to manage the funds until the time the trust states that the child has full control of the funds. A trustee can be a financial institution or an individual person or a combination of both.

## Advance Medical Directives

Advance Medical Directives include Living Wills, Power of Attorney, and Health Care Proxy (also known as Health Care Power of Attorney). These documents allow you to dictate your treatment wishes should you become incapacitated as well as name individuals to act on your behalf during your incapacitation.

## Guardianship

Establishing a guardian for your minor children in event of your death is important. With children who have already lost so much in their early life, making sure they are well taken care of in the event of another catastrophic loss, is crucial. With your will you can name a guardian for your minor children. Typically, the court will appoint the person you name.

Here are some questions to consider when choosing a guardian:
- Will you choose a family member or a trusted friend?

- Is this person familiar with adoption/kinship issues?

- Is this person familiar with your current kinship caring situation and the relationship with the child's parents?

---

### Resources on Wills

Estate Planningwww.estateplanning.com/

Crash Course on Wills and Trusts www.aarp.org/money/estate-planning/

### Advance Medical Directives

www.medicinenet.com/script/main/art.asp?articlekey=7814

### Resources on Guardianships

Choosing a Guardian www.jensenestatelaw.com/articles/estate-law/43-12-tips-for-choosing-a-guardian-for-your-children

Guardianship www.childwelfare.gov/permanency/guardianship.cfm

### Resources on Life Insurance

Life Insurance Trust www.rjmintz.com/types-of-trusts/life-insurance-trust/

Understanding and Choosing Life Insurance financialplan.about.com/cs/insurancl/a/LifeInsurance.htm

Using Life Insurance to Provide for Your Kids www.nolo.com/legal-encyclopedia/using-life-insurance-provide-children-29613.html

- Where do they live? Close to you or would your child have to move out of state?

- Do your parenting styles match?

- If you have more than one child, will your guardian be able to take in all of your children?

- Will your child(ren) have an ongoing relationship with the designated guardian in the here-and-now?

- Have you talked with your family about your choice and wishes?

On the advice of the lawyer who drew up our wills, my husband and I sent our family members a letter stating who we had established as guardians, trustee, and executor of our wills. We stated in the letter that we trusted our family to honor our wishes in the event of an untimely death. Additionally, we sent copies of our will to the named guardians, the trustee, and the executors of the wills.

Guardianship is an issue you will want to revisit as time goes on. People you choose when your child is young may not be appropriate as your child ages.

## Life Insurance

The key questions with life insurance are do you have it and is it enough? Your life insurance may need to provide for your minor child's living expenses if you die before he/she reaches the age of majority. You should not rely solely on the named guardians to provide financially for your child. Additionally, you may need your life insurance to cover the cost of your child's college education.

*Tia Marsh, an adoptive mother of two daughters, works in product development for the electronic payments industry by day, and puts her technology and communication skills to use at night volunteering in her community.*

*C.J. Lyford, Esq is an attorney in private practice who works with domestic and international adoptive families on issues of wills, guardianship, trusts, and citizenship. Her website is www.lyfordlaw.com.*

# Wanda's Story

*By Wanda Crabtree*

Pregnant with my first child at 17, life seemed to be a struggle. My boyfriend was incredibly abusive and I was just starting my addiction. Without a lot of guidance at home, I struggled to get on my feet and raise my daughter Amanda. During her early years I bounced around to a couple of different communities trying to get myself out from under her father's influence and straighten my life around. Unfortunately, I wouldn't have much success until he ended up going to prison.

Throughout this time, I leaned on my family to help me with my daughter. I'd leave her for months at a time with my parents or my sister. I always felt that I loved her enough that I knew I had to keep her in a safe place when my using got out of control. During Amanda's early childhood I bounced from negative relationship to negative relationship, working and selling drugs and using on the side. I just didn't want her in it or around the drugs, so I kept her at my mom and dad's as much as possible. It was a crazy time.

Then, just a few months after I got pregnant with my second child, I met my current husband. At that time, Ollie and I were battling our demons. We were both drug addicts. When Thomas was born, I was in jail on a possession charge. After he was born, the doctor put a hold on my son and he entered foster care. It was very devastating to me and my entire family. While I had the opportunity to hold him, no one else in the family was allowed to. And the most awful part is that the minute I left the hospital I went to get high. My baby had just been taken from me and all I wanted to do was get high.

For the next six months, I was required to work my case plan, stay clean, and provide a stable environment for my son in order to get him back. But the day I was supposed to get Thomas back, Ollie and I had a huge fight. The caseworker, who was supportive and helpful to me, told me I needed to stay away from Ollie. Fortunately, I was able to get Thomas back, but I failed to change much in my life.

For the next three years, Amanda and Thomas lived with me pretty much full time, but I was using again and my life was out of control. During that time Amanda and Thomas were around the drugs most of the time because we had our own place. I put them through so much, it is heartbreaking to think about all the things they were exposed to. Then, my life changed forever when I was charged with dealing drugs. I went to jail until I was sentenced about a year later and had to spend almost five years of my life in prison.

During this time, Amanda and Thomas went to live with my parents. Three-year-old Thomas was quite a handful for my parents and when it was determined that I would be spending so much time in prison, I knew I had to come up with another option for Thomas. At first I wanted him to live with my sister Tina, but when she and her husband decided they just couldn't do it, I turned to my sister Julie. There's nothing better than having your children stay with your family.

Unfortunately, Amanda was a tender 15-year-old when I was incarcerated and really struggled with my absence. Despite all that I had put her through, we were very close. For the next few years she struggled living with my parents, and eventually moved in with some family friends. I feel bad that I wasn't there for her. She became a mom at age 18, while I was still in prison. I know she had it pretty rough and I feel bad for all that I put her through.

For Thomas, while living with Julie and her family was a good thing for him, I know it was a struggle for everyone. Thomas was a handful and Julie did her best to find help for him and support him through some tough times. I think Julie did the best she could, but we still butted heads on some things because I still wanted to have a say in my son's life, but I really couldn't because I wasn't there dealing with everything she was dealing with. I had no control. Even still, it's hard for me to understand what all Julie went through taking care of Thomas. He was going through a lot of issues and Julie was having to deal with all of that.

I spent 58 months in prison, which gave me plenty of time to realize what I really wanted out of life. It was very impacting being locked up and unable to be there for my children. Before it was easy to know I had a problem but not really do anything about it. When I was in prison I had a lot of time to just think about all the things I had done wrong. I realized how important my family was and how great it was that they were helping me care for my children.

When I got out, I spent a lot of time talking to my children. My daughter was 20 and Thomas was 9. I had missed out on so much, but I wanted to rebuild our relationship. Thomas spent a year at my sister Tina's while I lived in a halfway house close by. I had the opportunity to see him every week and we slowly got to know each other again.

After I left the halfway house, my ex-boyfriend Ollie came back into my life. In a better place, he took Thomas and I several states away — away from the negative environment we had been around before. And now my life is completely transformed. I can't believe I spent 20 years of my life the way I did. Today Thomas is 12 and I have a new 15-month-old baby girl Zuriel. I'm a stay-at-home mom and I'm so blessed to be drug-free and enjoying motherhood from an entirely different perspective. It's a blessing and sometimes I feel sad I couldn't give that parenting to my other children.

Now life is just normal. I can't say how much better it is for all of us and for Thomas. He now has parents. It's been an adjustment for all of us, but we're healing. Today, I'm just so grateful for my family and my husband. I'm thankful that my family stepped up and helped me parent my children when I couldn't. Without them, I probably would have lost them to the system. There are no words to express how grateful I am that they took care of my children. It was the good Lord that saved me and my children. I love that God has changed my life.

*Wanda Crabtree is the mother of three children: Amanda is 23 with two children of her own, Thomas is 13 and Zuriel is 19 months old. She has lived in Wyoming for most of her life until she spent five years incarcerated and was in multiple locations. Her children were cared for by family and she praises God for that. After her release, she was reunited with her children and moved to Louisiana to start their new life with her current husband Ollie. She had three and a half years of probation that was successfully completed. She also went to college and received an office clerk certificate with a 3.6 gpa. She had an amazing wedding and then gave birth to her precious daughter. Now she is experiencing life and motherhood from a new and wonderful perspective. "I am finally a success story and hope that I can inspire others to feel that it is possible to live life sober and be happy and grateful every day."*

# My Adoption Journey Went A Little Like This...

*By Michelle L. Martin*

As "empty nesters" my husband and I were planning another cruise and looking forward to spending quality time together. Adoption was the furthest thing from our minds. Our granddaughter was born in September of 2003 and the emotional roller coaster came roaring in. I was happy with my feet planted firmly on the ground and at that moment the persistent tugging began.

Our granddaughter was born with Stickler Syndrome, a genetic condition she inherited from her biological mother. So, when she was born her tongue flipped back and cutoff her airway. She was immediately taken to PICU and there she remained for 61 days. Her parents, our son and his girlfriend, didn't have a clue as to how serious things were going to get. They tried to take care of her, but failed miserably, and soon she was in foster care. I cried just about every day and the tugging continued. As her grandparents, we were given first choice as to whether or not we wanted to foster to adopt her. During this time, my granddaughter was placed in a foster home, which broke my heart. Her foster parents wanted so much to adopt her, but I felt her slipping away. It was a difficult decision because we felt that we needed to cut ties with our son, at least until he could make better decision in his life. During this time, it was like an out of body experience for me but the tugging sensation persisted. Our marriage of 24 years was strained. In the end, we had to do what we thought was best for our granddaughter. After fostering her for several months and with the help of prayer, family, and the support of many others we adopted our granddaughter in December of 2006. Instead of another cruise, we went to Walt Disney World. I now know that the persistent tugging sensation was "my heartstrings."

It has been seven years and my granddaughter is nine years old. We still have our ups and downs. However, finding the Grandparents Raising Grandchildren and the Special Needs Adoptive Parent (SNAP) support groups helped me find both support, resources, and most importantly people who "get it." There's judgment, just understanding and an empathetic ear.

It has been my goal to educate and support others who find themselves in similar situations. My husband and I have spoken on several parent panels through our adoption agency. It is both humbling and rewarding. Three years ago I was afforded the opportunity to work for a wonderful post-adoption support organization as an adoptive parent consultant. I have great pleasure in supporting other kinship families and will continue to do so as long as I am able!

*Michelle Martin is a kinship caregiver with her husband. The couple lives in Michigan.*

# Keeping Connected to Kin —
*One foster/adopt dad shares his story of reconnecting his children to their biological extended families*
By Kim Combes, LBSW, MEd

Children in the foster care system carry invisible and painful wounds coming in part from the separation from biological loved ones. In the 30 years I have been in the human service arena I have interacted with children and adults who struggle with the question, "who am I?" as a result of being adopted, even some who were legalized into another's family as infants. There seems to be a gnawing wonder about those with whom they are related by blood. I've heard many a story, both good and bad, about finding biological family after a court's decision to terminate parental rights and a new family is subsequently found. The following is our story.

It numbers among one of the worst weekends of my life. Tears flowed freely as I anticipated telling my adopted sibling group of four that I had received word that their biological mother was dead. DNA tests confirmed that the bones found four months earlier were indeed those of their mom.

I received the call on Thursday at 4 p.m. My heart sank as I struggled with how to tell four children I loved so much that their dream of someday being reunited with their mother was now crushed forever. I would have to wait until Friday morning to inform them of this news since Matt, the oldest, was at work and wouldn't be home until after the youngest were in bed.

Watching the movie Pay it Forward that night only provoked more tears. My kids looked at me as if to say, "Yeah, Dad, it's a sad movie, but not that sad." Little did they know what was to come in less than 12 hours.

Having been a state social worker in the 80's I recalled how children in the foster care system pined for their biological parents or family members. Knowing this, I had plugged my children's maternal grandmother's phone number, which the worker gave me long ago, into my cell phone for future reference. It was upon getting the call regarding their mom's death that I decided to risk the phone interaction at this sad time for both of us.

"You don't know me, but I am calling to tell you how sorry I am to hear of your daughter's death. I just want you to know that my wife and I have adopted four of her five children and that they are OK."

Tears came readily for both of us as she explained how she had been looking for her precious grandchildren, wondering for more than half a decade if they were together, healthy, and thriving wherever they might be placed. Grandmother asked permission to give my number to her youngest daughter so she could contact me also. Permission was granted. "Gramma" also informed me that there would be a memorial service for Mom on September 19, when an ordained minister uncle from Ohio would be in Iowa as he wanted to perform the service. I let her know that we would do everything possible to be there with the kids.

During that six-week period between the initial call and the family reunion, Matt, Jose, and I met with Aunt Jackie, who was thrilled to see her nephews. She filled in many of the blanks of the boys' life for all of us. The boys were reticent on the 90-

minute drive home, but content to have once again connected with a biological family member, who was gracious and supportive of my wife and me for keeping her family together through adoption.

Two weeks prior to the memorial service, a cousin found through Facebook an older biological half-sister who was living with her father's mother in Texas. Gramma Mary drove from southern Texas so the kids could be reunited once again for the remembrance of Mom. To say the day was "bittersweet" would be an understatement.

Diane and I were nervous as we witnessed this emotional event. However, upon receiving the hugs and many "thank yous" from those who were genuinely grateful that the children landed in a Christian home where parents were so willing to allow them contact with blood relatives, our fears were relieved.

Gramma Mary and sister Crystal drove to our home for supper that night. There was not a dry eye in the place as the kids said goodbyes, not knowing when they would see each other again. We vowed to keep in touch.

Fast forward six months. Matt, being 16, struggled with the "who am I" question. He was restless here and needed to find himself. Thus, Gramma Mary, Diane, and I agreed that Matt would go to Texas for an indefinite period of time when school released for the summer. I told Matt I loved him enough to "let him go." The months prior to him leaving were difficult, at best, between the two of us because separation anxiety reared its ugly head. It is often easier to leave when everyone is angry with each other, a phenomenon that I have seen repeatedly in my human service career.

*He realized that "family" was more than just a blood connection — the emotional connection was significant as well.*

Matt left in June for a new chapter in his life and ours. It was difficult fearing Matt would grow to love his biological family more than he loved us and thus perhaps choose to stay in Texas. I was many times on my knees in prayer for him during his absence.

My family was able to take an extended vacation in October to stay with Matt and his family down South. It had been four months since we had seen him and didn't have much contact with him prior to that time because I gave him his space as I told him I would. We discovered a new maturity in Matt since he left Iowa. As much as he loved his biological family there, he wanted to come back with us, but knew that wasn't possible to keep the credits he needed to graduate on time in Iowa.

Matt returned to our home in March last year. The nine months he was gone helped refocus his priorities. He realized that "family" was more than just a blood connection — the emotional connection was significant as well. His stint in Texas was a great experience for him and drew us closer, rather than apart, as I had initially imagined. Matt has developed into a fine young adult for whom Diane and I are quite proud.

We continue to keep in touch with our children's biological family both in Iowa and Texas. Crystal, now 20, is planning a trip to Iowa this spring. We look forward to her visit, again enhancing the biological connection between siblings, which we have seen to have healing properties for all involved. Iowa grandmother and aunt are involved with us, as is their family in Texas — supporting us when things get rough as they sometimes do.

As a follower of Jesus, I trust God's word, and have seen it play out…"all things work together for good for those that love the Lord and are called according to His purpose." (Romans 8:28) The tragedy of Mom's death was not an end, but a beginning…the beginning of some healing that might not have otherwise taken place in the hearts of my children.

I think the signature line on Matt's thank you letter to Iowa Gramma for the $50 Wal-Mart card he received for Christmas speaks volumes, not just from our 18-year-old adoptee, but for many who have been separated from families: "Love you forever and always! — Matti."

*Kim Combes, LBSW, MEd, is a private practice counselor and national presenter, as well as a former foster dad to 40-plus teenage boys since 1994. Currently he and wife, Diane, live in Colo, Iowa, with their five adopted children who range in age from 11 to 18. To contact Combes, write to kcombes@netins.net. Reprinted with permission from* **Fostering Families Today** *magazine.*

# Julie's Story: *Caring for a Sister's Son*
*By Julie Carpenter*

Married only a few months, I was busy blending my new family together that included two stepsons and my son from a prior relationship. We were also expecting a new baby, and while life was good, our plates were full.

As my family life was blossoming, my younger sister's life was derailing. Arrested on federal drug charges, Wanda was serving a five-year prison sentence while her son Thomas lived with my parents. Trying to help as much as possible, but living two hours away, I began to see the toll caring for a busy four-year-old was having on my parents, especially my mom who was fighting her own terminal illness. I could see that Thomas was going to be more than they could handle due to the effects of his early childhood.

After some discussion, my husband and I felt there wasn't another option for Thomas. Thomas would need to come live with us. So, just a few months after welcoming our new baby girl to our family, we also welcomed Thomas.

From the get-go things were a challenge. Thomas had experienced a lot of negative things in his short life and I really didn't have the tools to handle all of the issues. Even though she was in prison a thousand miles away, Wanda challenged my decisions and my parenting frequently. Somehow, we muddled through it and things seemed to go well during his kindergarten year.

However, when we transferred him to a different school, it was evident he needed some additional support. A busy, hyper child, who struggled to understand personal boundaries, we had him tested for ADHD and saw some profound positive changes for Thomas once he was on medication. While his mom wasn't pleased that we'd had him tested, Thomas himself was excited about the positive effects the medicine had on his life. He told me, "Aunt Julie, I like those little pills — they help me." After a while, Thomas began to make friends, do better in school, and have a more positive attitude.

Even with the ADHD diagnosis and treatment, parenting Thomas was still a challenge. He and my son Morgan really clashed. And because Thomas needed so much, it really affected my relationship with Morgan. And really, I think I had unrealistic expectations for Morgan. I expected him to understand why Thomas was there and to appreciate all that he had that Thomas didn't. I didn't realize how much more Morgan needed because he, too, was experiencing all of this change and chaos. Those expectations and the impact of Thomas living with us on Morgan is something that still hurts me very much today.

It just really wasn't easy for any of us. We all looked forward to the summer months when Thomas would spend extended time with my oldest sister, giving us time to refocus on our own family. And my heart ached for Thomas who had experienced so much trauma at such a young age, was separated from his mom, and never really felt like he had a home even though he lived with us for four years.

When I look back on that time, I realize how unprepared I was to parent a child from a tough place. We were just beginning to find our way as a family, when Thomas came to live with us and the challenges he presented were difficult. I wish I had access to more resources and had more tools to better meet his needs.

While difficult, I do think we provided Thomas with the consistency and unconditional love he needed during a difficult time for him. Even though his mother loved him very much, sometimes her drug dependencies got in the way of her parenting abilities. We showed Thomas what it was like to be in a typical family, experiencing all the things a child should — Boy Scouts, riding bikes, family vacations, and much more.

Letting Thomas go was equally difficult and almost a relief at the same time. When he lived with us I was stressed out and tired. My heart still aches because I love him and miss him, but I'm really happy to note that today Thomas and Wanda are reunited after five years apart. My sister is now married, in a healthy relationship and recently welcomed a baby girl into the world.

Looking back on our experience, I know I would have taken in Thomas again, but I don't know that the rest of my family would make the same decision. It was a challenging time and affected us all. I know I would tell others considering taking in a relative to ask for help and utilize resources. I'd tell them to think about the impact it will have on their own children and let them know that they are just as important as they were before the other child came along. And finally, I would tell them to pray. I know at times, it was the only thing that got me through some of the challenges we faced.

*Julie Lynn (Mills) Carpenter is 42, married to a man who was made just for her. She is a mother to four amazing children and grandmother to one beautiful boy. Carpenter works at Youth Emergency Services in their mentorship program and she finds generous, positive, caring people to place in the lives of youth in her community. She believes she has been blessed to find work that is rewarding and helps her make a difference in this world.*

## Our Life is Rearranged
*By Martha Hooper*

When we got the call early on the morning of October 9, 2009 we had no idea how this sweet baby would change our lives and our lifestyle. We knew she didn't need to go home with her momma due to serious drug habits. What we didn't know was how we could prevent this from happening and keep this baby safe. Momma tested positive for drugs. The new baby had to be placed in pediatric intensive care for the next 12 days. The state determined she would go home with us. While we were grateful we wondered, "what's next?" We are busy people involved with our state's system of care and on a national level. Yet we didn't know the "what's next" answer.

Next came visits from workers at our home, making sure things were safe for the baby. Next came doctor visits, WIC visits, and a lot of sleepless nights. Then came court dates to determine a reunification plan. During this time our daughter decided she would rather us adopt the baby than continue the process. She signed her rights to us and the "next" meant we were then able to adopt the baby a year after her birth.

Now the next reality really sank in! We are at the age of old and older we are now parents of a beautiful, sweet (sometimes) baby girl. We are now responsible to meet each and every one of her needs. There are no grandparents to help us. We are both parent and grandparent.

Four years later we are still adjusting. She calls me Momma and my husband Papaw. Looks! Oh, yes we do get them. She also happens to be biracial. How do we handle the stares and questions, both spoken and unspoken? Quietly and honestly.

Question #1 - yes, she is our granddaughter, I'm way past child bearing years.

Question #2 - yes, she is adopted. Yes, we do realize there are a lot of young parents that would love to have her. Yes, I feel a little guilty to be so blessed.

Question #3 - yes, he is my husband and not my daddy even though she calls me Momma and him Pawpa. We laugh because you gotta have humor.

Question #4 - is it hard to manage at our stage in life to be parents again to a small child, of course it is. Raising children is hard no matter the age or stage of life we are in. We know this for a fact. We raised four biological, one adopted (now two) and fostered many. Do the blessings outweigh the struggles? Yes, but it is hard.

We have served several parenting roles and I must say kinship is the hardest. You definitely need good support. That can come from family, friends, or support groups. And last but not least, know your state's position on kinship care. There may or may not be help offered.

Tonight we've got child care, food for them to eat, clothes laid out for tomorrow, her hair is done, and she's had her bath. Now we gotta go provide training for foster, adoptive, and kinship care providers! Yes, indeed our life is rearranged...for the better! She just told me, "I'm going to miss you Momma."

*We have served several parenting roles and kinship is the hardest.*

*Martha and Buddy Hooper have been married 46 years they have 4 biological children and 2 adopted children, they have 14 grandchildren. They began fostering in 1989 and became adoptive parents in 2000. They became kinship care providers in 2009. During their time as foster parents they fostered more than 40 children.*

*Hooper has served on the Alabama Foster & Adoptive Parent board for more than 10 years and the past 8 as chair of the advocacy committee. She has trained foster parents in a variety of subjects for the past 8 years, including foster parent bill of rights, advocacy, IEP's, nurturing bonding and letting go, partnership with DHR and birth families, and many others. She has trained foster parents at the National Foster Parent Association conference as well as Tennessee, Georgia, and Florida state conferences. Hooper also served as founder and executive director of Cullman Caring for Kids, a child abuse prevention and family resource center for 16 years. She served on the Cullman County Multi Needs board, Juvenile Justice board, DHR quality assurance board, and Mental Health advisory board. Hooper currently serves on the AFAPA board and is the chair of Advocacy Committee for AFAPA. She was recently named as advisor to the National Foster Parent Association board for region 4, which includes 8 southeastern states.*

# The Blessing of Raising Charles
*By Lynda Hickok*

I retired when Charles was finishing the ninth grade. The special needs classes he had been assigned to that year included little or no provision for interaction with the general student body and he was offered little academic education. Yet, watching him I could see that he was not only able to learn, he also loved to learn. I decided to enroll him in the small school district where we lived. The administration was hesitant about enrolling him, partly because they had no special needs class. Again I dug in my heels. And again I studied the state law regarding public education, obtained a copy of the local school district admission policy, and thankfully was finally able to convince the school that they really had no option but to admit him. Their first proposal was to bus him 30 miles every day to the larger district where he had been. I insisted that he become part of the local school system. This move turned out to be the best thing that could have happened. Both of us have been thrilled with the way the experience finally turned out.

Charles spent his days with other children his age. The teacher assigned to him took the time to take him into the hall during class changes and taught him how to appropriately greet the students. He liked the students and they liked him. He was so well-accepted that he was voted homecoming prince after two months at the school. He showed talent in art, especially sculpting. His PE teacher began by having Charles run laps during times he was unable to participate in the daily activity. Before long he found other things for Charles to do that kept him part of the class. He could be a line judge during volleyball, a base coach during baseball, etc. Not only was it good for Charles to interact with the other students, it was also good for them to learn about people like Charles. I have nothing but appreciation and admiration for the school staff and the students.

Charles is a happy young man. He enjoys people and talks to everyone. We say that he has never met a stranger. One day soon after he started school in Waterville he got a ride home with another student. I told him that he couldn't ride with people he didn't know. A few days later he got a ride home with another student. When I reminded him that he could only ride with people we knew he said it was alright as he had asked the young driver his name. But as much as he enjoys people, he also values time alone. When he has spent an hour or so with a crowd, even family, he searches out a solitary location.

All juniors were required to work at the concession stand during high school games to raise money for their senior trip. Though Charles would not join them on the trip he was required to do his share of the work. His job during his first shift was to keep the pop bins full. By the end of his second shift he was able to wait on customers, take money, and make change. What an exciting opportunity and achievement for a special needs young man.

I had been asking about some sort of job experience for Charles since he began attending the local school. At the beginning of his junior year his teacher contacted a local manufacturing company to see if they would be interested in taking him on for a limited number of hours. The company had provided that type of training before they moved to our small town and said they would like to meet Charles. The manager liked him and asked if he would like to work there. Charles was excited and enthusiastic. He began to spend two

*It is truly a blessing to raise Charles. Charles tells me that I am his heart. He is truly mine.*

hours every school day at the company. He loved it. His duties were simple and repetitious, which was perfect for him. Near the end of the school year the company manager asked if Charles could work there over the summer for a few hours per week. It was so encouraging to watch Charles navigate the workplace and enjoy work.

Charles' religious education has been ongoing. He attended church with me each week and was interested in what was going on there. At age 10 he was baptized. He was somewhat confused by the term "Father" that Catholics use when addressing priests as it is also the opening line in the Lord's Prayer. After his baptism ceremony was over and we were leaving the church he turned to the priest and called out, "Goodbye God." A few months later he happened to see a priest in street clothes and was awe struck. He said, "He looks like a real man."

After watching other parishioners receive communion he wanted to participate. Several months of classes prepared him and he was ready to take his First Communion at age 11, a special occasion for a Catholic. He began serving as an altar server shortly after but that was relatively short lived. He just had too much fun on the altar. He would dance around, give the priest high fives and thumbs up, pick lint off the floor, and, in general, entertain the congregation and embarrass me. The parishioners had been wary of Charles when he first began to attend church with me, but they soon learned to love and treasure him. He is always happy to attend church. One priest remarked that he wished everyone was as happy to be at church as Charles is.

Charles quickly picked up all the prayers said at church though the words arc sometimes a little different from those everyone else says. He loved all the songs. He never misses saying the blessing before supper. At one point, an aunt was visiting and said the blessing while we held hands, which isn't something Catholics normally do. The aunt's blessing was quite long as she asked blessings on everything and everyone. A few days later we had supper with the same aunt and Charles took it upon himself to say the blessing. He held hands and said, "In Watervllle we say a different prayer" and proceeded to recite our short blessing.

Charles has been loved by several priests. One in particular was a Philippine priest named Father Bonnie Salvana. This priest died shortly before Charles' First Communion. I was worried that Charles would have a hard time with that death, but it didn't really seem to faze him. So many people have come and gone in his life that he doesn't seem to expect to have people around too long. What a sad thing to be unable to count on the people in your life. I have made a special effort to ensure that he knows I will be around for as long as I live. However, I do what I can to prepare him for an independent life when I am no longer around - and constantly reassure him of how much I love him.

Not only have many people drifted through Charles' life, but things, too, have appeared and disappeared. When he was with his father, toys would routinely be traded away for drugs. This happened so often that when he gets anything from clothes to toys he is proud of them. Yet, he doesn't seem upset if the item disappears. Similarly, the first several years he lived with me he never asked for anything. He loved to look at toys in stores but never asked for any. It didn't occur to me for some time that he wasn't asking for things. When I became aware of this I would offer small toys, books, or other items occasionally so he would know that he was worthy of having things. And the things he got stayed around until he was ready to donate them to another child. He was generous with his things and took pleasure in giving to others, including me. He offers me his toys sometimes and routinely shares his treats with me. I am proud of that.

Charles is especially fond of his bike. Puzzles and transformer toys are his favorites as he seems to see the world as a series of shapes. He rides his bike during the summer and keeps an eye on it when it is put up for the winter. He received a basketball hoop and stand when he was 16 and was proud and protective of it — keeping the water and dirt off it. However, he doesn't play with it.

Charles has an unusual take on the world around him. After telling him several times why we have Easter he explained it this way. "We have Easter because that is the day Jesus got up from being dead, put on a bunny costume and went from house to house with candy." I imagine Jesus got a chuckle out of that. At age 18 he still believed in Santa Claus, but was aware that most of the Santas he sees are just helpers. He insists that the real Santa lives in Waterville.

Physically, Charles has always been strong. He has learned to operate some machinery such as the lawn mower and snow blower, yet in some ways he is weak. He is unable to lift much and has little endurance. When swimming he makes good time crossing the pool, but the return trip is slow, and any further trips require several rest periods. He makes his own bed when required and puts away his own clothes. He likes to vacuum and is good at it. He likes cooking shows on TV but shows no interest in actually cooking.

In early June 2009 Charles began acting depressed and tired. I questioned him about possible bullying at school but he said he was having no trouble at school. He seemed to have no energy or interest in anything. After he declined a swimming trip and was unable to play a full round of miniature golf, both activities he enjoys, I took him to the doctor. Blood tests revealed some potentially serious problems and within a few hours we were in an ambulance on our way to Seattle Children's Hospital. Additional tests there revealed that he had Acute lymphoblastic leukemia. We spent the next seven months in the hospital and the Ronald McDonald House. We returned home in early 2010 though Charles remained on a maintenance program which was to last three years.

Once Charles returned home he returned to school and once again adjusted well. He was given special recognition at his graduation and as he received his diploma substitute that is issued to special needs students, the entire class and audience gave him a standing ovation. They truly loved him.

Charles began to feel ill again and was ill during his graduation in June. He was diagnosed with pneumonia a couple of days following the graduation. He spent most of the following week in the hospital, a condition he was well familiar with.

Shortly before Charles' graduation, my partner, Jim died following a long battle with cancer. The role of pall bearer was explained to Charles and he was asked if he would like to do that. He thought about it for a minute and said yes, but Jim sure was heavy. He thought he was expected to carry to casket alone. When asked about Jim he tells people that Jim is in heaven but his body is in the cemetery. It took a while for Charles to adjust to Jim's death. For a while he refused to let anyone talk about him. Within a year-and-a-half he would talk about him freely and often. Charles understands that I will die one day. He wanted to know what ladies would be my pall bearers.

In the spring of 2011 we moved from Waterville to Wenatchee in order to be nearer medical care for both of us. He looked on the move as an adventure and happily settled into his new home. His last day at the Waterville school the administration gave him a party and all the high school and middle school students attended. Many of the teachers cried as they were going to miss his happy face and upbeat attitude.

It had always been in the plans to place Charles in a group home as he grew up. I was getting older and I wanted him to begin a separate life before it became physically impossible for me to care for him. After a long search, a wonderful new home was located about 30 miles from home. It took some time to get him admitted to the home but it was exactly what I wanted for him and it turned out to be a perfect fit. He moved in during the summer of 2011 and loved it. He was finally able to have close friends. The residents get along well and participate in many activities.

My custody of Charles ended when he turned 18, but he still needed help and guidance. So I petitioned the court to become his guardian. That took two attorneys, one for me and one for him and several interviews. The guardianship was granted with me as his guardian and his aunt Mary as my second.

I firmly believe that Charles is with me because that was God's plan. God has helped us so much as we learn to navigate his special needs, his interests, and the world's acceptance of him. I pray every day that God continues to guide me in Charles' development and care. I will continue to pray that any decisions I make regarding Charles are in accordance with God's plans for him.

It is truly a blessing to raise Charles. Charles tells me that I am his heart. He is truly mine.


*Linda Hickock is the grandmother to Charles whom she raised as a single grandparent. While she didn't have any books or other guidance to help raise him, she had a lot of determination and a lot of encouragement from a Grandparents Raising Grandchildren group which she recommends that you find and join in your local area.*

# Resources

Additional resources can be found at www.emkpress.com

## 1. The Unexpected Role

*The Post-Adoption Blues: Overcoming the Unforseen Challenges of Adoption* by Karen J. Foley, MSN, PhD, RN

**The Grandfamilies State Law and Policy Resource Center**
A national legal resource in support of grandfamilies within and outside the child welfare system.
**www.grandfamilies.org**

**Foster Kinship**
Foster Kinship is a local nonprofit exclusively focused on serving kinship families and the over 19,000 children in kinship care in Nevada. To improve outcomes for children in kinship care, Foster Kinship empowers kinship caregivers to provide the safest, most stable and permanent placements for the children in their home.
**www.fosterkinship.org**

Jan Wagner's Blog
**jdwags.blogspot.com**

## 2. Getting Organized

**GrandFamilies: The Contemporary Journal of Research, Practice and Policy**
An online, peer review journal dedicated to topics related to grandparents raising grandchildren. *GrandFamilies: The Contemporary Journal of Research, Practice and Policy* provides a forum for quality, evidence-based research with sound scholarship, knowledge, skills and best practices from the field for scholars, clinicians, policymakers, educators, program administrators and family advocates.
**scholarworks.wmich.edu/grandfamilies**

**National Research Center on Grandparents Raising Grandchildren**

It was established in 2001 at Georgia State University and is now a collaborative initiative between Georgia State and Western Michigan universities.It's mission is to improve the well-being of grandparent-headed families by promoting best practices in community-based service delivery, and advancing the work of practitioners and scholars in the development, implementation and evaluation of new knowledge in the field.
**www.wmich.edu/grandparenting**

## 3. Your Legal Toolbox
**Generations United**

For nearly three decades, Generations United has been the catalyst for policies and practices stimulating cooperation and collaboration among generations, evoking the vibrancy, energy and sheer productivity that result when people of all ages come together. We believe that we can only be successful in the face of our complex future if generational diversity is regarded as a national asset and fully leveraged. The National Center on Grandfamilies is a critical part of Generations United's mission and strives to enact policies and promote programs that support relative caregivers and the children they raise.  **www.gu.org**

**Grandfamilies of America.com**
The Only National Organization Whose Membership and Administrative Staff Is Comprised Totally Of Relatives Caring 24/7 for Their Relative Children.
**www.grandfamiliesofamerica.com**

## AARP
Has a series of Grandfact sheets done by state.
www.grandfactsheets.org

## Interstate Compact Information (ICPC)
Information for each individual state can be found here.
www.icpcstatepages.org

## The Children's Defense Fund
The Children's Defense Fund (CDF) is a non-profit child advocacy organization that has worked relentlessly for more than 40 years to ensure a level playing field for all children. We champion policies and programs that lift children out of poverty; protect them from abuse and neglect; and ensure their access to health care, quality education and a moral and spiritual foundation. Supported by foundation and corporate grants and individual donations, CDF advocates nationwide on behalf of children to ensure children are always a priority.

www.childrensdefense.org/child-research-data-publications/data/kinship-care-resource-kit.pdf

# State by State Resources
Please note that kinship navigator programs and other kinship services change frequently based on funding levels. Each state has their own legal requirements so make sure the information you are relying on is specific to your state. A wonderful starting place is www.grandfactsheets.org. At presstime, the links below were operational. Please email info@emkpress.com if one is broken or you are aware of an additional resource that could be shared with others.

## Alabama
www.aces.edu/urban/FamilyWebsite/RAPP.html

## Arizona
www.azkincare.org
www.arizonakinship.org

## Arkansas
www.arkansasvoices.org

## California
www.edgewood.org/kssp
www.kinshiphelp.org
www.yfs.ymca.org/programs/kinship-support-services/kinship-navigator.html

## Connecticut
www.seniorresourcesec.org/programs-services/grandparent-support
www.infoline.org/focus/kinshiplist.asp

## Delaware
www.dhss.delaware.gov/dhss/dsaapd/kinshipnavigator.html

## Florida
www.floridaschildrenfirst.org/?p=4226

## Georgia
dhs.georgia.gov/node/1970
www2.gsu.edu/~wwwalh/index.html

## Hawaii
www.familyprogramshawaii.org

## Idaho
www.idahograndparentsasparents.org/resources

## Illinois
www.state.il.us/aging/1intergen/grg.htm

Kansas
www.kdads.ks.gov/Services/Programs/
rapp.htm

Kentucky
www.chfs.ky.gov/dail/familycaregiver.htm

Maine
www.familiesandchildren.org/maine-
kids-kin.html

Michigan
www.kinship.msu.edu

Minnesota
www.lssmn.org/raising-relative-children

New Hampshire
www.extension.unh.edu/Vulnerable-
Families/Kinship-Families

New Jersey
www.nj.gov/dcf/families/support/kinship
www.chsofnj.org/kinship-services

New York
www.nysnavigator.org

North Carolina
www.fullcirclecare.org/grandparents/
welcome.html

Ohio
www.kinshipohio.org

Pennsylvania
www.asecondchance-kinship.com

South Carolina (Resource Guide)
www.aging.sc.gov/SiteCollectionDocume
nts/G/GrandparentsRaising
GrandchildrenGuide.pdf

Washington
www.kinshipnavigator.org

www.dshs.wa.gov/kinshipcare

Wisconsin
www.dcf.wisconsin.gov/children/kinship
www.uwex.edu/ces/flp/grandparent/

West Virginia
www.wvdhhr.org/bcf/children_adult/
foster/kinship.asp

Wyoming
www.calc.net/wyoming_kinship_advoca-
cy.asp

## 4. Your Financial Toolbox
*Money Matters: The Get it Done in One Minute Workbook* by Shay Olivarria

**Bigger than your Block**
Was founded in 2007and works to broaden the perspectives of youth and adults via financial education using workshops and books.
www.biggerthanyourblock.com

**Epona Financial Services**
The company is dedicated to helping their clients develop the confidence and clarity to make sound decisions and reach their financial goals.
www.eponafs.com

## 5. Our Changing Family
*Families at Risk* by Jodee Kulp

**Raising H Blog**
Jan Wagner's blog about raising her grandson.
www.jdwags.blogsopt.com
**C.A.S.E. - The Center for Adoption Support and Education**
C.A.S.E. was created to provide post-adoption counseling and educational services to families, educators, child welfare staff, and

mental health providers in Maryland, Northern Virginia, and Washington, D.C. In addition, C.A.S.E. is a national resource for families and professionals through its training, publications, and consultations. C.A.S.E. is a private, non-profit adoptive family support center. Its programs focus on helping children from a variety of foster care and adoptive backgrounds to receive understanding and support which will enable them to grow into successful, productive adults.
www.adoptionsupport.org

### Better Endings
Provides hope for children, teens, and adults living, laughing, learning and loving through the challenges before birth — including alcohol exposure (fetal alcohol spectrum disorders-FASD) and other toxins.
www.betterendings.org

## 6. Guilt, Shame, & Love
*The Quest for Peace in a Broken World* by Julie Alvarado

### Casey Family Programs
At Casey Family Programs, we support and assist child welfare systems in their efforts to protect children and create strong families. Children do best in stable families and familiar environments. This gives them the best chance to grow into successful adults. With a variety of programs focused on the child-welfare system, Casey Family Programs is a treasure trove of facts and guides.
www.casey.org

### Fostering Families Today
Magazing covering areas of interest for fostering and kinship families.
editor@adoptinfo.net
www.fosteringfamiliestoday.com

### Coaching for Life
Coaching for LIFE! teaches organizations, families and individuals trauma informed and necessary skills for creating and maintaining peaceful systems where healing is ever-present.
www.coaching-forlife.com

### Raising Kin Blog
RaisingKin raises awareness about kinship care - relatives and close family friends who are raising a relative's child or children.
www.raisingkin.org

## 7. Perspective Of the Child
*Succeed Because of What You've Been Through* by Rhonda Sciortino
*The Prayer That Covers It All* by Rhonda Sciortino

### In Family Services
This is the website for Beth Powell, LCSW who specializes in helping traumatized children and the families who raise them to heal.
www.infamilyservices.net

### Forever Families
At Forever Families, learn practical strategies from the blogs, how to heal your child's pain from The Adoptive & Foster Parent Guide, and join our wise and loving group of parents in the Community.
www.forever-families.com

### Children's Home Society of North Carolina
CHS has one of the most comprehensive and seamless offerings of child welfare and family support services in North Carolina – providing programs in parenting education, family preservation, teen pregnancy

prevention, foster care, and adoption - all from one agency.
www.chsnc.org

## 8. Finding Support

*Taking a Break: Creating Foster, Adoptive and Kinship Respite in Your Community* find the guide here:
www.nrcdr.org/_assets/files/NRCRRFAP/ resources/taking-a-break-respite-guide.pdf

*Are We There Yet: The Ultimate Road Trip, Adopting & Raising 22 Kids* by Sue Badeau

*Love and Mayhem: One Big Family's Uplifting Story of Fostering and Adoption* by Dr. John DeGarmo

*Fostering Love: One Foster Parent's Journey* by Dr. John DeGarmo

**Sue Badeau's website**
Contains resources, tips, a blog, books and even freebies to download.
**www.suebadeau.com**

**Dr. John DeGarmo's website**
Contains articles, resources, links, excerts from his books and other great items.
**www.drejohndegarmo.com**

**HALOS**
Provides support and advocacy to abused and neglected chiden and kinship caregivers.
**www.charlestonhalos.org**

## 9. Parenting Children from Tough Starts

*Boy Who was Raised as a Dog* by Maia Szalavitz and Bruce Perry

*Attaching in Adoption, Tools for Today's Parents* by Deborah Gray

*ADHD: The Great Misdiagnosis* by Julian Stuart Haber

*From Fear to Love* by B. Bryan Post

*New Families, Old Scripts* by Caroline Archer and Christine Gordon

*Trauma, Attachment and Family Permanence* by Caroline Archer and Alan Burnell

*Parenting the Hurt Child: Helping Adoptive Families Heal and Grow* by Gregory Keck and Regina M. Kupecky

*Creating Ceremonies: Innovative Ways to Meet Adoption Challenges* by Cheryl A. Lieberman, PhD and Rhea K. Bufferd, LISCW

*The Body Remembers: The Psychophysiology of Trauma and Trauma Treatment* by Babette Rothschild

*Birds + Bee + YOUR Kids – A Guide To Sharing Your Beliefs About Sexuality, Love + Relationships* by Amy Lang

*Protecting the Gift: Keeping Children and Teenagers Safe (and Parents Sane)* by Gavin de Becker

*It's So Amazing!: A Book about Eggs, Sperm, Birth, Babies, and Families* by Robie Harris and Michael Emberley

*It's Perfectly Normal: Changing Bodies, Growing Up, Sex, and Sexual Health* by Robie Harris and Michael Emberley

**Resources for Parents and Caregivers to Learn about Trauma**
www.nctsn.org/resources

www.projectabc-la.org/parents

www.multiplyconnections.org

www.angriesout.com

**National Child Traumatic Stress Network**

The mission of the National Child Traumatic Stress Network is to raise the standard of care and improve access to services for traumatized children, their families www.nctsn.org

**Rise Magazine**
A magazine by and for parents affected by child welfare system. This specific magazine issue has trauma information
www.risemagazine.org/PDF/ Rise_issue_11.pdf
**www.risemagazine.org**

**Attachment & Trauma Network**
Hope and Healing for Traumatized Children and their Families includes resources and podcasts.
**www.attachtrauma.org**

**Project ABC**
Project ABC is a collaborative partnership among professionals in child welfare, mental health and community services designed to create a system of care for young children.
**www.projectabc-la.org**

**Multiplying Connections**
Resources for parents and professionals understanding the impact of trauma on children.
**www.multiplyingconnections.org**

**Kate Oliver's Blog**
**www.help4yourfamily.com**

**Stress Free Kids®**
Has products designed to help children, teens, and adults decrease stress, anxiety, and anger. These books and CDs will introduce you and your children to the proven techniques of deep breathing, progressive muscular relaxation, visualizations, and affirmations/positive statements. This unique

storytelling format has been embraced by psychologists, doctors, child life care specialists, yoga instructors, teachers, counselors, parents, and most importantly... children.
**www.stressfreekids.com**

**Inward Bound**
Inward Bound offers counseling, consultation/coaching, and training with the express purpose of compassionately helping couples, families, and individuals find their way into the relationships they long for.
**www.inwardbound.com**
**Sexual Abuse Resources**
**Stop it NOW!**
(888) PREVENT
or www.StopItNow.org

**PEACE of Mind**
**www.POMWA.org**

**Darkness to Light**
(866) FOR-LIGHT
**www.D2L.org**

**Birds + Bees + Kids**
**www.BirdsAndBeesAndKids.com**

**Prevent Child Abuse America**
500 North Michigan Ave. Suite 200
Chicago, IL 60611
(312) 663-3520
(800) 244-5373
mailbox@preventchildabuse.org
**www.preventchildabuse.org**

# 10. Understanding Attachment

*Creating Capacity for Attachment* edited by Arthur Becker-Weidman, PhD and Deborah Shell, MA, LCMHC

*Principles of Attachment Parenting* by Arthur Becker-Weidman, PhD

*Toddler Adoption: The Weaver's Craft* by Mary Hopkins-Best

*Parenting the Hurt Child: Helping Adoptive Families Heal and Grow* by Gregory Keck and Regina M. Kupecky

*First Steps in Parenting the Child Who Hurts* by Caroline Archer

*Attaching in Adoption, Practical Tools for Today's Parents* by Deborah Gray

**Center for Family Development**
Specializing in the treatment of adopted and foster families with trauma and attachment disorder.
www.Center4FamilyDevelop.com

**Christine Moers Videos on Parenting from Tough Places**
www.youtube.com/user/christinemoers

**A Forever Family**
www.a4everfamily.org

**ATTACh** – www.attach.org

**Kate Oliver's website**
www.help4yourfamily.com

# 11. Behavior & Discipline
*Behavior With a Purpose* by Charley Joyce, LICSW and Rick Delaney, PhD

*Assessing Youth Behavior* Charley Joyce, LICSW, contributing author

*1-2-3 Magic: Effective Discipline for Children 2-12* by Thomas W. Phelan, PhD

*How to Talk so Kids Will Listen and Listen so Kids will Talk* by Adele Faber and Elaine Mazlish

*Parenting With Love and Logic: Teaching Children Responsibility* by Foster Cline, MD and Jim Fay

*The Connected Child: Bring Hope and Healing to Your Adopted Family* by Karyn Purvis, PhD, and David Cross, PhD

*Building the Bonds of Attachment* by Daniel Hughes, PhD

*Creating Ceremonies: Innovative Ways to Meet Adoption Challenges* by Cheryl A. Lieberman, PhD and Reha K. Bufferd, LICSW

**Parenting by Connections**
Hand in Hand Parenting works with parents of young children providing resources, training, and lots of support. Our Parenting by Connection approach has given parents practical tools to resolve universal family challenges. Unlike other parenting methods, which rely on systems of rewards and punishment, our philosophy is centered on children's strong, innate desire to love and be loved.
www.handinhandparenting.org

**Hearts for Families**
To strengthen families and those that serve families with nurturing parenting education.
www.heartsforfamilies.org

**Piszchala Associates**
Specializing in Crisis Intervention Training for Community Service Providers, Foster & Adoptive Parents
www.piszchala-associates.com

# 12. Working With Schools
*Welcome Home, Forever Child: A Celebration of Children Adopted as Toddlers, Preschoolers, and Beyond* by Christine Mitchell

*Family Day: Celebrating Ethan's Adoption Anniversary* by Christine Mitchell

*A Foster-Adoption Story: Angela and Michael's Journey* by Christine Mitchell and Regina M. Kupecky, MSW

*For Parents with Special Needs Children in School Wrightslaw: From Emotions to*

*Advocacy The Special Education Survival Guide* by Peter W.D. Wright and Pamela Darr Wright

*How to Compromise With Your School District Without Compromising Your Child: A Field Guide For Getting Effective Services For Children with Special Needs* by Gary Mayerson

**The Legal Center For Foster Care & Education**
It serves as a national technical assistance resource and information clearinghouse on legal and policy matters affecting the education of children in the foster care system.
ccleducation@staff.abanet.org
**www.abanet.org/child/education.**

**Christine Mitchell's website**
Resources for families fostering and adopting out of fostercare.
**www.christine-mitchell.com/ adoption_and_school_assignments**

## 12. The Teen Years
*The Five Love Languages of Children* by Gary Chapman and Ross Campbell

*The Five Love Languages of Teens* by Gary Chapman

*Recognizing and Managing Fetal Alcohol Syndrome/Effects: A Guidebook ; Parenting The Story of An Older Child Adoption* by Brenda McCreight, PhD

*Eden's Secret Journal: The Story of An Older Child Adoption* by Brenda McCreight, PhD
*Positive Discipline for Teenagers* by Jane Nelsen, EdD, Lynn Lott, M.A, M.F.T

*Brainstorm: The Power and Purpose of the Teenage Brain* by Daniel J. Siegel, M.D

**You Gotta Believe!**
Older Child Adoption Agency and

Homelessness Prevention Program
**www.yougottabelieve.org**

**Brenda McCreight, PhD, RSW**
Therapist working children and families facing issues such as sexual abuse, family violence, adoption, and foster related concerns
**www.theadoptioncounselor.com**

**John H. Chafee Foster Care Independence Program Administration for Children and Families**
370 L'Enfant Promenade, SW
Washington, DC 20447
**www.acf.hhs.gov/programs/cb/pro-grams_fund/state_tribal/jh_chafee.htm**

## General Resources
*Families Change: A Book for Children Experiencing Termination of Parental Rights (Kids Are Important Series)* by Julie Nelson

*Maybe Days: A Book for Children in Foster Care* by Jennifer Wilgocki, Marcia Kahn Wright and Alissa Imre Geis

*Kids Need to Be Safe: A Book for Children in Foster Care (Kids Are Important series)* by Julie Nelson

*My Foster Family: A Story for Children Entering Foster Care* by Jennifer Levine

*The Dandelion Seed* by Joseph P. Anthony and Cris Arbo

*The Boy Who was Raised as a Dog: And Other Stories from a Child Psychiatrist's Notebook: What Traumatized Children Can Teach Us About Loss, Love and Healing* by Bruce D. Perry, MD, PhD, and Maia Szalavitz

*Lifebooks: Creating a Treasure for the Adopted Child* by Beth O'Mallery

*My Foster Care Journey* by Beth O'Mallery

*For When I'm Famous: A Teen Foster/Adoption Lifebook* by Beth O'Mallery

*Talking with Children About Loss* by Maria Trozzi

*Healing Loss in the Traumatized Child* by Marilyn Schoettle, MA and Ellen Singer, LCSW-

*The Foster Parenting Toolbox* edited by Kim Phagel Hansel

**Fostering Families Today Magazine**
541 E. Garden Dr. Unit N
Windsor, CO 80550
(888) 924-6736
(970) 686-7413
editor@adoptinfo.net
**www.fosteringfamiliestoday.com**

**Foster Focus Magazine**
Monthly magazine about foster care issues edited by a foster care alumni, Chris Chmielewski
chris@fosterfocusmag.com
www.fosterfocusmag.com

**Lifebook Resources**
Foster/kinship children's lifebook resources & lifebook tips
**www.adoptionlifebooks.com**

**Child Welfare Information Gateway**
Children's Bureau/ACYF
1250 Maryland Avenue, SW 8th Floor
Washington, DC 20024
(800) 394-3366
info@childwelfare.gov
**www.childwelfare.gov**
Child Welfare Information Gateway connects professionals and the general public to information and resources targeted to the safety, permanency, and well-being of children and families.

**Child Welfare League of America (CWLA)**
Headquarters
1726 M St. NW, Suite 500
Third Floor
Washington, DC 20036
(202) 688-4200
The Child Welfare League of America (CWLA) is the oldest national organization serving vulnerable children, youth, and their families. CWLA provides training, consultation, and technical assistance to child welfare professionals and agencies while also educating the public on emerging issues that affect abused, neglected, and at-risk children. **www.cwla.org**

## Kinship Resources
**Kinship Center**
124 River Road
Salinas, CA 93908
(831) 455-9965
(800) 4kinship
Kinship Center provides the full spectrum of family-centered support to strengthen the families and communities we serve.
**www.kinshipcenter.org**

**Casey Family Programs**
2001 Eighth Avenue, Suite 2700
Seattle, WA 98121
(206) 282-7300
At Casey Family Programs, we support and assist child welfare systems in their efforts to protect children and create strong families. With a variety of programs focused on the child-welfare system, Casey Family Programs is a treasure trove of facts and guides.
**www.casey.org**

**EMQ Families First**
251 Llewellyn Ave.
Campbell, CA 95008-1940
(408) 379-3790
They help children and families in need
through innovative programs that make a
real difference in people's lives.
**emqff.org**

**Youth Communication**
**NY Center, Inc.**
224 W. 29th Street
New York, NY 10001
(212) 279-0708
info@youthcomm.org
The mission of Youth Communication is to
help teenagers, including foster youth,
develop their skills in reading, writing,
thinking, and reflection, so they can acquire
the information they need to make
thoughtful choices about their lives.
**www.youthcomm.org**

**Represent Magazine**
224 W. 29th St
New York, NY 10001
(212) 279-0708
Written by and for teens in foster care,
Represent provides them a voice to share
personal experiences, to plan for their
future, and to help them negotiate the present.
**www.representmag.org**

# CEU Quizzes

On the following pages you will find CEU quizzes for each chapter. These are "open book" quizzes. As you read the articles identified in each of the questions, you should be able to answer the questions. Once you have completed the questions for the chapter, photocopy or tear out the completed pages, **attach your essay on a separate sheet of paper** (it may be typed or handwritten), send to the address below with the correct processing fee. **Be sure to check with your placement agency to see if they will credit you for completing the CEU Quiz.** You will be mailed a Certificate of Completion for each completed quiz.

**Downloadable copies of these forms are available at www.emkpress.com/KPCEUquizzes.html**

**Mail them to:**
EMK Press
16 Mt Bethel Road #219
Warren, NJ 07059
A processing fee of $5.00 for each quiz can be paid by check payable to EMK Press.

**Fax them or email them to:**
732-469-7544 or scan and email them to info@emkpress.com. Need a lot of CEU hours? Please email for quantity discounts on certificates of completion.

**Please include the following information when you send in each completed quiz (this is at the bottom of each quiz):**

Name_____

Address_____

City _____State _____Zip _____

Private or State Agency Contact_____

Office Address/PO Box _____

City _____State _____Zip _____

Learning Objective: to increase foster and/or adoptive parents' ability to apply and respond to new information and conceptual frameworks to their work with children in their care. Please rate the following on a scale of 1-4 (1 is poor, 4 is excellent):

The information was informative: ( 1-2-3-4 )

The information was useful/helpful in my role as a foster/adoptive parent: ( 1-2-3-4 )

The information was thought-provoking, ( 1-2-3-4 ) especially the story on page(s)

_____

## Chapter 1:
## The Unexpected Role CEU Quiz

1. According to the article, More Than Stand-ins: Real Parents and Real Struggles,” by Karen J. Foli, MSN, Ph.D., RN, which of the following are strategies to fight depression.

    a. Let yourself grieve.
    b. Know and use tangible resources.
    c. Take antidepressants.
    d. Limit your intake of caffeine.

2. According to the article, Seven Tips for New Kinship Caregiver,” by Alison O'Donnell Caliendo, which of the following are among the seven tips?

    a. Decipher local labels and acronyms.
    b. Beat frustration with preparation.
    c. Learn about child-only TANF.
    d. Understand how programs define you.
    e. All of the above.
    f. None of the above.

3. Which of the following statements is FALSE, based on the article, “From a Satin Duvet to a Washable Bed Spread by Phyllis Stevens?

    a. When a child is taken into foster care, the goal for that child is to be reunited with his or her birth mother or father.
    b. Missing a conference call that had been planned for weeks is not important.
    c. “Jon” has taught me what is important in life and what is not.
    d. All of the above.
    e. None of the above.

4. According to the article, “Kinship Toolbox,” by Jan Wagner, which of the following tips are offered to kinship caregivers?

    a. Don't stress yourself out.
    b. Hire a good babysitter.
    c. Listen intently.
    d. Be a good role model.

5. According to the article, "To Grandmother's House We Go," by Ron Huxley, LMFT, and Catie Hargrove, MS, which of the following are unanticipated emotional challenges kinship caregivers face?

    a. Holding onto child rearing practices that may conflict with current and social standards and from the child welfare system.
    b. Depression at having to parent at an older age.
    c. Confusion about who has final say on the welfare of the child.
    d. Struggle helping your child with Algebra homework.

6. According to the article, "Kinship Care – The History of a Name," by Eileen Mayers Pasztor, DSW, where did the name kinship care originate?

    a. A frustrated grandmother.
    b. Carol Stack's "All Our Kin: Strategies for Survival in a Black Community."
    c. A CWLA conference.
    d. A meeting with child welfare professionals.

7. Essay: How did you become a kinship caregiver? Please use a separate sheet of paper.

_____

Please print clearly:

Name _____

Address _____

City _____ State _____ Zip _____

Private or State Agency Contact _____

Office Address/PO Box _____

City _____ State _____ Zip _____

Learning Objective: to increase foster and/or adoptive parents' ability to apply and respond to new information and conceptal frameworks to their work with children in their care. Please rate the following on a scale of 1-4 (1 is poor, 4 is excellent):

The information was informative: ( 1-2-3-4 )

The information was useful/helpful in my role as a foster/adoptive parent: ( 1-2-3-4 )

The information was thought-provoking, ( 1-2-3-4 ) especially the story on page(s)

_____

See page 313 for payment and mailing details to earn Certificates of Completion.

## Chapter 2:
## Getting Organized CEU Quiz

1. Which of the following are among the 10 things caregivers need, according to the article by Allison Davis Maxon, MS, LMFT?

 a. Resources
 b. Parenting support
 c. Sense of humor
 d. Empathy
 e. All of the above
 f. None of the above.

2. According to the article, "Relatives and Kin Raising Children," by Beth Powell, which of the following are common needs of kinship caregivers
?

 a. Complimentary or low-cash recreational opportunities.
 b. Gift cards to Starbucks.
 c. Knowledge of resource families can apply for and most importantly, how relatives are supposed to apply for potential resources.
 d. Affordable daycare.

3. According to the article, "Kinship Care for a Son's Brother," by Tonya Barker, which of the following statement is FALSE?

 a. Kinship care is shared parenting to the max.
 b. Understanding the process is easy.
 c. Respite is a must.
 d. One day it will be over, the records closed and the papers in hand.
 e. All of the above.
 f. None of the above.

4. According to the article, "Asking Others for Help," by Beth Powell, which of the following statements is TRUE?

 a. In America today, there are about 13.7 million single parents raising more than 21 million children.
 b. 84 percent of single parents are female.
 c. 26 percent of children are younger than 21 in America today.
 d. Single caregivers need help raising the children they have in their care.
 e. All of the above.
 f. None of the above.

5. According to the article, "Keeping Track: Where Do I Stand?" by Andrea B. Smith, PhD, and Linda L. Dannison, PhD, who are some of the "players" on your child's team?

    a. Teacher
    b. Circuit court judge
    c. Clergy member
    d. Therapist/counselor

6. Which of the following are things to consider DURING an appointment, according to the article, , "Keeping Track: Where Do I Stand?" by Andrea B. Smith, PhD, and Linda L. Dannison, PhD?

    a. What are the eligibility requirements?
    b. Have a pencil and paper handy to jot down what you learn from your phone call.
    c. Name of person you will meet with.
    d. What information and documents you need to bring.
    e. All of the above.
    f. None of the above.

7. Essay: What are some things you do that help you stay organized in your parenting duties? Please use a separate piece of paper.

_____

Please print clearly:

Name _____

Address _____

City _____ State _____ Zip _____

Private or State Agency Contact _____

Office Address/PO Box _____

City _____ State _____ Zip _____

Learning Objective: to increase foster and/or adoptive parents' ability to apply and respond to new information and conceptal frameworks to their work with children in their care. Please rate the following on a scale of 1-4 (1 is poor, 4 is excellent):

The information was informative: ( 1-2-3-4 )

The information was useful/helpful in my role as a foster/adoptive parent: ( 1-2-3-4 )

The information was thought-provoking, ( 1-2-3-4 ) especially the story on page(s)

_____

See page 313 for payment and mailing details to earn Certificates of Completion.

## Chapter 3:
## Your Legal Toolbox CEU Quiz

1. According to the article, "Formal vs. Informal Kinship Care," By Jan Wagner, what is considered formal kinship care?
>    a. The placing of children in the home of a relative or close friend with a familial relationship temporarily.
>    b. The temporary guardianship of a child under court order.
>    c. The placing of children in the home of a relative or close friend with a familial relationship through the child welfare system and by the court.
>    d. Taking care of your grandchildren while your children go on a vacation.

2. Which of the following statement sis TRUE based on the article, "Legal Relationship Options," by Generations United?
>    a. Legal custody is similar to guardianship, but is usually granted by a different court with varying procedures.
>    b. Guardianship does not sever the biological parents' rights and responsibilities.
>    c. An option of standby guardianship exists in more than a third of states.
>    d. About a third of the state have educational consent laws which effectively allow children being raised by relatives to attend public school free of charge.
>    e. All of the above.
>    f. None of the above.

3. According to the article, "The Interstate Compact on the Placement of Children," by Janna Annest, JD, which of the following statements is FALSE?
>    a. The ICPC applies to the placement of any child in state custody, regardless of the relationship between the child and the adoptive parents.
>    b. ICPC requests can be approved without a completed homestudy.
>    c. Each state's ICPC office maintains a checklist of information it requires.
>    d. If the child is not in state care, adoptive parents may receive approval within a week or two of submitting all of the documents required by the sending and receiving states' ICPC administrators.
>    e. All of the above.
>    f. None of the above.

4. According to the article, "Basic Etiquette for Courtroom Attendance," by Andrea B. Smith and Linda L. Dannison, Ph.D., which of the following are among the guidelines for courtroom etiquette?
>    a. Interrupt the judge if you aren't allowed to speak.
>    b. Make sure you share all of the negatives about the child's birth parents.
>    c. If invited to speak, always address the judge directly and begin with, "Thank you, your Honor," then continue.
>    d. Take notes while you are there.

5. According to the article, "See You in Court," by Beth O'Malley, M.Ed., what can you do to prepare yourself or a child for court?
> a. Role play the court event.
> b. Avoid talking about it so no one gets nervous.
> c. Remind children that judges can be young, old, man, woman and any race.
> d. Eat a lot of sweets before going so everyone is in a good mood.

6. According to the article, "Kin Care," by Melissa D. Carter, JD; Christopher E. Church, Esq.; and Thomas B. Hammond, JD, what are the benefits of formalizing a kinship care arrangement?
a. Relatives are responsible for all expenses.
b. Allows the caregiver to access additional sources of financial assistance, programs and services.
c. Children can't be kidnapped.
d. Relative foster parents receive foster care subsidy to offset the costs.

7. Essay: What helped you tackle all of the legal aspects of caring for your kin? Please use a separate sheet of paper.

_____

Please print clearly:

Name _____

Address _____

City _____ State _____ Zip _____

Private or State Agency Contact _____

Office Address/PO Box _____

City _____ State _____ Zip _____

Learning Objective: to increase foster and/or adoptive parents' ability to apply and respond to new information and conceptual frameworks to their work with children in their care. Please rate the following on a scale of 1-4 (1 is poor, 4 is excellent):

The information was informative: ( 1-2-3-4 )

The information was useful/helpful in my role as a foster/adoptive parent: ( 1-2-3-4 )

The information was thought-provoking, ( 1-2-3-4 ) especially the story on page(s)

_____

See page 313 for payment and mailing details to earn Certificates of Completion.

## Chapter 4:
## Your Financial Toolbox CEU Quiz

1. According to the article, Financial Resources for Relative Caregivers," by Generations United, which of the following are potential sources of financial assistance for relatives raising children?

    a. An online fundraiser.
    b. Supplemental Security Income.
    c. Guardianship Assistance Program.
    d. Other family members.

2. According to the article, "Financial Resources for Relative Caregivers," by Generations United, which of the following are among the two basic types of grants a relative caregiver can receive under TANF?

    a. Foster care payments.
    b. Supplemental Nutrition Assistance Program.
    c. Family Grant.
    d. Child-Only Grant.

3. According to the article, "Financial Planning," by Claudia Mott, CFP, which of the following steps are involved in creating a budget?

    a. Set both short- and long-term goals.
    b. Create an account for your savings.
    c. Track your spending.
    d. All of the above.
    e. None of the above.

4. Which of the following are among the "Danger Signals in Money Management?"

    a. Unable to save for upcoming expenses – back to school clothes, birthdays, holidays.
    b. Calls from the collection agency.
    c. Ran out of money before the end of the month.
    d. One-third of your income saved for a "rainy day."

5. Which of the following statements is TRUE based on the article, "Kinship Care Finances," by Shay Olivarria?

    a. 65 percent of families involved in kinship care live below the poverty line.
    b. Almost half of all families involved in kinship care live below the federal poverty line.
    c. Between 25 percent and 75 percent of caregivers are single.
    d. 32 percent of kinship caregivers don't have a high school diploma.

6. According to the article, "Kinship Care Finances," by Shay Olivarria, what can be done to help kinship caregivers gain access to financial resources available to them?
    a. Kinship caregivers should receive funding from family and friends.
    b. Kinship caregivers have to be made aware of financial resources available to them.
    c. Kinship caregivers should be provided contact information for each financial resource.
    d. Kinship caregivers should have meetings with their financial advisers.

7. Essay: Who has been the most helpful in connecting you to financial resources? Please use a separate sheet of paper.

_____

Please print clearly:

Name _____

Address _____

City _____ State _____ Zip _____

Private or State Agency Contact _____

Office Address/PO Box _____

City _____ State _____ Zip _____

Learning Objective: to increase foster and/or adoptive parents' ability to apply and respond to new information and conceptual frameworks to their work with children in their care. Please rate the following on a scale of 1-4 (1 is poor, 4 is excellent):

The information was informative: ( 1-2-3-4 )

The information was useful/helpful in my role as a foster/adoptive parent: ( 1-2-3-4 )

The information was thought-provoking, ( 1-2-3-4 ) especially the story on page(s)

_____

See page 313 for payment and mailing details to earn Certificates of Completion.

## Chapter 5:
## Our Changing Family CEU Quiz

**1. Which of the following statements is TRUE based on the article, "Kinship Care and Strings Attached," by Kim Combes, LBSW, M.Ed.? 0**

   a. Workers and others in the system need to be reminded that we all have free will and that even those raised in the best of families can choose a wrong road and vice versa.

   b. Federal laws dictate that the placing worker much first attempt to place a child in a relative home.

   c. Kinship care, at least theoretically, is the best option when a child must leave the parental home.

   d. All of the above.

   e. None of the above.

**2. According to the article, "The Complex Relationships of Kin Care," by Mary-Jo Land, CPT, CDDP, what is one way to reduce pressures to clearly and in writing define everyone's roles, responsibilities and duties?**

   a. Keep a journal.

   b. Family group conferencing.

   c. Meet regularly with a CASA.

   d. Join a support group for kinship caregivers.

**3. Which of the following are among the things to remember when communicating with your adult child, according to the article, "Tips for Dealing with Your Adult Child?"**

   a. Give age-appropriate information.

   b. Obtain a restraining order.

   c. Only communicate through attorneys.

   d. Provide large pieces of information rather than details.

   e. All of the above.

   f. None of the above

**4. Which of the following are among the suggestions for visitation, according to the article, "Visitation Tips?" 0**

   a. Try to make your interactions with your adult child as positive as possible.

   b. Do not compete for your grandchild's affection.

   c. Talk bad about your adult child to your grandchild.

   d. Bring food for your adult child.

5. According to the article, "What's in a Name," By Madeleine Krebs, LCSW-C, which of the following statements is FALSE? 0
    a. Changes in relationships and titles take time.
    b. When children are adopted at older ages, it is natural for them to face difficulty in making the transition to calling their relative "Mom" and "Dad."
    c. School personnel need to know that the adopted child's "story" is open to the public.
    d. All of the above.
    e. None of the above.

6. According to the article, "Begin with Kin but Honor the Bond," which of the following are among the five consecutive choices or options when charges of abuse or neglect are substantiated against birth parents?0
    a. The second choice is to move the child to a group home.
    b. The fourth choice is adoption by the psychological parent.
    c. The first choice is to maintain the birth home when possible.
    d. The fifth choice is to reunify the child with birth family.

7. Essay: Who has been the most helpful in connecting you to financial resources? Please use a separate sheet of paper.
_____

Please print clearly:

Name _____

Address _____

City _____State _____Zip _____

Private or State Agency Contact _____

Office Address/PO Box _____

City _____State _____Zip _____

Learning Objective: to increase foster and/or adoptive parents' ability to apply and respond to new information and conceptual frameworks to their work with children in their care. Please rate the following on a scale of 1-4 (1 is poor, 4 is excellent):

The information was informative: ( 1-2-3-4 )

The information was useful/helpful in my role as a foster/adoptive parent: ( 1-2-3-4 )

The information was thought-provoking, ( 1-2-3-4 ) especially the story on page(s)
_____

See page 313 for payment and mailing details to earn Certificates of Completion.

## Chapter 6:
## Guilt, Shame, & Love CEU Quiz

1. Which of the following statements is TRUE based on the article, "Emotional Rollercoaster," by Betty Hanway?

    a. I am so glad I get to parent my grandson, we have a great relationship.
    b. I am Grandma to two and Grandma/Mom to one and it's not fair to any of them.
    c. All arrangements are complicated because we have "joint managing conservatorship" with both biological parents.
    d. My next step is for my daughter to move in with us and start parenting again.

2. According to the article, "What to Do When You are Mom to your Child's Mom," by Jan Wagner, which of the following statement is FALSE?

    a. The greatest impact of raising my grandson has been with my own biological children and their children.
    b. I desperately love my other grandkids, but my focus is on the one we are raising.
    c. Boundaries need to be set.
    d. The saving grace for me is acceptance.
    e. All of the above.
    f. None of the above.

3. According to the article, "'Grand' Parenting" by Noelle Hause, Ed.D., LPC, which of the following feelings may a kinship caregiver experience?

    a. Anxiety
    b. Disappointment
    c. Embarrassment
    d. Fear
    e. All of the above.
    f. None of the above.

4. Which of the following are among the things you cannot giveaway, according to the article, "I Cannot Giveaway That Which is No Mine to Give," By Juli Alvarado?

    a. I cannot provide love it I do not feel loved.
    b. I cannot provide safety to my child, if I do not feel safe inside.
    c. I cannot create calm if chaos is erupting around me.
    d. I cannot expect my children to obey me, because we are right.

5. Which of the following benefits did author Amy Radtke experience in joining a support group in the article, "Kinship Care: A Journey Through Sorrow?"

    a. I understand the challenges and feelings the members described.
    b. It helped me to lose weight.
    c. I felt I had "come home" to a group of people, who understood 100 percent what I was feeling.
    d. It helped me solve all my problems.

6. According to the article, "The Safety Net of Kinship Care," by Amy Radtke, MA, which of the following statements is TRUE?

    a. Although kinship care certainly comes with many challenges, it does carry certain joys.
    b. I personally carry certain regrets for how I parented my daughter.
    c. We fill the void of the missing parent.
    d. There is no incentive to be the safety net.
    e. All of the above.
    f. None of the above.

7. Essay: What have been some of the most difficult feelings you have struggled with as a kinship parent? Please use a separate sheet of paper.

_____

Please print clearly:

Name _____

Address _____

City _____State _____Zip _____

Private or State Agency Contact _____

Office Address/PO Box _____

City _____State _____Zip _____

Learning Objective: to increase foster and/or adoptive parents' ability to apply and respond to new information and conceptual frameworks to their work with children in their care. Please rate the following on a scale of 1-4 (1 is poor, 4 is excellent):

The information was informative: ( 1-2-3-4 )

The information was useful/helpful in my role as a foster/adoptive parent: ( 1-2-3-4 )

The information was thought-provoking, ( 1-2-3-4 ) especially the story on page(s)

_____

See page 313 for payment and mailing details to earn Certificates of Completion.

## Chapter 7:
## Perspective of the Child CEU Quiz

**1. According to the article, "From a Child's View," by Lee Sperduti, which of the following statements is FALSE?**
   a. I needed someone to tell me that my situation was not my fault.
   b. People seem to generally believe that everyone was taught and understands basic life and social skills.
   c. Occasional interventions by professionals may have also given me validation to my thoughts and feelings.
   d. Much of the guilt that I had shouldered for way too many years may have been relieved had I been told that my parents' problems were among themselves and had mothering to do with my brother and me.
   e. All of the above.
   f. None of the above.

**2. According to the article, "A Traumatized Child's Hierarchy of Needs," by Beth Powell, LCSW, letting kids run the household because they come from a hard place, creates which of the following?**
   a. Anger
   b. Resentment
   c. Insecurity
   d. Entitlement
   e. All of the above.
   f. None of the above.

**3. According to the article, "Kinship Adoption: Family Provides Vital Information," by Carol Lozier, LCSW, which of the following statement is TRUE?**
   a. The U.S. Department of Health and Human Services estimates that one-half of children in the foster care system live with a relative.
   b. AARP states that 5.2 million of our nation's households are headed by grandparents or other relatives providing care for one or more children.
   c. In a kinship adoption, unlike other adoptions, families often possess informatio that children yearn to know.
   d. According to the U.S. Department of Health and Human Services Social Security Act, relatives are given the last consideration for child placements.

**4. According to the article, "The Good, the Bad and the Ugly of Kinship Parenting," by Rhonda Sciortino what is the point of the article according to the author?**
   a. Grandparents are always the best choice for a child who can't live with his or her parents.
   b. Foster care can be a positive experience for some children.
   c. CASAs and mentors can have a positive influence on a child's life.

    d. If a social worker had taken a closer look at my grandparents and the way they lived, he or she would have seen that they were not fit to raise a child.

**5. Which of the following statements is TRUE, according to the article, "Family Finding Fulfilling our Promise," by Matt V. Anderson, MSW?**
    a. There are more than 400,000 children living in foster care.
    b. 45,000 children age out of foster care every year.
    c. 150,000 children are waiting for a family to call their own.
    d. Children who age out of foster care often attend college and find successful careers.

**6. According to the article, "Kinship – Finding Our Place in the Circle," by Sandy White Hawk, which of the following statements is FALSE?**
    a. In Lakota culture the grandparents are the teachers to the family and young parents.
    b. Grandparents offer nothing to their grandchildren.
    c. The care of children – the next generation – was always a priority.
    d. If the parent-child relationship is a trusted one, young parents can avoid any pitfalls in their relationship.

**7. Essay: What have you learned about parenting from listening to the child you are caring for? Please use a separate sheet of paper.**

Please print clearly:

Name _____

Address _____

City _____State _____Zip _____

Private or State Agency Contact _____

Office Address/PO Box _____

City _____State _____Zip _____

Learning Objective: to increase foster and/or adoptive parents' ability to apply and respond to new information and conceptal frameworks to their work with children in their care. Please rate the following on a scale of 1-4 (1 is poor, 4 is excellent):

The information was informative: ( 1-2-3-4 )

The information was useful/helpful in my role as a foster/adoptive parent: ( 1-2-3-4 )

The information was thought-provoking, ( 1-2-3-4 ) especially the story on page(s)

_____

See page 313 for payment and mailing details to earn Certificates of Completion.

## Chapter 8:
## Finding Support CEU Quiz

1. According to the article, "United We Stand...Divided We Fall," which of the following statements is TRUE?

    a. In times of trouble and difficulty we become separate units with many words.
    b. We understand in our hearts the meaning of – divided we stand, united we fall.
    c. We discovered that our dreams and plans were filled with potholes.
    d. We can repair the neurological and physical damage of prenatal exposure to our adopted daughter.

2. According to the article, "Respite," what is the definition of respite?

    a. A new Nestle candy.
    b. A response children from traumatic backgrounds often have.
    c. A support group for kinship caregivers.
    d. A temporary beak, given to caretakers, that provides a period of rest and renewal.

3. According to the article, "Kinship Support Groups," which of the following are concerns/issues of the focus group?

    a. Financial assistance.
    b. Respite care.
    c. Legal representation.
    d. Counseling.

4. According to the article, "Self-Care for Kinship Caregivers," which of the following are ways caregivers can keep their stress level at a healthy level ?

    a. Schedule free time for your day.
    b. Practice saying, "no, thank you."
    c. Reduce the amount of time you spend with technology.
    d. Find inspiration.
    e. All of the above.
    f. None of the above.

5. According to the article, "Self-Caring for Caregivers," what are some tools that you might find helpful in your toolkit?

a. Schedule a weekly massage.
b. Make room for grief.
c. Attend regular support group meetings.
d. Laugh, play, breathe, relax.

6. **Which of the following are among the "10 Ways to Happiness?"**

a. Allow yourself to be dependent at times.
b. Read a book every week.
c. Create unique family activities.
d. Live at peace with memories.

7. **Essay: In what ways have you found support as a kinship caregiver? Please use a separate sheet of paper.**

_____

Please print clearly:

Name _____

Address _____

City _____State _____Zip _____

Private or State Agency Contact _____

Office Address/PO Box _____

City _____State _____Zip _____

Learning Objective: to increase foster and/or adoptive parents' ability to apply and respond to new information and conceptal frameworks to their work with children in their care. Please rate the following on a scale of 1-4 (1 is poor, 4 is excellent):

The information was informative: ( 1-2-3-4 )

The information was useful/helpful in my role as a foster/adoptive parent: ( 1-2-3-4 )

The information was thought-provoking, ( 1-2-3-4 ) especially the story on page(s)

_____

See page 313 for payment and mailing details to earn Certificates of Completion.

## Chapter 9:
## Parenting Children From Tough Starts CEU Quiz

1. According to the article, "'Smart Enough' Parenting," by Sue Badeau, which of the following are red flag behaviors a child may exhibit?

    a. Holding hands with friends while playing.
    b. Preoccupation with images of death, violence and gory, graphic details.
    c. Talking about difficult moments in their past.
    d. Extreme difficulty with forming peer friendships.

2. According to the article, "Sensory Integration," by Barbara Elleman, OTR/L, BCP, which of the following symptoms of dysfunction of sensory integration do young children exhibit?

    a. Poor self-concept.
    b. Clumsiness or difficulty with coordination.
    c. Slow to achieve developmental milestones.
    d. Difficulty tolerating changes in position.

3. Which of the following are the four stages of "good grief," according to the article, "Healing Loss in the Traumatized Child," by Ellen Singer, LCSW-C?

    a. Anger, frustration, grief, sadness
    b. Relief, calming, tears, transition
    c. Understanding, grieving, commemorating, moving on
    d. Transformation, processing, perspiring, grieving

4. According to the article, "Hidden Differences Shout Loudly," by Jodee Kulp, what does every child with FASD need?

    a. Patience and understanding
    b. Discipline
    c. Rules and enforcement
    d. Medication to remain stable

5. According to the article, "Life Links: Transitioning Children with Less Trauma," by Jennifer Winkelmann, which of the following statements is FALSE?

    a. Moves usually happen on an emergency basis, where the child has little, if any, notice.
    b. Just before, during and after transition is the worst time for the players to change.

   c. Children are often removed from the care of their parents by a person who is
      a stranger.
   d. A child's belongings are often left behind or lost in transit.
   e. All of the above.
   f. None of the above.

**6. According to the article, "To Be Concerned or Not to Be Concerned? That is the Question!" by Noelle Hause, Ed.D., LPC, what are some questions to ask yourself if you are concerned about your child's behavior?**

   a. What's wrong with my child?
   b. Does my child lack the appropriate skills to be successful?
   c. Have I been emotionally available to my child?
   d. Why can't my child be more like my friend's child?

**7. Essay: What are some things you have learned about raising a child from a tough start and how have you changed your parenting style to accomodate those needs? Please use a separate sheet of paper.**

_____

Please print clearly:

Name _____

Address _____

City _____State _____Zip _____

Private or State Agency Contact _____

Office Address/PO Box _____

City _____State _____Zip _____

Learning Objective: to increase foster and/or adoptive parents' ability to apply and respond to new information and conceptal frameworks to their work with children in their care. Please rate the following on a scale of 1-4 (1 is poor, 4 is excellent):

The information was informative: ( 1-2-3-4 )

The information was useful/helpful in my role as a foster/adoptive parent: ( 1-2-3-4 )

The information was thought-provoking, ( 1-2-3-4 ) especially the story on page(s)

_____

See page 313 for payment and mailing details to earn Certificates of Completion.

## Chapter 10:
## Understanding Attachment CEU Quiz

1. According to the article, "Attachment 101," which of the following are among the principles to follow to facilitate attachment?

    a. Always say yes.
    b. Avoid saying no.
    c. It's about connections, not compliance.
    d. Do not punish the child.
    e. All of the above.
    f. None of the above.

2. According to the article, "Attachment 101," which of the following is among the four most important factors in placement stability?

    a. Foster parent's access to resources and supports.
    b. Foster parent's ability to love without condition.
    c. Foster parent's ability to be sensitive and responsive to the child.
    d. Foster parent's commitment to the child.

3. Which of the following are ways you can help a child manage his or her body, according to the article, "10 Ways to Help Children Feel Less Anxious," by Martha B. Straus, Ph.D., and Melanie Ernould, MA?

    a. Feeling awareness
    b. Yoga
    c. Exercise
    d. Regular playdates

4. Which of the following are among the "10 Ways to Help Children Feel Less Anxious," by Martha B. Straus, Ph.D., and Melanie Ernould, MA?

    a. Don't listen when worries come.
    b. Practice mindful awareness.
    c. Worry well, but only once.
    d. All of the above.
    e. None of the above.

5. According to the article, "PLACE Parenting," by Kate Oliver, MSW, LCSW-C, what does PLACE stand for
?

       a. Peace, luck, acknowledge, creative, employment
       b. Playful, loving, accepting, curious, empathy
       c. Poise, likeness, ability, courage, elegance
       d. Poignancy, learning, agreement, calm, engage

6. According to the article, "PLACE Parenting," by Kate Oliver, MSW, LCSW-C, which of the following statements is FALSE?

       a. A way to really get playful is to learn from a parent who gets this stuff.
       b. Do not engage in an argument.
       c. Get curious about the children in your care.
       d. Empathy is being able to see something from the viewpoint of another person.
       e. All of the above
       f. None of the above.

7. Essay: What are some things you do to build attachment with the children you care for? Please use a separate sheet of paper.

_____

Please print clearly:

Name _____

Address _____

City _____State _____Zip _____

Private or State Agency Contact _____

Office Address/PO Box _____

City _____State _____Zip _____

Learning Objective: to increase foster and/or adoptive parents' ability to apply and respond to new information and conceptual frameworks to their work with children in their care. Please rate the following on a scale of 1-4 (1 is poor, 4 is excellent):

The information was informative: ( 1-2-3-4 )

The information was useful/helpful in my role as a foster/adoptive parent: ( 1-2-3-4 )

The information was thought-provoking, ( 1-2-3-4 ) especially the story on page(s)

_____

See page 313 for payment and mailing details to earn Certificates of Completion.

## Chapter 11:
## Behavior & Discipline CEU Quiz

1. According to the article, "Appropriate Boundaries in Parenting," by Sue Laney, which of the following are among the three styles of parenting?

    a. Gentle nurturer
    b. Brick wall
    c. Stern captain
    d. Deep-rooted tree

2. According to the article, "Don't Use an Elephant Gun to Shoot a Mouse," by Walt Piszchala, which of the following are included among the five-step approach to setting limits?

    a. Give them some time.
    b. Be prepared to enforce.
    c. Use language that calms.
    d. Review the consequences.
    e. All of the above.
    f. None of the above.

3. According to the article, "Child Neglect and Hoarding Food," by Charley Joyce, MSW, LICSW, which of the following are among the interventions designed to focus on the function of neglect-based food hoarding?

    a. Coupling nurturing with food.
    b. Limit the number of snacks.
    c. Lock up food between meal times.
    d. Teach food regulation.
    e. All of the above.
    f. None of the above.

4. According to the article, "Foster Children and the Cruelty to Animals," by Charley Joyce, MSW, LICSW, what should be included in a treatment model for children who are cruel to animals?

    a. Constant contact with animals.
    b. Move the child to a home without animals.
    c. Continue to allow the child to harm the animal until he or she has worked out the problem.
    d. Create a unique game with the animals and child to encourage bonding.
    e. All of the above.
    f. None of the above.

5. According to the article, "Lying: Why and What to do About it," by Charley Joyce, MSW, LICSW, which of the following are among the reasons why children lie?

    a. To create connection.

    b. Because it has become a pattern of behavior.

    c. As a way to feel important.

    d. As a way to avoid boredom.

6. According to the article, "Helping Older Children with Bathroom Related Issues," by Kate Oliver, MSW, LCSW-C, which of the following questions should you ask to help figure out what a child is having enuresis or encopresis issues?

    a. Does this child have trauma associated with the bathroom?

    b. Is this child pissed off?

    c. Is this a child who is fearful of connection to others?

    d. Was this child properly potty-trained?

    e. All of the above.

    f. None of the above.

7. Essay: What have been some ways you have learned to successfully discipline the children you care for? Please use a separate sheet of paper.

_____

Please print clearly:

Name _____

Address _____

City _____State _____Zip _____

Private or State Agency Contact _____

Office Address/PO Box _____

City _____State _____Zip _____

Learning Objective: to increase foster and/or adoptive parents' ability to apply and respond to new information and conceptal frameworks to their work with children in their care. Please rate the following on a scale of 1-4 (1 is poor, 4 is excellent):

The information was informative: ( 1-2-3-4 )

The information was useful/helpful in my role as a foster/adoptive parent: ( 1-2-3-4 )

The information was thought-provoking, ( 1-2-3-4 ) especially the story on page(s)

_____

See page 313 for payment and mailing details to earn Certificates of Completion.

## Chapter 12:
## Working With Schools CEU Quiz

1. According to the article, "Supporting Kinship Care Children in a Classroom" by Christine Mitchell, which of the following statements is TRUE?

    a. Changes in routine, such as vacations, field trips or substitute teachers can be difficult for a student with a history of instability.
    b. Children who have experienced multiple moves and caregivers may have intense anxiety with stability.
    c. Because children spend a great deal of time at school, their school experience does not play a significant role in their future and self-worth.
    d. Children in kinship care situations may be more likely to have speech and language delays, learning disabilities, developmental delays and emotional or mental health issues.

2. According to the article, "Making Sense of the Letters," by Christine Mitchel, what is the definition of IDEA?

    a. A document which spells out the components of a child's special education.
    b. The federal legislation behind most of the rights guaranteed to children with learning issues.
    c. Designed to protect individuals with "handicaps" from denial of benefits or discrimination from any program receiving federal funds.
    d. Provides testing accommodations for learning disabled students.

3. According to the article, "Bullying," by Sherryll Kraizer, Ph.D., which of the following are common forms of social bullying?

    a. Kicking
    b. Mimicking
    c. Internet harassment
    d. Ganging up on someone

4. According to the article, "Overcoming Difficult Comprehension Challenges," by Lee Tobin McClain, what are some ways you can help at home with your child's reading skills?

    a. Call the teacher frequently.
    b. Ask questions.
    c. Make reading a priority.
    d. Work on math facts.

5. According to the article, "Troublesome Family-based School Assignments," by Christine Mitchell, which of the following school assignments might be troublesome for a child living in kinship care?

     a. Write about your birth.
     b. Autobiographies and family history assignments.
     c. Family tree assignments.
     d. VIP, superstars student of the week projects.
     e. All of the above.
     f. None of the above.

6. According to the article, "Special Education 101" by June Bond, MSW, and Mary Eaddy, what should a child's IEP contain?

     a. Annual goals for your child.
     b. Address testing modifications or changes in how the tests are administered.
     c. Learning challenges and extra therapy required to fix them.
     d. Description of the child's home life.

7. Essay: What ways have you found beneficial in helping your child succeed at school? Please use a separate sheet of paper.

_____

Please print clearly:

Name _____

Address _____

City _____ State _____ Zip _____

Private or State Agency Contact _____

Office Address/PO Box _____

City _____ State _____ Zip _____

Learning Objective: to increase foster and/or adoptive parents' ability to apply and respond to new information and conceptual frameworks to their work with children in their care. Please rate the following on a scale of 1-4 (1 is poor, 4 is excellent):

The information was informative: ( 1-2-3-4 )

The information was useful/helpful in my role as a foster/adoptive parent: ( 1-2-3-4 )

The information was thought-provoking, ( 1-2-3-4 ) especially the story on page(s)

_____

See page 313 for payment and mailing details to earn Certificates of Completion.

## Chapter 13:
## The Teen Years CEU Quiz

1. According to the article, "Parenting the Hormonally Challenged: Teens & Sexuality," by Denise Goodman, Ph.D., which of the following are the 3 c's for use in an emergency?
>   a. Close, create, collaborate
>   b. Case, coordinate, conduct
>   c. Courage, communicate, control
>   d. Calm, confront, correct

2. According to the article, "Adolescence: Surviving and Thriving," by Brenda McCreight, Ph.D., which of the following statements is TRUE?
>   a. The adolescent brain undergoes a massive change beginning about 10 and finally finishes its work by age 30.
>   b. With adolescence continuing to evolve, parenting has also had to change with each generation.
>   c. Areas associated with fairly basic functions, including the motor and sensory areas, mature late in the process.
>   d. The brain grows massively and the parts that are underused are basically pruned off, while the parts that are regularly used and stimulated are allowed to grow and shape the personality of the youth.
>   e. All of the above.
>   f. None of the above.

3. According to the article, "Teenage Kincare," by Sherry Howard, what advice is offered to anyone parenting in a kinship arrangement?
>   a. Enforce rules without guilt.
>   b. Keep the communication open with the parents and keep your home open to them if possible.
>   c. Use your maturity to your advantage: you know better than to sweat the small stuff.
>   d. Respect the need for quiet time to soothe the inner chaos.
>   e. All of the above.
>   f. None of the above.

4. According to the article, "What's with Those Teenagers?" by Penny G. Davis, MA, which of the following are tools and strategies that are helpful with teens with trauma backgrounds?
>   a. Have clear rules, expectations and limits.
>   b. Vary curfew times depending on activities teens are involved in.
>   c. Require at least one extracurricular activity.
>   d. Focus on solutions.

5. According to the article, "How to Handle Teen Lying," by Drs. James and Mary Kenny, which of the following are ways to curtail your teen's lying?
    a. Ground your child until he or she tells the truth.
    b. Verify your child's activities from outside sources.
    c. Take away the payoff for lying.
    d. Interrogate your child when he or she returns from an outing.

6. According to the article, "Let's Talk About It," which of the following are important things to discuss when a youth enters your home?
    a. Who will purchase their clothes?
    b. When do they have to move out?
    c. Will they be involved in family activities and family vacations?
    d. Can their friends come over?

7. Essay: What are some things you've learned about parenting teens? Please use a separate sheet of paper.

_____

Please print clearly:

Name _____

Address _____

City _____ State _____ Zip _____

Private or State Agency Contact _____

Office Address/PO Box _____

City _____ State _____ Zip _____

Learning Objective: to increase foster and/or adoptive parents' ability to apply and respond to new information and conceptual frameworks to their work with children in their care. Please rate the following on a scale of 1-4 (1 is poor, 4 is excellent):

The information was informative: ( 1-2-3-4 )

The information was useful/helpful in my role as a foster/adoptive parent: ( 1-2-3-4 )

The information was thought-provoking, ( 1-2-3-4 ) especially the story on page(s)

_____

See page 313 for payment and mailing details to earn Certificates of Completion.

**Chapter 14:**
**Tying Up Loose Endss CEU Quiz**

1. According to the article, "Kinship Care is Complicated," by Casey Mills, what is the benefit of being raised by kin?

    a. Maintaining connection to family.
    b. Being raised with biological siblings.
    c. Having to explain family dynamics.
    d. Knowing our story.

2. Which of the following points should be considered about kinship care before leaping to the conclusion kinship care is the preferred solution, according to the article, "Kinship Care: Look Before You Leap," by June Bond, M.Ed.?

    a. Blood is thicker than water.
    b. Is the kinship placement more cost effective than foster care?
    c. Is the kinship placement safe?
    d. Is kinship care consistent with the bonds that are already established for the child?

3. According to the article, "Wanda's Story," by Wanda Crabtree, what did the author learn from her time in prison?

    a. How to sell more drugs once she got out.
    b. How important family was.
    c. How to better care for her children.
    d. How to fight with her sister.

4. What has author Kim Combes, LBSW, M.Ed., what has he learned from maintaining kinship relations for his children?

    a. Maintaining kinship relationships is harmful.
    b. Kinship relations confuse children.
    c. Kinship relationships have healing properties for all involved.
    d. Maintaining kinship relationship is challenging.

**5. According to the article, "Julie's Story," by Julie Carpenter, what did the author wish she had more access to when parenting her nephew?**

      a. Access to more funding.
      b. More respite care.
      c. More resources.
      d. More tools to better meet his needs.

**6. According to the article, "Our Life is Rearranged," by Martha Hooper which of the following questions does the author commonly get asked about her granddaughter/daughter?**

      a. Is she your granddaughter?
      b. Why did you say yes to raising your granddaughter?
      c. Is it hard to manage at your stage in life to be parents again to a small child?
      d. Can we help you sometimes?

**7. Essay: What has been the most challenging thing you've faced as a kinship caregiver? Please use a separate sheet of paper.**

_____

**Please print clearly:**

**Name** _____

**Address** _____

**City** _____ **State** _____ **Zip** _____

**Private or State Agency Contact** _____

**Office Address/PO Box** _____

**City** _____ **State** _____ **Zip** _____

**Learning Objective: to increase foster and/or adoptive parents' ability to apply and respond to new information and conceptual frameworks to their work with children in their care. Please rate the following on a scale of 1-4 (1 is poor, 4 is excellent):**

The information was informative: ( 1-2-3-4 )

The information was useful/helpful in my role as a foster/adoptive parent: ( 1-2-3-4 )

The information was thought-provoking, ( 1-2-3-4 ) especially the story on page(s)

_____

page 313 for payment and mailing details to earn Certificates of Completion.

About the Publisher:

**EMK Press:**
Resources and books for families like yours.

16 Mt. Bethel Road, #219
Warren, NJ  07059
732-469-7544
732-469-7861 fax

### Titles currently in print:

*The Kinship Parenting Toolbox*

*The Foster Parenting Toolbox*

*Adoption Parenting: Creating a Toolbox,
Building Connections*

*I Don't Have Your Eyes*

*We See the Moon*

*At Home in This World, A China Adoption Story*

*Pieces of Me: Who Do I Want to Be?*

We publish books for families formed by adoption, foster, and kinship situations
www.emkpress.com

Please advise us if a link listed in this book is broken or not working.

To reach us via email:

info@emkpress.com

Quantity discounts are available for this book,
visit www.emkpress.com/kinshiptoolbox.html for pricing and details.